persistence

of

history

the persistence of history

cinema, television, and the modern event

edited by
vivian sobchack

routledge
new york and london

Published in 1996 by
Routledge
29 West 35th Street
New York, NY 10001

Published in Great Britain in 1996 by
Routledge
11 New Fetter Lane
London EC4P 4EE

Printed in the United States of America
Typography: Jack Donner

Library of Congress Cataloging-in-Publication Data
The persistence of history : cinema, television, and the modern event / edited by Vivian Sobchack

p. cm. — (AFI film readers)

Includes bibliographical references and index.

ISBN 0–415–91083–8. — ISBN 0–415–91084–6 (pbk.)

1. Motion pictures and history. 2. Television and history. I Sobchack, Vivian Carol. II. Series.

PN1995.2.P47 1995

302.23'4—dc20 95–30070

cip

to bill

for sharing history

contents

acknowledgments ix

introduction: history happens 1
vivian sobchack

part one: the historical event

1. the modernist event 17
hayden white

2. cinematic shots: the narration of violence 39
janet staiger

3. historical consciousness and the viewer: *who killed vincent chin?* 55
bill nichols

4. "i'll see it when i believe it": rodney king and the prison-house of video 69
frank p. tomasulo

part two: historical representation and national identity

5. antimodernism as historical representation in a consumer culture: cecil b. demille's *the ten commandments*, 1923, 1956, 1993 91
sumiko higashi

6. modernism and the narrative of nation in *jfk* 113
robert burgoyne

7. *andrei rublev*: the medieval epic as post-utopian history 127
denise j. youngblood

8. subject positions, speaking positions: from *holocaust*, *our hitler*, and *heimat* to *shoah* and *schindler's list* 145
thomas elsaesser

part three: the end(s) of history

9. **historical *ennui*, feminist boredom** 187
patrice petro

10. **the future of the past: film and the beginnings of postmodern history** 201
robert a. rosenstone

11. **interrotroning history: errol morris and the documentary of the future** 219
shawn rosenheim

12. **the professors of history** 235
dana polan

contributors 257

index 259

acknowledgments

Two institutions and many colleagues made this volume possible. I extend my gratitude to the American Film Institute, which laid the conceptual ground for this project when, several years ago, it invited meta-historian Hayden White to give the AFI's annual Patricia Doyle Wise Lecture (a series in which scholars from disciplines other than film and media studies consider issues related to the moving image). It was in this extraordinary lecture that White first addressed the notion of the "modernist event" and its transformation of contemporary historiography—not only initiating the basis for his own contribution to the pages that follow, but also, and more significantly, serving as a provocation for the volume as a whole. I am deeply appreciative of both his inspiration and his continuing friendship. My thanks go also to the Committee on Research of the Academic Senate of the University of California, Los Angeles, which served a more practical function in its support of the invaluable research assistance of Lisa Kernan. Quite simply, this volume could not have been realized without her considerable editorial skills, her good sense, and her astute critical sensitivity.

Edward Branigan and Charles Wolfe, the editors of the AFI Film Reader series, and Bill Germano and Eric Zinner of Routledge all have my deep appreciation for their unflagging support and enthusiasm—and for their considerable grace in moving the project along.

Finally, I am especially grateful to my colleages and friends who are the authors of this volume—not only for their impressive contributions to an important and timely dialogue about the nature and function of "history" and historical representation, but also for their extraordinary understanding and patience during the lengthy delay caused by my recuperation from a personally historic surgery. I am in their debt for being so much in their concern and care.

introduction history happens

vivian sobchack

Writing in a recent issue of the *New Yorker*, Roger Angell reviews *Forrest Gump* (Robert Zemeckis, 1994), the immensely popular film about a simpleton hero triumphing over the vicissitudes of American history which captured the hearts (if not the minds) of most Americans and the Academy of Motion Picture Arts and Sciences. The film, he tells us, is a "moony" and "fantastic" dream in which ignorance and niceness win out over historical consciousness and meaning. *Forrest Gump* presents "the shambles and the horror of our recent American past made harmless and sweet because the protagonist doesn't understand a moment of any of it." Angell goes on to note, however, that at the same time, the film contains nary a trace of "what used to be called without irony the American dream: the faith that we all belonged somewhere in a rational and forgiving system" that provided not only one's just deserts, but also historical and ideological surety.[1] In essence, although Angell does not grant the film credit for its contradictions, the sweet *Forrest Gump* also presents a not-so-sweet vision of history and one's "rational place" within it. The complexity of diverse individual trajectories and their nodal coalescence in the massive "historical events" we see foregrounded as the film's background are ironically revealed as nothing less (while something more) than confusion: that is, notions of both rationality and system are undermined by the visible evidence that "History" is the concatenated and reified effect of incoherent motives and chance convergences.

Forrest Gump, then, manifests ambivalent attitudes about the meanings of "history" and the "historical event" currently held by many contemporary Americans; I would argue that the film is less simple- (or single-) minded than its Candide-like hero—who, unlike Candide, in, and after, the long run (and there is such a "long run" dramatized in the film) learns nothing he did not know at the beginning. In the first instance, *Forrest Gump* tells us with great sincerity not to worry: one can be *in* history, can *make* history, without paying attention and without understanding. Like the feather that begins and ends the film, the historical actor is blown by the winds of chance, must of existential necessity be somewhere at some time, engaged in some act that may or may not be considered remarkable or historically motivating in a present or future moment. Thus, reflection and reflexivity are a waste—rather than an expansion—of time: there is no point to comprehending the overwhelming complexity of motives and acts and material causes that make up history since, in the long run, history will comprehend and confer meaning on even the most simple-minded of us. In the second instance, however, *Forrest Gump* tells us with reflective and condensed bumper-sticker irony (and with something akin to the long view of the *Annales* school of history that deals with "long-term equilibriums and disequilibriums" through the minute detailing of everyday life and its "conjunctures"[2]), "Shit happens." The temporally inflated notion of something we might once have called the "historical event" is deflated and its specificity reduced to generalized matter—not because events are now considered trivial, but because they are now considered indeterminate in their boundaries and their "eventual" historic importance.

On the one hand, then, Forrest Gump—the character, not the film—denies the hermeneutic necessity (perhaps even the hermeneutic possibility) of understanding the significance of that "larger" temporal spread we live and narrativize socially (rather than individually) as "History" or "histories." Since history can't happen without us, the film seems to say through its putative hero, we've played our part simply by "being there." We don't have to know or care what it means. On the other hand, however, one could argue that *Forrest Gump*—the film, not the character—is historically conscious: ironic and playful, its thematics, mise-en-scène, and modes of representation make visible the breakdown of the segmentation that, in a previous age, secured for us the borders and value between "significant" and "trivial" events, between fact and fiction, between past and present, between experience and its representation. The paradox of the film's narrative is that it makes a sharp distinction between the personal and historical event / the historically trivial and significant action and simultaneously collapses this distinction, pointing to the conflation of personal and historical, trivial and significant. Furthermore, this narrative paradox is also figured as a representational paradox. Digitally inserting its fictional hero into documentary footage and into an interactive relation with "real" historical events and persons, *Forrest Gump* confuses the fictional with the historically "real" in an absolutely seamless representation—and yet it does not, for a second, presume that its audience will be at all categorically confused. Indeed, it depends for its humor on the audience's conscious recognition of the distinct terms of this confusion.

In sum, *Forrest Gump* stands as both symptom of and gloss upon a contemporary—and millennial—moment in which history (with either upper- or lower-case *h*, in the singular or plural) and historical consciousness have been often described on the one hand as "at an end," and on the other hand have been the object of unprecedented public attention and contestation. One could, in fact, suggest that *Forrest Gump* is a one-joke movie, absolutely dependent for its humor and irony upon historically (self-) conscious viewers who have been immersed in questions about the boundaries, meanings, and place of history in their daily lives, as well as about their own possible place in history. While one can certainly argue its marking the dissolution and "end" of history (as well as the responsibility for it), *Forrest Gump* can be argued also as marking (and dependent upon) a new and pervasive self-consciousness about individual and social existence as an "historical subject."

In this regard, it is important to note that the year in which *Forrest Gump* appeared in theaters was also a year noted for heated debates about the "national history standards" for secondary education proposed by UCLA's Center for History in the Schools. It was a year that united ordinary citizens (most of whom had probably watched every episode of Ken Burns's nostalgic 1990 PBS epic *The Civil War*) and academic historians in a vigorous and successful campaign to defeat Disney's construction, in Virginia, of an historical theme park to be built near actual historic Civil War battlefields. It was a year in which charges of historical revisionism were leveled by veterans at the Smithsonian Air and Space Museum's planned (and somewhat apologetic) exhibition surrounding the Enola Gay, the plane that dropped the atomic bomb on Hiroshima. This was the same year, too, in which television gave us the incessantly touted "trial of the century"—the O. J. Simpson proceedings—in which traumatic and trivial "events" and "evidence" were intertwined and conflated not only in questions of what should count as mattering in the case, but also in their simultaneous representation as on the one hand "special" and "historic" and on the other hand as diurnal and temporally repetitive. And, this was the year in which The History Channel appeared on cable, its promotional material telling us, "If you couldn't be there the first time, here's your second chance," its trademark slogan promising "All of History. All in One Place.™"[3]

Forrest Gump, the Disney controversy, the O. J. trial coverage, The History Channel, all tell us something about our present moment and the relatively recent escalation in the public sphere of a qualitatively new self-consciousness about history. One might say we are in a moment marked by a peculiarly novel "readiness" for history among the general population. That is, people seem to carry themselves with a certain reflexive phenomenological comportment toward their "immediate" immersion in the present, self-consciously grasping their own objective posture with an eye to its imminent future possibilities for representation (and commodification) as the historical past.

In this volume, Hayden White discusses the particularly novel events of the twentieth century that have challenged traditional and coherent historiographic narratives and their entailment with new modes of representation. Indeed, one could argue that the "events" of the twentieth century are less inherently novel than the novel technologies of representation that have transformed "events" by bringing them to unprecedented visibility and magnitude, and that have narrated them in ways that have made the very mechanisms of narration explicitly visible. Over the course of the century and at an accelerating pace, first cinema, and then television, camcorders, and digital media have brought both the arbitrary and motivated segmentation of time to public awareness. The possible manipulation of events through representation and narration, their editorial potential as trivial or traumatic, their abstraction as "shots" or "bits," and their inherent underdetermination even as they are overdetermined through use are all, by now, common knowledge. Thus, the audience—who also saw the Zapruder film in *JFK*, sat at home through the many uses of the Rodney King tape, and recognized the recreation of Holocaust footage in *Schindler's List*—is always in on the joke of *Forrest Gump*. The once arcane lesson of White's *Metahistory*—that historiography is about arranging and telling stories, not about delivering objective truth—is, by now, also common knowledge. This explains, perhaps, the public's fascination and playfulness, as well as its cynicism and suspension of all belief, with the "status" of the historical event and the "event" of historical representation.

Furthermore, by virtue of their increasing representational immediacy, these new twentieth century technologies of representation and narration (most significantly, television) have increasingly collapsed the temporal distance between present, past, and future that structured our previously conceived notion of the temporal dimensions of what we call history (as the latter is differentiated from experience). That is, event and its representation, immediacy and its mediation, have moved increasingly toward simultaneity. Early in the century, we thought history was something that happened temporally "before" and was represented temporally "after" us and our personal and immediate experience. For an event to "become" History, an "appropriate" period of time for reflection upon it seemed necessary. This seems no longer the case. Today, history seems to happen right now—is transmitted, reflected upon, shown play-by-play, taken up as the stuff of multiple stories and significance, given all sorts of "coverage" in the temporal dimension of the present as we live it. Correlatively, there seems a sense in which we believe we can go right out and "be" in history: hence, the people who flocked to the sides of the freeway to watch—and be in—the "historic" parade led by O. J.'s Ford Bronco, who knew that they—as well as O. J.—might make the five-o'clock "news"; hence, too, the people who stood outside of Nicole Simpson's Brentwood condo and told reporters they were there because they wanted to be "part of history."

It is easy to think such actions and such desire pathetic or deluded—or to reduce and explain them away in terms of Andy Warhol's comment that, in such a highly mediated and media-filled world, anyone can be a celebrity for fifteen minutes. It is harder to think of the more positive aspects of such actions and such desire, but these aspects can—and perhaps must—be conceived if we are to admit the value of that something we call history to the present moment, and if we are to see any viable future in the representation of the past. From a phenomenological perspective, the popular location of history as possible "at any moment" in the present and the self-consciousness of one's comportment as an historical actor redeem to us a vibrant connection of present to past and a sense of agency in the shaping of human events. Furthermore, the popular apprehension of the traumatic and grand "historical event" as a potentiality in the trivial temporality of the everyday (common and extensible enough to "include one in") can be seen as signaling not merely the "end" of History as a distinct temporal category, but also (and alternatively) an emergent and novel form of historical consciousness—in sum, as a very real and consequential "readiness" for history.

What is both poignant and heartening about this novel form of historical consciousness is that it has no determinate "object." In great part, the effects of our new technologies of representation put us at a loss to fix that "thing" we used to think of as History or to create clearly delineated and categorical temporal and spatial frames around what we used to think of as the "historical event." Thus, White is apposite in ending the essay which begins this collection by quoting Gertrude Stein. In the age of television, camcorders, and seamless digital manipulation, when anyone can be caught and filmed and interviewed or digitized into a "historic" crowd scene, riot, or significant event, the "rare and peculiar cases" Stein mentions, "when the outside breaks through to be inside because the outside is so part of some inside that even a description of the outside cannot completely relieve the outside of the inside," are no longer very rare and peculiar.

However, and again as an effect of our new technologies of representation, this loss of a "fix" on History and of the stable temporal and spatial framing of events as "historical," the loss to historical consciousness of an historical object, can also be seen as a gain. That is, this loss of a firm grasp of its object forces into the foreground of our current existence the constitutive quality of consciousness as it engages the objective world. Now objectively indeterminate, History cannot be "taken up" by consciousness, but, rather, must be subjectively "made out." This is not to deny the world its spatial solidity nor the temporal event its reality—that is, its material causes and consequences. (There is a difference between "making something up" and "making it out.") It is, rather, to recognize—as I think most people do today—that we are subjectively implicated in and responsible for the histories we tell ourselves or others tell us and that, while these are just representations, their significance has both value and consequence to our lives. Hence the contemporary and widespread contentiousness around categories, boundaries, exclusions, and inclusions, ordering and re-membering History, history, herstory, histories.

At the present moment, the loss of a determinate historical object and the correspondent and conscious hunger for history has led to the most disheartening and hopeful of conditions. On the one hand, for the most cynical, History has become a commodity—something to be "fixed" according to maximum consumer desire (that is, not only made secure, but also "neutered," "altered," and "doctored up"). Exemplary is Disney's recent movie *Pocahontas*, "which for the first time in the history of Disney animation is based on American history." In a recent *Entertainment Weekly*, we are not only told of what are now commonly expected consumer product tie-ins: "Nestlé (candy bars), Mattel (Pocahontas, Barbie-style), Payless Shoesource (moccasins), and Burger King (kids' meals)." We are also told of Disney's emphases of certain aspects of the "story": Pocahontas "cooling the tempers of her Virginia tribe and the British settlers because of her love for Capt. John Smith (voice by Mel Gibson)." However, most cynical of all—and most indicative of Disney's awareness of the public's heightened historical consciousness—are Disney's attempts to forestall potential criticism. "Since any film dealing with history is a target for controversy in these PC times," we are told, "Disney has buffered itself against attack. It consulted with historians and Native American groups during the making of the film, and recruited Russell Means (*The Last of the*

Mohicans) to provide one of the voices."[4] Here, it is clear that the contemporary loss of a determinate and fixed historical object has been replaced with an overdetermined and reified commodity. Furthermore, that Russell Means is cited not for his actual historical contributions as a Native American activist but, rather, for his appearance as a character in the film adaptation of a historical novel seems the ultimate confirmation of Guy Debord's critique of the twentieth-century "society of the spectacle": that "everything that was lived directly has moved away into a representation."[5]

On the other hand, there does seem reason to counter cynicism (which is usually unproductive and self-congratulatory) with hope. While it is certainly true that the hunger for a lost historical object has led to History as *commodity*, to both *Pocahontas* and The History Channel ("All of History. All in One Place.™"), it is also true that such hunger has led to a widespread recognition of history and its representation as *process*, to both *JFK* with its multiple constructions of a traumatic national event and C-SPAN with its coverage of momentous, trivial, and often geologically paced legislative negotiations. Popular audiences have become involved in and understand the stakes in historical representation, recognize "history in the making," and see themselves not only as spectators of history, but also as participants in and adjudicators of it. Current debates around the nature, shape, and narration of history are no longer only the province of academic historians and scholars of film and literature. "History happens" now in the public sphere where the search for a lost object has led not only to cheap substitutes but, in the process, also to the quickening of a new historical sense and perhaps a more active and reflective historical subject.

All of the essays in this volume deal with transformations in the sense and representation of history which emerged at the beginning of the twentieth century, correlative with the birth of cinema, modernity, and "modernism." This transformation has arguably found its fullest expression in the current "postmodern" moment, which is marked by the dominance of televisual and other electronic forms of communication and representation as well as an unprecedented awareness of representation itself. All of the essays that follow deal with the ways in which film and televison respond to, interrogate, and create contemporary history. In one way or another, all ask what kinds of narration are adequate to express the manner in which we relate to—as Thomas Elsaesser puts it—a "prevalence of events at once so apparently senseless and so predictably routine that neither narratives nor images seem to encompass them" in their "ungraspable singularity."

Thus, the questions foregrounded in Part 1, "The Historical Event," relate new media technologies as well as new modes and practices of narration to the problem of the adequacy of representation to historical matter. According to Hayden White in the essay that opens the section, historical matter, particularly in its status as significant or discrete "event," has "dissolved as an object of a respectably scientific *knowledge,*" and there are now "no limits" on what can "be legitimately said about it." Considering the extraordinary controversy surrounding Oliver Stone's *JFK*, White argues, in "The Modernist Event," that the traumatic events unique to the twentieth century—events of such magnitude or singularity that they can neither be completely forgotten nor adequately remembered—can only find their appropriately tenuous representation in the "de-realization" effected by modern media and modernist forms such as collage and fragmentation. The human agency, causal structures, and closure which grounded realist historical narratives, he suggests, are not commensurable with the twentieth-century experience of events—which is, itself, an experience of "experiential shortcomings"—nor with the need to "mourn" the loss of historical explanation and comprehension.

Janet Staiger's "Cinematic Shots: The Narration of Violence" further interrogates the controversy surrounding *JFK*. Asking if Stone is really doing anything formally unusual or particularly "adequate" to the traumatic event it treats (and she thinks he is not), Staiger explores historical re-enactments and reality TV as well as the relations between "official" and "popular" versions of history. At stake in the *JFK* controversy, she suggests, is not its modernist form so much as it is the replacement in the public mind of the official Warren Commission story with the alternative and popularly "authorized" story of violence and conspiracy that admits no satisfying resolution. Thus, Staiger argues with White, and suggests that the question of historical representation is less one of textual forms than of textual effects. Indeed, she warns against confusing formal tropes with their social and cultural functions in specific historical contexts. Staiger concludes that *JFK* is a "postmodern" history, not because of its editing strategies, but rather because of "the reading strategies" of its viewers who, "like the postmodern historiographer, ... have learned the rules of representation" and "recognize that the movie is a subjective version of the past."

Bill Nichols, in "Historical Consciousness and the Viewer: *Who Killed Vincent Chin?*", both engages and goes beyond the dialogue between Staiger and White in his discussion of what he calls "the most important political documentary of the 1980s." He highlights the dialectical process inherent in what White has called elsewhere "the content of the form."[6] Nichols sees certain modes of narration as conducive to, though not determinate of, the emergence of the spectator's historical consciousness and consequent self-recognition as a potential historical actor. Differentiating between representation and explanation, demonstrating that the "historical event" is "up for grabs," marking a crisis in representation through its collage of multiple versions, voices, and conditional and subjunctive moods, the formal strategy of *Who Killed Vincent Chin?* may provoke in us as spectators "the felt and active experience of *making sense* of what we see and hear." Further, by "dint of passage through a more experiential domain," we may come to knowledge of a different and more active order. *Who Killed Vincent Chin?* is a "performative discourse" that "invites us to grasp our present as history in order to keep alive the idea of a radically transformed future."

Frank Tomasulo's "I'll See It When I Believe It": Rodney King and the Prison-House of Video" takes a very different approach to the relation of representational forms to their historical matter—and to their mattering. Suggesting that historicism has become "a replacement for history" and recalling Fredric Jameson's dictum that "History is what hurts," Tomasulo revisits the Rodney King videotape as "a controversial site for interrogating some basic historical, political, and pedagogical" issues. Arguing that the contemporary and dominant practice of teaching everything as "text" and "discourse"—including the "historical event" in which "a black man is being beaten"—leads to "a diminution of materialism as a philosophy and a weakening of political will to fight injustice." Tomasulo insists on the difference between the real and its representation and, in his critique of much poststructuralist thought, points to the "ultimate irony" that surrounds the King videotape: namely, "that scholars who had welcomed close textual analysis as a tool for spinning elaborate ideological readings and rereadings of film/TV texts for decades suddenly had to confront defense attorneys on the opposite side of the political spectrum who used the same tools of visual analysis to convince a jury" that what they were seeing was a visual "text" open to interpretation.

In Part 2, "Historical Representation and National Identity," formal issues do not disappear, but become part and parcel of a discussion of various representational strategies that are used not only to narrate historical events, but also to narrate "the nation." While the films addressed by the authors in this section are diverse, what unites the essays is their concern with and critique of the traditional conjunction of history and nation in something akin to "sermonization": the narration of past events and nation-building in coherent moral tales. Also running through these essays are questions of spectacle and melodrama and their "propriety" in relation to the "appropriate" representation of history. As Thomas Elsaesser notes, "Much of the force of the injunction against misrepresentation ... relies implicitly on a religiously grounded *Bilderverbot* (iconomachy), itself at least in part an acknowledgment of the power of images to elicit 'effects of melodrama, sentimentality, prurience.'" It is this injunction that the cinema, in its very existence, transgresses.

Indeed, Cecil B. DeMille gloried in the "transgressions" of both cinematic spectacle and melodrama in his Biblico-historical epics. Thus, Sumiko Higashi argues, his films bridged the gap between premodern (or antimodern) characteristics of sentimentality, prurience, and the sure sense of the progressive trajectory of history and the consumerist sensibilities and commodity fetishism of modern and postmodern audiences. In "Antimodernism as Historical Representation in a Consumer Culture: Cecil B. DeMille's *The Ten Commandments*, 1923, 1956, 1993," Higashi claims that DeMille's "oversized spectacle" was "antimodernist," but promoted "a modern consumer ethos" that the films "legitimated within a religious and pedagogical framework." The silent *Ten Commandments*, its 1956 sound remake during the Cold War, and the frequent re-runs of the latter on contemporary television which interrupt the Israelites' trek on foot through the desert with car commercials, contain and are contained by the specific historical moment of their national exhibition. Nonetheless, along with their use of "historical pageantry as a form of commodity fetishism," their long-running appeal can also be located in their sermonizing equation of the Promised Land with America and their linear historical narrative of "the rise and fall of empires ... culminating with the founding of America as the world's beacon."

Decades later, Oliver Stone's *JFK* also finds resolution of its historical and representational crisis in a culminating and traditional narrative of nation and the rise and fall of empires. In "Modernism and the Narration of Nation in *JFK*," Robert Burgoyne argues that, despite its modernist form and broken narrative, the film "holds onto the very ideal of a coherent narrative of nation that its own formal structure seems to repudiate." On the one hand, *JFK* maintains a traditional view of history as fixed—even if obscured by lies and deception. This history is a "universal imperial" one that links "Caesar, the Crucifixion, the killing of kings," and conspiracy plots to a master-narrative of the nation. Burgoyne points out that although *JFK* defamiliarizes "social reality by narrating the past as a site of contradictory, mundane, and abstracted details," its modernist form is "overarched by an almost biblical sense of prefiguration and fulfillment." On the other hand, *JFK* "resists the reductiveness of a single, official history and defends the role and power of differentiated memories." Nonetheless, while its "greatest strength is its use of the disjunctive style ... to appeal to national identity in a way that recognizes the media as a crucial terrain," the film's greatest weakness is its "desperate need" to recuperate a unified and fixed view of history so as to secure what is commonly thought to be the only foundation for the formation of national identity and community.

We move to quite a different relation between history and nation in Denise Youngblood's "*Andrei Rublev*: The Medieval Epic as Post-Utopian History." Tarkovskii's film, Youngblood argues, "mocks the unreality and myth-making of Socialist Realism and ... debunks the idea, cherished by Russians, that their history is a 'Holy Mystery'" and presents, instead, Russian history as an unfathomable enigma. Using the cinema as "an alternate discourse for history telling," Tarkovskii gives us "an experimental history of medieval times that confronts the truisms of positivist history" with the haphazard and irresolute quality of the chronicle, the decontextualized fragment—forms of selection and attention to temporality that "challenge" the "Anglo-German 'scientific' narrative tradition of historical writing." Youngblood not only defends *Andrei Rublev*—"a film that is invented from beginning to end" and "mocks long-standing historical conventions"—as a legitimate historiographic work about the Russian nation, but also defends it as a film whose vision of history is "profoundly postmodern, or post-utopian."

The section comes to a close with Thomas Elsaesser's far-ranging "Subject Positions, Speaking Positions: From *Holocaust*, *Our Hitler*, and *Heimat* to *Shoah* and *Schindler's List*." Elsaesser traces the history of the representation of fascism through a variety of modes and national cinemas, focusing on two central and complex issues relating to "appropriate" historical representation—in particular, to the representation of the Holocaust. The first issue is a question of representational mode and the other, of national identity and "identity politics." In a complex and persuasive discussion, Elsaesser tracks the move away from realism in the representation of fascism and argues for melodrama as a narrative mode appropriate to the work of mourning. Melodrama, he argues, is able to represent the "obsession, fantasy, and trauma" that attaches to certain historical events of which sense can never be made, and is particularly capable of engaging "with matters of life and death on the part of those whom history has given the role of spectators, but also of those who are charged with passing on compassion and preserving memory." Thus, *Schindler's List* is as valid in its mourning work as is *Shoah*. Elsaesser also raises a question that is central to the emergence of German cinema's speaking positions in response to the representation of fascism and the Holocaust by national and cultural "others": namely, "Whose history is it?" Appropriated by and appropriate to both German and (American) Jew, the historical event of the Holocaust is subject to and spoken of in incompatible stories from incompatible speaking positions—stories that narrate nations as they also narrate history.

Part 3 of this volume is titled "The End(s) of History." Its four essays are all purposefully eccentric and emphasize on the one hand the "dead end" of historiography as it has been traditionally conceived and practiced, and raise on the other the question of historiography's "ends" or functions. As Robert Rosenstone puts it, there is now a pervasive sense "that traditional history has in this century run up against the limits of representation." But this sense of ending brings with it the constructive task of creating a new kind of history and forging a usable past that speaks both to the present and of a future.

Patrice Petro, prompted by the discourse of "exhaustion" and "boredom" now surrounding contemporary feminist film theory, attempts to think a novel form of history that will take up boredom as a constructive force and an antidote to the "banal" novelty of modernism. In "Historical *Ennui*, Feminist Boredom," Petro argues that "modernism, like feminism itself, is best understood, not as a *novel* way of representing history but as a *banal* way of representing novelty as well as gender difference." She goes on to demonstrate the gendered nature of *ennui* and melancholia, temporal states figuring lack and loss that "themselves have a long and venerable history" in which "male losses were transformed into representational gains." Boredom, however, has been linked both with female sensibility and, most significantly in terms of historiographic representation, with a temporal significance that "fails to happen." Feminist boredom, then, has constructive historiographic possibilities: it privileges the banal and the everyday, refuses postmodern melancholia at the "end" of history, takes a stance of "active waiting," and sees a "flux of meaning" in repetition and in the very commonplaces previously excluded from the domain of historiography.

Robert Rosenstone also looks to the radical transformation of traditional historiographic practice, finding this transformation in visual rather than print media. In "The Future of the Past: Film and the Beginnings of Postmodern History," Rosenstone points to the overproduction of written works of postmodern historiographic theory and the underproduction of written postmodern history. That new, postmodern history, he argues, occurs in other media—now predominantly film and video, soon perhaps on CD-ROMs and the Internet. In an essay whose own postmodern form embraces digression, confession, pastiche, and concatenation, Rosenstone offers a gloss on a variety of films and videos that respond to the postmodern critique of traditional historiography. These works reject traditional and linear story development, privilege "self-reflexivity," offer "a multiplicity of viewpoints," and are "irreverent." They "intermix contradictory elements ... and indulge in creative anachronism." They also accept their own partisanship and rhetorical character, "refuse to focus or sum up" in totalizing narratives or "alter and invent incident and character," feel free to use fragmentary and poetic knowledge, and "never forget that the present is the site of all past representation and knowing." Citing Beckett's "I can't go on, I'll go on" as the new historiographer's credo, Rosenstone speaks to the necessity of the historical enterprise and to the emergence of a new historiographic "middle" voice that "refuses to take as the lesson of Auschwitz the notion that historical understanding is no longer possible."

Shawn Rosenheim, in "Interrotroning History: Errol Morris and the Documentary of the Future," looks to the intervention of television in history which, he argues, has irrevocably altered both historical events and historiography. Contrasting the sentimental, mythologized, "self-congratulatory affirmation of loss and redemptive nationhood" figured by Ken Burns's *The Civil War* with the O. J. Simpson trial in which "the crime and its consequences have remained shapeless and badly told, as journalists have attempted to master the situation through repetition, meaningless updates, and mutual self-reference," Rosenheim turns as an alternative to the historiographic practices of "documentarian" Errol Morris. Focusing on pilot programs for the yet unaired series, *Errol Morris: Interrotron Stories*, Rosenheim highlights not only Morris's "invention" of a new technology of communication between filmmaker and subject, but also his commitment to "dubious points of view," "stylistically ambiguous narration," and the destabilization of the spectator's "perception of what televisual history is made of." Murder cases, in particular, serve for Morris as "a model of historical inquiry." They are "properly" inflected by "tabloid interest," "sensational representations of scandal," evidence that "quickly proves tainted or inconclusive," and re-enactments that show not what really happened but rather "illustrate the slipperiness of memory." In comparing Morris's televisual historiography to Carlo Ginzburg's in *The Cheese and the Worms*, Rosenheim sees *Interrotron Stories* as a radically new form of "*mentalité* television"—historiography for the future.

The concluding essay in the volume is Dana Polan's "The Professors of History." Interrogating the representation of the academic "professor" in literature and film, Polan wonders at the differences articulated among professors of science, literature and creative writing, and history and finds that in the popular consciousness the "professors of history" are seen as superfluous or ridiculous. Furthermore, given their perceived status as merely "re-presenters" (rather than interpreters) of significant events, they seem particularly redundant—especially in the cinema, which depends in great part on drama and embodied action. Indeed, as Polan notes, "there is something essentially uncinematic about the work of history." Thus Polan points to *Bill and Ted's Excellent Adventure* as a film that both criticizes "the inert irrelevance" of traditional historiography and simultaneously "supports its underlying empiricism." Looking at the gap between current popular interest in the historical past and the lack of interest in the work of the historian leads Polan to conclude that "[h]istory as a professional activity appears to have little place in public consciousness precisely at a moment ... in which the question of the potentially public nature of history is of burning pertinence."

The Persistence of History, the title of this collection, is meant to signal this "burning pertinence"—even as History has supposedly come to a postmodern end. Evoking both Dali's *The Persistence of Memory*, with its melting watches, its loss of objective time, and its barren landscape, and the notion of "the persistence of vision" that, however incorrectly, has historically explained the apparent retention of moving cinematic images on the retina, "the persistence of history" names both a moment of re-membering the past and a moment of re-visioning that projects into the future. If history—like shit—"happens," it happens only in the present, in the temporal space between the past and the future. But "the persistence of history" suggests a temporal connection and spread that confers on "history" (differentiating it from "shit") a magnitude and significance that emerges from historiographic reflection and makes out of that present unshaped material something that deeply matters.

notes

1. Roger Angell, "Two Dreams," *The New Yorker*, March 13, 1995, 7.
2. Fernand Braudel, *Afterthoughts on Material Civilization and Capitalism*, trans. Patricia M. Ranum (Baltimore and London: The Johns Hopkins University Press, 1977), 5.
3. Advertisement in *TV Guide*, March 18, 1995, 9.
4. Pat H. Broeske and Jessica Shaw, "The Pocamotion," *Entertainment Weekly*, February 3, 1995, 9.
5. Guy Debord, *Society of the Spectacle* (Detroit: Black and Red, 1983), n.p.
6. Hayden White, *The Context of the Form: Narrative Discourse and Historical Representation* (Baltimore and London: The Johns Hopkins University Press, 1987), ix–xi.

part one

the historical event

one

the modernist event

hayden white

"History does not break down into stories but into images."
—Walter Benjamin

"The coming extinction of art is prefigured in the increasing impossibility of representing historical events."
—Theodor Adorno

It is a commonplace of contemporary criticism that modernist literature, and, by extension, modernist art in general, dissolves the trinity of event, character, and plot which provided the staple both of the nineteenth-century realist novel and of the historiography from which nineteenth-century literature derived its model of "realism." In particular, the tendency of modernist literature to dissolve the event has especially important implications for understanding the ways in which contemporary Western culture construes the relationship between literature and history. The invention of a subject-less and plot-less historiography in the twentieth century has amply demonstrated that modern historical research and writing could get by without the notions of character and plot.[1] But the dissolution of the event as a basic unit of temporal occurrence and building-block of history undermines the very concept of factuality and threatens therewith the distinction between realistic and merely imaginary discourse. This dissolution undermines a founding presupposition of Western realism: the *opposition* between fact and fiction. Modernism resolves the problems posed by traditional realism, namely, how to represent reality realistically, by simply abandoning the ground on which realism is construed as an opposition between fact and fiction. The denial of the reality of the event undermines the very notion of "fact" informing traditional realism. Therewith, the taboo against mixing fact with fiction, except in manifestly "imaginative" discourse, is abolished. And, as current critical opinion suggests, the very notion of "fiction" is set aside in the conceptualization of "literature" as a mode of writing which abandons both the referential and poetic functions of language use.

It is this aspect of modernism that informs the creation of the new genres, in both written and visual form, of *post-modernist*, para-historical representation, called variously "docu-drama," "faction," "infotainment," "the fiction of fact," "historical metafiction," and the like.[2] These genres are represented by books such as Capote's *In Cold Blood* (1965), Mailer's *The Executioner's Song* (1979), Doctorow's, *Ragtime* (1975), Thomas' *The White Hotel* (1981), De Lillo's *Libra* (1988), and Reed's *Flight to Canada* (1976); the television versions of *Holocaust* (1978) and *Roots* (1977); films such as *The Night Porter* (Cavani, 1974), *The Damned* (Visconti, 1969), *Our Hitler* (Syberberg, 1976–77), *The Return of Martin Guerre* (Vigne, 1982), and more recently Stone's *JFK* (1991) and Spielberg's *Schindler's List* (1993). All deal with historical phenomena, and all of them appear to "fictionalize" to a greater or lesser degree the historical events and characters which serve as their referents in history.

These works, however, differ crucially from those of their generic prototype—the nineteenth-century historical novel. That genre was born of the interference between an "imaginary" tale of romance and a set of "real" historical events. The interference had the effect of endowing the imaginary events with the concreteness of reality, while at the same time endowing the historical events with the "magical" aura peculiar to the romance.[3] The relationship between the historical novel and its projected readership was mediated by a distinctive contract: its intended effects depended upon the presumed capacity of the reader to distinguish between real and imaginary events, between "fact" and "fiction," and therefore between "life" and "literature." Without this capacity, the affect in which the familiar (the reader's own reveries) was rendered exotic while the exotic (the historical past or the lives of the great) was rendered familiar could not have been produced.

What happens in the postmodernist docu-drama or historical metafiction is not so much the reversal of this relationship (such that real events are given the marks of imaginary ones while imaginary events are endowed with reality) as, rather, the placing in abeyance of the distinction between the real and the imaginary. Everything is presented as if it were of the same ontological order, both real and imaginary—realistically imaginary or imaginarily real, with the result that the referential function of the images of events is etiolated. Thus, the contract that originally mediated the relationship between the nineteenth-century (bourgeois?) reader and the author of the historical novel has been dissolved. And what you get, as Gertrude Himmelfarb tells us, is "History as you like it," representations of history in which "anything goes" (to the detriment of both truth and moral responsibility, in Himmelfarb's view).[4] This is exactly the sort of accusation which has been so often directed at Oliver Stone since the appearance of *JFK*.

Stone was criticized by journalists, historians, politicians, and political pundits for his treatment of the events surrounding the assassination of President John F. Kennedy. In part, this was a result of the "content" of his film. He was accused, among other things, of fostering paranoia by suggesting that President Kennedy's assassination was a result of a conspiracy involving highly placed persons in the United States government. But also—and for some critics even more seriously—Stone's film seemed to blur the distinction between fact and fiction by treating an historical *event* as if there were no limits to what could legitimately be said about it, thereby bringing under question the very principle of objectivity as the basis for which one might discriminate between truth on the one side and myth, ideology, illusion, and lie on the other.

Thus, in a review of *JFK* which appeared in the *Times Literary Supplement*, entitled "Movie Madness," Richard Grenier wrote:

> And so Oliver Stone romps through the assassination of John Kennedy, inventing evidence that supports his thesis [of conspiracy], suppressing all evidence that conflicts with it, directing his film in a pummelling style, a left to the jaw, a right to the solar plexus, flashing forward, flashing backward, crosscutting relentlessly, shooting "in tight" (in close), blurring, obfuscating, bludgeoning the viewer until Stone wins, he hopes, by a TKO.[5]

Note that Grenier objects to the ways in which Stone slants evidence concerning the assassination, but he is especially offended by the form of Stone's presentation, his "pummelling" and "bludgeoning" style which apparently distorts even those events whose occurrence can be established on the basis of historical evidence. This style is treated as if it were a violation of the spectator's powers of perception.

Another film critic, David Armstrong, was also as much "irked" by the form as he was by the content of Stone's movie. He excoriated what he called Stone's "appropriation of TV car commercial quick-cutting" and reported that, for him, "watching *JFK* was like watching three hours of MTV without the music."[6] But Armstrong disliked "the film as a film" for other reasons as well, reasons more moral than artistic. "I am troubled," he says, "by Stone's mix'n'match of recreated scenes and archival footage..." because "young viewers to whom [Stone] dedicates the film could take his far-reaching conjectures as literal truth." Armstrong suggests, in a word, that Stone's editing techniques might destroy the capacity of "young viewers" to distinguish between a real and a merely imaginary event.[7] All of the events depicted in the film—whether attested by historical evidence, based on conjecture, or simpy made up in order to help the plot along or to lend credence to Stone's paranoid fantasies—are presented as if they were equally "historical," which is to say, equally real, or as if they had "really happened." And this in spite of the fact that Stone is on record as professing not to know the difference between "history" and what people "make up," in other words, as viewing all events as equally "imaginary," at least insofar as they are *represented*.[8]

Issues such as these arise within the context of the experience, memory, or awareness of events which not only could not possibly have occurred before the twentieth century but the nature, scope, and implications of which no prior age could even have imagined. Some of these "holocaustal" events—such as the two World Wars, the Great Depression, a growth in world population hitherto unimaginable, poverty and hunger on a scale never before experienced, pollution of the ecosphere by nuclear explosions and the indiscriminate disposal of contaminants, programs of genocide undertaken by societies utilizing scientific technology and rationalized procedures of governance and warfare (of which the German genocide of 6,000,000 European Jews is paradigmatic)—function in the consciousness of certain social groups exactly as infantile traumas are conceived to function in the psyche of neurotic individuals. This means that they cannot be simply forgotten and put out of mind, but neither can they be adequately remembered; which is to say, clearly and unambiguously identified as to their meaning and contextualized in the group memory in such a way as to reduce the shadow they cast over the group's capacities to go into its present and envision a future free of their debilitating effects.[9]

The suggestion that the meanings of these events, for the groups most immediately affected by or fixated upon them, remain ambiguous and their consignment to "the past" difficult to effectuate should not be taken to imply in any way that such events never happened. On the contrary, not only are their occurrences amply attested to, their continuing effects on current societies and generations which had no direct experience of them are readily documentable. But among those effects must be listed the difficulty felt by present generations of arriving at some agreement as to their *meaning*—by which I mean, what the facts established about such events can possibly tell us about the nature of our own current social and cultural endowment and what attitude we ought to take with respect to them as we make plans for our own future. In other words, what is at issue here is not the facts of the matter regarding such events but the different possible meanings that such facts can be construed as bearing.

The distinction between facts and meanings is usually taken to be a basis of historical relativism. This is because in conventional historical inquiry, the "facts" established about a specific "event" are taken to *be* the "meaning" of that event. Facts are supposed to provide the basis for arbitrating among the variety of different meanings that different groups *can* assign to an event for different ideological or political reasons. But the facts are a *function* of the meaning assigned to events, not some primitive data that determine what meanings an event can have. It is the anomalous nature of modernist events—their resistance to inherited categories and conventions for assigning them meanings—that undermines not only the status of facts in relation to events but also the status of "the event" in general.

But to consider the issue of historical objectivity in terms of an opposition of "real" and "imaginary" events, on which the opposition of "fact" and "fiction" is in turn based, obscures an important development in Western culture which distinguishes modernism in the arts from all previous forms of realism. Indeed, it seems as difficult to conceive of a treatment of *historical* reality that would not use fictional techniques in the representation of events as it is to conceive of a modernist fiction that did not in some way or at some level make claims about the nature and meaning of history.[10] And this is true for a number of quite obvious reasons. First, the twentieth century is marked by the occurrence of certain "holocaustal" events that bear little similarity to what earlier historians conventionally took as their objects of study and do not, therefore, lend themselves to understanding by the commonsensical techniques utilized in conventional historical inquiry nor even to representation by the techniques of writing typically favored by historians from Herodotus to Arthur Schlesinger. Nor does any of several varieties of quantitative analysis, of the kind practiced in the social sciences, capture the novelty of such events.[11] Moreover, these kinds of events do not lend themselves to explanation in terms of the categories underwritten by traditional humanistic historiography, in which human "agents" are conceived to be in some way fully conscious and morally responsible for their actions and capable of discriminating clearly between the causes of historical events and their effects over the long as well as the short run in relatively commonsensical ways—in other words, agents who are presumed to understand "history" in much the same way as professional historians do.

But beyond that, the "historical" event, by which one used to mean something like "the assassination of the thirty-fifth president of the United States," has been dissolved as an object of a respectably scientific *knowledge*. Such events can serve as the "contents" of bodies of *information*, but as possible objects of a *knowledge* of history that might lay claim to the status of scientific lore, they are of interest only as elements of a statistical series. Indeed, such singular events as the assassination of a head of state are worthy of study only as a hypothetical presupposition necessary to the constitution of a documentary record whose inconsistencies, contradictions, gaps, and distortions of the event presumed to be their common referent itself moves to the fore as the principal object of investigation. As for such singular events *of the past*, the only thing that can be said about them is that they *occurred* at particular times and places.[12]

An event such as the assassination of President John F. Kennedy will inevitably continue to generate the interest of "history buffs" and even of professional historians as long as it can be made to seem relevant to current political, ideological, or group- or individual-psychological concerns, as the case may be. However, any attempt to provide an objective account of the event, either by breaking it up into a mass of its details or by setting it within its context, must conjure with two circumstances: one is that the number of details identifiable in any singular event is potentially infinite; and the other is that the "context" of any singular event is infinitely extensive or at least is not objectively determinable.[13] Moreover, the historical event, traditionally conceived as an event which was not only observable but also observed, is by definition an event that is no longer observable, and hence cannot serve as an object of a knowledge as certain as can a present event which can still be observed. This is why it is perfectly respectable to fall back upon the time-honored tradition of representing such singular events as the assassination of the thirty-fifth president of the United States as a story and to try to explain it by narrativizing (fabulating) it—as Oliver Stone did in *JFK*.[14]

But this is where the distinction between the "fact" as opposed to the "event" of modernism must be addressed. The notion of the "historical event" has undergone radical transformation as a result of both the occurrence in our century of events of a scope, scale, and depth unimaginable by earlier historians and the dismantling of the concept of the event as an object of a specifically scientific kind of knowledge. The same is true however, for the notion of the "story"; it has suffered tremendous fraying and an at least potential dissolution as a result of both that revolution in representational practices known as cultural "modernism"[15] and the technologies of representation made possible by the electronics revolution.

On this last point, we can consider the power of the modern media to represent events in such a way as to render them, not only impervious to every effort to explain them but also resistant to any attempt to represent them in a story form. The modern electronic media can manipulate recorded images so as literally to "explode" events before the eyes of viewers. The uses made in courtroom presentations of television images of Los Angeles police beating a black man (Rodney King) had the effect of making this seemingly unambiguously documented event virtually unintelligible *as an event*. The very precision and detail of the imagistic representation of the event are what threw it open to a wide variety of interpetations of "what was really going on" in the scene depicted. The contingency of the videographic recording of the event (the videographer "happened" to be within sight of the scene with camcorder available, loaded, functioning, etc.), precluded the fiction that the events recorded followed a specific "scenario," script, or plot-line. It is no accident, as it used to be said, that accidents have traditionally served as the very archetype of what historians formerly thought of as "events." But the "accidents" in question were always of a certain kind, namely, the sort that yielded to the imperatives of storytelling and followed the rules of narrativization.

But not only are *modern* post-industrial "accidents" more incomprehensible than anything earlier generations could possibly have imagined (think of Chernobyl), the photo and video documentation of such accidents is so full that it is difficult to work up the documentation of any one of them as elements of a single "objective" story. Moreover, in many instances, the documentation of such events is so manipulable as to discourage the effort to derive explanations of the occurrences of which the documentation is supposed to be a recorded image. "It is no accident," then, that discussions of the modernist event tend in the direction of an aesthetics of the sublime-and-the-disgusting rather than that of the beautiful-and-the-ugly.

An example of what I have in mind is provided by an article published in a recent issue of the periodical *1-800*. Here Michael Turits analyzed the hermeneutic gymnastics inspired by media coverage of two amply documented techno-air disasters: the collision of three Italian MB 339A (*Frecce tricolori*) jet planes in an air show over Ramstein, Germany, in August 1988, killing 50 and injuring 360; and the explosion in 1986 of the NASA Challenger space shuttle just after lift-off, in full view of a live "audience" and millions of television viewers. In his analysis of the media's presentations of these events, Turits likens the impact of their endless re-presentations on TV to the ambiguating effects of those televised "replays" of crucial events in sporting contests. Turits observes that "when the [Challenger] blew up and the *Frecce tricolori* collided, ... the optical geometries yielded by endless replays far outran the capacities of the network techno-refs to make a call." What had been promised to be a clarification of "what happened" actually produced widespread cognitive disorientation and a despair at ever being able to identify the elements of the events in order to render possible an "objective" analysis of their causes and consequences. Thus Turits notes:

> Like an out-of-control computer virus somehow lodged in the network's video editing desks, the Ramstein collision and the Challenger explosion could do nothing but frantically play themselves over and over.... The frame-by-frame re-runs that followed [the Challenger explosion] for months served the same purpose as the media's obsession with the deep-sea recovery of the shuttle and astronaut remains—to reconstruct the too brief event as *a visually intelligible* accident.[16]

The networks played the tapes of the Challenger explosion over and over. In response to the question of why they had done so, the news commentator Tom Brokaw said: "What else could we do? People wanted answers."[17] But as Turits remarks, the tapes certainly provided no answers. All that the "morphing" technology used to re-present the event provided was a sense of its evanescence. It appeared impossible to tell any single authoritative story about what really happened—which meant that one could tell any number of possible stories about it.

And this is why the issues raised in the controversy over *JFK* could be profitably set within a more recent phase of the debate over the relation of historical fact to fiction peculiar to the discussion of the relation between modernism and postmodernism. For literary (and for that matter filmic) "modernism" (whatever else it may be) marks the end of storytelling—understood in Walter Benjamin's sense of "the tale" by which the lore, wisdom, and commonplaces of a culture are transmitted from one generation to another in the form of the followable story. After modernism, when it comes to the task of storytelling, whether in historical or in literary writing, the traditional techniques of narration become unusable—except in parody.[18] Modernist literary practice effectively explodes the notion of those "characters" who had formerly served as the subjects of stories or at least as representatives of possible perspectives on the events of the story; and it resists the temptation to "emplot" events and the "actions" of the "characters" so as to produce the meaning-effect derived by demonstrating how one's end may be contained in one's beginning. Modernism thereby effects what Fredric Jameson calls the "de-realization" of the event itself. And it does this by consistently voiding the event of its traditional narrativistic function of indexing the irruption of fate, destiny, grace, fortune, providence, and even of "history" itself into a life (or at least into some lives) "in order to pull the sting of novelty" and give the life thus affected at worst a semblance of pattern and at best an actual, transsocial, and transhistorical significance.[19]

Jameson shows how Sartre, in a typically modernist work like *Nausea*,[20] thematizes the experience of time as a series of instants which either fail to take on the form of a story or fall apart into shards and fragments of existence. The thematization takes the form of a representation of the ineradicable differences—indeed, the opposition—between "ordinary" life and a putatively "adventurous" one. Thus, in a scene analyzed by Jameson, the protagonist Roquentin reflects to himself:

> I have never had adventures. Things have happened to me, events, incidents, anything you like. But no adventures.... I had imagined that at certain times my life could take on a rare and precious quality. There was no need for extraordinary circumstances: all I asked for was a little precision.... [F]rom time to time, for example, when they play music in the cafes, I look back and tell myself: in the old days, in London, Meknes, Tokyo, I have known great moments, I have had adventures. Now I am deprived of this. I have suddenly learned, without any apparent reason, that I have been lying to myself for ten years. And naturally, everything they tell about in books can happen in real life, but not in the same way. It is to this way of happening that I clung so tightly. (53–55)

Roquentin's problem is that, to him, in order for an event to have the meaning of an adventure, it would have to resemble the kinds of events met with in adventure *stories*. Events would have to be "narratable." Here is how Sartre represents Roquentin's desire for story-events:

> This is what I thought: for the most banal event to become an adventure, you must (and this is enough) begin to recount it. This is what fools people: a man is always a teller of tales, he lives somehow surrounded by his stories and the stories of others, he sees everything that happens to him through them; and he tries to live his own life as if he were telling a story.

But you have to choose: live or tell.

Roquentin's melancholy stems from his realization that:

> Nothing *happens* while you live. The scenery changes, people come and go out, that's all. There are no *beginnings*. Days are

tacked on to days without rhyme or reason, an interminable, monotonous addition.... That's living. But everything changes when you tell about life; it's a change no one notices: the proof is that *people talk about true stories.* As if there could possibly be true stories; things happen one way and we tell about them in the opposite sense. You seem to start at the beginning: "It was a fine autumn evening in 1922. I was a notary's clerk in Marommes." And in reality you have started at the end. It was there, invisible and present, it is the the one which gives to words the pomp and value of a beginning. (56–7; my emphases) ... I wanted the moments of my life to follow and offer themselves like those of a life remembered [as in Proust!]. You might as well try to catch time by the tail. (58)

And this realization leads him to conclude:

> This feeling of adventure definitely does not come from events: I have proved it. It's rather the way in which the moments are linked together. I think this is what happens: you suddenly feel time is passing, that each instant leads to another, this one to another one, and so on; that each instant is annihilated, and that it isn't worth while to hold it back, etc., etc., And then you attribute this property to events which appear to you in the instants: *what belongs to the form you carry over to the content.* You talk a lot about this amazing flow of time but you hardly see it.... [my emphasis]
>
> If I remember correctly, they call that the irreversibility of time. The feeling of adventure would simply be that of the irreversibility of time. But why don't we always have it? Is it that time is not always irreversible? There are moments when you have the impression that you can do what you want, go forward or backward, that it has no importance; and then other times when you might say that the links have been tightened and, in that case, it's not a question of missing your turn because you could never start again." (80)

These passages from Sartre today seem dated, melodramatic, even hackneyed—as the *recent* past always does—but they usefully point out the modernist apprehension that the meaning, form, or coherence of events, whether real or imaginary ones, is a function of their narrativization. Jameson concludes that the modernist de-realization of the event amounts to a rejection of the historicity of all events and that this is what throws the modernist sensibility open to on the one hand the attractions of myth (the myths of Oedipus, Ulysses, Finnegan, and so on), or on the other hand the extravagances of melodrama (typically institutionalized in the genre of the detective, spy, crime, or extraterrestrial alien story). In the former case, the meaning of otherwise unimaginable events is seen to reside in their resemblance to *timeless* archetypal stories—like the death of the young hero-leader, JFK. In the latter case, meaning is rendered spectral, seeming to consist solely in the *spatial* dispersion of the phenomena that had originally seemed to have converged only in order to indicate the occurrence of an event.

Sartre's treatment of the event is a representation (*Vorstellung*) of a thought about it, rather than a "presentation" (*Darstellung*) of the event itself. A similarly modernist presentation of the event is found in a passage from Virginia Woolf's last novel, *Between the Acts*.[21] The title itself indicates a typical concern of High Modernism, namely, an interest in what, if anything, goes on in the "intervals" between those rare instants in our lives in which something "eventful" seems to be happening. But the story thematizes the insubstantiality not only of the intervals between events, but also of those events whose seeming occurrence renders possible the apprehension of what comes between them *as* an interval.

In *Between the Acts,* the life of the Oliver family seems to be as orderly as the pageant which is to be performed by the villagers on the family estate on that single "day in June in 1939" which frames the non-action of the story. The pageant is depicted, however, as differing from the real world by its possession of a discernible plot; its intervals mark the "acts" which themselves represent identifiable "periods" of English history from the Middle Ages to the present. In the intervals between the acts of the pageant, the members of the Oliver family and their guests disperse and recombine in moments of what always turn out to be failed epiphanies, so that in reality the events which might have served to mark out a plot in their lives never quite occur. What happens "between the acts" is nothing at all; indeed the difference between the acts and the intervals which occur between them is progressively smudged and finally erased. The principal difference we are left with is that between the pageant, with all its acts marked by events, and the real life of the spectators, in which no events whatsoever occur. An eventful instant of time would have been one that collected and condensed the vagrant events that are experienced more as intervals than as occurrences, and endowed them with pattern and cohesion, if only for a moment. But there are no such events in this story. All of the events that take place before, during, between, and after the "acts" of the pageant itself are shown to have been as insubstantial as what takes place between the individual frames of a movie film and as fictitious as those "historical" events depicted in the pageant.

The passage I referred to as exemplifying the typically modernist approach to the representation of an event appears in the second "scene" of the story (there are no chapter designations). The central figure of the novel, Isabella

(Mrs. Giles) Oliver, has just entered the library of the family house, located "in a remote village in the very heart of England," on the morning of the pageant. Her father-in-law, Bart Oliver, a retired civil servant, is already there, reading the newspaper. As she enters, she recalls a phrase uttered by a woman visitor to the library some years earlier:

> "The library's always the nicest room in the house," she quoted, and ran her eyes along the books. "The mirror of the soul," books were.... *The Faerie Queene* and Kinglake's *Crimea*; Keats and *The Kreutzer Sonata*. There they were, reflecting. What? What remedy was there for her at her age—the age of the century, thirty-nine—in books? Book-shy she was, like the rest of her generation; and gun-shy, too. Yet as a person with a raging tooth runs her eye in a chemist shop over green bottles with gilt scrolls on them lest one of them may contain a cure, she considered: Keats and Shelley; Yeats and Donne. Or perhaps not a poem; a life. The life of Garibaldi. The life of Lord Palmerston. Or perhaps not a person's life; a county's. *The Antiquities of Durham*; *The Proceedings of the Archaeological Society of Nottingham*. Or not a life at all, but science—Eddington, Darwin, Jeans.
>
> None of them stopped her toothache. For her generation the newspaper was a book; and, as her father-in-law dropped the *Times*, she took it and read: "A horse with a green tail ..." which was fantastic. Next, "The guard at Whitehall ..." which was romantic and then, building word upon word, she read: "The troopers told her the horse had a green tail; but she found it was just an ordinary horse. And they dragged her up to the barrack room where she was thrown upon a bed. Then one of the troopers removed part of her clothing, and she screamed and hit him about the face ..."
>
> That was real; so real that on the mahogany door panels she saw the Arch in Whitehall; through the Arch the barrack room; in the barrack room the bed, and on the bed the girl was screaming and hitting him about the face, when the door (for in fact it was a door) opened and in came Mrs. Swithin carrying a hammer.
>
> She advanced, sidling, as if the floor were fluid under her shabby garden shoes, and, advancing, pursed her lips and smiled, sidelong, at her brother. Not a word passed between them as she went to the cupboard in the corner and replaced the hammer, which she had taken without asking leave; together—she unclosed her fist—with a handful of nails. (19–20)

Notice that quite a few (and for the most part mundane) "events" are registered here: Isabella "peruses" the bookshelves for a possible "remedy" for the ills that afflict her generation—significantly marked by a date: 1939. She "considers" poetry, biography, history, science, and turns away from them all to the newspaper where she "reads" an account of an event, a rape, an event so surreal that she "sees" it "on the ... panels" of the library door. But the image of the event, which happened in the past, metamorphoses, without a break in grammar or syntax, into that of Mrs. Swithin, Bart's sister, "entering" the library in the fictive present: " ... and on the bed the girl was screaming and hitting him about the face, when the door (for in fact it was a door) opened and in came Mrs. Swithin carrying a hammer."

The image of the girl being raped leaks into that of the quite ordinary event of Mrs. Swithin entering the library and contaminates it, endowing it with a sinister, phantasmagoric aspect: Mrs. Swithin "*advanced, sidling,* as if the floor were *fluid* under her *shabby* garden shoes, and, *advancing, pursed her lips* and *smiled, sidelong,* at her brother. Not a word passed between them and she went to the cupboard in the corner and replaced the hammer, which she had taken without asking leave; together—she unclosed her fist—with a handful of nails." (My emphases.) The two events, the rape of the girl and the entrance of Mrs. Swithin into the library, are endowed with an equal measure of significance, or rather of ambiguity, of meaning. There is no way of distinguishing between their respective phenomenal aspects or their different significances. Both events flow out of their outlines and flow out of the narrative as well. The effect of the representation is to endow *all* events with spectral qualities. Mrs. Swithin's replacement of the hammer leads to an exchange between herself and her brother that Isabella recognizes—uncannily—as having taken place every summer for the last seven years.

> Every summer, for seven summers now, Isa had heard the same words; about the hammer and the nails; the pageant and the weather. Every year they said, would it be wet or fine; and every year it was—one or the other. The same chime [of the clock] followed the same chime, only this year beneath the chime she heard: "The girl screamed and hit him about the face with a hammer." (22)

The outside phenomenal aspects, and insides of events, their possible meanings or significances, have been collapsed and fused. The "meaning" of events remains indistinguishable from their occurrence, but their occurrence is unstable, fluid, phantasmagoric—as phantasmagoric as the slow-motion, reverse angle, zoom, and rerun of the video representations of the Challenger explosion. This is not to say that such events are not representable, only that techniques of representation somewhat different from those developed at the height of artistic realism may be called for.

Contemporary discussions of the ethics and aesthetics of representing the Holocaust of the European Jews—which I take to be the paradigmatic "modernist" event in Western European history—provide insights into the modernist view of the relationship between history and fiction. With respect to the question of how most responsibly to represent the Holocaust, the most extreme position is *not* that of the so-called Revisionists, who deny that the event ever happened;[22] but rather, those who hold that this event is of such a kind as to escape the grasp of *any* language even to *describe* it and of *any* medium—verbal, visual, oral, or gestural—to *represent* it, much less of any merely historical account adequately to *explain* it. This position is represented in George Steiner's oft-quoted remark, "The world of Auschwitz lies outside speech as it lies outside reason."[23] It is also represented in the remark of the philosopher Emile Fackenheim: "The Holocaust ... resists explanation—the historical kind that seeks causes, and the theological kind that seeks meaning and purpose.... The Holocaust, it would appear, is a qualitatively unique event, different in kind even from other instances of genocide. One cannot comprehend [the Holocaust] but only confront and object."[24]

The historian Christopher R. Browning addresses questions and assertions such as these in a remarkably subtle reflection on the difficulties he had to face in his efforts to reconstruct, represent, and explain a massacre of some 1,500 Jews—women, children, elders, and young men—by German Army Reserve Battalion 101 on July 13, 1942 in the woods outside the Polish village of Jozefów. Browning has spent years pondering the documents that attest to the facts of this event and interviewed 125 members of the battalion who, neither regular soldiers nor members of the SS, took on the role of "professional killers" in the course of their service as anonymous executors of the genocidal policy conceived and implemented by their Nazi leaders. Browning's aim was to write the history of one day in the life of the "little men" who were the perpetrators of specific crimes against specific people at a specific time and place in a past that is rapidly receding from living memory and passing into "history." And in his report on his research, Browning asks:

> Can the history of such men ever be written? Not just the social, organizational, and institutional history of the units they belonged to. And not just the ideological and decision-making history of the policies they carried out. Can one recapture the experiential history of these killers—the choices they faced, the emotions they felt, the coping mechanisms they employed, the changes they underwent?[25]

He concludes that such an "experiential history" of this event, all too typical of all too many events of the Holocaust, is virtually impossible to conceive.

The Holocaust, he reminds us, "was not an abstraction. It was a real event in which more than five million Jews were murdered, most in a manner so violent and on a scale so vast that historians and others trying to write about these events have experienced nothing in their personal lives that remotely compares." And he goes on to assert that "Historians of the Holocaust, in short, know nothing—in an experiential sense—about their subject." This kind of "experiential shortcoming," Browning points out,

> is quite different from their not having experienced, for example, the Constitutional Convention in Philadelphia or Caesar's conquest of Gaul. Indeed, a recurring theme of witnesses [to the Holocaust] is how "unbelievable" [that event] was to them even as they lived through it.[26]

This experiential shortcoming pertains to the *nature* of the events under scrutiny; these events seem to resist the traditional historian's effort at the kind of empathy which would permit one to see them, as it were, from the inside; in this case, from the perpetrators' perspective. And the difficulty, Browning argues, is not methodological. It is not a question of establishing the facts of the matter, but of *representing* the events established as facts in such a way as to make those events believable to readers who have no more "experience" of such events than the historian himself.

Browning, in short, draws back from suggesting what appears to me to be the obvious conclusion one might derive from this problem: namely, the problem is indeed not one of method but rather one of representation, and this problem of representing the events of the Holocaust requires the full exploitation of modernist as well as pre-modernist artistic techniques for its resolution. Browning draws back from this possibility because, like Professor Saul Friedlander and other experts in the study of representations of the Holocaust, whether in writing, film, photography, monuments, or whatever, he fears the effects of any "aestheticization" of this event. By making the Holocaust into the subject matter of a narrative, it becomes a story which, by its possible "humanization" of the perpetrators, might "enfable" the event—render it fit therefore for investment by fantasies of "intactness," "wholeness," and "health" which the very occurrence of the event *denies.*

According to Eric Santner, the danger of yielding to the impulse to "tell the story" of the Holocaust—and by extension any other "traumatic" event—opens the investigator of it to the danger of engaging in "narrative fetishism," which is, in his view, a "strategy of undoing, in fantasy, the need for mourning by simulating a condition of intactness, typically by situating the site and origin of loss elsewhere."[27] In short, the threat posed by the representation of such events as the Holocaust, the Nazi Final Solution, by the assassination of a charismatic leader such as Kennedy or Martin Luther King or Gandhi, or by an event such as the destruction of the Challenger, which had been symbolically orchestrated to represent the aspirations of a whole community, is nothing other than the threat of turning these events into the subject-matter of a narrative. Telling a story, however truthful, about such traumatic events might very well provide a kind of "intellectual mastery" of the anxiety which memory of their occurrence may incite in an individual or a community. But precisely insofar as the story is identifiable *as a story*, it can provide no lasting "psychic mastery" of such events.

This is why the kinds of anti-narrative non-stories produced by literary modernism offer the only prospect for adequate representations of the kind of "unnatural" events—including the Holocaust—that mark our era and distinguish it absolutely from all of the "history" that has come before it. In other words, what Jameson calls the "psychopathologies" of modernist writings and film, which he lists as "their artificial closures, the blockage of narrative, [their] deformation and formal compensations, the dissociation or splitting of narrative functions, including the repression of certain of them, and so forth,"[28] might offer the possibility of representing such traumatic events as being produced by the monstrous growth and expansion of technological "modernity" (of which Nazism and the Holocaust are manifestations) in a manner less fetishizing than any traditional representation of them could ever be.

What I am suggesting is that the stylistic innovations of modernism, born as they were of an effort to come to terms with the anticipated loss of the peculiar "sense of history" which modernism is ritually criticized for not possessing, may provide better instruments for representing "modernist" events (and for pre-modernist events in which we have a typically modernist interest) than the storytelling techniques traditionally utilized by historians for the representation of those events of the past that are supposed to be crucial to the development of their community's identity. Modernist techniques of representation provide the possibility of de-fetishizing both events and the fantasy accounts of them which deny the threat they pose, in the very process of pretending to represent them realistically. This de-fetishizing can then clear the way for that process of mourning which alone can relieve the "burden of history" and make a more, if not totally realistic perception of current problems possible.

It is fortunate, therefore, that we have in the work of one of the greatest of modernist writers a theorization of this problem of representing events in the narrative. In four lectures entitled *Narration*,[29] delivered at the University of Chicago in 1936, Gertrude Stein reflected on the unreality of the "event" in contrast to "things which have really existed." An event, she suggested, was only an "outside without an inside," whereas a thing which has "existed" has its outside inside itself. When "the outside is outside," she said, "it is not begun and when it is outside it is not ended and when it is neither begun nor ended it is not either a thing which has existed it is simply an event." She went on to contrast both journalistic and historical treatments of events with a specifically modernist artistic treatment of them, on the basis of the failure of the former kind to put "the outside inside":

> In real life that is if you like in the newspapers which are not real life but real life with the reality left out, the reality being the inside and the newspapers being the outside and never is the outside inside and never is the inside outside except in the rare and peculiar cases when the outside breaks through to be inside because the outside is so part of some inside that even a description of the outside cannot completely relieve the outside of the inside.
>
> And so in the newspapers you like to know the answer in crime stories in reading crime and in written crime stories knowing the answer spoils it. After all in the written thing the answer is a let down from the interest and that is so every time that is what spoils most crime stories unless another mystery crops up during the crime and that mystery remains.
>
> And then there is another very peculiar thing in the newspaper thing it is the crime in the story it is the detective that is the thing.
>
> Now do you begin to see the difference between the inside and the outside.
>
> In the newspaper thing it is the crime it is the criminal that is interesting, in the story it is the story about the crime that is interesting. (54)

As for historical representation, she has this to say:

> Anyone can see that there is more confusion that is to say perhaps not more confusion but that it is a more difficult thing to write history to make it anything than to make anything that is anything be anything because in history you have everything, you have the newspapers and the conversations and letter writing and the mystery stories and audience and in every direction an audience that fits anything in every way in which an audience can fit itself to be anything, and there is of course as I have been saying so much to trouble any one about any one of any of these things. (54)

It was, Stein argued—or rather poetized—because of the specifically "modern" awareness of the exteriority of events that their narrative treatment was so difficult:

> We talked a great deal all this time how hard it is to tell anything anything that has been anything that is, and that makes a narrative and that makes history and that makes literature and is history literary.
>
> Well how far have we come.
>
> Can history be literature when it has such a burden a burden of everything, a burden of so many days which are days one after the other and each has its happening and still as in the newspaper what can make it matter is it is not happening to-day, the best thing that can happen about that happening is that it can happen again. And that makes the comfort of history to a historian that history repeats itself, that is really the only comfort that a historian can have from anything happening and really and truly it does not happen again not as it used to happen again because now we know really know so much that has happened that really we do not know that what has happened does not happen again and so that for poor comfort has been taken away from the historian.
>
> What I mean is this, history has gotten to be so that anybody can if they go on know that everything that happened is what happened and as it all did happen it is a very serious thing that so much was happening. Very well then. What would be the addition to anything if everything is happening, look out of any window, any window nowadays is on a high building if it happens right and see what is happening. Well enough said, it is not necessary to go on with recognition, but soon you do know anybody can know, that it is all real enough. It is all real enough, not only real enough but and that is where it is such a diffilcult thing not real enough for writing, real enough for seeing, almost real enough for remembering but remembering in itself is not really an important enough thing to really need recalling, insofar as it is not seeing, but remembering is seeing and so anything is an important enough thing for seeing but it is not an important enough thing for writing, it is an important enough thing for talking but not an important enough thing for telling.
>
> That is really the trouble with what history is, it is important enough for seeing but not important enough for writing, it is important enough for talking but not important enough for telling. And that is what makes everybody so troubled about it all about what history is, because after all it ought to be important

enough for telling for writing and not only important enough for talking and seeing, it really ought to be, it really ought to be, but can it be. Cannot it really be. (59)

Now the same thing is true when the newspaper tells about any real thing, the real thing having happened it is completed and being completed can not be remembered because the thing in its essence being completed can not be remembered because the thing in its essence being completed there is no emotion in remembering it, it is a fact like any other and having been done it is for the purposes of memory a thing having no vitality. While anything which is a relief and in a made up situation as it gets more and more exciting when the exciting rises to being really exciting then it is a relief then it is a thing that has emotion when that thing is a remembered thing.

Now you must see how true this is about the crime story and the actual crime. The actual crime is a crime that is a fact and it having been done that in itself is a completion and so for purposes of memory with very rare exceptions where a personality connected with it is overpowering there is no memory to bother any one. Completion is completion, a thing done is a thing done so it has in it no quality of ending or beginning. Therefore in real life it is the crime and as the newpaper has to feel about it as if it were in the act of seeing or doing it, they cannot really take on detecting they can only take on the crime, they cannot take on anything that takes on beginning and ending and in the detecting end of detective stories there is nothing but going on beginning and ending. Anybody does naturally feel that that a detective is just that that a detective is just that that it is a continuity of beginning and ending and reality nothing but that. (42)

I will resist the impulse to comment on this passage since it is composed in such a way as to collapse the distinction between its form and its semantic content on which the possibility of commentary pretending to clarify what the passage "means" is based. But as I write this essay, the newspapers are filled with accounts of another "trial of the century," in this case, preliminary hearings in the case of a famous Afro-American athlete and movie personality, O. J. Simpson, suspected of brutally murdering his (white) wife (mother of his two children) and her male companion (a male model and aspiring actor, white and Jewish). These court proceedings were themselves preceded by a bizarre incident in which Simpson, apparently contemplating escape from the country, led police on a slow-moving "chase" on the freeways of Los Angeles to the accompaniment of television cameras, nationwide radio and TV coverage, and the same kind of "commentary" as that which attended the explosion of the Challenger or the very athletic events in which Simpson had made his fortune. Few events of such notoriety have been so amply documented as this chase, which featured live spectators who had rushed to the route of the flight to cheer Simpson, thereby being transformed into "actors" in the "scene" by the television camera's eye.

What is the "inside" and what the "outside" of this "event"? What the "beginning" and what is the "end"? Although the trial of Simpson, which is imminent, is intended to determine the specific role played by him in the crime of double murder, it is evident that this trial will be a separate "event" rather than a continuation of the event that it occasioned it. Interestingly, the prosecuting attorneys have announced that they will not seek the death penalty for Simpson if he is convicted of the crime, indicating that, given the American public's affection for this hero, any effort to seek the death penalty would prejudice the possibility of a jury's convicting him. The crime-event is already being detached from the trial-event, almost as if to suggest that they belong to different universes of occurrence. In fact, the trial will have the purpose of providing a scenario compatible with a commonplace of the discourse of justice, namely, that everyone is equal under the law but that the law of the rich and famous is one thing and that of the poor and obscure quite another.

notes

This paper is a version of the Patricia Doyle Wise Memorial Lecture annually commissioned by the American Film Institute and delivered at UCLA on Wednesday, April 8, 1992, in co-sponsorship with the UCLA Film and Television Archive. I want to thank the Institute for inviting me. I am especially grateful to Vivian Sobchack, editor of this volume for her introduction to the lecture, her great conversation over the ten years we were colleagues, and her counsel for the subsequent development of this essay.

1. Fredric Jameson, "Metacommentary [1971]," in *The Ideologies of Theory: Essays, 1971–86* (Minneapolis: University of Minnesota Press, 1988), ch. 1.
2. Linda Hutcheon, *A Poetics of Postmodernism; History, Theory, Fiction* (New York and London: Routledge, 1988), 76. Hutcheon notes that in Postmodern novels, the focus is on the "process of event becoming fact." Reflecting on Hutcheon's remark, I could not help but relate it to Linda Williams's description of what she calls "the new documentary" film, which, like *Shoah* or *Roger and Me,* are less about "facts" than they are about the filmmaker's search for the facts. She points out also that these films "are, *as Stone's film isn't,* documentaries...." This suggests that *JFK* ought not be assessed by the criteria we would use to evaluate documentaries. I would suggest that *JFK* is neither factual nor fictional but rather "figurative" and should be assessed as a "figure" first and foremost. Cf. Linda Williams, "Mirrors Without Memories: Truth, History, and the New Documentary," *Film Quarterly* 46, no. 3 (Spring 1993); 13.
3. Cf. Jameson, "Magical Narratives," in *The Political Unconscious: Narrative as a Socially Symbolic Act* (Ithaca: Cornell University Press, 1981), ch. 2.
4. Cf. Gertrude Himmelfarb, "History as You Like It," *Times Literary Supplement,* October 16, 1992, 12–15.

5. "Movie Madness," *Times Literary Supplement*, January 24, 1992, 16–17. Grenier goes on to report that: "Never in the history of Hollywood has a motion picture been slammed so vehemently by America's political class. Politicians and political writers of every political hue have condemned *JFK* as irresponsible and even crazed: hard left, right, centre." He then remarks on the difference between the responses of politicians and political writers and that of "film critics, who identify with the country's 'artistic' class." "On the whole," he says, these critics "have rather liked the movie, which sets them conspicuously apart from other American commentators, columnists, journalists, who, with truly extraordinary unanimity, have been absolutely appalled by the film." And from this contrast of responses, he concludes that "Perhaps one should not buy a used car from a film critic." (16)
6. David Armstrong and Todd Gitlin, "Killing the Messenger," *Image*, Sunday, February 16, 1992, 14. These are separate essays, published under a single title and with the questioning subtitle "Why Did The Press React So Furiously Over Stone's Movie?" See also the remarks of Michael Rogin, "'Make My Day!': Spectacle as Amnesia in Imperial Politics," *Representations* 29 (Winter 1990): 99–123.
7. Armstrong and Gitlin, "Killing the Messenger." The critic's concern for the sensibilities of the young is telling; when critics start expressing concern for the corruption of youth, it is always a good sign that a work of art has hit a collective nerve.
8. Stone presumably knows the difference between the events of the Vietnam War and various representations of it. He does not seem to be arguing that the events of the war did not happen, only that in representations there is little difference between factual and fictional accounts of those events. His views of "history" are another matter. In an interview, Stone is quoted to the following effect: "What is history? Some people say it's a bunch of gossip made up by soldiers who passed it around a campfire. They say such and such happened. They create, they make it bigger, they make it better. I knew guys in combat who made up shit. I'm sure the cowboys did the same. The nature of human beings is that they exaggerate. So, what is history? Who the fuck knows?" (*Esquire*, 116, no. 5 [November 1991], 93).
9. The inclusion of the Holocaust in this list may be questioned by scholars of that event who insist on its uniqueness, if not in all of history, then at least in the history of genocides. In my view, all historical events are *by definition* unique, one of a kind, but still comparable with other events of the same species. The other events in my list are similarly unique of their species. My point is that the events in this list are all *uniquely twentieth-century* and belong, therefore, to the same *genus*.
10. Cf. Sidney Monas, "Introduction: Contemporary Historiography: Some Kicks in the Old Coffin," in *Developments in Modern Historiography* ed. Henry Kozicki (New York: St.Martin's Press, 1992), 1–16.
11. See Zygmunt Bauman, *Modernity and the Holocaust* (Ithaca: Cornell University Press, 1989), 122.
12. Cf. Krzysztof Pomian, "Evento," in *Enciclopedia Einaudi* (Torino: Giulio Einaudi editore, 1978), VIII, 972–993; and Edgar Morin, ed., *Teorie dell'evento*, Italian translation of *Le retour de l'événement* (Milano: Bompiani, 1972)
13. I have discussed the problem of context in "Geschichte erklären. Formalistische und kontextualische Strategien," *Neue Rundschau* 105, Heft I (1994), 41–56.
14. And here we may note that posters for Stone's film, not mentioned by any of the reviews I have read as having any particular significance present the title as: "*JFK: The Story that Won't Go Away*." Taken literally, then, the title indicates that the "subject" of the film is not an event but a "story"—a story, moreover, that insists itself into the conciousness of a whole generation as a response to a trauma and that can therefore be neither closed and forgotten nor precisely remembered as *merely* an event of the past.
15. Thus, Jameson defines literary modernism as a product of a double crisis; on the

one hand, a "social crisis of narratable experiences" and on the other, a "semiotic crisis of narrative paradigms." Fredric Jameson, *Sartre: The Origins of a Style* (New York: Columbia University Press, 1984), 211. I want to make clear that by the term "modernism" I am not referring to that program of dominating nature through reason, science, and technology supposedly inaugurated by the Enlightenment; I refer, rather, to the literary and artistic movements launched in the late nineteenth and early twentieth centuries against this very program of modernization and its social and cultural effects—the movement represented by writers such as Pound, Eliot, Stein, Joyce, Proust, Woolf, and so on.

16. Michael Turits, "Moment of Impact: Three Air-Crashes," *1–800* (Fall, 1989): 34
17. Turits, 35.
18. Craig Owen has argued that postmodernism is characterized by a revival of allegorical representation, though of a kind quite different from that repudiated by Romantic aesthetics in the name of the Symbol in the nineteenth century. See "The Allegorical Impulse: Toward a New Theory of Postmodernism,"in *Beyond Recognition: Representation, Power, and Culture* (Berkeley and Los Angeles: University of California Press, 1992), 52ff.
19. Jameson, "The Nature of Events," *Sartre*, ch. 2.
20. Jean-Paul Sartre, *Nausea*, translated from the French by Lloyd Alexander (Norfolk: New Directions, [1964]). Page references are inserted parenthetically in the text.
21. Virginia Woolf, *Between the Acts* (San Diego, New York, London: Harcourt Brace, 1970). Page references are inserted parenthetically in the text.
22. I want to stress the difference between the modernist problematization of the "event" and the effort on the part of a group of parahistorians known as "Revisionists" to *deny* that the event known as the Holocaust ever happened. It should be noted that the Revisionists have a very traditional notion of both historical events and evidence. What they wish to establish on the basis of a very literalist interpretation of the evidence is that the occurrence of the Holocaust cannot be proven. They are rather like Fundamentalist Christians interpreting the evidence for evolutionism.
23. George Steiner, quoted in Berel Lang, *Act and Idea in the Nazi Genocide* (Chicago: University of Chicago Press, 1990), 151.
24. The literal import of Steiner's remark is echoed in the answer to the question; "How is the unspeakable to be spoken about?", proposed by Alice and A. R. Eckhardt: "Certainly," they say, "we ought to speak about it, but how *can* we ever do so?" See also George Kren's assertion that "The meaning of the Holocaust can never be grasped from the historical record"; and Elie Wiesel's, "We shall never understand how Auschwitz was possible." All quotations are taken from Alan Rosenberg and Gerald E. Meyers, eds., *Echoes from the Holocaust: Philosophical Reflections on a Dark Time* (Philadelphia: Temple University Press, 1988).
25. Christopher R. Browning, "German Memory, Judicial Interrogation, Historical Reconstruction," in *Probing the Limits of Representation: Nazism and the Final Solution*, ed. Saul Friedlander (Cambridge: Harvard University Press, 1992), 27
26. Browning, 25. Cf. Martin Jay, "Experience Without a Subject: Walter Benjamin and the Novel," in *New Formations*, 20 (Summer 1993): 145–155.
27. Eric Santner, "History Beyond the Pleasure Principle," in *Probing the Limits of Representation* 146.
28. Jameson, *Sartre*, 210.
29. Gertrude Stein, *Narration: Four Lectures, with an Introduction by Thornton Wilder* (Chicago: University of Chicago Press, 1993). Page references are inserted parenthetically in the text.

two

cinematic shots

the narration of violence

janet staiger

In the essay opening this volume, historian Hayden White tackles the issue of how to represent history in moving images, dealing in part with Oliver Stone's 1991 film, *JFK*.[1] Previously, White asked whether moving images could represent historical *thinking*, concluding that moving images can do just so.[2] Now he is interested in considering whether a particular time period (the twentieth century—or at least what he marks as certain "modernist" moments in it) can be represented. He wonders, for instance, if the twentieth century has witnessed events unlike those that nineteenth-century historians had as their subjects, events such as massive famines, ecological disasters, nuclear explosions, or the Holocaust. These violent experiences are not only difficult to *describe* verbally but also impossible to *explain* in terms of traditional human agency. The nature, scope, and implications of these events give them a new dimension.

At the same time, White argues that modernism and what he considers its extension, postmodernism, provide new ways to represent and investigate such twentieth-century events and catastrophes.[3] In a (post)modernist representation of real events, meaning and event run together, producing new genres such as the "docu-drama," "faction," "infotainment," "the fiction of fact," and historical metafiction such as Doctorow's *Ragtime* (1975), Thomas's *The White Hotel* (1981), Syberberg's *Our Hitler* (1977), Visconti's *The Damned* (1969). These metafictions are about events that cannot be remembered *nor* can they be forgotten.

JFK, for White, is symptomatic of these new metafictions. Critics castigated the film because it "seemed to blur the distinction between fact and fiction by treating an historical *event* as if there were no limits on what could legitimately be said about it...." In particular, White remarks on the critical reception of the film by David Armstrong, who chastises *JFK* for the "'mix 'n' match of recreated scenes and archival footage,'" or by Richard Grenier, who writes that Stone directs "'his film in a pummelling style, a left to the jaw, a right to the solar plexus, flashing forward, flashing backward, crosscutting relentlessly, shooting "in tight," blurring, obfuscating, bludgeoning the viewer until Stone wins, he hopes by a TKO.'"[4]

An implicit psychoanalytical dimension to White's thesis parallels the homology being created here between the content of the violent acts and the brutal style of shooting and editing. If people do try to describe such unrepresentable events through a more traditional, linear narrative, the attempt itself could be seen to produce a fetishism of the event. Since such a description is impossible, the substitute narrative serves as the description's replacement, trying to fill in for the lack of an ability to describe or explain the events. This attempt to narrativize thus undoes the necessary process of mourning for the loss of explanation. In trying to master the impossible story, the historian unwittingly and ironically is unable to *psychically* master the event. Thus, only anti-narrative nonstories of the literary (post)modernist kind are able to represent such traumatic events; the anti-narrative form of representation is not totalizing and permits mourning to occur.

White's grand allegory is typical of the kind of provocative work he has produced for historiographers for the last quarter century. As usual, the proposition he has produced is an intriguing one, capable of generating a rather interesting narrative about twentieth-century representations of modernity's historical realities. What I wish to consider, however, is not the truth of White's narrative, but whether, in fact, Oliver Stone did something particularly unusual in his docu-drama practice in *JFK* and whether that supposed unusual practice is (post)modernist—for White leaves the answers to these questions tantalizingly unclear. In proceeding with this investigation, then, I shall have some more angles from which to (re)view shots—both historical and edited—in *JFK*.

First of all, did Oliver Stone do something unusual in his docu-drama practice in *JFK*? To answer this question, I think it is necessary to pose a series of four subquestions which together seem to me to characterize discussions about docu-dramas, re-enactments, films which mix types of source material, and adequate subjects for re-presentation in film.

is it unusual to dramatize historical events?

Is it reality? No. It's better.

—Tom Shales, 1989, on television documentaries

Narrativizing historical events is as old as the Bible or the *Iliad* and the *Odyssey*. In fact, Jerome Bruner argues in "The Narrative Construction of Reality" that narrative is one of several "cultural tool kits" that permits mastery and transfer of knowledges and skills from person to person, culture to culture. Bruner claims that

> we organize our experience and our memory of human happenings mainly in the form of narrative—stories, excuses, myths, reasons for doing and not doing, and so on. Narrative is a conventional form, transmitted culturally and constrained by each individual's level of mastery.... Unlike the constructions generated by logical and scientific procedures that can be weeded out by falsification, narrative constructions can only achieve verisimilitude."5

While White may be accurate in describing the psychological desire to narrativize events as connected to the Oedipal complex, the death principle, and issues of aggression and mastery, Bruner claims the narrativizing process is also ecologically necessary for social order.

This subquestion about dramatizing historical events, however, is not really precisely about narrative but instead about *dramatization*—or about interpretation. One might claim that narrating is "normal" but that anything other than a virtual copy of the real event must emphasize certain aspects of the events and neglect others, and thus produce both drama and a point of view.

Thousands of instances of dramatizing reality exist in print and moving images. In fact, as soon as movies started, they began dramatizing contemporary affairs. An early silent film such as *The Sampson-Schley Controversy* might be considered an interpretive docu-drama. In 1901, Edwin S. Porter, who had produced many short films based on real events, filmed a three-shot movie but in a way so that he took a position about a controversy over whether Captain Schley had inappropriately exceeded his command during the Battle of Santiago Bay and deserved to be court-martialed for cowardice. Porter aligned his point of view with that of the *New York Journal*, whose editorial cartoon served as the source of Porter's visual imagery. In the first two shots, Porter depicted Captain Schley commanding the battleship that led the fray against the enemy and fighting alongside his sailors. Porter then cut to a third shot showing Admiral Sampson drinking tea several hundred miles away.[6]

Why would Porter bother to organize the narrative by cross-cutting to Sampson? Because dramatizing and interpreting the events are not only inherently necessary (all narratives are selective) but are much more engaging if the drama produced emphasizes conflict between individuals. In this case, the conflict was merely political and legal, but conflict that becomes physically violent is an even more fascinating spectacle. Echoing centuries of Western dramatic theory, books on how to write movies continue to emphasize conflict as the fuel for viewer interest because the causes for and effects of conflict and violence are debatable, reproducing aggression or mastery among spectators who struggle over the depictions and points of view. Like the accusations made against Stone for his cutting in *JFK*, Porter dramatically jabbed at the opponent Sampson, landing a quick right to his chin. Was it reality? No, it was better. Even at the start of cinema, narration through editing provided a specific dramatization of conflict, with the filmmaker taking his shot at explaining and interpreting a historical event.

if dramatizing historical events with editing is standard cinematic practice, is it unusual to mix documentary footage with re-enactments?

Hollywood has never been the land of footnotes.

—Bob Katz, 1991, review of *JFK*

The activity of combining moving images shot at the time as an event has occurred (i.e., documentary footage) with staged scenes (i.e., what is called in the industry, "re-enactments") is a practice nearly as old as the movies, with early newsreels employing the two types of materials to create a narrative of the events for the viewer.[7] However, this practice has become a major issue during the past several years, in part because of the significant rise of so-called "reality-based television."

Reality-based television has been remarkably successful in audience ratings and in syndication. As of April 1993, at least fourteen reality shows were on the four major networks, including, for example, *Rescue: 911*, *Unsolved*

Mysteries, *Cops*, and *How'd They Do That?*[8] Industry personnel consider these programs to have emerged from documentary practice and to have taken off during the six-month writers' strike in 1988 when the networks turned to them in order to fill airtime.

Reality-based TV producers make a major distinction between their genre and the docu-drama. On the one hand, the docu-drama is seen as a "pure" re-enactment of a historical event. Examples might include the movie bio-pic *The Glenn Miller Story* (Anthony Mann, 1954) or the three television versions of the Amy Fisher story. Docu-dramas are based on real events but the entire text is re-enacted.

On the other hand, reality TV uses the interview and voices of original historical people to tell the story of the event. Moreover, reality TV *mixes* documentary footage, still photos, news clips, and sound bites with re-enactments. The re-enactments are based upon "what actually happened" but they use actors instead of the original people or, lately, the original people may even play themselves in a reconstruction of the event. In discussing this practice, Arnold Shapiro, a producer of some of these documentaries, suggests that such a mixture goes back in U.S. television news practices to at least the 1950s and the show *You Asked For It*. The reason proferred for doing these re-enactments is, however, not merely to give narrative information but to create dramatic interest. Although producers of these programs claim to be very careful not to create dialogue that is unsubstantiated, some producers have also indicated that they will create a re-enacted dramatization *even when they have archival footage of the event*. This happens when it is determined that the re-enactment will produce a better visual impact or is stronger dramatically than the documentary footage.[9] Such re-enactments must adhere to the same network standards for veracity which pertain when no documentary footage is available.

Obviously, given the audience popularity of reality-based TV, the question of blurring fact and fiction has taken on an urgency for TV networks. Shapiro points out that "in the past, documentary makers labeled all dramatizations as such," but lately that convention has ceased. Another way to differentiate the ontological status of the material has been to shoot in black and white for the dramatized past and in color for the current interviews. Even that practice has disappeared. Documentary filmmaker Harrison Engle, who is also president of the International Documentary Association, points out that *The Thin Blue Line* (Errol Morris, 1988), "blended what one critic called 'the B-movie re-enactment' of a bizarre Texas murder with the traditional talking heads of those involved in the crime." Engle's own latest documentary "mixes re-enactments with archival footage."[10]

The question of the mixing of documentary and re-enactment material is not that mixing creates any more or less *accurate* interpretation of the event. What results is still thought to be a point of view. Rather, the issue is that the mixing may confuse the audiences as to what is documentary evidence versus what is speculation or hypothesis by the filmmaker. It is supposed that audiences will be less capable of judging the validity of the interpretation if they are confused into perceiving the re-enactment as an authentic "trace" of the real. What is at stake is the credibility of the image as it relates to spectatorial understanding of the technology of the camera, for even if the meaning of the image is ambiguous (as it appears to have been in the case of the Rodney King footage) that is quite a different matter than its credibility claims if it is a re-enactment rather than an inscription of the original event. Audience perception and memory are what matters.[11]

Evidence does exist that audiences are not particularly discriminating viewers. Statistics indicate, for example, that "almost half the watchers considered ... *America's Most Wanted* ... to be news."[12] Thus, problems exist because of the presumption of audience gullibility and the belief that a re-enactment is "more subjective" than documentary footage—as well as likely more dramatic and entertaining. Consequently, networks have faced a dilemma about how to deal with such popular and revenue-generating programs. What is causing their difficulty is that viewers often refuse to distinguish between entertainment and news in the way networks feel obliged to insure that they do.

One way for producers to avoid the problem of meeting network standards for the authenticity of material for news programs is to move any questionable programs out of news and into "entertainment." Networks maintain little documentation for docu-dramas—only enough to prevent the threat of law suits for infringement on personal story rights. Thus, a solution for the news ethics problem has been recategorizing many reality-based programs and consequently implying different standards for referring to the real. A striking recent example of this is when a producer for NBC's *Dateline* (a "news" program) enhanced a story about a Chevy pickup truck by adding explosives to the vehicle and failing to make evident that the subsequent crash had been staged. Besides firing the executive producer, NBC shifted *Dateline* from its news division to the entertainment section to prevent any further innuendo that NBC's standards for news practices were degenerating.

A second protective strategy has been to label the re-enactment (or the docu-drama) as having been derived from a specific person's point of view. Here, (post)modernist practices of recognizing and representing the existence of various subjectivities enter and are co-opted by commercial interests. While *Rashomon* and many other twentieth-century texts may have challenged the idea that any cohesive representation of reality can be said to exist, now television and movies can appropriate the multi-perspective narrational device to their own purposes. Three made-for-TV movie versions of the Amy Fisher story make perfect sense. One is Amy Fisher's; one is Joey Buttafuoco's, and the third represents the court transcription.

Such a *Rashomon*-like strategy has already been parodied. During April 1993 in the "Doonesbury" comic strip, Uncle Duke stages his own dramatic rescue from an avalanche in hopes of selling the story to television. But, his version is scooped by versions from the rescue crew and from his assistant, Honey. This satire is even funnier if the reader recalls that the character Duke is based on Hunter Thompson, founder of "gonzo journalism," itself an earlier example of the journalistic dramatizing of fact. Additionally, a new comic-book series, "He Said/She Said," provides a cartoon version of the Fisher/Buttafuoco story. One side tells "her story in her words"; the flip side is "his story." Apparently a Mia Farrow/Woody Allen comic is in preparation.[13]

Thus, the practice of mixing documentary and re-enacted footage for entertainment purposes is widespread, even if somewhat debated as a legitimate practice for use in the news division on network TV. In the case of *JFK*, we cannot consider the controversy that erupted as generated by merely the film's cross-editing of shots of mixed heritage. Moreover, aligning a dramatization with a particular perspective is so common as to be susceptible to satire. Stone positioned *JFK* as Garrison's version of the events, and, as I shall discuss below, reviewers routinely took the film to be from his perspective. Moreover (although after the fact), Stone and co-writer Zachary Sklar published the script *with footnotes* to substantiate every re-enacted scene in the movie as reality-based, thus claiming to adhere to traditional standards of authenticating claims. We never asked such a proof for the Amy Fisher stories. Something else besides the hybridizing of material for dramatizing the narrative must be involved.[14]

is it unusual to represent violence as the product of a conspiracy?

The President's brain is missing.

—Jim Hoberman, 1991, review of *JFK*

Perhaps it really is the subject matter of *JFK* that was the unusual practice. Is this perhaps the first case of a major Hollywood studio making a reality-based movie that claims a conspiracy was behind certain violent historical events? Well, again the answer is no. However, comparison with an earlier film which does so may be particularly helpful in thinking about why such a controversy developed around *JFK*.

In 1939, Warner Bros. produced *Confessions of a Nazi Spy* (Anatole Litvak, 1939). As described in *Hollywood Goes to War*, "*Confessions* was based on a real incident: Nazi spies who came to the United States had been caught and convicted by a federal court in New York City."[15] According to Clayton Koppes and Gregory Black, when Warner Bros. sent the script to the Production Code office, "a hot debate" ensued.

> One faction objected strenuously, arguing that the screenplay depicted Hitler and his government unfairly. There was no proof that German agitators had come to the United States with the intention of seizing control of the country; after all, they said, every country has spies. Nor was it fair to show Hitler only as "a screaming madman." The film should acknowledge "his unchallenged political and social achievements." Such European events as the dismemberment of Czechoslovakia and the abolition of Christian schools in the Third Reich were "extraneous" to the spy story. Even if everything in the script were true, this group said, it would be "one of the most lamentable mistakes ever made by the industry."[16]

Warner Bros. proceeded with the film which "identif[ied] the German-American Bund as an arm of the German government whose purpose was to destroy the American Constitution and Bill of Rights."[17] Moreover, they populated the film with major studio stars—Edward G. Robinson, George Sanders, Paul Lukas—and gave it to Anatole Litvak to direct. As Koppes and Black point out, the critical response was mixed, and the film enjoyed only moderate box-office success. Among the negative comments were those of the *Variety* reviewer who scoffed at the melodrama presented:

> Brutality, calloused inhumanity, kidnapping, beating, kicking in the groin and every evidence of disagreeable behavior is included. Two dominant impressions of the film may perhaps be: (a) that every outgoing German liner has kidnapped victims of Nazi sadism hidden away in dungeons, and (b) that the bunds are expressions of open treason. A third over-all impression is that any cafe with the waiters in leather shorts and tables in checkered linen is a nest of conspirators. It should be bad for biz in such taverns.[18]

Confessions of a Nazi Spy is similar to *JFK* in that it too mixes documentary footage with re-enactments. The *New York Times* reviewer describes this: "...the film's quasi-documentary character has been supported by its employment of newsreel shots of Hitler haranguing his Brownshirts, a commentator's voice, maps and other factual pictorial matter." The reviewer continues, "But its editorial bias, however justified, has carried it to childish extremes."[19]

Editing in *Confessions*, then, functioned much like Stone's editing strategy of intercutting documentary footage with re-enactments to fill in gaps and connect the conspiratorial players into a coherent, masterful plot. Missing shots were supplied to create a causal chain rhetorically explaining the Germans' violence. Thus, just as with *JFK*, *Confessions* suggested that it could reveal how events seemingly unconnected and threatening to the integrity of the United States were actually related to one another. In such conspiracy discourse, covert activities in the real world are presumed capable of being plotted into a master narrative in which every sinister event relates.[20]

Shortly after the film's opening, Fritz J. Kuhn, president of the German Bund, initiated a request for an injunction against distribution of the film in advance of a five-million-dollar libel suit against Warner Bros., claiming the Bund was a "loyal American organization." Warner Bros. responded by indicating that they would prove that the "scenes of spying and perversive activity portrayed there are true."[21] The injunction was denied, although Kuhn was allowed to proceed with the libel suit. Unfortunately for Kuhn, he was arrested at about the same time on perjury charges connected to other events.[22]

JFK follows in a line of conspiracy stories, most of which are wholly fictional, that focus on a group's intent to subvert a government and its representatives. A number of these appeared in the 1970s, including *The Parallax View* (Alan Pakula, 1974), *Marathon Man* (John Schlesinger, 1976), and *Three Days of the Condor* (Sydney Pollack, 1976). Most of the conspiracy movies were made after the conspiracy in question had been proven to be true, and eventually Watergate generated its own docu-drama, *All the President's Men* (Alan Pakula, 1976).

Confessions, however, is somewhat unusual in the history of movies in its claims to dramatize a true conspiracy. *Confessions* was under Congressional investigation in 1941 when the bombing of Pearl Harbor cut short the need to prove the charges against the Nazis. At this point state policy changed, making the plot not only credible, but useful in mobilizing public sentiment for war. But like the case of *JFK*, however, when the history was not the official history, it was contested.

is it unusual to present unofficial versions of history?

Doublespeak Appendix

Conspiracy Theory: A critique or explanation I find offensive.
Historical Lies: Lies, partial lies, or truths that conflict with
well-established official lies....

—Edward S. Herman, 1992, on *JFK*

Usually unofficial versions of history are not released by major studios.

They tend to like authorized ones. Many of the statements of concern over *JFK* employ various worries that the movie manipulated viewers into accepting Stone's thesis. In one version of this, it is held that if viewers think a re-enactment has documentary status, they may become confused about what is known as a fact and what is, as yet, merely a speculative assertion. Additionally, viewers might miss the point that the story is told from one person's point of view (in the case of *JFK*, from Garrison's perspective). Finally, rapid editing is considered to be particularly aggressive. Recall Grenier's vocabulary about *JFK*'s editing: Stone directs "'his film in a pummelling style, a left to the jaw, a right to the solar plexus, flashing forward, flashing backward, crosscutting relentlessly, shooting 'in tight,' blurring, obfuscating, bludgeoning the viewer until Stone wins, he hopes by a TKO.'" These worries hinge on the assumption that viewers have to be tricked or even beaten up to accept the conspiracy thesis.

This might be the case if viewers actually did believe the official version of Kennedy's assassination. However, adequate evidence exists that massive portions of the U.S. population already assume that Oswald was not the sole author of Kennedy's death. A Gallup poll in July 1991 indicated that only 16 percent of Americans thought that Oswald acted alone. Seventy-three percent "suspect others were involved."[23] A *Washington Post* survey in May 1991 revealed that 56 percent of the population believed in a conspiracy; only 19 percent agreed with the official Warren Commission's thesis.[24] Further, it is not only recently that significant numbers of Americans have believed in a conspiracy theory in regard to the assassination. Less than a year after Kennedy's death, "in the spring of 1964, one-third of Americans believed Lee Harvey Oswald acted in concert with others. Within two years the figure had doubled. Every poll taken over the last quarter century has shown between 60 percent and 80 percent of the public favoring a conspiratorial explanation."[25]

What Stone has provided, then, is not merely an unofficial version of the assassination but one that happens to be a very popular version. As Andrew O'Hehir suggests, "Those who are enraged at Oliver Stone's film *JFK* for its heavily fictionalized blending of various assassination theories are missing the point. As Stone has apparently grasped in his blockhead populist way, the J. F. K. killing has been fiction for a long time." O'Hehir proposes that "[Kennedy's assassination is] the creation myth we use to understand the discords of contemporary America: the tale of the fall from grace, for which we keep vainly seeking redemption. If it hadn't happened, we would have had to invent it."[26]

While I do not wish to argue that Kennedy's assassination has become fictional—it did really happen—I do believe that most individuals in the United States already embrace some dramatic plot for the events of that day. Individuals may attribute parts of the conspiracy to various institutions or persons or they may just generally think more of the story exists than has been recognized officially.

What is at stake in the *JFK* controversy, then, is not a bludgeoning of the spectator by the editing style or the hybrid documentary/re-enactment material, but fear that in the fight between the official version and the popular one, the official Warren Commission story will finally fall to a new and popularly produced "authorized" history. This fear is particularly obvious in the way an article in the *Washington Post* presents a series of interviews with persons coming out of the film.

> —"I came out of the movie feeling different about the government," said Russell Reed, 21....
> —"I really see what the movie said could be possible," said Amanda Peel, 17....
> —"The government should unlock the documents and let people find out what is in the documents," said David Buell, 30....[27]

Clearly, by stressing the ages of the interviewees, the *Washington Post* proposes that while the generation of baby-boomers may believe the story of a conspiracy behind the Kennedy assassination, *JFK* threatens to promote that belief into the next generation.

Some writers have pointed out that the media attack on Stone may have been a defensive move by certain journalists out to protect their failure to criticize the government's version of the assassination. Two *Village Voice* writers argue, "The bashing of Oliver Stone's movie *JFK* by the bastions of the American media—CBS, *The New York Times*, *Time*, *Newsweek*, and *The Washington Post*—is said to spring from the sincere desire on the part of the keepers of American's memory to see that our sacred history does not fall prey to revisionist charlatans. While Stone's film does take serious liberty with history, the virulence with which the film has been attacked seems to say more about a defensive press that missed and continues to miss a major story than it does about any flaws in *JFK*."[28]

If, then, we return to my first question, whether Oliver Stone did something particularly unusual in his docu-drama practice in *JFK*, I think we have to conclude that he did not. Dramatizing historical events, mixing documentary footage with re-enactments, representing conspiracy theories, and telling unauthorized histories have all occurred in the past. They have not occurred without incident or question, but they are normal media practices, as are other of Stone's dramatic strategies. These would include hiring Kevin Costner, who has dinner with George Bush and dances with wolves, to play the sympathetic lead actor.

All of these observations, however, do not necessarily suggest a negative answer to the second large question: are these practices (post)modernist? After all, all of my examples are derived from two quintessential twentieth-century media—film and television. Perhaps, as White suggests, these examples are merely instances of (post)modernist responses to the traumas of the era. In which case, I think we need to move to that question.

unsolved mysteries

Thus, *should we understand any of these practices as (post) modernist*? I think that this question ultimately implies a textual effects hypothesis and not a formalist analysis of style and content. To consider certain practices of cinematic or televisual editing as symptomatic of (post)modernism as White does is to miss the point. What is really at stake is the *effect* of a potentially (post)modernist strategy of mixing documentary shots and re-enactments. Is the *effect* on the audience one of confusing fact and fiction, commenting on the medium of inscription, and thus leaving the event untotalized—which would make it (post)modernist? Or is the effect something else?

Modern theory warns us against master narratives, narratives that attempt to essentialize specific historical events into an every-time-and-every-place. I would suggest that we should never confuse a formal device such as rapid editing or editing together materials of different ontological status with the device's social or cultural functions nor ignore such a device's function within its historical context. Editing of hybrid material might leave an event ambiguous, but it might also permit the confirmation of what many spectators already believe to be real: in the case of *JFK*, Oswald was either a patsy or part of a conspiracy of some small or larger scale.

In reading critical responses to the movie, I observe that consistently the negative reviewers simply disagree with the story they perceive Stone is telling. That is, they are not confused and know that what is on the screen is *Stone*'s mixture of documentary and re-enactment footage cast into a dramatic narrative.[29] Moreover, they believe the story of Kennedy's assassination *is* tellable and explainable. The debate is not about whether one can describe the event verbally or visually because *everyone thinks he or she can*. They just do not think the Stone/Garrison story is correct. Nor are they (more than slightly) confused about what they think Stone/Garrison is claiming. For example, the *Newsweek* writer describes the film's plot:

> The assassination ... was a grand conspiracy involving the CIA, the FBI, the Army and Navy, anti-Castro Cubans, New Orleans lowlifes and the Dallas police force. The motive: to thwart the dovish tendencies of John F. Kennedy who, if he had lived,

would have pulled all American troups out of Vietnam, settled the cold war with the Soviet Union and patched up relations with Castro's Cuba.[30]

Furthermore, whether critical or admiring of the film, reviewers do not find Kennedy's assassination an event equivalent to the Holocaust or nuclear war, although many consider it to have produced a national trauma. A sense of causality is also apparent. For those holding the madman-Oswald-did-it-alone point of view, a psychiatric discourse operates to explain human agency. For those holding the Oswald-as-patsy-or-conspirator point of view, a conspiracy discourse functions to fill in the missing parts of the Zapruder footage.

In a discussion about social drama, Victor Turner argues that three phases characterize social relations during a conflict among members of a group. The first phase "begins with a breach of regular norm-governed social relations, signalized by a public transgression of a salient rule normally binding on members of the group." This breach is followed by a crisis and finally by the deployment of "adjustive and redressive mechanisms ... to seal off or heal the breach—a phase call[ed] 'redress.'" Turner notes that each participant in the social conflict creates a social drama. "Soon I realized," he writes, "that it was their very bias that was of central importance. For the aim of the social drama is not to present a seemingly objective recital of a series of events; it is concerned, rather, with the different interpretations put upon those events, and the ways in which these give subtle expression to divergent interests or switches in the balance of power."[31] Turner continues that psychological factors are also involved in the drama presented.

Thinking about the representation of a historical event as a subjective social drama between contesting sides is not a new idea. It is, however, very different from the radical notion that history is itself fictional. In her work on postmodernist literature as "historiographic metafiction," Linda Hutcheon suggests that postmodern works are those that "deny the possibility of a clearly sustainable distinction between history and fiction."[32] This does not mean that historical events did not happen but that authors of postmodern literature are pointing out that history texts are interpretive dramatizations, that history texts are sites of contestation and social drama. As Hutcheon writes,

> In challenging the seamless quality of the history/ fiction (or world/art) join implied by realist narrative, postmodern fiction does not, however, disconnect itself from history or the world. It foregrounds and thus contests the conventionality and unacknowledged ideology of that assumption of seamlessness and asks its readers to question the processes by which we represent

> our selves and our world to ourselves and to become aware of the means by which we make sense of and construct order out of experience in our particular culture. We cannot avoid representation. We can try to avoid fixing our notion of it and assuming it to be transhistorical and transcultural.[33]

The reviewers of *JFK* certainly seem to have operated at a metafictional level in responding to the film. However, they have done so not specifically because of its "(post)modernist" editing style but rather because the reviewers were already accustomed to the notion that history is dramatized from various points of view and thus debatable.[34]

The overt and metafictional recognition of the interpretive activities of those engaged in creating and reading social dramas like *JFK* does not, however, explain a disturbing finding: 22 percent of adults polled in the U.S. in April 1993 thought it possible that the Holocaust had never happened. In the postmodernist theory, the distance between the representation and the real has become such a widely available and misunderstood notion that it is possible for people to doubt accounts of events of the magnitude of those described by White as a "(post)modernist event."[35]

However, questioning the actual existence of a past event is not what happened in the case of *JFK*, whose reviewers and audiences clearly read the movie as a drama about a real past. White may be right about his allegory for events such as the Holocaust—trying to represent them as coherent narratives attributed to human agency may delay the mourning process or allow them to be ignored altogether. But the assassination of Kennedy does not belong to that category of events and responses. *JFK*'s represented violence is still considered real and explainable, even if debatable. We are still attempting to dramatize, master, and heal the breach of that traumatic event. We are still in conflict over that violence with various members of the audience who take a metafictional reading stance that looks at the film as presenting only one perspective on the past, a social drama with which they do or do not associate themselves.

Thus, White may be right in seeing that *JFK* poses a problem for postmodern historiography, but for the wrong reason. Like the postmodern historiographer, critics and spectators of twentieth century histories have learned the rules of representation. They can read the movie as a dramatic narration. Thus it is not the formal properties of the editing strategies that makes the movie (post)modern; rather, it is the reading strategies of the viewers who recognize that the movie is a subjective version of the past, created through shots put together by some agent. What is undecidable, finally, is who is appropriately authorized to fill in the missing narrative material. Spectators of the assassination have not stopped struggling over the story of Kennedy's violent death, permitting every version to stand as equally an official drama. Thus, White may be right in his psychoanalytical reading of our relation to the historical event: we are not yet able to let that past event go, to move on to mourning the loss of JFK. This is because we still think we might be able to represent with some verisimilitude that event. Like the program that stimulated "reality-based TV," the assassination remains a violent plot whose cinematic shots do not yet produce a satisfying narrative resolution—it is still an "unsolved mystery."

notes

I would like to thank the audience at the Institute for Humanities, State University of New York at Stony Brook, for their comments on a draft of this paper.

1. Hayden White, "The Modernist Event," in this volume.
2. Hayden White, "Historiography and Historiophoty," *American Historical Review* 93, no. 5 (December 1988): 1193–99.
3. I do not personally agree with theorizing "postmodernism" as an extension of "modernism" but arguing the point here is unnecessary; I will accept White's position.
4. David Armstrong and Todd Gitlin, "Killing the Messenger," *Image*, Sunday, February 16, 1992; Richard Grenier, *TLS*, 24 January 1992, quoted by White, "The Modernist Event."
5. Jerome Bruner, "The Narrative Construction of Reality," *Critical Inquiry* 18, no. 1 (Autumn 1991): 4.
6. Charles Musser, *Before the Nickelodeon: Edwin S. Porter and the Edison Manufacturing Company* (Berkeley, CA: U. of California Press, 1991), 182.
7. "Faking the Early News Films," in Raymond Fielding, *The American Newsreel, 1911–1967* (Norman, OK: U. of Oklahoma Press), 37–45. Fielding uses the term "faking" as though he assumes the producers hoped the viewers would be unable to differentiate between the documentary and re-enacted footage. More work on assumptions about viewers and goals of the producers is necessary before concluding that "faking," as we might take the term to mean, is an adequate description of the situation. Additionally, in this essay I am assuming two points: 1) that historical events have happened; we are concerned not to prove their existence but to understand the problems of retrieval of descriptions and interpretations of meaning; and 2) that while documentary footage is selective and thus interpretive, it does have an ontological status different from re-enactments of historical events.
8. Steve Coe, "Networks serve up heavy dose of reality," *Broadcasting & Cable*, 12 April 1993, 26.
9. Mike Mathis, producer-director for "Unsolved Mysteries," Directors' Guild of America Workshop, August 1992; *Nightline*, ABC, 6 February 1990; Diane Haithman, "Drawing the Line Between Tabloid TV and Re-Enactments," *Los Angeles Times*, 20 February 1989, part 6, 1.
10. Haithman, "Drawing the Line." Because of the re-enactments, *The Thin Blue Line* was ruled ineligible for inclusion in the documentary category for awards from the Academy of Motion Picture Arts and Sciences.
11. Andre Bazin's arguments about the ontology of the photographic image can be turned to here.
12. Thomas B. Rosenstiel, "TV Blurs Facts and Filminess; Infotainment: Seeing

Really is Believing," *Los Angeles Times*, 3 December 1989, part M, 4. The source is unclear about how TV genres were defined in the survey; hence, it is not known if audiences had choices beyond "news" and "entertainment." Obviously, this information would help in interpreting these results.

13. This "Doonesbury" strip was published during April 1993. The comic book described was also published in April 1993. It asserts "the events depicted herein have been presented in the exact order and manner in which they occurred. Character dialogue is based solely on statements made by the persons involved in the affair. First Amendment Publishing attests to the veracity and accuracy of the activities and events portrayed in this comic book."
14. *Malcom X*, released after *JFK*, has had something of the same trouble, although the adherence by Spike Lee to the authorized autobiography perhaps muted the potential for controversy.
15. Clayton R. Koppes and Gregory D. Black, *Hollywood Goes to War: How Politics, Profits, and Propaganda Shaped World War II Movies* (NY: Free Press, 1987), 27.
16. Koppes and Black, *Hollywood Goes to War*, 28.
17. Koppes and Black, *Hollywood Goes to War*, 29.
18. "Land," "*Confessions of a Nazi Spy*," *Variety*, 3 May 1939.
19. Frank S. Nugent, *Confessions of a Nazi Spy*, *New York Times*, 29 April 1939, 13.
20. See Richard Hofstadter, *The Paranoid Style in American Politics and Other Essays* (New York: Knopf, 1965); Paul Michael Rogin, *Ronald Reagan, The Movie* (Berkeley: University of California Press, 1987).
21. "German Bund Sues," *Motion Picture Herald*, 20 May 1939, 9; "Answers Kuhn," *Motion Picture Herald*, 9 September 1939, 9.
22. The Federal Court ruled that no injunction could be issued to prevent or stop the publication of something deemed libelous; if libel exists, the party can file a damage suit and merits of fact would be heard at the trial. *Kuhn v. Warner Bros.*, 19 June 1939, District Court, S. D. *New York Federal Supplement* 29 (1940): 800.
23. Tamar Vital, "Who Killed J.F.K.?", *Jerusalem Post*, 31 January 1992.
24. "Twisted History," *Newsweek*, 23 December 1991, 46.
25. Jefferson Morley, "The Political Rorschach Test," *Los Angeles Times*, 8 December 1991, rpt. in *JFK*, ed. Stone and Sklar, 231.
26. Andrew O'Hehir, "*JFK*: Tragedy into Farce," *San Francisco Weekly*, 18 December 1991, rpt. in *JFK*, ed. Stone and Sklar, 270.
27. Robert O'Harrow Jr., "Conspiracy Theory Wins Converts," *Washington Post*, 2 January 1992, rpt. in *JFK*, ed. Stone and Sklar, pp. 370–71.
28. Robert Hennelly and Jerry Policoff, "*JFK*: How the Media Assassinated the Real Story," *The Village Voice*, 31 March 1992, rpt. in *JFK*, ed. Stone and Sklar, 497.
29. Whether they perceive this to be "news" or "entertainment" is another issue.
30. "Twisted History," *Newsweek*, 23 December 1991, 46.
31. Victor Turner, *On the Edge of the Bush: Anthropology as Experience* (Tucson, AZ: U. of Arizona Press, 1985), 121.
32. Steven Connor summarizing Hutcheon's position in *Postmodernist Culture: An Introduction to Theories of the Contemporary* (Cambridge, MA: Basil Blackwell, 1989), 127.
33. Linda Hutcheon, *The Politics of Postmodernism* (London: Routledge, 1989), pp. 53-4.
34. If we really wanted to find a film that in a postmodern way blurred fiction and fact we might turn instead to Haskell Wexler's *Medium Cool* [1969], a movie in which an integral shot "contains" both documentary narrative and fictional narrative. Since the fiction story existed along side the real events in the Chicago park, the fiction may have even affected the reality.
35. Michiko Kakutani, "When History Is a Casualty," *New York Times*, 30 April 1993, C1 and 31. To lay the lack of belief in the Holocaust having occurred directly at the feet of deconstructionism, as Kakutani does in the essay, is, however, irresponsible.

three

historical consciousness and the viewer

who killed vincent chin?

bill nichols

The memory of past time depends on the present project of the subject: the intentionalization of the past changes with the intentionalization of the future.

—Anthony Wilden, *System and Structure*

Who Killed Vincent Chin? (Renée Tajima and Chris Choy, 1988) examines the murder of Vincent Chin by Ronald Ebens and his stepson in 1982. Ebens was an out-of-work autoworker in Detroit who was reported to have mistaken Chin for Japanese. Ebens blamed Chin for his own lack of work and, in a street fight, killed him. The film uses a wide variety of source materials not only to raise questions not only about the structural conditions that might give rise to Ronald Ebens's specific form of social consciousness, but also to propose novel alternatives to the prevailing forms of historical representation found in nonfiction cinema.

Taking less than ten minutes of screen time, the opening succession of shots presents: topless dancers from the Fancy Pants bar describing their jobs; a policeman recounting how Ronald Ebens and his stepson, Michael Nitz, beat Vincent Chin to death with a baseball bat in a McDonald's parking lot near this bar; Mrs. Chin on the Phil Donahue show, choking back tears at the loss of her son; neighbors of Ebens saying he and his family are "good people" and it (the murder) was "just one of those things [that] could happen to anyone"; Ronald Ebens, on a Detroit TV show denying that he has ever been a racist; men streaming out of an auto factory with an African-American quartet singing "Get a Job" on the sound track; shoppers at a mall listening to groups sing ditties about "their city," Detroit; a friend of Ebens describing his and Ebens's ethic, "You work hard and you play hard"; Mrs. Chin, against a background of traditional Chinese music, recounting the shocks, hardship, and racism she discovered in America, such as being driven from a Detroit baseball stadium by (white) fans who refused to tolerate the presence of Asians; Ebens telling of his own courtship and marriage and the couple's move to Detroit as the same African-American quartet croons "How sweet it is to be loved by you..."; and a group of auto workers who go from work to a bar where they talk about how the Japanese undercut American car prices by paying workers less for their labor.

If the future, like the past, is made and remade in terms of our changing present situation, it cannot be known in advance and made subject to dicta, dogma or any other teleological imperative. And yet the future cannot be abandoned as merely unknowable or our decisions and actions would become meaningless. Intentionality, as Wilden's epigraph indicates, is that (phenomenological) process by which consciousness constitutes and addresses a world, by which consciousness is always *consciousness of* something.[1] That something, here, is the future, that time in which we act upon what we learn now. It is the ceaseless dialectic of past, present, and future that sustains historical consciousness for the historical actor as well as the historical spectator. It is the construction of such actors within a viewing context that provides the present focus of this essay. Political art needs to "convey the sense of a hermeneutic relationship to the past which is able to grasp its own present as history only on condition it manages to keep the idea of the future, and of radical and Utopian transformation, alive."[2]

For the film spectator, this "present" is the present moment of viewing. At issue, then, is the relation between this moment and previous moments (our past, including earlier moments within the film itself) as they coalesce into an intentionalization of the future (a consciousness of a necessary correspondence between now and what has yet to come). My claim is that *Who Killed Vincent Chin?* is the most important political documentary of the 1980s. It is so because it establishes a present moment of viewing in relation to what has already taken place in the film, such that we regard our own present as past, or, more conventionally, as prologue to a future outside the film which, through the very process of viewing, we may bring into being. I use the conditional mood and the phrase "*may* bring into being" because it remains a question of the content of the form as we apprehend it. Form guarantees nothing. Its content, the meaning we make of it, is a dialectical process taking place between us and the screen and between present, past, and future. The viewing process provides an analogy for a larger historical process. Our present, aligned to the film's re-presentation of past events, may construct a dialectical "will to transform" as our specific intentionalization toward the future. This is not to say that the engendering of a historical consciousness is determined by our apprehension of certain film forms; only that such a consciousness *may* follow from such apprehension, and that the content of *Who Killed Vincent Chin?*'s collage form seems especially conducive to this result.[3]

This claim—that *Who Killed Vincent Chin?* constructs a dialectical will to transform as an intentionalization toward the future—borrows from what Freud called *Nachträglichkeit* and White called "willing backwards" to describe a viewing experience that suspends us in time, between past and present, present and future. As prompted by *Who Killed Vincent Chin?* and certain other films, this experience stands distinctly apart from the form of historical consciousness arising from classic realist representation with its sense of linear causality and teleological determination. Here, by contrast, the future remains unknowable but simultaneously up for grabs. *Nachträglichkeit* joins more squarely with the question of modernism, as posed by White, and of postmodernism, as posed by Jameson.[4] As we view a film retrospectively, in the mode of "willing backward," we model a future on the basis of our present situation as it is mediated by how we now understand our past situation. The collage structure of *Who Killed Vincent Chin?* invites such a reading and as we retro-spect, re-read, re-construct, we assemble a story (*histoire*) from our present perspective that is mediated by what we now understand of past events in the plot, in "the story so far...."

The sense of working a boundary that impinges on realism has fundamental importance to documentary film representation and historical consciousness (the fragments that comprise the film are themselves usually realist in construction whereas the assembly of the fragments resembles collage more than classic narrative realism). Within this border zone, the assembly of fragments, such as those presented during the first ten minutes of *Who Killed Vincent Chin?*, allows for the evocation of what is not manifestly present, what cannot be named or represented literally without shifting to a different, meta-communicative level (such as the one here). Collage, though comprised of realist fragments, has a distinct "content" from that of the classic realist narrative. The paradoxical status of realism as a mode of representation that attests to knowledge and to aesthetic pleasure remains acute: the fragments appear "merely" to replicate what already exists; the collage announces itself as a distinctive form of representation. To resolve this paradox in either direction so that a text is made transparent to the world, as unmediated knowledge, or rendered opaque, as a realm of aesthetic signification, is to dull the very edge that gives realism its power and continuing use-value. Collage, such as we find in *Who Killed Vincent Chin?*, retains the paradox while simultaneously aiming it in the direction of a will to transform.

Realism alone clearly will not suffice. *Who Killed Vincent Chin?* derails narrative without destroying it; it reconstitutes realism without abandoning it. Retardations, delays, slippages, diversions, incomplete reasonings, unfinished arguments, partial proposals, competing claims, jarring or strange juxtapositions, fissures, jumps, gaps, or other *perepetias* mark this distinct inflection of realist narrative. The film's form ties the present moment of viewing intimately to what has already been viewed as we actively try to make connections left unstated by the film. Various modes of documentary representation, distinct fragments, or units interlace with one another in configurations we might call sedimented, laminated, or marbled.[5] Disparate elements must be reread and reworked. Strange juxtapositions and unexpected fissures require us to fit fragments into place within a shifting field of reference. As Robert Burgoyne puts it regarding historical narrative (but the same would hold true for collage), "In short, historical narrative is seen as a performative discourse, a product of the same kinds of actions that produce historical events; the investing of the world with symbolic meaning."[6]

The contemporary search for alternative forms of representation parallels a waning of historical consciousness itself. A crisis of representation ensues from the failure of classic realist narrative models to convince us of their commensurability with the reality we experience beyond them. Different models arise and contend. The modern event (massively demonstrated in disasters, catastrophes, and social holocausts) eludes traditional historical understanding. Things happen but without identifiable agency, without a clear causal chain, without explanatory linkage. Questions arise that cannot be answered by traditional storytelling techniques. Too much of that excess magnitude we explain by saying that "history" remains unaccounted for; too much noise or dissonance, too many loose ends and dangling uncertainties remain. The (narrative) center will not hold. As Hayden White puts it,

> But not only are *modern*, post-industrial "accidents" more incomprehensible than anything earlier generations could possibly have imagined

(think of Chernobyl), the photo and video documentation of such accidents is so full that it is difficult to work the documentation of any one of them up as elements of a single "objective" story. Moreover, in many instances, the documentation of such events is so manipulable as to discourage the effort to derive explanations of the occurrences of which the documentation is supposed to be a recorded image.[7]

Thus, *Who Killed Vincent Chin?* provides a surface upon which to inscribe both the sense and the senselessness of Chin's murder. The film presents surface traces of an absent subject. It is one of many films to do so: *Hotel Terminus: The Life and Times of Klaus Barbie* (Marcel Ophuls, 1988), *Roger and Me* (Michael Moore, 1989), *Far From Poland* (Jill Godmilow, 1984), and *Sari Red* (Pratibha Parmar, 1988) are a few others. This tactical choice reinforces the sense that these traces lack the "grit," the points of attachment, that would hold them within a given frame of reference or explanatory matrix. To re-present the event is clearly *not* to explain it. Multiple interpretations and meanings seem to explode outward. The event—up for grabs, decontextualized or de-realized—produces a crisis for historical representation. The fractured, fragmented surface mirrors back assigned meanings ironically: it refracts them and denies them the closure or objective truth value that might otherwise be claimed for them.

Who Killed Vincent Chin?, with its superficial resemblance to an MTV visual style, poses the risk of sliding toward a discourse not of sobriety, but delirium.[8] The film presents us with: a fraying away of the historical event from an explanatory frame; the logical impossibility of explaining the whole by means of any part; the reluctance to name the framework in which apparent disorder can assume pattern and meaning (intensified by an aversion to "master narratives"); the analytic impossibility of determining causality, intentionality, or motivation from the visual record; the heightened intensity brought to bear on the isolated event itself as though it *ought* to yield up its secrets, its meaning. All of these factors burden the interpretation of the event with an excess that threatens to become pure delirium.

Signs of this potential delirium appear in the film's complex array of source materials as well as in its remarkably diverse set of moods (subjunctive, conditional, performative), tenses (past, present, future) and voices (active, passive, middle). The film joins together home movies, interviews shot by the filmmakers, interviews conducted by others but reused by the filmmakers, photographs, "behind the scenes" observational footage of network news journalism, the reproduction of broadcast news and talk shows, cartoons, advertisements, and press conferences.

The film includes a diversity of moods each of which contributes to its fragmented construction. These will each be described in turn. The first mood is the subjunctive, which *Webster's Third New International Dictionary* defines as "a set of verb forms that represents an attitude toward or concern with a denoted act or state not as fact but as something entertained in thought as contingent or possible or viewed emotionally (as with doubt, desire, will)...." Such a definition is entirely in keeping with the dominant stress of performative documentary and historical fictions like *Who Killed Vincent Chin?*, where the effect of the absent subject and collage form prompts both interviewees and the viewer, respectively, to construct thoughts of what might have happened that fateful night, what should have happened in the courts, what may yet happen to the persistence of racism in our land.

The conditional mood, devoted to matters of supposition, and the ablative absolute case, specifying "time, cause, or an attendant circumstance of an action," also propose themselves as linguistic models for the types of text/event/viewer relations (hermeneutic relations) discussed here. For example, *if* the testimony of Starlene, one of the dancers at the Fancy Pants club had been admitted in court, it *may have contributed* to a very different outcome. Similarly, *if* the courts were not so overburdened, there *might have been* time to insist that such testimony be considered. These sentences, in the conditional mood, loosely correspond to the retrospective construction we place on some of the fragments dealing with Ronald Ebens's trial and the subsequent appeals. (These conditional claims are implied, are not stated as such.) The move away from conventional declarative structures appears to correspond to a move away from "rationality," or linear causality, and toward something closer to chaos theory (the discovery of pattern within apparently entropic processes by reframing or recontextualizing them). This is distinct from classic notions of "deep structure" or "structuring absence" where what is not seen or given materially can still be specified within a routine linguistic protocol: It can be named or specified even if it cannot be represented.

The performative mood involves those aspects of the film that deflect our attention away from the referential claims of the text to the more expressive, poetic or rhetorical dimensions of the text *per se*. This deflection does not target the organizational properties of the text or the viewer's apprehension of them in the way formal or political reflexivity does; performativity is, instead, an insistence on the expressive gesture itself. There is a strongly performative quality to the opening minutes of *Who Killed Vincent Chin?*, for example, where various types of source material kaleidoscopically invoke the social milieu of Detroit in 1982 without feigning any transparency to this milieu. The performative mood is more than stylistic flourish. It counters the ideological effect of a text: instead of surreptitiously substituting a sign system (realism, for instance) for the historical referent this system appears to capture or present, the performative mood heightens our awareness of how referential meanings are themselves produced without entirely dispensing with the meanings so produced.

Of particular interest in *Who Killed Vincent Chin?* is the use of the middle voice in addition to the more conventional active and passive voices. Middle voice originates in Greek grammar and refers to those verb forms that indicate an effect on the subject occasioned by the action described by the verb. "I take," for example, may become "I choose" in middle voice, carrying with it both a sense of self-agency and of heightened moral consciousness. In terms of this film, the interviews with Ronald Ebens that are conducted by Renée Tajima move from "I interview" to "I offer testimony of what another said." Similarly, the viewer's involvement shifts from "I see" to "I witness or understand." Such changes lack the linguistic markers that the middle voice would have in writing and thus they remain more speculative; I nonetheless believe this concept to be an apt one for the type of effect *Who Killed Vincent Chin?* produces.[9]

Through a collage of this rich array of moods, tenses, voices, and sources, *Who Killed Vincent Chin?* achieves a distinct linkage between the general and the particular. It evokes those conceptual categories by which we generalize from particular instances (racism, sexism, class conflict) but does not name them. As Robert Burgoyne comments regarding Bertolucci's *The Conformist*, "Moments of struggle are recoded in such a way that local, historical events acquire a secondary referent. The double coding can be understood as a kind of shift in perspective, manifested through the temporal and point of view structure of the film."[10] Filmmakers Choy and Tajima adopt a similar strategy, involving much more radical shifts than Bertolucci's, to bring into being an intentionality marked by the will to transform.

Their approach also differs sharply from that of Oliver Stone, a cinematic historian working in a more recognizably fictional mode. If Stone's recent film *JFK* seeks to find a frame that, in retrospect, will prove a fascist conspiracy behind Kennedy's assassination and risks sliding into paranoia along the way, *Who Killed Vincent Chin?* invokes a retrospective framing of Chin's murder precisely in terms of those complex social mediations that paranoia denies or represses.

Like *JFK*, *Who Killed Vincent Chin?* begins with an embedded, implicit explanation of what caused a specific murder built from a welter of fragments, a panoply of images and voices drawn from a wide range of sources. What the opening segment of *Who Killed Vincent Chin?* described above does is imply linkages that remain unstated. There is no voice-over commentary to orient us; scenes exhibit that "peculiar dispersal of documentary across a heterogeneous series of objects" without the guiding hand of a narrator.[11] The heterogeneity of images and sounds grows in intensity, signalling a double refusal: the film will neither play a surrealist game with the historically real (through an insistence on the strangeness of its juxtapositions) nor uphold realist epistemology (through the organizing unity of verbal commentary or continuity editing). *Who Killed Vincent Chin?* searches for a historical frame greater than a strict sequence of events with their presumably inexorable causality. The latter would have conveyed a very different, and outmoded, sense of history or culture. The film seeks out instead a frame that cannot be named, at least not without the risk of making the apparently paranoid leap that dooms Jim Garrison in *JFK*. To name that global form of agency that "determines" local events is to reify and naturalize. These names—"global economy," "social conditions," "capitalism," "the ruling class"—all invoke an imaginary agent rather than a symbolic process. Through its form, *Who Killed Vincent Chin?* challenges us to intuit, sense, or inferentially grasp, and thereby understand, the frame or perspective that gives this act of "random" violence its fullest meaning.

In the act of viewing the film, *Who Killed Vincent Chin?* pivots dialectically between past and present, present and future, and among issues of race, class, masculinity, sex, work, pleasure, and death. This pivoting upholds a tension between the particular and the general, the local and the historical, the need for abstract or conceptual knowledge, and the desire to impart a knowledge rooted in the concrete. *Vincent Chin*'s investigative action supports an epistemological genealogy that holds embodied (local, concrete, experiential) and disembodied (general, abstract, conceptual) knowledge together without blending them into a unity or diminishing them through hierarchy. If Vincent Chin's murder is to be understood in relation to the more abstract categories of class, race, and gender (already embedded but not named in the opening sequence), it must be understood in all its specificity and existential horror. And if this horror, or terror, is to be understood dialectically, it must be understood in relation to an embodied intentionality that activates the abstract principle of a will to transform.

The full embodiment of knowledge hinges on the interpretive understanding of the spectator, not on any stated meanings in the realist fragments that come before us. Even the actual murder of Vincent Chin is never spelled out at any one place in the film. Any realist description of the murder which is presented becomes only one part of the story that we retrospectively construct from what the plot places before us. I resort to the description which follows since my goal is not to replicate the form and structure of the film but to understand it; the effect of the following account, therefore, is quite distinct from the effect produced by the film. The fatal event, as retroactively constructed by the viewer is as follows:

Ron Ebens shouts encouragement to a black stripper, Starlene, at the "Fancy Pants" club, but Vincent Chin makes a derogatory comment. They start to argue with each other at the bar.

Ebens, "It's because of you little motherfuckers that I'm out of work."

Chin, "Don't call me a fucker."

Ebens, "I'm not sure if you're a big fucker or a little fucker."

A fight ensues. Chin knocks Ebens down and leaves. Ebens tracks Chin down and beats him to death with a baseball bat while his step-son holds Chin in place as a target.

The "cause" of the murder is also destabilized and found dispersed through the film, particularly in different fragments of Ronald Ebens's comments:

"If you want to construe [my 'motherfucker' remark] as a racial slur, I don't know how you could do that, but I didn't say that.

"It was like this was pre-ordained to be, I guess; it just happened.

"It's not something you plan on happening, but it happens.

"I've never been a racist. And God is my witness, that's the truth.

"I felt like a real jerk, being in jail, knowing the next day was Father's Day.

"[Protest by the American Citizens for Justice] is selfish, a way for Asian-Americans to get ahead, overcome their alleged plight, alleged because I know very few Asians, very few...."

Ebens's statements represent a knowledge all too fully embodied, all too totally tied to immediate, personal experience and local context. Instead of a dialectical will to transform, there is a strong desire for permanence. Like Sartre's anti-Semite, Ebens wishes

to be massive and impenetrable ... not to change. Where, indeed, would change take [anti-Semites]? We have here a basic fear of oneself and of truth. What frightens them is not the content of truth, of which they have no conception, but the form itself of truth, that thing of indefinite approximation.... They do not want any acquired opinions; they want them to be innate.[12]

"The bigot's reduction" (the segregation of Us from Them across the social imaginary) represses the passionate urge to question and know. If anything, we glimpse the failure to make an imaginative leap toward uncertainty and speculation at all. Such a leap would catapult the viewer/historian toward the conceptual but unnamed perspective that the film itself requires of its viewers. Unlike the social paranoid who also leaps beyond facts, details and other minutiae, but toward irreversible certainty, Ronald Ebens cannot embrace the explanatory frames of racism or jingoism openly.[13] The film itself, however, chooses to leave unnamed what Ebens represses. It retains the form of indefinite approximation, leaving it for us to fill in and complete what the text's gaps and fissures address but do not identify.

Ebens's refusal of the metaphorical dimension of language, his need to cling to the metonymic contiguities of literalism, fit more precisely with the profile of classic schizophrenia than paranoia (and contrast radically with the metaphorical work of collage evident in the film as a whole). He who has admitted killing another man uses as his means of defense a *refusal to see* (to frame, to bracket, to contextualize)—a ploy that *Who Killed Vincent Chin?* makes almost impossible for its viewers. For Ronald Ebens, retrospection, willing backwards, serves only to reinforce his profound sense of non-agency. Events take place in which those who exercised agency no longer recognize themselves as agents. "It was like this was ordained to be, I guess; it just happened."[14]

This may be Ebens's perspective, but it is clearly not the film's. Choy and Tajima take a position not of nostalgic passivity, but of passionate revision. Ronald Ebens clings to the literal model of the chronicle, unwilling to make the leap beyond an ahistoricized sense of destiny. The film, however, invites bold conjecture with every cut, every new juxtaposition, every shift and change of frame. Choy and Tajima reject the monad-centered, judicially required demand for *a guilty individual*. They take no interest (not even skeptical interest) in projects to inculcate the acceptance of personal responsibility for crimes by those who commit them.[15] Although they do not let Ebens off the hook, they avoid the sense of global conspiracy a paranoid view of racism might entail and do not create the debilitating sense of victimization that an Althusserian structuralism would produce as an "ideological effect."

The oblique subject brought into being by the viewer, by means of the collage principle at work in the film, clearly entails race, class, and gender—three words *not* spoken in the film itself but omnipresent in what the collage *shows* (in the interaction between shots and scenes). Willing backward, *Nachträglichkeit*, means aiming toward a future state in which these terms achieve the full expressivity of embodied knowledge; when the meaning and effect of such terms are liberated from the chains of abstraction and brought to realization in the hearts of people.

The *experience* of the text, then, is integral to grasping the content of its form. *Who Killed Vincent Chin?* proposes an alternative form of knowledge that may have recourse to abstractions such as "race" or "class" but that depends on a return to the concrete. This involves not only an evocation of the horror of an isolated killing, but, even more, the felt and active experience of *making sense* of what we see and hear.

Leslie Devereaux, writing in relation to debates within anthropology, critiques dominant representational strategies; her remarks have application here:

> The conventions of scientific writing work against the portrayal of experience in favor of elicited systems of thought, and observed regularities of public behavior, usually reported *as* behavior, that is, with the emphasis on action rather than interaction, and prescription rather than contingency, which amounts to grave distortion of human actuality. In this rhetorical form it becomes hard not to render people homogeneous and rule following [or breaking], no matter the disavowals we utter about this. Our scientized standards of evidence privilege speech over feeling and bodily sensation, which is assimilated to the personal. The personal, the putatively private, is an indistinct category of suspicious character.[16]

Who Killed Vincent Chin? opts to eschew the conventions and standards of scientific writing and of juridical procedure, moral judgment, and traditional, or realist-based Marxist analysis. Feeling and bodily sensation occupy a central place in this alternative strategy of collage and *Nachträglichkeit*. What concepts and abstractions arise do so by dint of passage through a more experiential domain, and the knowledge that ensues may well be of a different order.

The film's dynamic editing, the technique responsible for the collage effect, functions to emphasize the "portrayal of experience," less Ronald Ebens's experience than our own as we take up the process of making sense of what we see and hear. The editing, through what it juxtaposes and what it omits, fosters a will to transform that revolves around a cry for justice which the judicial system has yet to hear. More obliquely, it presents as its subject a white racism that cannot speak its own name. White racism recognizes no name for itself insofar as it can be subsumed within the domain of what "was ordained to be."

Approximating Marx's challenge to rise from the abstract to the concrete, and charged with the intensity Jameson associates with existential historicism where the past retains a "vital urgency," *Who Killed Vincent Chin?* compels us to approximate the truth Ronald Ebens represses.[17] Ebens's petty-bourgeois aspirations; masculinist sense of pride and chauvinism; his history of alcoholism; the implicit sexism in his choice to "let off steam" by visiting a striptease bar with his step-son; his ignorance of Asian cultures and people; the reinforcement of family, friends, work, a distinct sub-culture in which Ebens lived (in which, for example, people take turns bashing a Japanese car with a sledge hammer in a televised spectacle of frustration and anger), and official policies (which portray the Japanese as workaholics, incapable of pleasure, and indifferent to others) clearly contribute to the overdetermination of what actually happened (each factor could provide an answer to the question posed by the film's title).[18]

Choy and Tajima juxtapose these elements in ways we, if not Ebens, cannot fail to apprehend. Vincent Chin's murder required all these factors, acting in concert, through the "medium" of Ebens. Where, then, does agency reside? Everywhere and nowhere. It is in how we make sense of the juxtaposition or conjunction of these factors, just as a will to transform resides in the way we make sense of the gaps and fissures of the film's collage form. This is what makes the film's mixture of realist fragments and modernist collage so distinct and innovative within documentary film practice. To attribute responsibility or guilt to monadic agents (Ebens) or naturalized abstractions ("class conflict," "racism") would reify; to place it in "what's ordained to be" would mystify. Instead, *Who Killed Vincent Chin?* situates agency within the web of conflict surrounding overdetermined events itself.[19] This web consists of relationalities more than things. "Things happen," but less because of providence than because of the condensation of forces at strategic nodal points.

Who Killed Vincent Chin? poses its issues and questions of the historicality of an "event" with exceptional force. Its oblique (unnamed) subject (white racism) eludes both naming and address. And yet the film's result is very far from a lapse into quietism. We are called upon to complete elsewhere the story begun by the film. "Please, all you good and honest people," Mrs. Chin pleads near the film's conclusion, in response to the final judicial decision, which leaves Ronald Ebens a free man. Thanks to the meaning and effect of the film's form, we are left in a position where we, as both film viewers and historical actors, experience the potential to respond in our present, which is the film's future, to Mrs. Chin's plea. "It's up to you," says Jim Garrison at the end of *JFK*, looking toward this camera and hence toward us. But the challenge presented there, to identify and name those specific figures who did the dirty deed, to see that justice as already defined will yet be done, gives way, here, to a transformative intentionality of much greater magnitude. To paraphrase Jameson, *Who Killed Vincent Chin?* invites us to grasp our present as history in order to keep alive the idea of a radically transformed future. This is an achievement that earns the film singular distinction within the domain of historical representation.

notes

1. For additional discussion of intentionality in relation to film, see Vivian Sobchack, *The Address of the Eye: A Phenomenology of Film Experience* (Princeton: Princeton University Press, 1992).
2. Fredric Jameson, "Marxism and Historicism," in *The Ideologies of Theory: Essays 1971–1986*, vol. 2, *The Syntax of History* (Minneapolis: University of Minnesota Press, 1988), 148–177.
3. This essay is strongly indebted to Hayden White's writing on history, particularly to his book *The Content of the Form: Narrative Discourse and Historical Representation* (Baltimore: Johns Hopkins University, 1987) and to White's Patricia Wise Lecture, "The Modernist Event," in this volume. In his book, White takes on the central place of narrative in the construction of meaning about the world presumed to exist outside it. My concern here with the form of *Who Killed Vincent Chin?* as a collage text explores a type of narrative that White discusses in greater detail in "The Modernist Event." In either case, a prefatory comment by White helps clarify the centrality of the "content of the form" and its difference from such conventional notions as style: "[N]arrative, far from being merely a form of discourse that can be filled with different contents, real or imaginary as the case may be, already possesses a content prior to any given actualization of it in speech or in writing. It is this 'content of the form' of narrative discourse in historical thought that is examined in the essays of this volume" (*Content of the Form*, xi).
4. Hayden White, "The Modernist Event," and Fredric Jameson, *Postmodernism, or, The Cultural Logic of Late Capitalism* (Durham: Duke University Press, 1991).
5. I discuss modes of documentary representation in *Representing Reality: Issues and Concepts in Documentary* (Bloomington: Indiana University Press, 1991). Jameson argues that new modes of narrative do not supersede previous ones but produce sedimentations in which previous modes continue to exist alongside more recent ones. See *The Political Unconscious: Narrative As a Socially Symbolic Act* (Ithaca: Cornell University Press, 1981), particularly 98–102. The corresponding notion that we are ourselves, as subjects, not unified entities, entirely available to consciousness, is the subject of my essay, "We, the People: Form, Rhetoric and Ideology," in *PostModern Discourses of Ideology*, ed. Mas'ud Zavarzadeh and Teresa Ebert (Gainesville: University Press of Florida, 1995).
6. Robert Burgoyne, *Bertolucci's 1900: A Narrative and Historical Analysis* (Detroit: Wayne State Press, 1991), 41.
7. Hayden White, "The Modernist Event," in this volume. 23
8. I adopt the term "discourse of sobriety" in *Representing Reality* (3–5) for expository discourse that regards its relation to the historical world as unproblematic and instrumental. Such discourse is unreceptive to fictive representations (hence the avoidance of fictional experimentation in traditional historiography and the rhetorical construction of the news anchor as "father knows best"). Such discourse takes the tropes of realism literally. Discourses of sobriety make their operational or explanatory moves in relation to the historically real through metaphors (like all discourse) but here these metaphors are meant to be real, to "capture" with fidelity both characteristics of the world and what to do about them. This has the aura of a "serious" enterprise quite distinct from the "fun" implied by fictional representations despite the common use of metaphor and narrative.
9. For more on this point, see White, "The Content of the Form," in *The Content of the Form*, especially 190–193. See John Peradotto, *Man in the Middle Voice: Name and Narration in the Odyssey* (Princeton: Princeton University Press, 1990) for more on the nature of middle voice. These thoughts on mood and voice are indebted to informal conversations with Hayden White and Karen Bassi.
10. Robert Burgoyne, *Bertolucci's 1900*, 11.
11. Raúl Ruiz, *Of Great Events and Ordinary People*. This comment is made on the soundtrack in voice-over. It is meant as a critique of the tradition whereby an array of images could be stitched together into a meaningful statement by means of voice-

over commentary. Ruiz opts to insist on a heterogeneity that attests to the structural disjunctions in consciousness produced by pseudo-totalizations like the nation-state.

12. Jean-Paul Sartre, *Anti-Semite and Jew* (New York: Schocken, 1948), 19–20.
13. See Richard Hofstadter, "The Paranoid Style in American Politics," in *The Paranoid Style in American Politics* (New York: Knopf, 1966).
14. This line of reasoning, if we may call it that, also figured heavily in the defense lawyer's arguments in the case of the Rodney King beating. The Los Angeles Police Department officers argued that Mr. King "was in control" of the situation (and that they were not). They only "responded to" what Mr. King did. Willing backwards becomes an exercise in willing oneself into passivity, at best an agent of fate, or here, of police policy and procedures. I discuss the Rodney King case in greater detail in *Blurred Boundaries* (Bloomington: Indiana University Press, 1994).
15. This contrasts with the work of films like *El Chacal de Nahueltoro* (Miguel Littin, Chile, 1969) and *Death By Hanging* (Nagisa Oshima, France/Japan, 1976) which work to expose the enormous investment the judiciary and the state generally have in guaranteeing that the individual criminal accept responsibility for his or her crime. Without a sense of guilt, the premise of individual responsibility breaks down. When guilt is not evident, recourse is typically made to medicine and one or another concept of insanity as the explanation for a lack of guilt. Such recourse continues to remain localized at the level of the individual; it provides an alibi for sidestepping the more disruptive question of collective guilt or systemic responsibility, precisely the type of questions raised by *Who Killed Vincent Chin?*.
16. Leslie Devereaux, "Experience, Re-presentation and Film," (unpublished ms.), 7.
17. Fredric Jameson, "Marxism and Historicism," 157.
18. Neither the film nor any subsequent commentary that I have seen stresses the fact that the most proximate cause of the initial quarrel between Chin and Ebens was not the effect of Japanese cars or workers on the American economy but the quality of a stripper's performance. Starlene, a relatively new, African-American performer, claims that it was Chin's disparagement and Ebens's defense of her dancing that began the argument that led to Chin's death. (She was not called to testify at the original trial but did testify at the second, federal trial where Ebens was charged with violating Chin's civil rights; her testimony and that of another dancer in this venue apparently had an important effect on the jury.) Chin's failure to appreciate Starlene's dancing together with assumptions Ebens may have held about Japanese workers and their denial of pleasure (even though Chin was Chinese-American and, of course, a patron of the Fancy Pants bar himself) complicates issues of racism with those of sexism and class as they pertain to nightclubs, striptease, audience involvement, banter, and the body.
19. The term "web of conflict" comes from Georg Simmel, "The Web of Group Affiliations," *Conflict* (Glencoe, Illinois: Free Press, 1955). Simmel's synchronic theory of conflict seems highly commensurate with contemporary notions of the divided and split subject, with relations of affinity, and with a politics of identity. These all render classic concepts of a binary class struggle chimerical. His theory complements the diachronic theory of sedimentation as one mode of production leaves vestiges of itself (such as patriarchal relations) within the mode that succeeds it. (Together, these theories also suggest parallel sedimentations and conflicts among forms of artistic production.) Such models call for the complementary concept of a dominant—that specific concatenation of factors that transforms existing, conflictual relations decisively. In this case, the dominant would seem to be the global economy as it implants itself in the tacit knowledge and schizophrenic worldview of one Ronald Ebens. Simmel's model is often regarded as a conservative one since the competing forces within the conflictual web may cancel each other out, sustaining the status quo; Choy and Tajima demonstrate how such a web can be represented to promote a transformative intentionality.

four

"i'll see it when i believe it"

rodney king and the prison-house of video

frank p. tomasulo

> Any given set of real events can be emplotted in a number of ways, can bear the weight of being told as any number of different kinds of stories. Since no given set or sequence of real events is intrinsically tragic, comic, farcical, and so on, but can be constructed as such only by the imposition of the structure of a given story type on the events, it is the choice of the story type and its imposition upon the events that endow them with meaning.
>
> —Hayden White, *The Content of the Form*

Hayden White's notion of "emplotment" as a form of historical storytelling defines a major approach to the contemporary study of history (and historiography). For White, the narratives imposed on "real events" constitute "appropriate ways of endowing human processes with meaning."[1] Thus, history is defined as the discourse *around* events, rather than as those original events that prompted the discourse in the first place. Whether White intended it or not, this reconceptualization has been taken to mean that discursivity is the essence of history and that the question of the truth value of the materiality of lived history should not be addressed.[2] He even goes so far as to say, "It does not matter whether the world is conceived to be real or only imagined, the manner of making sense of it is the same."[3] To the extent that scholars conflate writing about historical events and the events themselves, histori*cism* becomes a replacement for history.

This paradigm has been particularly valorized by some members of the current generation of historians and media scholars, some of whom have even gone so far as to question the very use of the terms "fact," "reality," and "real event" to discuss history. As White points out: "Thinkers—from Valéry and Heidegger to Sartre, Lévi-Strauss, and Michel Foucault—have cast serious doubts on the value of a specifically 'historical' consciousness, stressed the fictive character of historical reconstructions, and challenged history's claims to a place among the sciences."[4]

For poststructuralist thinkers, history is never unmediated by discourse, and all events are narrativized "stories" or "texts" that only *purport* to represent historical occurrences. The accuracy or inaccuracy of those accounts is not subject to verification. Thus, knowledge is partially divorced from reality and is necessarily and totally subject to polysemous interpretation. New Historicist Dominick LaCapra has critiqued this approach on two grounds. For one, he claims that it depends on "an indiscriminate reliance on techniques of fragmentation, decentering, and associative play"; for another, he questions the motives of the poststructuralists: "Derrida, Foucault, and Lyotard attempt to intensify a legitimation crisis in modern society."[5]

Although Hayden White does not have those radical motives, one intent of historicism is to amend the goal of trying to organize the events of modern life into a single coherent narrative pursuant to a single meaning: "It will be lived better if it has no single meaning but many different ones."[6] In extreme variants of this polysemic schema, any one version of making sense of events is as "truthful" as any other. Such currently fashionable conceptions of history as historicism seem entirely appropriate to an age that has been called "the society of the spectacle,"[7] a term that no doubt derives from the ubiquity of suspect media representations in all avenues of contemporary twentieth-century life (that is, the era of late capitalism).

Indeed, increasingly, the postmodern world has been called upon to rely on cinematic and electronic evidence for its depiction and understanding of historical events. In short, our concepts of historical referentiality (what happened), epistemology (how we know it happened), and historical memory (how we interpret it and what it means to us) are now determined primarily by media imagery. The newsreel footage of the explosion of the dirigible

Hindenburg (1937), the Zapruder film of the assassination of President John F. Kennedy (1963), the televised shooting of alleged assassin Lee Harvey Oswald (1963), the nationally televised riots outside and proceedings inside the Democratic Party convention (1968, "the whole world is watching"), the NASA-transmitted moon landing (1969), the surveillance camera recording of heiress Patty Hearst participating in a Symbionese Liberation Army bank robbery (1974), the televised Watergate (1973), Irangate (1987), Clarence Thomas-Anita Hill (1991), and O. J. Simpson (1994) hearings, and hidden government videotapes of prominent individuals caught committing scandalous acts (John DeLorean [1985], Abscam congressmen [1988], Marion Berry [1990]) all suggest our increased reliance on media imagery to define and verify daily news events and the historically real in the modern epoch. If "seeing is believing," as the saying goes, then contemporary history in the era of global media capitalism is increasingly being "written" on film and videotape.

As Hayden White cautioned, however, "The analysis of visual images requires a manner of 'reading' quite different from that developed for the study of written documents."[8] The mere fact that cameras are everywhere and the whole world *is* watching in the late twentieth century suggests a level of technological mediation that may make all the difference between these two models of historical inquiry. As Guy Debord has observed, electronic culture experiences its historical moment as if "everything that was lived directly has moved away into a representation."[9] The "reality effect" of seeing quotidian historical events taking place within the historiographic space of a motion picture or television screen is decidedly different from that of the historian's clay tablet, cuneiform, quill, pen, or typewriter. The "indexical wham"[10] of viewing real-life events on television—as they occur in real time, shortly after they have transpired, and/or in slow motion or freeze-framed replay—creates a strong tendency to assume such visuals are transparent, easily read off their surfaces. As Roland Barthes put it, "Pictures ... are more imperative than writing, they impose meaning at one stroke, without analyzing or diluting it."[11] There is an assumption here that the spectator of media imagery is a passive, ahistorical effect-of-the-text, rather than an active, critical subject with real, historically specific attributes and attitudes such as gender, social class, intelligence, and race. Thus, mediated transmissions or reproductions have been regarded as veritable "historiogemes"—that is, as defining units of public history—especially when those media images are not accompanied by overt narration or commentary.

The classical realist film theories of André Bazin—loosely based on the phenomenological epistemology and ontology of Maurice Merleau-Ponty and filtered through Bazin's mystical Catholicism—represent an attempt to define the relationship between the profilmic event and mediated media discourse. Bazin believed that film's photochemical and photographic basis, its existential optical bond to the antecedent reality taking place in front of the camera lens, made the cinema an "asymptote to reality," especially when the spatiotemporal continuum of reality was preserved in a single, uninterrupted long take.

Two questions emerge from Bazin's ontology of film: Given its two-dimensional reproduction of a three-dimensional world, as well as the distorting capabilities of lenses, shot scale, camera angle, editing, and other techniques, how close to the "reality axis" does the parabola of cinema get? And is it true that "the objective nature of photography confers on it a quality of credibility absent from all other picture-making," that, "in spite of any objections our critical spirit may offer, we are forced to accept as real the existence of the object reproduced"?[12]

Indeed, Bazin went to the reductionistic extreme of saying that "the photographic image *is* the object itself, the object freed from the conditions of time and space that govern it."[13] This metaphysics of presence has been an important theoretical consideration in any analysis of documentary film, although Bazin meant for it to apply to purely fictional works as well. Ironically, Bazin was interested in preserving the spatiotemporal continuum of life, not to *fix* it (as does still photography) but to reveal and respect "the ontological ambiguity of reality."[14] Still photographs (and, by extension, the motion picture and video artifact) are as much *iconic* signs as they are *indexical* ones, in Charles Sanders Peirce's terminology, because they not only have an existential bond with but also possess some of the properties of the object represented.[15] As Umberto Eco has noted, "Iconic signs reproduce some of the conditions of perception."[16] As such, they are not pure *reproductions* of a preexistent or contemporaneous "reality," but prima facie *transformations* of the world before the camera lens.

This point has been made repeatedly about film and video depictions of historical events, especially by many contemporary film and television scholars who advocate poststructuralism, deconstructionism, Derridean analysis, and/or polysemiotics. Implicitly or explicitly, these academics have theoretically denied the very existence of historical "facts" and realities outside the realm of visual mediation and other mediating discourse. The critique of representation is "the fundamental slogan of poststructuralism."[17] In this realm, indeterminacy, polysemy, and the endless play of signifiers reign supreme. Even the ancient tradition of the "Western metaphysics of presence" has been called into question by Friedrich Nietzsche, Martin Heidegger, Paul de Man, Jacques Derrida, and their followers. If, as they have asserted, what we regard as objective reality and meaning do not inhere in the things and events of this world, and if we have no direct knowledge of these things and events, then perhaps all

machine. Here, a sort of Heisenberg Uncertainty Principle of Video was operative, in which the acts of recording, transmitting, and viewing the event on videotape changed the event. The role of the observing consciousness transformed what was perceived and conceived. Ultimately, then, through the confrontation of his/her consciousness with the phenomenal, material reality shown on the televised videotape, each viewer assigned whatever degree of authenticity and value to the images he/she deemed appropriate, based on his/her degree of identification with a particular demographic group.

One demographic group that reacted to the first King verdict was the Society for Cinema Studies (SCS), the international organization for film/television scholars. The group's annual conference in April 1992 coincided with the announcement of the "Not guilty" verdict and the riots that followed. A petition was drawn up, distributed, and signed by many in attendance:

> (1) The verdict to acquit four white Los Angeles Police Department officers contradicts powerful visual evidence—video evidence of excessive police brutality seen globally.
>
> (2) The reaction in the streets of Los Angeles and other cities is fueled by the jury's deliberate refusal to "see" this visual evidence the way that most of us—regardless of color—saw these images.
>
> (3) But how did they "see" this video? They saw it repeatedly, repeatedly—desensitized to its power and effect. They saw it in slow motion, analytically—as the defense supplied a "reading" of the appropriateness of each officer's reaction. This demonstrates how close readings can incur misreadings. Our outrage is that, even with visual evidence, Blacks' experience of police brutality does not count.
>
> (4) As media educators, we must voice our outrage at this verdict and endorse all efforts to indict the LAPD officers for civil rights violations.[48]

As a political statement expressing outrage, there is little to criticize in the SCS resolution; indeed, the statement was in substantive agreement with public statements issued by both then-President George Bush and Los Angeles Police Chief Daryl Gates, who criticized the outrageous Simi Valley verdict. As an epistemological document, however, the basis for the moral judgments in the hastily drafted SCS document is fraught with problematic principles, not the least of which involves the reemergence of the specter of positivism that the film studies discipline had been trying to exorcise for years. It seemed particularly contradictory for the SCS to make such a statement because, as Vivian Sobchack notes, "Contemporary theory was emphasizing the inaccessibility of direct experience and focused on the constitutive processes and mediating structures of language."[49]

First, the idea that the King videotape contained "powerful visual evidence of police brutality" assumes that the legal case could be made solely on the basis of the surface appearances of the blows as seen on the video—apart from the legalistic questions of whether proper Los Angeles Police Department procedures were followed or not. Second, the notion that "the way *most of us*—regardless of color—saw these images" (emphasis added) should be the basis for rendering jury verdicts is highly suspect, implying that juridical decisions can and should be made by referendum, without trial, on the basis of videotaped evidence. Third, it has never been proven—empirically or otherwise—that slow-motion examinations of violent scenes "desensitize" spectators to the horror of physical brutality. Although it has been argued that slow motion minimizes the effects of a violent scene because in the real world a faster blow is a harder one and that freeze-frame viewing reduces the visual impact of violence by making the baton strokes seem less relentless, the slow-motion technique might have even *monumentalized* the baton blows, thereby exaggerating their violent force in the minds of jurors. Indeed, jurors who convicted two officers in the federal trial admitted that watching the videotape "forward, backward, frame by frame" fifteen to twenty times a day convinced them of the guilt of Sgt. Stacey Koon and Officer Laurence Powell.

Fourth, if "close readings can incur misreading," then much of the theoretical superstructure of poststructuralist film theory needs to be modified, because if there is such a thing as a "misreading," then there must perforce be a correct or preferred reading inherent in the text, above and apart from discourse. Whatever Jacques Derrida intended to convey, his maxim, "*il n'y a pas de hors-texte*"[50] (there is nothing outside the text), has become a rationale for intratextual narcissism (if not solipsism) and an endorsement of the unbridled play of polyvalent signifiers. The SCS statement seems to dismiss close textual analysis as an anachronistic residue of bourgeois formalism but, as Dominick LaCapra has so astutely pointed out, "a text may also render its contexts in critical and potentially transformative ways that close reading may disclose."[51] Finally, the idea that a videotape record provides access to or can act as the postmodernist arbiter of the absolute truth or eidetic reality (let alone juridical meaning) of what happened in front of George Holliday's zoom lens is a positivist fantasy, contradicting decades of mediation theory in cinema and television scholarship.

The ultimate irony is that scholars who for decades had welcomed close textual analysis as a tool for spinning elaborate ideological readings and rereadings of film/TV texts suddenly had to confront defense attorneys on the opposite side of the political spectrum who used the same tools of visual analysis to convince a jury that their clients acted properly according to the LAPD's "escalating force" policy. When one's political ox is gored, one's theoretical and epistemological *partis pris* change to accommodate inconvenient realities. In short, if an academician believes in the ultimate indeterminacy of truth (and is especially skeptical about the role of media as guarantor of truth), how can he/she conclude with any certainty that Rodney King was the victim of a prototypical racist beating by the police?

This contradiction raises some very interesting issues of central importance not only to the film/television studies discipline but to the body politic as well. Those who question the reality of history are, in a way, condemned repeatedly to revise it. Although a healthy epistemological skepticism about written accounts and interpretations of the past is an important corrective to dominant ideology, extreme nihilism toward history can undermine belief in even the most settled of historical facts, such as the existence of slavery or the Holocaust. Certainly, slavery and the Holocaust can be analyzed and interpreted endlessly, but denying their reality or attributing the discourse surrounding them solely to the ideological interests of Blacks or Jews is pure revisionism. Karl Marx's point that "men make their own history, but...they do not make it under conditions chosen by themselves"[52] is ironically true of Rodney King, but poststructuralist historians and media scholars who espouse a constructivist view of the past seem to deny that "men make their own history"; they substitute the notion that *historians* make (up) history. Thus, if the postmodern historian makes no meaningful distinction between the historical and the imaginary, thereby denying the facticity of the tragic beating of Rodney King in favor of an illusive ficticity of media representations of that assault, he/she would be hard-pressed to offer the "compelling visual evidence" of the videotape as proof to support an irrefutable "guilty" verdict for the LAPD officers.

Most courtroom decisions (and historical events) are laden with ambiguities. The "absolute" truth sought in most fictionalized courtroom dramas represents a convention that real-life jurors imagine as the goal of real-life cases; more often than not, *Rashomon* (Akira Kurosawa, 1950) becomes the practical model. But although the truly open-and-shut case is rare, jurors do make dispositions on a wide variety of matters every day, based on the rules of evidence and their own best judgment and experience. More important, most of the factual events were not in dispute in the Rodney King case (although the tape evidence of a head blow by Officer Powell was inconclusive, even with video enhancement techniques). All parties agreed that King had been speeding and that the police officers had Tased, swarmed, beaten, and arrested him. What was at stake in the first trial were the procedures and motives involved in

King's apprehension and whether the physical force was appropriate or excessive from the point of view of a "reasonable" police officer.

These subjective matters were not explicit or "visible" in the videotaped images seen by the nation on the nightly news broadcasts. As Bill Nichols astutely points out: "A photographic image represents the visible event, not the motivation. Subjectivity eludes its grasp."[53] Nevertheless, although the subjective states of mind of *the participants* may not have been amenable to video dissection, the subjectivity of *the spectators of the videotape* is relevant to the issue at hand. Different interpretive communities saw the same tape differently (e.g., the Black and white communities, Los Angeles and Simi Valley, civilians and cops). Yet it is not necessarily a foregone conclusion what any individual member of any demographic group will perceive in a given situation. For instance, one African-American officer on the scene, Officer Love, testified that no excessive force was used against Rodney King.

conclusion: "i'll see it when i believe it"

No apprehension is merely momentary and ephemeral ... the object is pregiven with a new content of sense, it is present to consciousness with the horizon of acquired cognitions.

—Edmund Husserl, *Experience and Judgment*

According to Husserlian phenomenology, subjects experience objects dialectically in the cognitive act, yet the object always already remains and exists independent of the subject. There is ample room in Husserl's theories for levels of mediation unthought of by André Bazin. For Husserl, the perceptual and meaning-making operations of human consciousness are highly structured interpretive acts, although he conceded that perception is often based on what he termed "products of historically sedimented subjectivity" unless a preliminary bracketing step was taken.

Human beings rarely enter a situation, historical or otherwise, with a fresh, untainted perspective. In other words, people generally do not come to believe things *after* seeing them; they see things only when they *already* believe them—based on their prior *Lebenswelt* and media exposure. Thus, consciousness, even though it is never fixed, is also never arbitrary, as some deconstructionists would have us believe. More often than not, spectators based their individual reactions to the Rodney King video on their pretextual identities, attitudes they had formulated well *before* they viewed the tape. There is a critical difference between deriving meaning *from* history and attributing meaning *to* history as a way of justifying one's own antecedent beliefs. Even if the historical "facts" represented on the videotape are conceded, the meanings ascribed to them are contestable, because "the facts are a *function* of the meaning assigned to events, not some primitive data that determine what meanings an event can have."[54]

If history is indeed "up for grabs," as Hayden White once suggested, then liberating people from the tyranny of facts by promoting a Cartesian systematic doubt or a Ricoeurian hermeneutics of suspicion may be progressive. But if professional educators begin to empower individuals to open their eyes and minds to the possibility of alternative readings or "reading against the grain" of a text's overt meaning, they should be aware that such a pedagogical strategy may also lead to inadvertent consequences, namely, that their students may adopt political positions at odds with the prevailing wisdom or "political correctness" of their professors.

The very basis of close textual analysis is to see beyond the surface appearances of media phenomena (the nightsticks pounding King, for instance) and to put images in social and historical context (black victim of racist brutality and/or guilty resister of lawful authority). A text without a context is a pretext for misunderstanding political and historical events. Even though the status of historical knowledge has been problematized in the age of electronic reproduction, exaggerating the extent to which we live in a "media society" or "electronic society" has social consequences. If everything is a text without a referent, and a narrativized text at that, then it can hardly be argued that injustice and exploitation really exist. Reducing the King video to the play of the arbitrary sign disconnects it from any ontological ground. As Vivian Sobchack explains, "Film makes sense by virtue of its very ontology. That is, its existence emerges embodied and finitely situated."[55]

Fredric Jameson's ontology also emphasizes a belief in reality: "I have argued for the presence and existence of what seems to me a palpable referent—namely, death and historical fact, which are ultimately not textualizable."[56] Jameson's rationale is political. With the breakdown of historicity that accompanies a loss of the historical referent and the concomitant undecidability of representation comes a diminution of materialism as a philosophy and a weakening of political will to fight injustice. But, as Linda Williams observed: "The contradictions are rich: on the one hand the postmodern deluge of images seems to suggest that there can be no a priori truth of the referent to which the image refers; on the other hand, in this same deluge, it is still the moving image that has the power to move audiences to a new appreciation of previously unknown truth."[57]

With this dialectic in mind, it is important to avoid a simplistic and reductive conclusion that there is reality and there is media mediation and never the twain shall meet. Historical facts and cultural expression mingle and interact on a daily basis, especially in the modern world. The media have become part of the material world; superstructure has become base.[58] Guy Debord has expressed this notion most forcefully: "The spectacle is not a collection of images, but a social relation among people, mediated by images."[59] As a commodity in the material world, the video image "is *capital* to such a degree of accumulation that it becomes an image."[60] To quote Jameson again, "Culture itself is one of those things whose fundamental materiality is now not merely evident but quite inescapable.... Culture has become material, a social institution."[61] Making history or making news on television has become so embedded as social practice in our daily lives that it has reached the ultimate fate of postmodern culture: commodification. If history has become a commodity, then television news programming has become its sales pitch. It is both journalism and show business, history and dramatic entertainment.

Media representations need not be absolutely equated with historical facts in every instance. Distinctions need to be made between what is shown and what is edited out, and attention must be paid to the workings of ideology in a class society. Todd Gitlin proposes a conspiracy theory of media: "For the most part, television ... shows us only what the nation already presumes, focuses on what the culture already knows—or more precisely, enables us to gaze upon something the appointed seers think we need or want to know."[62] If this claim is true, how, then, can we make the claim that we live in a racist society with a racist master narrative when most viewers believed, having seen the televised tape of the beating, that Rodney King was unjustly beaten? On the one hand, there is Hayden White's explanation that "the outside phenomenal aspects, and insides of events, their possible meanings or significances, have been collapsed and fused ... unstable, fluid, phantasmagoric—as phantasmagoric as the slow-motion, reverse angle, zoom, and rerun of the video representations of the Challenger explosion."[63] On the other hand, perhaps the recent tendency to dissolve events into a nihilistic specter of postmodernist nonmeaning has not been accepted by ordinary citizens, who draw on their own experiences of life and media rather than on the pseudohistorical hypotheses of scholars when evaluating events broadcast into their living rooms.

Media scholars need to realize that how people analyze and draw historical conclusions from TV newscasts is projective and purposeful, based more on their horizon of expectation and what they bring to the experience than what they get from it. The notion advanced by Christian Metz that spectators' primary identification is with the technological apparatus of image-making (cameras, projectors, TV sets) rather than with the on-screen characters and events needs to be reinvestigated.[64] If one identifies narcissistically with the act of looking, then that gaze of consciousness assists us in establishing ourselves as subjects-in-the-world, as well as subjects-of-the-tube. But it cannot be forgotten that, as Julia Kristeva put it, "the knowing subject is also the desiring subject," that is, how we experience the world can be dependent on our attitudes. Put another way, our perceptions may be conditioned by our (pre?)conceptions. In phenomenological terms, any perception is also an intention.

Kaja Silverman has argued that "a cinematic text will satisfy the viewer's desire for reality only if both text and viewer inhabit what Jacques Rancière would call the same 'dominant fiction.'"[65] The dominant fiction in the Rodney King affair may well have been that the legal guilt or innocence of the four officers on trial was the *sine qua non* of meaning, while the structural problems of an entire society (crime and punishment, as well as racial injustice) were displaced onto the individuals captured on videotape.

The French silent filmmaker Jean Epstein is said to have rhapsodized about the truth-seeking abilities of the new motion-picture apparatus. Epstein opined that the veracity of courtroom witnesses could be determined by training a slow-motion camera on them. Writing about the films of Erich von Stroheim, André Bazin expressed a similar view of the camera's ability of detection: "Reality lays itself bare like a suspect confessing under the relentless examination of the commissioner of police. [Stroheim] had one simple rule for direction. Take a close look at the world, keep on doing so, and in the end it will lay bare for you all its cruelty and its ugliness."[66]

George Holliday's amateur videotape took a close (albeit fuzzy) look at the urban world and it laid bare the cruelty and ugliness of modern life on America's mean streets. Perhaps the day will come when some sort of video polygraph will be admissible evidence in a court of law (or even in the court of public opinion). Such a technological breakthrough would certainly represent a true Bazinian "asymptote to History." Until that time, however, fallible human beings will have to rely on fallible technology and their own experiences to adjudge the truth value of events in the world or the legal guilt and/or innocence of individuals and entire societies. And it may well be, as historian Maurice Mandelbaum suggests, that "any event is far too complex and ambiguous to sustain any single meaning."[67] If complexity and ambiguity are our lot, people will continue to impute meanings based on their own life situations, for, as Hayden White admits, "[there] appears to be an irreducible ideological component in every historical account of reality."[68]

notes

1. Hayden White, *Tropics of Discourse: Essays in Cultural Criticism* (Baltimore: Johns Hopkins University Press, 1978), 61.
2. To White, even the most apparently factual historical account should be treated as a literary artifact. See especially Hayden White, "The Historical Text as Literary

Artifact," in *The Writing of History*, ed. Robert H. Canary and Henry Kozicki (Madison: University of Wisconsin Press, 1978), 41–62.

3. White, "The Historical Text," 61.
4. Hayden White, *Metahistory: The Historical Imagination in Nineteenth-Century Europe* (Baltimore: Johns Hopkins University Press, 1973), 1–2.
5. Dominick LaCapra, *Soundings in Critical Theory* (Ithaca, N.Y.: Cornell University Press, 1989), 1, 17.
6. White, *Tropics of Discourse*, 50.
7. Guy Debord, *The Society of the Spectacle* (Detroit: Black and Red, 1983).
8. Hayden White, "Historiography and Historiophoty," *American Historical Review* 93:5 (December 1988): 1193.
9. Debord, *The Society of the Spectacle*, sect. 1.
10. Bill Nichols, "Visible Evidence" (paper presented at Society for Cinema Studies conference, New Orleans, 13 February 1993). Nichols's use of the term "indexical" derives from Charles Sanders Peirce's distinction between linguistic signs: index, icon, and symbol. The index has an existential bond to its referent (weather vane, blood pressure, etc.); the icon resembles its referent through similarity (the portrait); and the symbol has an arbitrary relationship to the referent. For an application of these terms to the cinema, see Peter Wollen, *Signs and Meanings in the Cinema* (Bloomington: Indiana University Press, 1984), 116–54.
11. Roland Barthes, "Myth Today," *Mythologies*, trans. Annette Lavers (New York: Hill and Wang, 1972), 110.
12. André Bazin, *What Is Cinema?*, 2 vols, ed. and trans. Hugh Gray (Berkeley: University of California Press, 1967, 1971), I: 13.
13. Bazin, *What Is Cinema?*, I: 14 (emphasis added).
14. Bazin, *What Is Cinema?*, II: 68.
15. Charles Sanders Peirce, *Peirce on Signs: Writings in Semiotics by Charles Sanders Peirce*, ed. James Hoopes (Chapel Hill: University of North Carolina Press, 1991), 239–51.
16. Umberto Eco, "Articulations of the Cinematic Code," in *Movies and Methods*, ed. Bill Nichols (Berkeley: University of California Press, 1976), 594.
17. Fredric Jameson, "Architecture and the Critique of Ideology," in *Architecture/Criticism/Ideology*, ed. Joan Ockman (Princeton: Princeton Architectural Press, 1985), 56.
18. Bill Nichols, *Representing Reality: Issues and Concepts in Documentary* (Bloomington: Indiana University Press, 1991), 177.
19. Dominick LaCapra, *History and Criticism* (Ithaca, N.Y.: Cornell University Press, 1983), 11.
20. Hayden White, "Method and Ideology in Intellectual History," in *Modern European Intellectual History: Reappraisals and New Perspectives*, ed. Dominick LaCapra and Steven L. Kaplan (Ithaca, N.Y.: Cornell University Press, 1982), 305.
21. Nichols, *Representing Reality*, 109.
22. Nichols, *Representing Reality*, 110.
23. Fredric Jameson, *The Political Unconscious: Narrative as a Socially Symbolic Act* (Ithaca, N.Y.: Cornell University Press, 1981), 35, 102.
24. Fredric Jameson, *Postmodernism, or the Cultural Logic of Late Capitalism* (Durham, N.C.: Duke University Press, 1992), 18.
25. Jameson, *Postmodernism*, 26.
26. Jameson, *Postmodernism*, ix.
27. "Swarming" is a technical term in L.A.P.D. jargon for the tactical method used to subdue resisting suspects. It involves surrounding the individual, then moving in closer, and using "escalating force" to handcuff the perpetrator.
28. On June 11, 1993, U.S. District Judge Irving Hill ruled in Los Angeles that George Holliday's $100 million violation of copyright lawsuit against CNN, ABC, CBS, and NBC had no merit. The judge described the King videotape as being of "great

social import." For details, see "King Beating Videographer's Suit Dismissed," *Atlanta Journal-Constitution*, 12 June 1993, A5.

29. "9 1/3 Minutes Changed Life of Videotaper," *Atlanta Journal-Constitution*, 24 April 1993, A3.
30. Needless to say, contemporary theory cannot shoulder the entire blame for the first jury verdict. Other considerations were clearly involved: the precise nature of the state charges, the fact that King did not testify, the demographics of the Simi Valley jury, and other legal determinants.
31. White, *Metahistory*, 434.
32. In film theory, a "structuring absence" is an unsaid element in (or outside) a text that nonetheless is crucial to its constitution. The concept was introduced to cinema studies in a famous essay by the *Cahiers du Cinéma* editors: "John Ford's *Young Mr. Lincoln*," in *Movies and Methods*, 493–529.
33. Bazin, *What Is Cinema?*, I: 29.
34. Régis Durand, "Event, Trace, Intensity," trans. Lynne Kirby, *Discourse* 16.2 (Winter 1993-94): 123.
35. John Hess, Chuck Kleinhans, and Julia Lesage, "After Cosby/After the L.A. Rebellion: The Politics of Transnational Culture in the Post Cold War Era," *Jump Cut* 37 (1992): 2.
36. Mike Mashon, "Losing Control: Popular Reception(s) of the Rodney King Video," *Wide Angle* 15.2 (April 1993): 16.
37. "Verdict Suggests Jury Came to View Beating through Police 'Eyes,'" *Washington Post*, 30 April 1992, A25.
38. Nick Browne, "The Spectator-in-the-Text: The Rhetoric of *Stagecoach*," *Film Quarterly* 29.2 (Winter 1975/76): 26–38. For an application of Browne's analysis of authorial inscription and spectator positioning to the television medium, see Frank P. Tomasulo, "The Spectator-in-the-Tube: The Rhetoric of *Donahue*," *Journal of Film and Video* 36.1 (Spring 1984): 5–12.
39. Hayden White, "The Value of Narrativity in the Representation of Reality," in *On Narrative*, ed. W. J. T. Mitchell (Chicago: University of Illinois Press, 1980), 14–15.
40. Mashon, "Losing Control," 14.
41. The pun on Judge Learned Hand's name is intended. Carrying it further, one might speak of the invisible *fist* of police brutality.
42. Jameson, *Postmodernism*, 186.
43. Sigmund Freud, "A Child Is Being Beaten: A Contribution to the Study of the Origin of Sexual Perversions," in *The Standard Edition of the Complete Psychological Works of Sigmund Freud*, 24 vols., trans. and ed. James Strachey (London: Hogarth, 1953–66), 17: 179–204.
44. Martin Luther King, Jr., quoted in David J. Garrow, *Protest at Selma: Martin Luther King, Jr., and the Voting Rights Act of 1965* (New Haven, Conn.: Yale University Press, 1978), 111.
45. Louis Althusser, *Lenin and Philosophy*, trans. Ben Brewster (New York: Monthly Review Press, 1971), 142–48.
46. "Looking Past the Verdict," *Newsweek*, 26 April 1993, 23–24.
47. "Batons in the Jury Room: The Reaching of a Verdict," *New York Times*, 24 April 1993, A9.
48. "The Society for Cinema Studies Resolution," *Jump Cut* 37 (1992): 2.
49. Vivian Sobchack, *The Address of the Eye: A Phenomenology of Film Experience* (Princeton: Princeton University Press, 1992), xiv. A conversation with Vivian Sobchack about the petition at the 1992 SCS conference inspired the writing of this essay.
50. Jacques Derrida, *Of Grammatology*, trans. Gayatri Chakravorty Spivak (Baltimore: Johns Hopkins University Press, 1976), 158.
51. Dominick LaCapra, *History, Politics, and the Novel* (Ithaca, N.Y.: Cornell University Press, 1987), 206.

52. Karl Marx, *The Eighteenth Brumaire of Louis Bonaparte* (New York: International Publishers, 1963), 15.
53. Nichols, *Representing Reality*, 153.
54. Hayden White, "The Modernist Event," in this volume, 21.
55. Sobchack, *The Address of the Eye*, 12.
56. Jameson, *Postmodernism*, 94.
57. Linda Williams, "Mirrors without Memories: Truth, History, and the New Documentary," *Film Quarterly* 46.3 (Spring 1993): 10.
58. The classical Marxist base-superstructure relationship is a dichotomous one in which the economic forces and relations of production give rise to the ideological beliefs of a given historical period. In the contemporary world, the two antinomies interact more dialectically, in the sense that the mass media, especially television, constitute a sense of reality for most people in the society and thereby determine social consciousness. See Raymond Williams, "Base and Superstructure in Marxist Cultural Theory," *New Left Review* 82 (1973): 3–16.
59. Debord, *The Society of the Spectacle*, sect. 4.
60. Debord, *The Society of the Spectacle*, sect. 34.
61. Jameson, *Postmodernism*, xvii, 67.
62. Todd Gitlin, "Looking through the Screen," in *Watching Television*, ed. Todd Gitlin (New York: Pantheon Books, 1986), 3.
63. White, "The Modernist Event," in this volume, 29.
64. Christian Metz, *The Imaginary Signifier: Psychoanalysis and the Cinema*, trans., Ben Brewster (Bloomingon: Indiana University Press, 1982), 49–51.
65. Kaja Silverman, "Historical Trauma and Male Subjectivity," in *Psychoanalysis and Cinema*, ed. E. Ann Kaplan (New York: Routledge, 1990), 110.
66. Bazin, *What Is Cinema?*, I: 2.
67. Maurice Mandelbaum, "The Presuppositions of *Metahistory*," in *Metahistory: Six Critiques*, ed. George H. Nadel (Middletown, CT: Wesleyan University Press, 1980), 42.
68. White, *Metahistory*, 21.

part two

historical representation and national identity

five

antimodernism as historical representation in a consumer culture

cecil b. demille's *the ten commandments,* 1923, 1956, 1993

sumiko higashi

public history and american historiography

When Cecil B. DeMille released a remake of the silent version of *The Ten Commandments* in 1956 to culminate his decades-long career, a *Variety* critic commented, he "has broken new ground in terms of size, [but] he has remained conventional with the motion picture as an art form."[1] Acclaimed as one of Hollywood's most innovative directors in the 1910s and early 1920s, DeMille thereafter became a showman who reified spectacle in a visual style that remained relatively unchanged for decades. Yet he continued to break box-office records precisely because his mise-en-scène dated back to an antimodernist tradition that mediated the experience of twentieth-century modernity for generations of filmgoers. An amalgam of realism and sentimentalism—two conflicting but related modes that represented the conservative response of the genteel classes to modernization—DeMille's epics nevertheless functioned as spectacle for visual appropriation in a modern consumer culture.[2] The director was in fact well-known for having established fashion trends in Jazz Age films that became a primer for consumption, defined as refinement by the respectable middle class. Indeed, he was instrumental in commodifying and reifying the religious spirit itself in sensational biblical epics that rationalized materialistic values. Although separated by three decades, the silent and sound versions of *The Ten Commandments* attest to remarkable continuity in the dynamics of filmmaking in terms of the ideology of consumption: both films were cultural productions of postwar decades characterized on the one hand by unprecedented consumer spending, and on the other hand by American dominance of a global economy. DeMille's lavish production of biblical epics was in itself a form of commodity fetishism that paralleled spectacular scenes representing America as the land of milk and honey. And in more recent years, the annual telecast of the sound version during the Passover and Easter holidays represents yet another manifestation of the power of antimodernist narrative to promote patriotism in the form of consumption. Undoubtedly, DeMille did not himself envision the transformation of an epic that was a crowning achievement of the studio system into a televisual "supertext," but its singular revival in postmodernist form is a phenomenon worth considering.

Straddling the Victorian era and a modern consumer culture, DeMille represented a pictorial tradition that framed and thus contained spectacle, especially disquieting urban scenes, even as he transformed that legacy in a mass medium. Particularly relevant to a consideration of his antimodernist historical films is Richard Hofstadter's summation of America's "quarrel with history" as "the difficulty of combining the pastoral, or still worse the primitivist, sense of the ideal human condition with another equally deep intellectual craving: the belief in progress."[3] A response to the experience of modernization as rapid industrialization and development of capitalistic markets worldwide, demographic upheaval in chaotic urban centers, and increasing bureaucratization, antimodernism represented a nostalgic invocation of small-town values, experience, and horizons.[4] As such, it celebrated a republican civic culture that invoked a golden age of harmony expressing the will of divine providence. Although this idealized past eventuated in twentieth-century standardization and rationalization, antimodernists continued to assess contemporary developments, as David Glassberg argues, with a nostalgic glance backwards.[5] A sign of the aesthetic as well as the social and political values of the conservative elite, antimodernism became a significant force in the pageantry movement that culminated before the First World War. As civic theater, it provided early filmmakers like DeMille with a significant intertext in the production of historical drama enacted in the public sphere.

During the Progressive Era, the genteel classes sponsored public history in the form of civic drama not only to counter the attractions of commercialized amusement, but also to project a sense of community based on visions of an arcadian past. At the height of the movement in 1912, a half-million spectators witnessed four separate marathon performances of the Pageant and Masque of St. Louis. Widespread publicity including newsreels described the pageant—a series of reenactments of three centuries of local history—and the masque—an allegory regarding the cosmic significance of the rise and fall of civilizations—as expressions of civic pride. A representation of an antimodernist aesthetic, historical drama evolved from inspirational tableaux vivants in an era when culture was deemed sacrosanct. Contrary to modernist expressions that included worship of the machine aesthetic as well as autonomous and self-referential art objects, Arnoldian sensibility dictated that art fulfill a social function and exert a spiritual influence.[6] Accordingly, civic pageantry in immense outdoor settings reinforced a contemplative and respectful reception of the lessons of the past. Audiences were seated so far from elaborately constructed sets that they could scarcely distinguish between foreground and background or comprehend symbolic events without the aid of programs.[7] Civic drama, in other words, did not produce the modernist stylistic phenomenon that Daniel Bell criticizes as "an eclipse of distance between the spectator and the artist, between the aesthetic experience and the work of art." [8] As precepts steeped in nostalgic visions of the past, historical pageants reenacted inspirational scenes that contrasted with such disturbing signs of modernization as urban chaos and pluralism. Although some ethnic peoples were included in the movement's definition of civic community, social groups considered unassimilable, such as native Americans or labor unions with suspect ideological beliefs, were excluded. Significantly, the lower classes proved at least on one memorable occasion that they could appropriate the antimodernist cultural forms of the elite for their own purposes. In 1913 Italian, Polish, and Jewish silk workers reenacted scenes from an ongoing, protracted, and bitter labor dispute in the Paterson Strike Pageant staged in Madison Square Garden.[9]

Granted, the teleological concept of time endorsed by civic pageantry implied progress that reinforced the status quo and militated against social change, but there was nevertheless a relationship between public history and the New History of Progressive reform-era historians. Pageant officials, to be sure, subscribed to nineteenth-century historiography that, according to Hofstadter, "embodied the ideas of the possessing classes about industrial and financial issues, manifested the complacency of white Anglo-Saxon

Protestants about social and ethnic issues, and, on constitutional issues, underwrote the requirements of property and of national centralization."[10] Such an interpretation of the past accorded with proclamations of Manifest Destiny and spread-eagle diplomacy that civic pageants, albeit reenactments of local events, endorsed in a celebration of history as a wellspring for patriotism. As Glassberg argues, however, parallels did exist between historical pageantry and Progressive Era historiography as movements that emphasized contemporary uses of the past. Social and economic developments, for example, became as significant as political themes or the centrality of the nation-state. Yet the construction of history as a usable past that was associated with the pragmatist thought of John Dewey, as well as Progressive historians, hardly constituted a rupture with previous historiography; in fact, it even played into the hands of educators intent on Americanizing workers and immigrants. To this day, history as a discipline based on empiricist models of knowledge is part of a social studies curriculum designed in the Progressive Era to educate a useful citizenry. The basic assumptions of such a paradigm, as Peter Novick argues, are a "commitment to the reality of the past, and to truth as correspondence to that reality, a sharp separation between knower and known, between fact and value, and, above all, between history and fiction."[11]

Precisely because the issue of empiricism became a focus of contention, the convergence of professional and public forms of history, that is, the relevance of the New History to civic theater and civic education was short lived. After the First World War, Progressive historians like Carl Becker and Charles Beard questioned empiricist and inductivist models of scholarship and championed modernist approaches that historians today label relativism or pragmatic hermenuetics.[12] Such a rupture with orthodox epistemology did precipitate controversy within the historical profession, but debate was restricted to the halls of academe and failed to penetrate more public forums. In sum, professional historians not only lost ground to educators with respect to the definition of history in public schools, they also lost an increasing mass readership for historical works to amateurs and journalists.[13] Ultimately, the conceptualization of history as progress that was perpetuated in social studies curricula and mass market publications laid the ground work for filmmakers like DeMille who constructed historical consciousness in the form of narratives of national emergence.

the consumption of spectacle: *the ten commandments*, 1923

Although the silent version of *The Ten Commandments* does not constitute a teleological narrative of national emergence, its significance for the commodification of spectacle cannot be underrated. DeMille reinforced the consumer ethos as the basis of an American way of life at a time when society was deeply divided by class, ethnicity, religion, geographical region, and gender. The immediate postwar events of the Red Scare, which included militant unionism and strikes, deportation of radicals, and alienation of the middle class, left Americans an unsettling legacy.[14] Within a broadly defined middle class, moreover, a cultural war was being waged between small-town fundamentalists and city dwellers espousing a more modernist sensibility.[15] DeMille's lavish spectacles contributed to the definition of American consumption as personal fulfillment and uplift and thus to the secularization of liberal Protestantism.[16] Consumer values increasingly provided the social cement in a world subject to the centrifugal forces of modernity.[17] Given the divisiveness of American society in the decade following the First World War, *The Ten Commandments* was a milestone because the director constructed a historical film that, unlike his first epic, *Joan the Woman* (1916), appealed to a national film audience rather than a segmented market.

Despite its success in a mass market, the Biblical Prologue of *The Ten Commandments* unquestionably appealed to the genteel classes whom DeMille had courted before the war with feature films constructed as intertextual modes of address. Set decoration in *The Cheat* (1915), for example, replicated World's Fair pavilions, museum exhibits, and fashionable department stores frequented by the well-to-do. Similarly, *The Ten Commandments* invoked not only the celebrated tradition of historical pageantry but also the King James Version of the Bible, in particular the expensive, gilt-edged edition illustrated by Gustave Doré. A definitive work by the nineteenth-century French illustrator, the Doré Bible, with its emphasis on theatricality, realism, and Orientalism, was an important source of inspiration for artists working in the pictorial tradition. Also significant as an intertext related to DeMille's epic were news reports of the discovery of Tutankhamun's tomb in November 1922, an event characterized as one of the most sensational and longest-lasting stories in modern journalism.[18] Although the Biblical Prologue, which comprised a lengthy introduction to a Modern Story set in the Jazz Age, appealed on an intertextual basis to a cultivated audience, the film as sheer spectacle excited the masses as well. DeMille built extraordinary sets with huge monuments to recreate the grandeur that was Egypt, orchestrated immense crowd scenes in a vast, arid landscape, and employed special effects for miraculous events like the parting of the Red Sea. Furthermore, he continued to experiment with the Handschiegl process, which required expensive application of color upon completion of photography, and used two-strip Technicolor in addition to standard tinting and toning for scenes of the exodus and of Moses receiving the Ten Commandments on Mount Sinai.

Unlike the Modern Story about a romantic triangle, the Biblical Prologue appears regressive in terms of its visual style due to a preponderance of long and extreme long shots, punctuated by occasional medium shots to show individuals reacting to tumultuous events. DeMille's shot scale, in other words, fails to resolve the narratological dilemma of historical pageants viewed as a macrocosm from such a distance that audiences had to read their programs to comprehend the spectacle. Yet the director's use of monumental sets, huge crowd scenes, special effects, and color processes explains the high ratio of extreme long shots. A contemporary screening of the black and white prints in circulation is thus extremely misleading. As the Hebrews leave the City of Rameses in the Handschiegl version of the film, for example, a thin vertical strip of blue appears in the center of footage tinted sepia and increases in width in succeeding shots to convey a sense of liberation. A sequence of masses of people walking into the desert, which concludes with a fade-out leaving a blank screen in red, is toned in that flaming color to give a sensation of intense heat. Significantly, the massive stone wall in the background of the art titles citing the Book of Exodus disappears upon the liberation of the Hebrews, whereas a bright orange curtain of flames entraps the legions of the Pharaoh in mid-pursuit. Symbolizing the clash between cultures are elements of fire and water sensationalized by the use of color and special effects. Although the body of water parted as an escape route is named the Red Sea, the Pharaoh and his awed charioteer continue their chase as they are outlined against an enormous pastel colored wall of bluish-tinted green waves.[19]

When *The Ten Commandments* premiered in New York, a chorus of approval resounded in trade journals, fan magazines, and newspapers. James R. Quirk proclaimed in *Photoplay* that the film was "the best photoplay ever made" and "the greatest theatrical spectacle in history." *The New York Times* announced, "It is probable [that] . . . no more wonderful spectacle has ever been put before the public." *Moving Picture World* echoed, "This Paramount production easily occupies the position at the top of the ladder of screen achievements."[20] Critics especially applauded the extraordinary use of color in the film, the latest technological advance in pictorial realism that had already occasioned debate among the nation's cultural stewards. The genteel classes, for whom culture was sacrosanct, had long expressed concern that the addition of color to established forms of iconography would pander to the vulgar taste of the masses. Indeed, the rapid proliferation of halftones in literary texts in the late nineteenth century had caused similar alarm about the debasement of traditional art.[21] DeMille's expensive use of color processes, however, was an aspect of filmmaking that had been anticipated by historical pageantry as a form of commodity fetishism. Publicity material as well as news and magazine articles about civic drama emphasize the enormous expense and quantity of resources required to stage marathon pageants. Similarly, trade journals, fan magazines, and souvenir progams read like fact sheets about the twenty-four-square-mile tent city that DeMille constructed on location, complete with a utilities system supplying water, electricity, and communication to house the 2,500 people and 3,000 animals assembled for the Biblical Prologue.[22]

What does the attention paid to the squandering of huge quantities of matériel to reenact history in the public sphere signify in a modern consumer culture? What was the significance, in other words, of the intersection of antimodernist spectacle and urban commercialized amusement? As social and cultural historians have demonstrated, the transition from a producer to a consumer economy occurred unevenly and over a considerable period of time. DeMille proved instrumental because he mediated the experience of modernity for twentieth-century filmgoers with representations of an antimodernist aesthetic that emphasized moral instruction. Consumer behavior was thus legitimated within a religious and pedagogical framework. Specifically, the director constructed spectacle for visual appropriation as a legacy of pictorialism based on realistic representation and on sentimental values extolling uplift. The Biblical Prologue, for example, consists mostly of a series of instructive tableaux with intertitles lifted chapter and verse from the Book of Exodus. As such, the epic was not meant to produce the "eclipse of distance" representative of modernism but exemplified a didactic tradition.[23] Yet the spectacular use of sets, crowd scenes, special effects, and color did indeed elicit feelings of excitement and sensations that characterized reception of modernist art. The calculated production of emotional affect, as distinct from Protestant emphasis on self-denial and restraint, thus became the basis of spectacle that was antimodernist but promoted a modern consumer ethos.

Aesthetic contradictions are also apparent in DeMille's articulation of space in a work divided into two distinct narratives in different time periods and with separate casts. As previously noted, a theatrical as opposed to a cinematic rendering of space distinguishes the Biblical Prologue with its emphasis on tableaux vivants in extreme long shot. By contrast, the director exhibits a dazzling use of editing, camera angles, and variations in shot scale in the Modern Story, a melodrama of two brothers, one an atheist and the other a straight arrow. Yet the moralizing tradition of Victorian pictorialism links the prologue with the Jazz Age narrative. Indeed, the Modern Story concludes with a flashback to the biblical era that mitigates the "eclipse of distance" produced by melodramatic focus on a romantic triangle. The recapitulation of an anecdote in which Christ, with his back to the camera, heals a woman afflicted with leprosy is photographed not only in extreme long shot but in low-key lighting so that the scene has a painterly composition. A comparison of this scene with a sequence in *The King of Kings* (1927), in which Christ heals a blind girl, illustrates how DeMille later employed the tradition of pictorial realism to commodify images for modern consumption. The director cuts from an extreme long shot of a crowd of expectant travelers, gathered before the humble home of the carpenter, to a series of medium shots and medium close-ups of the blind girl seeking to be healed. When she finally opens her eyes for the first time, the face of Christ comes into focus in a medium close-up that represents not only her point of view but that of the audience as well. A two-shot then shows the carpenter embracing the young girl in a moment meant to reinforce spectator identification with the humanity of Christ. Such a representation of the New Testament not only exemplifies the "eclipse of distance" effected by the conventions of melodrama, but also illustrates the extent to which sentimental uplift was coopted in the process of transforming religious spectacle into a cultural commodity.

Ultimately, DeMille contributed not only to the secularization of evangelical Protestantism, but also to its reification as spectacle for mass consumption.[24] Granted, film reception was mediated by variables such as gender, class, and ethnicity that dictated local exhibition practices, but demographic differences were in turn subject to the homogenizing influence of a consumer culture. An especially ironic instance of the leveling impact of consumption was visible in the commercial uses of religious art that influenced the director's work. A costly and treasured possession among well-to-do Victorian families, the Doré Bible provided a familiar intertext for the Biblical Prologue of *The Ten Commandments*. Yet religious iconography that appealed to genteel readers, fascinated by theatrical representations of an Orientalized Middle East, eventually became acceptable to Catholics as well as Protestants. In 1945, a two-volume Catholic edition of the Bible, still based on St. Jerome's Vulgate rather than the Protestant King James Version, was published with Doré's illustrations.[25] More recently, an illustration of Moses by the French artist was recycled in a less dignified format as part of an advertising campaign conducted by a Jewish firm, Empire Kosher Poultry. And *TV Guide* used still another Doré engraving of the lawgiver to advertise a series titled *Ancient Mysteries* sponsored by Merrill Lynch; on the opposite page was an ad for a Billy Graham special.[26] DeMille's practice of reifying religious spectacle as a commodity—a strategy that influenced advertisers who preached spiritual uplift through consumption—ultimately proved that the custodians of culture were justified in their concerns about the debasement of traditional art.[27]

america's coming of age and cold war politics: *the ten commandments*, 1956

The clamorous reception accorded the sound version of *The Ten Commandments* as a narrative of national emergence that conflates the Promised Land with America can only be understood in the context of the Cold War.[28] Although the relationship between historiography and civic drama was not as evident in succeeding decades as it had been during the pageantry movement, the ideological requirements of the Second World War and its aftermath influenced scholarly as well as public representations of history. According to Peter Novick, empiricist and objectivist models of inquiry practiced in the sciences were touted during the postwar years as the hallmark of intellectual life in the free world. Consequently, the reputation of Progressive historians like Carl Becker and Charles Beard declined amidst charges of moral relativism and misguided presentism in an era of consensus history that stressed the "past for its own sake." Conservative intellectuals, including Catholic theologians, moreover, linked relativistic thought with totalitarian ideologies and practices. A large number of the historians among them were recruited to serve in the OSS during the war and remained active thereafter in the CIA and the Department of State. Consensus or counterprogressive historiography did produce scholarly agreement regarding issues such as the brutal nature of slavery and racism, previously subjects of the most acrimonious debate within the discipline. But it remained the task of a new generation of New Left historians to question the direction of American foreign policy in the postwar era. In 1959 William Appleman Williams lobbed a grenade into the conservative camp of diplomatic historians in the form of *The Tragedy of American Diplomacy*, an indictment that characterized American expansionism and maldistribution of income as related developments.[29] Coincidentally, DeMille died in the same year and so did not live to see his spread-eagle version of American history subject to revisionism.

Unquestionably, consensus history was a product not only of the ideological demands of the Cold War but of World War II. Chief among the producers of propaganda to promote the war effort were motion-picture studios such as Paramount (co-founded by DeMille in 1913) that distributed newsreels projected in theater chains throughout the country. Indeed, DeMille himself had produced a documentary titled *Land of Liberty* as the industry's contribution to the New York World's Fair and the Golden Gate International Exposition (1939–40). Columbia University historian James T. Shotwell had considerable input into the project as its consultant. Consisting of 126 excerpts from feature films (including DeMille's own work), short subjects, newsreels, and stock footage, the film was seen by twenty million viewers and later circulated in an eighty-five-minute version for classroom use. At the beginning, a title recalls the pageantry movement by declaring, "The Motion Picture Industry is proud of the fact that in providing entertainment for the millions, it has drawn so frequently upon the dramatic events of American history for themes and background and the existing film material could be thus assembled in historical continuity." A discourse differentiating between an Old World, dominated by a repressive class structure, and the "land of the second chance—a new home for the white man in his age-old migration Westward," the film celebrates Manifest Destiny. As such, it exemplifies consensus history or historical metanarrative that has since become outmoded; that is, it represents the American past primarily as an expansionist saga with emphasis on military conflict and diplomacy: the French and Indian War, the Revolutionary War, the Louisiana Purchase, the War of 1812, the Mexican War, the Civil War, the Spanish-American War, and the First World War. Although some rhetoric is devoted to racial equality, non-white peoples such as Native Americans represent obstacles to progress. Among the few references to slavery is a rather stylized musical number from *Show Boat* (1936) that features Paul Robeson singing "Old Man River." A few women like Dolly Madison and Clara Barton make token appearances as idealized visions. The conclusion of the film does concede that the nation has serious social problems, but only after a celebration of technological advancement in the "land of milk and honey." Not coincidentally, Jesse L. Lasky, Jr., son of one of the cofounders of the organization that became Paramount, coauthored the script of both *Land of Liberty* and the sound version of *The Ten Commandments*.[30]

The civic theater that DeMille reproduced in his historical epics reached its cinematic apogee in wartime newsreels and propaganda films. At the end of each year Paramount edited a compilation of footage of significant events to illustrate a specific theme. *Year of Decision* (1941) provides an intriguing preview not only of wartime propaganda works but also of *The Ten Commandments.* A film that recalls historical pageants staged in the Progressive Era, the newsreel represents history as a linear progression of events with a moral lesson. A father visits his son at an army camp, for example, to explain why the nation is at war. "America the Beautiful" plays on the soundtrack while a high-angle shot of the two men, photographed with their backs to the camera, encourages the audience to eavesdrop as well as identify with the characters. Such visual strategies in a newsreel attest that categories of fiction and non-fiction have been problematic since news events were first reenacted in early cinema (a practice now seen on tabloid television).[31] As the father calls his son's attention to "the Bible that your mother sent," a dissolve to the Ten Commandments and to the Bill of Rights equates the two documents. American freedoms are contrasted with tyranny exercised over the Japanese by "the gang that's running things over there." A rousing version of the "Battle Hymn of the Republic" is then heard as the camera pans across a painting of the Founding Fathers that includes Benjamin Franklin and George Washington. While the stern parent lectures his son about the

American way of life, a shot of Emperor Hirohito, described as an "overgrown monkey," elicits the comment: "They bow down to the little half pint like the ancient Egyptians had to bow to pharaoh." Paramount News thus conflates Western democracy with Christian doctrine in much the same way that American expansion was rationalized as Manifest Destiny in *Land of Liberty*. Significantly, Frank Capra's *The Battle of China* (1944) in the *Why We Fight* series, which included scenes from feature films, also preaches a history lesson that links the pyramids, Moses receiving the Ten Commandments, ancient Rome, the discovery of America, and Washington crossing the Delaware.[32] A decade later, *The Ten Commandments* provided a summation of the movie industry's representation of historical reality in both fiction and non-fiction films.[33] Biblical epics as well as documentaries, in sum, were constructed as public history that foregrounded the rise and fall of empires in a linear development culminating with the founding of America.

DeMille's extraordinary box-office success was the result of his ability to update the antimodernist tradition of sentimental uplift and evangelical Protestantism in historical films that rationalized Manifest Destiny. During the nineteenth century, the religious doctrine of the genteel classes had influenced the rhetoric of American foreign policy and expansion. Woodrow Wilson exemplified this tradition when he projected the moral rectitude of Progressive reformers onto a global scale by entering the First World War "to make the world safe for democracy." Albeit saturated with paranoia, World War II propaganda films like Paramount News also linked religious practice with foreign policy by warning that Hirohito and Hitler posed a threat to American churches. When DeMille announced plans to remake his silent classic in 1952, he thus affirmed that "the new adaptation will be 'in line with the spiritual reawakening of all nations of the free world in these troubled times.'"[34] The "troubled times" referred, of course, to the Cold War. Hence a souvenir program evoked postwar memories of an embattled Great Britain and the Iron Curtain speech by proclaiming, "Cecil B. DeMille is to motion pictures what Winston Churchill is to statesmanship." Another program declared that the conflict dramatized by the epic was "as modern as the headlines in the morning newspaper. Whether men shall be ruled by the whims of a dictator, or whether men are free souls under God's Law." The director's own description of the film was overblown with Cold War rhetoric:

> In the relationship between Moses and Rameses, we have the clash between two great opposing forces which have confronted each other throughout human history and which still . . . are engaged in mortal combat for the future of mankind.
>
> On the one hand there is the Pharaoh Rameses—worshipped as a god—the massive machinery of oppression at

his command, his people chattels, and his will their only law.

Opposing him stands Moses, armed only with a staff—and the unquenchable fire of freedom under God.[35]

Small wonder that one film critic referred explicitly to Cold War events when he concluded that the lesson of the film "could apply right now to the case of the Hungarians vs. the Russians."[36]

Interestingly, DeMille's research staff unearthed significant historical data that was used, as in wartime propaganda films, to link past, present, and future in the unfolding of a divine will. An illustration in a souvenir program, for example, shows Charlton Heston as Moses standing before the Liberty Bell. Inscribed on the monument is the prophet's declaration in Leviticus: "Proclaim liberty throughout the land unto all the inhabitants thereof." Also reproduced in the program is a copy of the seal of the United States encircled by a quote from Oliver Cromwell: "Rebellion to tyrants is obedience to God." Within the circle is a pictorial design, ascribed to Thomas Jefferson, of Pharaoh's mighty chariot hosts being drowned in the Red Sea.[37] A number of biblical as well as historical events, personalities, and symbols associated with the birth of America were thus invoked, as they had been during the Second World War, to reaffirm the nation's ideals.

DeMille's account of the sources that inspired his epic as a lesson relevant to a nation embattled against tyranny attests to his selective reading of the past. An admirer of Churchill—a name that both his father and brother bore—the director quoted the British statesman regarding the teaching of Moses as "the most decisive leap forward ever discernible in the human story." But DeMille's citation of a lecture about the lawgiver delivered by Henry George in 1878 is at first rather puzzling.[38] Author of *Progress and Poverty* (1879) and advocate of a single tax to redistribute wealth, George had been an influential reformer. DeMille's brother, William, had married George's daughter, Anna, but political differences between the two siblings had been one of the causes of a ruptured relationship. William was a liberal and a democrat with a small "d," whereas Cecil became aligned with conservatives. Consequently, the reproduction of George's lecture in a souvenir program is, on the surface, absurd. Cited as inspiration for a historical film whose subtext was stridently anti-communist, George's lecture is full of ringing denunciations of the inequities wrought by capitalism:

> It is not the protection of property, but the protection of humanity, that is the aim of the Mosaic code. . . . Moses saw . . . that to permit in land the same unqualified private ownership that by natural right attaches to the things produced by labour, would be inevitably to separate the people into the very rich and the very poor.[39]

Yet the oratorical tone of this particular text demonstrates the extent to which DeMille's sensibility harkened back to a Victorian age. George was able to translate the Sermon on the Mount for genteel urban reformers because his grandiloquence was biblical and his vision of social harmony nostalgic for an agrarian past.[40] DeMille cited the single-tax advocate, even though his own political views were reactionary, so that he could recast the rhetoric of American reform tradition in a postwar contest between good versus evil. Indeed, the filmmaker himself appears on a curtained stage in a two-minute prologue to *The Ten Commandments* not only to attest the historical veracity of the film, but also to link the biblical past to the Cold War.

A number of seamless transitions skillfully orchestrated at the beginning of the epic articulates the director's ideological message. After his appearance on a proscenium stage conveys a sense of theatrical space that is constructed throughout as a series of tableaux, a foreword recalling silent film intertitles appears on the screen. The Paramount logo (a scene of the Watsatch Mountains in Utah designed by founder W. W. Hodkinson) is next incorporated into a narrative that depicts the comparable rugged landscape of Mount Sinai, a site recalling the American West. During the ensuing credits, Elmer Bernstein's musical score conveys moods that are in turn spiritualist and mystical, Orientalist and sensual, militaristic and bellicose. Audiences then read the following three titles: "THOSE WHO SEE THIS MOTION PICTURE PRODUCED AND DIRECTED BY CECIL B. DEMILLE WILL MAKE A PILGRIMAGE OVER THE VERY GROUND THAT MOSES TROD MORE THAN 3,000 YEARS AGO," "IN ACCORDANCE WITH THE ANCIENT TEXTS OF PHILO, JOSEPHUS, EUSEBIUS, THE MIDRASH, AND," "THE HOLY SCRIPTURES." DeMille himself narrates the voice-over and begins by emphasizing the moral significance of light in the pictorial tradition:

> And God said let there be light and there was light. And from this light God created life upon earth. And Man was given . . . the power to choose between good and evil. . . . man took dominion over man . . . and freedom was gone from the world. So did the Egyptians cause the children of Israel to serve . . . and their cry came unto God and God . . . cast into Egypt . . . the seed of a man upon whose mind and heart would be written God's . . . commandments—one man to stand alone against an empire.

As the director speaks, a series of dissolves shows light beaming down from the clouds of a vast sky, masses of toiling Hebrew slaves, and the woman Yochabel placing her infant son Moses in a crib.

A narrative of the progressive emergence of a nation that telescopes past and present, *The Ten Commandments* draws on genre conventions of the Western, as Marc Vernet argues.[41] Archetypal values associated with the urban congestion of the East, as opposed to the "safety valve" of the West, reverberate in the contrast between the luxury of the Egyptian court and the starkness of Mount Sinai's granite. Scenes of the exodus include a vehicle resembling a covered wagon that crosses through the parted waters of the Red Sea, and music signifying the Pharaoh's pursuing chariots echoes a Western soundtrack. As the Pharaoh, moreover, Yul Brynner wears silver necklaces and a pigtail on the side of his head that recall Native American costumes as well as Chinese queues. An actor who attracted DeMille's attention in the title role of *The King and I* on Broadway, Brynner also wears leopard skin, as does an Ethiopian princess; in short, he represents a conflated image of the unassimilable "Other" whose presence on the frontier is as unwelcome as it had been in congested cities.[42] The vast, arid landscape traversed by the children of Israel on their way to the Promised Land, not coincidentally, resembles the mythic American plains. And it evokes the influential frontier thesis of Progressive historian Frederick Jackson Turner, who celebrated the West as the fount of American democratic values.[43] Fittingly, at the film's conclusion Moses appoints Joshua as a successor who will build an empire in the land of milk and honey and ascends the barren cliffs of a mountain. An extreme long shot shows him raising his left hand in salute, a final gesture that, as Michael Wood argues, converts him into a figure resembling the Statue of Liberty.[44]

As is the case in Westerns as a foundation ritual, DeMille's biblical epic is inflected with ambiguities and contradictions. At first glance the director equates Egyptian tyranny with Soviet totalitarianism—a reworking of the ideological production of wartime newsreels to suit postwar realignments—in contrast to the Promised Land and American liberty. Yet congruence between the Old World and the New explains why the children of Israel were so easily corrupted in bacchanalian revels and "all manner of . . . works of the flesh and . . . vile affections." Consumption, historically associated with the luxury of despotic Oriental empires, is ambiguously represented in the film as both a sign of decadence and an act of transcendence. Indeed, the biblical epic itself, photographed in Vista Vision and Technicolor, is commodified for the visual appropriation of awed spectators. Particularly significant in the film's ambivalence regarding consumption are shots that reinforce not only differences but similarities between the two antagonists. When Rameses expels Moses from Egypt, for example, he wears costly armament befitting his royal status, while he bestows on his scorned rival a coarse Levite robe and a staff. But as princely men who have been reared together like brothers, vying for the hand of Nefretiri and the Egyptian throne, they are both photographed in medium shots against a limitless landscape. Parallels also abound in scenes of Moses returning triumphant to lead his people out of bondage. As Egyptian chariots pursue the departing Hebrews, corresponding shots show Moses and Rameses standing on promontories opposite the Red Sea. DeMille, in short, constructs a number of symbolic oppositions that nevertheless function as part of the epic's homologous structure. The film thus registers more ambiguity about distinctions between the decadent Old World and the pristine New than its self-righteous and bombastic rhetoric concedes. Complicating this issue are scenes that conflate both the Old World and the New with the studio system as the site par excellence of American consumption. When Moses first crosses the desert after being expelled from Egypt, he nearly dies of thirst but finds "strength from a fruit-laden palm tree," silhouetted in a picture-postcard shot that evokes Los Angeles. A multi-million dollar epic, *The Ten Commandments* represented the restoration of what one critic labeled "the glory that was Hollywood," as if it were analagous to the grandeur that was Egypt. The lavish production of Orientalist spectacle, as Edward W. Said argues, was an expression as well as an instrument of imperialist power in both the Old World and the New.[45]

Such productions harkened back to the golden age of the studio system when film spectacle represented the commodification of history anticipated by Progressive Era civic pageantry. A three-hour-thirty-nine-minute epic whose cost escalated from eight million to well over over thirteen million dollars, *The Ten Commandments* was in 1956 the most expensive motion picture ever produced.[46] Filmed partly on location in Egypt, where DeMille personally directed a second unit, the spectacle was the subject of massive publicity that trumpeted such statistics as the recruitment of sixty-four assistant directors, thirty-one cameramen, fifty thousand animals, and ten thousand extras, not to mention the Egyptian cavalry corps. A list of small bits and parts for actors alone filled thirteen single-spaced typewritten pages in the script. The reconstruction of an Orientalized, despotic Egypt that ruled a far-flung empire meant the display of colossal monuments, palatial sets, and abundant treasure. For sequences filmed amidst the barren rocks of Mount Sinai and in vast expanses of desert—landscapes that were otherwise dull—DeMille orchestrated sensational special effects that won for the epic its only Academy Award. As a showman, then, he brought new dimensions to the production of spectacle as a form of commodity fetishism in a burgeoning postwar consumer culture.

A summation of a significant and underrated career, *The Ten Commandments* attests to DeMille's enduring appeal as a filmmaker. For decades, he had translated the genteel tradition of pictorial realism, characterized by objectification and commodification that was meant to be uplifting, to the motion picture screen. The director's mise-en-scène was thus intertextually related to spectacles orchestrated for the elite, that is, the proscenium stage, department-store windows, World's Fair pavilions, museum exhibits, and civic pageantry. A culmination of these cultural forms, the screen represented Western tradition dating back to the Renaissance when the position of the spectating subject was constructed in terms of perspectival space. Distance between the eye of the subject and the object being scrutinized was essential to the hegemony of vision and to empiricist modes of thought that have dominated bourgeois culture.[47] Conservative critics like Daniel Bell have thus expressed alarm regarding the "eclipse of distance" effected by modernist and postmodernist art, and the resulting loss of temporality and direction. Articulating these issues from a postmodernist perspective, however, Elizabeth Deeds Ermarth is not averse to the rendering of "historical time as a thing of the past." Significantly, she compares the concept of time as "a neutral, homogeneous medium" with "the space of pictorial realism in painting," and concludes that history as "the most powerful construct of realistic conventions . . . betrays its religious origin."[48] Although DeMille's antimodernist representation of the biblical past appears to be outmoded in a postmodern culture, such contrasts explain why his spectacle has remained compelling for so many decades.

To this day, *The Ten Commandments* exerts a powerful appeal because it sums up pictorial realism as a mode of representing the Protestant view of history as teleology. The spectator, in other words, witnesses a progression of events culminating in the founding of America as the will of divine providence. Critics, to be sure, still ridicule DeMille's visual style as excessively static, but his transformation of the motion-picture screen into an artist's canvas, especially in Vista Vision, rendered perspectival space a perfect medium for representing history in linear terms. Camera placement was usually perpendicular to the shot to emphasize the frontality, theatricality, and monumentality of scenes constructing the spectator as an eyewitness. Although reverse angle shots were used to represent the large-scale dimensions of spectacle, the director used two-shots rather than shot-reverse-shots to photograph dialogue, and seldom used angled shots. Since camera movement was minimal, a tracking shot such as the one following Rameses's chariot down the Avenue of the Sphinxes was extremely dramatic.[49] Granted, the remake employed the visual strategy of *The. King of Kings* to humanize biblical characters by cutting to medium shots and medium close-ups. But emphasis on static compositions produced the same distancing effect resulting from extreme long shots in the silent version of *The Ten Commandments* and thereby minimized the "eclipse of distance." Antimodernist historical film thus continues to exert a powerful influence by inviting successive generations of audiences to learn the lessons of the past while engaging in the pleasure of appropriating lavish spectacle.

the commodification of history: *the ten commandments* as a televisual "supertext," 1993

The annual telecast of *The Ten Commandments* during the Passover and Easter holidays demonstrates that a biblical epic based on empiricist notions of history may be significantly transformed on the small screen. A historical film constructed according to the antimodernist aesthetic of civic pageantry is recycled, by virtue of its dissemination through an electronic medium, in a postmodernist cultural form. Consequently, DeMille's televisual epic, which projects a theatrical space evocative of the past, now provides an ironic example of what Fredric Jameson describes as textual "flatness" or depthlessness," "the death of the world of appearances," and the waning of history. A spectacle based on pictorial realism and intertexually related to wartime newsreels, in other words, now signifies the inacessibility of reality as a historical referent.[50] Converted into network "programmed flow," a phenomenon first analyzed by Raymond Williams, the film as a televisual "supertext" incorporates commercials, program trailers, station identifications, and announcements. As Nick Browne and Sandy Flitterman argue, commercials not only constitute micronarratives that provide a resolution for dramatic tensions built up during the telecast, but also continue the flow of the televisual text.[51] A sequence in which Yochabel hides her infant son Moses to save him from death, for example, was followed in a 1993 telecast by these commercials involving family: a child describing her mother's Rice Krispies treat, a father using Armstrong floor cleaner before playing with his son, a working mother treating her children to a McDonald's dinner, and an elderly woman informing her granddaughter about Monro Muffler. During the course of the marathon telecast—programming that garnered high Nielsen ratings from seven to eleven-thirty on Sunday night—some commercial messages provoked unintended hilarity.[52] When, for example, the children of Israel follow Moses into vast expanses of desert on foot, ads for Chrysler Minivan, Toyota Camry, and Oldsmobile Achieva assume greater urgency. As a result of the narrative flow of a "supertext," then, the referent of the telecast version of *The Ten Commandments* is no longer history but a commodity, or, more precisely, a reaffirmation of the values of a consumer culture.

Since DeMille was a spokesman for the consumer ethos, aspects of his spectacle aptly lend themselves to functioning as part of a televisual "supertext" in ways he could not have anticipated. A seamless transition to ads is possible, for example, because *The Ten Commandments* is constructed, as are commercials, in the rhetorical form of a sermon. DeMille himself engages in the practice of directly addressing spectators, which is common on television, by appearing in a prologue and narrating the voice-over. Displacing the director during climactic moments in the film, God himself addresses Moses from a burning bush on Mount Sinai. When *The Ten Commandments* was telecast in 1983, a title with calligraphic lettering set against the golden glow of a diffuse light appeared before each commercial interruption. Appearing as an integral part of the epic's narration, it read, "We'll return after these messages." Consistent with the moral significance of light in the pictorial tradition, the products advertised were apparently enjoying a spiritual endorsement. More recently, the aural rather than visual dimension of television was emphasized when a stentorian Voice-of-God narrator announced, "The ABC Sunday Night Movie will return after these messages."

Apart from the convention of direct address that is replicated in commercials, DeMille provides lavish spectacle in an abundance of images for visual appropriation. Indeed, the magnificence of the Egyptian court provides a counterpoint to the ordinary household goods advertised in messages aimed at families with middle-class incomes. Although on one level the ads provide closure for narrative tensions in the film, on another they trigger the "Diderot effect," or consumer dissatisfaction resulting from the comparison of luxurious set and costume design with ads for ordinary products.[53] The insertion of commercials in opulent spectacles may in fact serve to heighten an appetite for upscale mechandise as opposed to mundane commodities. Since television exists to promote consumption, such an effect is indeed desirable for consumer capitalism. And insofar as the materialistic values of Western culture become global, *The Ten Commandments* once again assumes the dimensions of a narrative of national emergence and progression. "American, postmodern culture," as Jameson argues, "is the internal and superstructural expression of a whole new wave of American military and economic domination throughout the world."[54] Although DeMille inveighed against the tyranny of the Soviet Union, his representation of the pleasures of consumption proved to be the ultimate weapon in the arsenal of the free market. Antimodernist historical narrative, with antecedents in the civic pageantry movement as a form of commodity fetishism, still resonates in a postmodern consumer society.

notes

For a fuller discussion of DeMille's silent epics in relation to civic pageantry, see my *Cecil B. DeMille and American Culture: The Silent Era* (Berkeley and Los Angeles: University of California Press, 1994). I am grateful to Ned Comstock at the USC Cinema-TV Library and Andrea Kalas at UCLA Film and Television Archive for assistance with research on *Land of Liberty* and to Paolo Cherchi Usai at George Eastman House for a screening of the color print of the silent version of *The Ten Commandments.* I also wish to thank David Parker at the Library of Congress for a detailed explanation of early color processes.

1. "The Ten Commandments," *Variety*, 10 October 1956, in *The Ten Commandments* clipping file, Margaret Herrick Library, Academy of Motion Picture Arts and Sciences, Los Angeles (hereafter cited as AMPAS).
2. On realism, see Amy Kaplan, *The Social Construction of American Realism* (Chicago: University of Chicago Press, 1988); Alfred Habegger, *Gender, Fantasy, and Realism in American Literature* (New York: Columbia University Press, 1982). On sentimentalism, see Ann Douglas, *The Feminization of American Culture* (New York: Alfred A. Knopf, 1977); Jane Tompkins, *Sensational Designs: The Cultural Work of American Fiction 1790–1860* (New York: Oxford University Press, 1985). See also H. Barbara Weinberg, Doreen Bolder, and David Park Curry, *American Impressionism and Realism: the Painting of Modern Life, 1885–1915*, the catalogue for an exhibit held at the Metropolitan Musem of Art, New York.
3. Richard Hofstadter, *The Progressive Historians: Turner, Beard, Parrington* (New York: Alfred A. Knopf, 1968), 7.
4. On the distinction between modernization as social process and modernism as "visions and ideas that aim to make men and women the subjects as well as the objects of modernization," see Marshall Berman, *All That Is Solid Melts Into Air: The Experience of Modernity* (New York: Simon & Schuster, 1982), Introduction. On modern art and the ideology of modernization, see Andreas Huyssen, "Mapping the Postmodern," *New German Critique* 33 (Fall 1984): 5–53; repr. in Huyssen, *After the Great Divide: Modernism, Mass Culture, Postmodernism* (Bloomington: Indiana University Press, 1986), 178–221.
5. David Glassberg, *American Historical Pageantry: The Uses of Tradition in the Early Twentieth Century* (Chapel Hill: University of North Carolina Press, 1990), 147–48; Naima Prevots, *American Pageantry: A Movement for Art and Democracy* (Ann Arbor: UMI Research Press, 1990); Paul Boyer, *Urban Masses and Moral Order in America, 1820–1929* (Cambridge: Harvard University Press, 1978), 256–60. See also Michael Kammen, *Mystic Chords of Memory: The Transformation of Tradition in American Culture* (New York: Alfred A. Knopf, 1991).
6. See Robert M. Crunden, *Ministers of Reform: The Progressives' Achievement in American Civilization 1889–1920* (New York: Basic Books, 1982).
7. See Glassberg, *American Historical Pageantry*; Boyer, *Urban Masses.*
8. Daniel Bell, *The Cultural Contradictions of Capitalism* (New York: Basic Books, 1976), 99–119.
9. Linda Nochlin, "The Paterson Strike Pageant of 1913," *Art in America* 62 (May/June 1974): 68; Martin Green, *New York 1913: The Armory Show and the Paterson Strike Pageant* (New York: Macmillan, 1988), ch. 1; Anne Huber Tripp, *The IWW and the Paterson Silk Strike* (Urbana: University of Illinois Press, 1987), ch. 6; Steve Golin, *The Fragile Bridge: Paterson Silk Strike, 1913* (Philadelphia: Temple University Press, 1988), ch. 6.
10. Hofstadter, *Progressive Historians*, 27.
11. Glassberg, *American Historical Pageantry*; Peter Novick, *That Noble Dream: The "Objectivity Question" and the American Historical Profession* (Cambridge: Cambridge University Press, 1988), 1–2. See also John Higham, *History: Professional Scholarship in America* (Englewood Cliffs: Prentice-Hall, 1965); Cushing Strout, *The Pragmatic Revolt in American History: Carl Becker and Charles Beard* (New Haven: Yale University Press, 1958).
12. See Brook Thomas, "The New Historicism and other Old-fashioned Topics," in *The New Historicism*, ed. H. Aram Veeser, (New York: Routledge, 1989), 182–203; Thomas, *The New Historicism and Other Old-Fashioned Topics* (Princeton: Princeton University Press, 1991).
13. On postwar Progressive historiography, see Novick, ch. 7. For a useful critique of Novick, see James T. Kloppenberg, "Objectivity and Historicism: A Century of American Writing," *American Historical Review* 94 (October 1989): 1011–1030. See also Kloppenberg, *Uncertain Victory: Social Democracy and Progressivism in European and American Thought, 1870–1920* (New York: Oxford University Press, 1986).
14. See William Leuchtenburg, *The Perils of Prosperity, 1914–32* (Chicago: University of

Chicago Press, 1958); Paul A. Carter, *Another Part of the Twenties* (New York: Columbia University Press, 1973).

15. Daniel H. Borus, "New Perspectives on the 1920s in the United States," paper delivered at SUNY Brockport, April 1991.
16. See Richard Wightman Fox and T. J. Jackson Lears, eds., *The Culture of Consumption* (New York: Pantheon); Simon J. Broner, ed., *Consuming Visions: Accumulation and Display of Goods in America, 1880–1920* (New York: W. W. Norton, 1989).
17. On consumption and woman's sphere, See Linda Kerber, "Separate Spheres, Female Worlds, Woman's Place: The Rhetoric of Women's History," *Journal of American History* 75 (June 1988): 9–39.
18. James Stevens, ed., *A Doré Treasury: A Collection of the Best Engravings of Gustave Doré* (New York: Bounty Books, 1970); *The Doré Bible Illustrations* (New York: Dover, 1974); Philip Vanderberg, *The Golden Pharaoh* (New York: Macmillan, 1978); Thomas Hoving, *Tutanhkamun: The Untold Story* (New York: Simon & Schuster, 1978); souvenir program, in *The Ten Commandments* clipping file, AMPAS.
19. Unfortunately, the director's personal print at George Eastman House is decomposing. A second version that also employs the Handschiegl process has colored footage different from the one that was DeMille's personal print. Since this process was expensive, prints in distribution were photographed in Technicolor. On historical representation and melodrama, see John L. Fell, *Film and the Narrative Tradition* (Norman: Oklahoma University Press, 1974; Berkeley: University of California Press, 1986), 51–53.
20. "*The Ten Commandments*," in *New York Times Film Reviews* (New York: Arno Press, 1970), 22 December 1923; James R. Quirk, "The Ten Commandments," *Photoplay* (February 1924): 42; C. S. Sewell, "The Ten Commandments," *Moving Picture World* 5 (January 1924): 56.
21. On the use of color and halftones, see Neil Harris, "Color and Media: Some Comparisons and Speculations" and "Iconography and Intellectual History: The Halftone Effect," in *Cultural Excursions: Marketing Appetitles and Cultural Tastes in Modern America* (Chicago: University of Chicago Press, 1990), 304–336.
22. See Vivian Sobchack, "'Surge and Splendor': A Phenomenology of the Hollywood Historical Epic," *Representations* 29 (Winter 1990): 24–49.
23. Bell, *Cultural Contradictions*, 99–119.
24. On reification, see Georg Lukács, *History and Consciousness: Studies in Marxist Dialectics*, trans. Rodney Livinstone (Cambridge: MIT Press, 1971), 83–223; Guy Debord, *Society of the Spectacle* (Detroit: Black & Red, 1977); Fredric Jameson, "Reification and Utopia in Mass Culture," *Social Text* 1 (1979): 130–48.
25. I am indebted to Robert Gilliam for pointing this fact out to me.
26. *New York Times*, 12 March 1993, D16; *TV Guide* (September 4–10, 1993): 178–79. Capitalizing on the well-known slogan of entrepreneur Frank Perdue, "It Takes a Tough Man to Make a Tender Chicken," Empire Kosher Chicken countered with the caption, "It Takes an Even Tougher Man to Make a Kosher Chicken," under an illustration of Moses. Demonstrating a resistance to the cycle of exchange that characterizes modern consumption, Perdue Farms sought a federal injunction against Empire Kosher Chicken.
27. On consumption as spiritual uplift in advertising, see Roland Marchand, *Advertising the American Dream: Making Way for Modernity, 1920–1940* (Berkeley: University of California Press, 1985).
28. See Alan Nadel, "God's Law and the Wide Screen: *The Ten Commandments* as Cold War 'Epic,'" *PMLA* (May 1993): 415–430.
29. Novick, *Noble Dream*, Part III. See also William Appleman Williams, *The Tragedy of American Diplomacy* (New York: World Publishing Co., 1959).
30. Rudy Behlmer, "*Land of Liberty* a Conglomerate," *American Cinematographer* 72 (March 1991): 34–40; Allen W. Palmer, "Cecil B. DeMille Writes American History for the 1939 World Fair," *Film History* 5 (1993): 36–48. See also Jesse L. Lasky, Jr., *Whatever Happened to Hollywood?* (New York: Funk & Wagnalls, 1973), 191–193. Lasky

recounts a hilarious exchange between DeMille and Shotwell in which the director asserts he would rather sacrifice accuracy for drama.

31. See Charles Musser, *The Emergence of Cinema* (New York: Scribners, 1990).
32. See *Meet Frank Capra: A Catalog of His Work* (Palo Alto: American Film Institute, 1990), 42–43; David Culbert, "'Why We Fight': Social Engineering for a Democratic Society at War," in K. R. M. Short, *Film and Radio Propaganda in World War II* (Knoxville: University of Tennessee Press, 1983), 173–191.
33. Once ranked the third biggest moneymaker after *The Sound of Music* and *Gone with the Wind*, the epic is still listed in *Variety's* top-grossing film charts. Unlike the silent version, DeMille did not restrict the historical epic to a Biblical Prologue as an introduction to a separate narrative titled the Modern Story.
34. *Los Angeles Times*, 8 August 1952, in *The Ten Commandments* clipping file, AMPAS.
35. Souvenir programs, in *The Ten Commandments* clipping file, AMPAS.
36. *Los Angeles Examiner*, 15 November 1956, in *The Ten Commandments* clipping file, AMPAS.
37. Souvenir program, in *The Ten Commandments* clipping file, AMPAS.
38. Souvenir programs, in *The Ten Commandments* clipping file, AMPAS.
39. Henry George, "Moses," souvenir program, in *The Ten Commandments* clipping file, AMPAS.
40. Warren Susman, *Culture As History: The Transformation of American Society in the Twentieth Century* (New York: Pantheon, 1973), 90–91.
41. Mark Vernet, "Wings of the Desert; or, the Invisible Superimpositions," *The Velvet Light Trap* 28 (Fall 1991): 65–72. See also Charles Wolfe, "Cecil B. DeMille," in *American Directors*, ed. Jean Pierre Coursodon, vol. 1 (New York: McGraw-Hill), 98. Gianfranco Nolli argues that the Hebrews sought the right to worship their God rather than freedom in any modern sense, let alone the founding of a nation, in "La Sacra Biblia secondo Cecil B. DeMille," *Blanco e nero* 19 (July 1958): 13–19. Interestingly, Tim Burton reacts to the epic as if it were a horror film instead of a Western: "*The Ten Commandments*, which I love, was on TV last night. It's just like a horror movie: there was this guy Moses, he was a regular guy, then he turns into a zombie. He comes back spouting lines like 'It is written—so it shall be done!' He's like the exact opposite of what you would want if you were trying to get somebody into religion. I remember seeing it as a kid and thinking, 'I think I'll watch *Frankenstein* to get *my* religious fix!'" See "Heart and Darkness," *Vogue* (July 1992): 194.
42. *The Autobiography of Cecil B. DeMille*, ed. Donald Hayne (Englewood Cliffs: Prentice-Hall, 1959), 416.
43. The Turner thesis has fallen on hard times as revisionist frontier historians have painted a less flattering portrait of the West. See, for example, John Mack Farragher, "The Frontier Trail: Rethinking Turner and Reimagining the American West," *American Historical Review* 98 (February 1993): 106–117.
44. Michael Wood, *America in the Movies or, "Santa Maria, It Had Slipped My Mind!"* (New York: Basic Books, 1975), ch. 8.
45. Edward W. Said, *Orientalism* (New York: Random House, 1978), 123.
46. Following an example he had set with *The King of Kings*, DeMille donated all his earnings to a foundation established for charitable purposes. *Variety* reported this gesture in terms of Cold War rhetoric by claiming "he is not trying to put an H-bomb under the system that reared and enriched him."
47. See Debord, *Society of the Spectacle*.
48. Bell, *Cultural Contradictions*, 116, 110; Elizabeth Deeds Ermath, *Sequel to Time: Postmodernism and the Crisis of Representational Time* (Princeton: Princeton University Press, 1992), 13, 30. Bell characterizes postmodernism as an extention of modernism, especially in the 1960s, whereas Ermath conflates empiricism with modernism and describes postmodernism as a later movement with a different concept of temporality. See also Donald M. Lowe, *History of Bourgeois Perception* (Chicago: University of Chicago Press, 1982).

49. DeMille's visual style influenced contemporary filmmakers like Martin Scorsese, who confessed to having viewed *The Ten Commandments* forty or fifty times. See "Martin Scorsese's Guilty Pleasures," *Film Comment* 14 (September–October 1978): 63.
50. Fredric Jameson, "Postmodernism, or The Cultural Logic of Late Capitalism," *New Left Review* 146 (July/August 1984): 58–64; repr. "The Cultural Logic of Late Capitalism," in *Postmodernism, or, The Cultural Logic of Late Capitalism* (Durham: Duke University Press, 1991), 1–54.
51. Raymond Williams, *Television: Technology and Cultural Form* (New York: Schocken, 1975), ch 4. See also Nick Browne, "The Political Economy of the Television (Super) Text," *Quarterly Review of Film Studies* 9 (Summer 1984): 174–83; Sandy Flitterman, "The *Real* Soap Operas: TV Commercials," in *Regarding Television: Critical Approaches—An Anthology,* ed. E. Ann Kaplan, (Frederick, MD: University Publications of America, 1983): 84–96.
52. In 1993, *The Ten Commandments* lost out to *60 Minutes* and *Murder, She Wrote* for the first two hours of its viewing but thereafter earned higher ratings than programs on all the other networks, including Fox. See *Variety*, 12 April 1993, 24.
53. Grant McCracken, *Culture and Consumption* (Bloomington: Indiana University Press, 1990), 118–19.
54. Jameson, "Postmodernism," 57.

six

modernism and the narrative of nation in *jfk*

robert burgoyne

The debate over Oliver Stone's *JFK* has been framed to date largely within the discourse of historiography, with greatest attention being paid to issues concerning the limits of fact and fiction and the erosion of the presumed boundary between documentary and imaginative reconstruction.[1] Defenders of the film have usually argued from a deeply theoretical position, pointing out the permeable nature of the border between factual discourse and imaginative reconstruction, as well as the protean quality of even the most substantial documentary record of the past.[2] In this essay, I wish to shift the angle of approach to the film in order to consider another set of questions, revolving chiefly around the tension between the film's formal innovations and its explicit aim to articulate a narrative of national cohesion. The film's fragmentary form, I argue, can be revealingly seen as an expression of a national narrative in disorder and disarray, its collage-like narrative structure reflecting the disruption of the evolutionary or historical narrative that gives continuity to national identity. From this perspective, the film's notorious mixing of idioms conveys meanings that depart from issues of fact and fiction: rather, it expresses the fracturing of historical identity, the breaking apart of a once unified national text. The film thus recuperates its radically discontinuous style, I argue, by linking it to the loss of what Benedict Anderson called social "unisonance," to the absence of a unified national narrative that it nostalgically evokes as the foundation of community and the ground for all other narratives of human connection.[3]

The concept of nationalism has increasingly been tied to the development of particular narrative forms.[4] In writing of the nation as an "imagined community," for example, Anderson has linked the ideology of the modern nation to a specific sense of space and time expressed most clearly in the narrative forms of the realist novel. The temporal parallelism of the realist novel—the sense of temporal coincidence and simultaneity, of a multitude of unrelated actions occurring in a single community in what Walter Benjamin calls "homogeneous, empty time"—is directly related, in Anderson's view, to the image of the modern nation: "The idea of a sociological organism moving calendrically through homogeneous, empty time is a precise analogue of the idea of the nation, which is also conceived as a solid community moving steadily down (or up) in history."[5] Emerging as a strong form in tandem with the rise of nations, the realist novel, with its composite structure, its depiction of the one yet many of national life, and its temporal parallelism "allowed people to imagine the special community that is the nation."[6] As Anderson says, the structure of the realist novel and also the newspaper, both of which are crucial to the development of the "imagined community," can be seen as forming a "complex gloss upon the word 'meanwhile.'"[7]

By contrast, Hayden White has argued that modernist anti-narrative techniques, characterized by fragmentation, the exploding of the conventions of the traditional tale, and the dissociation or splitting of narrative functions, may be the most appropriate techniques for representing the historical reality of the contemporary period, with its unprecedented catastrophes and its compound global contexts.[8] His hypothesis—that there is a deep connection between the cultural genres of modernist aesthetic practice and the social dramas of the twentieth century—provides a suggestive contrast with Anderson's ideas about the cultural models of the nation-building past. White argues that the stylistic techniques of modernism, far from being ahistorical, or removed from history as so many critics have contended, provide better instruments for representing the recent events of the past than do the storytelling conventions of traditional historians, or, for that matter, the storytelling conventions of realism. Traditional forms of historical explanation, relying on concepts of human agency and causality, assume a kind of narrative omniscience over events which, by their scale and magnitude, elude a totalizing explanation. Modernist forms, in contrast, offer the possibility of representing, for the Western world, the traumatic events of the twentieth century—such as the two World Wars, the Great Depression, and the use of genocide as a state policy—in a manner that does not pretend to contain or define them.

In these pages, I will address the film *JFK* in terms of both of these models, hoping to show how *JFK* utilizes modernist, antinarrative techniques in order to express both the loss and the refiguration of a unified national identity. I argue that while the broken narratives and the profusion of stylistic forms in the film may seem at first appropriate to the catastrophic event of a presidential assassination and, indeed, convey a sense of a fractured social reality, they are ultimately recontained in a nostalgic image of social unisonance in the film's closing scenes.

The disjointed temporality and dislocated spaces of *JFK* can be read as reflecting the distorted and irrational sense of national identity and the fragmented social reality that the film finds at the heart of the United States in the post-Kennedy era. Far from seeing the nation as a "solid community moving steadily down (or up) in history," the spatial, temporal and narrative strategies of the film evoke division, rupture, and discontinuity between communities, individuals and their actions, and between events and their causes. Analysis of the temporal, register of the film in light of the idea of the nation as "imagined community" is especially revealing. The complex system of narrative temporality in *JFK*, to start with, is very far from the image of "homogeneous, empty time" filled up by the "steady, anonymous, simultaneous activity" conjured by the realist novel. Instead, the most striking characteristic of the film is its interweaving of past and present through an extraordinary combination of flashbacks, flashforwards, and achronic images—images that cannot be dated or assigned a temporal position. Moreover, time constitutes one of the principal thematic motifs in the film. Far from being seen as empty and homogeneous, time is thematized as heterogeneous and subject to human manipulation. Examples include the extensive newspaper report on Oswald that appeared in a New Zealand paper four hours before he was charged with Kennedy's murder; the *Life* magazine photo of Oswald with its contradictory times of day; the impossible chronology of the events of Oswald's day on the date of the assassination; the delay in bringing Oswald down into the lobby of the jail, which allowed Jack Ruby to take his place among the crowd; the phone lines into Washington that went out for hours immediately after the assassination; the live oak in Dealey Plaza that the Warren Commission claimed had unnaturally dropped its leaves in

November, affording Oswald an unobstructed view; the shots themselves, with the Zapruder film serving as the "clock" of the assassination, giving the lie to the "magic bullet" theory which would have us believe that a bullet could suspend itself in mid-flight for one and a half seconds. The overall picture of time that emerges is not one of uniform consistency but of simultaneity corrupted by inexplicable delays, gaps, compressions, accelerations, and contradictions. Rather than fostering a sense of the security of parallel lives moving along the same trajectory, the film evokes time as a dimension that can be manipulated, a dimension that is open to doubt, to ambiguity, and to suspicion.

A comparison of two scenes in the film illustrates the close connection the text makes between structures of temporality and concepts of the national narrative and national identity. At the beginning of the film, time and date are specified exactly through voice over, graphic titles, and overt period references. The historical portrait drawn by the film in its opening minutes depicts a society whose constituent elements are moving along parallel pathways in a homogeneous time, punctuated by clear-cut historical events. The recreation of the assassination that occurs several minutes into the film furthers the impression of temporal simultaneity, as the time of day is foregrounded by numerous, almost obsessive cut-aways to the clock overlooking Dealey Plaza. And when Jim Garrison (the New Orleans District Attorney whose investigation into the assassination serves as the basis of the film) is first introduced, directly after the gunshots, the time of the event is specified orally and underlined visually by rapid point of view cuts from Garrison's perspective to an antique clock. Throughout the opening sequences, then, the dominant temporal form is precisely that of simultaneity and parallelism. The film creates a snapshot of the nation at the moment of the assassination, forging a picture of a national community beset by tragedy, linked by the ubiquitous television broadcasts detailing the news of the assassination, the arrest of Oswald, and the swearing-in of Johnson.

This sense of simultaneity and parallelism, the impression the film creates of a community drawn together by a singular, punctual event, begins to dissolve as the investigation into the assassination proceeds. As the past is opened up through a series of character-narrations, the time scheme of the film becomes increasingly complex. For example, in the sequence that summarizes the various mysteries surrounding Oswald, several different layers of time are folded together. First, the scene begins in a reassuring, communal fashion as Garrison and his staff gather in a favorite restaurant to discuss what they have found so far. A sense of solid, social reality dominates the opening of the sequence, as the maitre d' anticipates Garrison's request for a drink, which has already been poured for him, and as various well-wishers exchange greetings. Then, as the Assistant D.A. on Garrison's staff discusses the oddities of Oswald's character, a summary of his life, consisting of black-and-white still photos, black-and-white film footage, and color "home movie" footage appears as illustration. Periodically, however, another set of images is inserted: color footage of a mysterious hand fabricating the photo of Oswald with a rifle that will appear on the cover of Life magazine; an image that will seal Oswald's guilt in the eyes of the public.

In addition to mixing images that are manipulated or highly ambiguous with images that seem stable and thus imply facticity, the film constructs time here in a way that undermines any sense of its linearity, causality, or embeddedness in social reality. By interrupting the flashback chronicle of Oswald's life with scenes that detail the construction of a composite photograph of Oswald, the film stages the narrative of Oswald's life as a construct detached from the realm of everyday reality and from the solid sense of social space insistently presented at the beginning of the scene. Social reality is abstracted and defamiliarized. The submerged past that begins to surface here will lead Garrison to say, at the close of the sequence, "[W]e're through the looking glass here. Black is white. White is black."

This manner of presenting the ambiguities associated with Oswald is a pattern that occurs throughout the movie. The character-narrations and subjective flashbacks defamiliarize social reality by narrating the past as a site of contradictory, mundane, and abstracted details, overarched by an almost biblical sense of prefiguration and fulfillment. As Garrison reads the testimony of the train-yard manager, Lee Bowers, for example—a witness who spotted suspicious activities taking place on the grassy knoll—the film provides a series of images, attended by Bowers's verbal description, that are specified exactly according to time, place and perspective. At the close of this narration, however, the film suddenly introduces a still photograph of the same man now dead, covered in blood and slumped over the wheel of a car. Only much later in the film will the suspicious circumstances of his death be revealed. Here the film uses a technique of temporality similar, although not identical, to the Oswald fabrication scene described above: it telescopes time by inserting an achronic, undated, almost unreadable image, an image abstracted from any temporal or spatial connection with the rest of the sequence, into a series of images whose chronology is precisely specified. The mundane and the portentous, the particular and the prophetic (a textual motif underlined in the two Cassandra figures who inaugurate the film, Eisenhower and Rose Charmaine, the beaten woman who warns her doctors of the impending assassination) are placed in direct proximity in a way that transforms the past into something other than a horizontal cause-and-effect chain. The time scheme that dominates the film is one of anticipation within retroversion: flashbacks that convey an instantaneous, but undatable, image of the future.[9]

Seen as a reflection of discontinuity and disorder in the national narrative, the temporal structure of *JFK* departs radically from the sense of continuity that traditionally defines the national past and from the parallelism and simultaneity binding together, in Anderson's view, the community of the modern nation. The temporal collage the film sets up communicates instead the message that the national narrative has become unraveled, that the shots in Dealey Plaza have produced a *caesura* in the narrative of nation akin to the blackening of the screen that occurs in the film directly after the assassination. Many of the character-narrations, moreover, come from socially marginal people whose testimony would not be seen as credible in a court of law. David Ferrie (a shadowy member of several extreme right-wing groups), Willie O'Keefe (a convicted homosexual prostitute), and the stripper from Jack Ruby's bar, to name a few, provide vivid and extensive character-narrations, which, we are told, will carry very little weight in a legal proceeding. However, by looking to the marginalized and excluded as a source of authenticity and truth, the film implies that a split between the public sphere and the sphere of "the people" has further eroded the concept of nation as "imagined community."

If, as Timothy Brennan says, the nation is an imaginary construct that depends for its existence on an apparatus of cultural fictions, then the disjunctive, fragmentary form of *JFK* suggests the shattering of social identity.[10] It encodes stylistic characteristics such as fragmentation, rupture, repetition, and the atomistic scattering of details as a sign of social morcellation, a mark of the falling apart of a once unitary nation. The message conveyed by the film's style thus intersects in complex ways with the argument, made in this volume by Hayden White, that modernist and postmodernist forms may provide the most effective methods for rendering the events of the recent past. While the film vividly illustrates the thesis White elaborates—that historical reality far exceeds the capacity of any realist form to comprehend it—it nonetheless also holds onto the very ideal of a coherent narrative of nation that its own formal structure seems to repudiate.

For White, the chief value of modernist techniques for representing the traumatic historical events of the twentieth century resides in the sense of doubt and uncertainty toward historical knowledge that a modernist approach to the past permits. Rather than assuming an illusory intellectual mastery over the event, a modernist style of historiography finds that the meaning of the past is contestable because the questions we ask of an event cannot be answered with any semblance of mastery or totality. Historical reality itself has been transformed in the twentieth century, he argues, by the occurrence of events of such a compound nature and magnitude that any objective account or rational explanation based solely on "the facts" can only be illusory, implying mastery over events and contexts that escape explanation. The effort to come to grips with the "modernist" event can only take place in an atmosphere of historiographic doubt.

While such a description clearly corresponds to *JFK*, with its mood of epistemological skepticism and lack of resolution, the film on the whole places a different kind of pressure on the question of modernism and historical representation. In terms of offering the cinematic equivalent of a sophisticated historiographic analysis, *JFK* is exemplary: it represents the event cubistically, from competing perspectives; it mixes film idioms, genres, and period styles (documentary, Soviet-style montage, Hollywood naturalism, domestic melodrama, to name a few) in order to represent the variety of overlapping contexts in which the event occurs; it foregrounds the artificial and provisional nature of any reconstruction of reality by refusing to predicate any single version of events. Nevertheless, in its overall concern for the relation between the past and an ongoing sense of national identity, the film seems to be split between its modernist form and its desire to reconstitute or recover a seamless national text. Although it uses the full panoply of modernist devices, it implies that a certain sense of history is part of the social imaginary and that historical ambiguity raises deeply disturbing questions about identity.

Certainly *JFK* questions history both as a mode of knowledge and as a means of understanding the present. However, by focusing obsessively on a historical event, it also affirms a desperate need for history as the foundation of national identity. It has been said that "[t]he interrogation of history is a stage in the search for identity."[11] Above all, *JFK* demonstrates the problematic nature of history in relation to identity, exposing the contradictory faces of a historical narrative that has ceased to function as an expression of the "imagined community."

The images of history evoked by *JFK* can be described in terms of two competing paradigms. In the first instance, as a result of its obsession with explaining the event, *JFK* appears to represent a traditional view that a unified and fixed historical reality exists, and could be recovered, were it not obscured by willfully deceptive stories and by the inaccessibility of the crucial facts. Seen in this way, the film sets itself the task of imposing a metanarrative to unify the disparate stories, rumors, and contexts of the Kennedy assassination into a coherent frame.

At other points, however, and closely similar to White's concept of the "derealization" of the event in the twentieth century, the film seems to represent the alternate paradigm of history as an "epistemic murk," an unstable discourse of fact and fiction, truth and illusion that discloses a fragmentation of contexts, motives, beliefs, and regimes of credibility.[12] From this perspective, the film's project might be described as an attempt to write a history that represents the incoherence, the contradictions, and the inconsistencies that characterize the historical text, exemplifying what we might call, to use Homi Bhabha's words, the "dissolution of history as fragmentary composition; the decomposition of narrative voice."[13] The film's insistence on explaining the historical event and thereby recovering a sense of the unisonance of the nation is thus contradicted by its violent polyphony, its filtering of the national history through the epistemic murk of rumor, fact, and illusion, conveyed through the complex temporality of the jump cut, the fast forward, the freeze frame, and the splitting of sound from image in which the past escapes any possibility of realignment in "homogeneous, empty time."

JFK oscillates between these competing paradigms, which are represented, more or less explicitly, through a series of character-narrations. In place of social unisonance, the film provides a series of readings of the assassination drawn from a wide range of social types. From the almost freakishly marginal David Ferrie to the seemingly informed speculations of "X," these readings exhibit common characteristics as well as telling differences: they adhere to the same code of explanation, but make different appeals to belief. Juxtaposed in the film in a way that invites comparison, the narrations of Ferrie and of "X" exhibit a striking lack of unisonance at the level of the signifier.

The confessional nature of Ferrie's account, the anguish and fear that permeate his monologue, conveys a strong sense of truth, underscored by the long-take camera work that seems to wish to offer itself as the equivalent of a visual polygraph test. His narration stands out for the simplicity of its scenic construction: in a film characterized by virtuoso editing and stylistic "thickness," this scene is rendered in a straightforward presentation: there are no cutaways, inserts, or dramatized illustrations attending his description. Rather than establishing a unifying frame for the murder, however, a metanarrative that would resolve the incompatibilities of different texts and contexts, Ferrie offers a reading of the event that is polysemic: "It's a mystery, inside a riddle, wrapped in an enigma." He concludes by stressing the incomprehensibility of the event, its vastness and obscurity, a plot in which "everyone is always flipping sides," and in which the machinations of the Cubans, the CIA, and the Mob are described as "fun and games. It's all fun and games."

By contrast, "X" offers the authority of an "inside view," and provides a sense of dispassionate analysis in which logic and history provide an explanatory framework. His narration charts a different route into the social imaginary. Continuously framed with the monuments of Washington, D.C. behind him, "X" speaks of a plot that centers on the control, suppression, and manufacture of information. Cover stories, secret documents, conversations "in the wind" delineate a plot that has been rationally constructed from start to finish, and which could, it appears, be uncovered with sufficient access to "the facts." "X"'s narration, however, is replete with all the techniques that have garnered *JFK* such a notorious reputation for dissembling: it is filled with imaginary reenactments and recontextualized documentary images that dramatize a far-flung conspiracy emanating from the highest reaches of power. "X", unlike Ferrie, concludes by telling Garrison that he can and must discover the truth, that his quest is "historical."

Drastically dissimilar appeals to belief are made in these readings: in one case, a straightforward scenic rendering of the character's version of events; in the other, a highly edited aggregation of existing footage, staged reenactments, and rumor made photographically concrete. In juxtaposing these two stories, both consisting of tenuous threads of information, the film exposes a cultural landscape in which different kinds of knowledge and different types of visual and verbal evidence abound. The different rhetorical strategies characterizing these two narrations of the plot to murder Kennedy, however, come together in a set of common dichotomies: both the testimony from "below" and the testimony from "above" shuttle between explanations based on personal acts of revenge versus collective political acts, between crime and subversion, between fanaticism and economic calculation, between inside agents and outside agitators.

Underlying the discourse about Kennedy's assasination, however, is the more elusive and oblique subject of the national narrative. In these two dialogues, different rhetorics of national identity, or, more precisely, different metaphors and myths of the nation are placed in uneasy proximity. Ferrie uncovers one such myth in his "confession" that all he wanted was to become a Catholic priest, to live in a monastery, to pray to God. One of Anderson's central theses concerning national identity is that "the dawn of nationalism at the end of the eighteenth century coincide[d] with the dusk of religious modes of thought," and that nationalism essentially extended and modernized "religious imaginings," taking on religion's concern with death, continuity, community, and the desire for origins.[14] For Ferrie, the centrality and communalism of the Church, especially that of the monastic life, stands as an example of collectivity only poorly replicated by the criminal and state-sponsored institutions that have replaced it. Ferrie seems to occupy in a complex way the position of the exile, nationalism's opposite. Referring to Oswald as a "wannabe, nobody really liked him," Ferrie brings to the surface of the text the desire for affiliation, for community, for the univocity of assent. The figure of the exile, seen here in the person of Ferrie hovering around the periphery of the national community, is, however, displaced, in a paradoxical fashion, into the center of the film's portrait of national life, extending ultimately to the figure of Garrison, who will, like Ferrie, be metaphorically "defrocked" and banished, at least temporarily, from the national community—a point made apparent in the slanted media coverage of Garrison's case against Clay Shaw. Moreover, Garrison's identification with Ferrie is figured directly in the subsequent scene at Ferrie's apartment, in which he looks into the mirror and imagines the circumstances of Ferrie's death. The dichotomy the film sets up between exile and the imagined community illuminates its narrative address: the film posits its viewer as a charter member of the community of nation who is simultaneously alienated from it; both insider and outsider, winner and loser, part of the whole yet driven to reject the premises upon which the national community has lately been established.

A very different myth of the nation than that exemplified by Ferrie, and a very different sense of cultural identification permeates the dialogue of "X". Here, the assassination of Kennedy is placed in a historical frame that encompasses not only the national narrative but the principal symbols of national identity. Beginning at the Lincoln Memorial and ending at the eternal flame marking Kennedy's tomb, the sequence details a secret history, a national past that has uncannily woven itself into the communal text.[15] "X" narrates a history consisting of covert operations in Italy, Tibet, Viet Nam, Cuba, that brutally extended and consolidated the reach of American power in the 1950s and early 1960s. The murder of Kennedy, and the national narrative in general, are described by "X" in terms of a universal imperial pattern: Caesar, the Crucifixion, the killing of kings are set out by "X" as the salient intertextual references for the U.S. narrative of nation.

Counterposed to this clandestine history of the national security state, however, is the implied narrative of national life represented by the monuments to Lincoln and Kennedy, who, the film suggests, are linked in a different chain of affiliation, connected to a different narrative of nation. This narrative of national life is referenced metonymically in the shots of two black children playing on the grassy embankment near Garrison and "X" and by the black father and son who are seen paying their respects at Kennedy's tomb at the end of the scene.[16] Blackness in *JFK* functions almost like a motif, the visible signs of an idealized national narrative characterized by racial and social progress, a narrative capable of binding the whole "national community" together. "X"s version of the narrative of nation—"The organizing principle of any society is for war. The authority of a state over its people resides in its war powers"—appears to be contradicted by the mise-en-scène, which evokes a national mythology and a historical life of "the people" that appears to be distinct from the martial authority wielded by the state. The mise-en-scène of this sequence illustrates a point made by Bhabha: "The living principle of the people as that continual process by which the national life is redeemed ... [t]he scraps, rags, and patches of daily life must be repeatedly turned into the signs of a national culture."[17]

Between these different representations of the national past and the national culture—one narrated, the other expressed through mise-en-scène—a major fissure exists. The "imagined community" portrayed in the film is clearly not fixed, visible, or unified horizontally, but is instead split into several separate and distinct nations: those "in the loop" and those who occupy the position of exile; those who are "faceless" and those who are marked by history. Split and divided, the idea of the nation becomes a kind of lost object in *JFK*, a unisonance once identified with patriotism and home—signified with exceptional nostalgic power in the lengthy montage scene that opens the film—now identified with loss and silence.

The modernist and postmodernist narrative techniques of the film express a sense of the splitting and division of a society and of the loss of the idealized symbols of national identity. If the development of a coherent narrative mode is essential for achieving a sense of history and of cultural identity, as Anderson and others have argued, the film's anti-narrative techniques would appear to signify identity's dissolution. If the realist novel is understood to serve a "nation-building function, equivalent to the institution of law," *JFK* would appear to display the divisions of culture, history, and symbolism that, the film implies, make our present sense of national identity so dissonant.[18]

On the other hand, the film's radically contestatory interpretation of the past can also be seem as a form of popular counter-memory, bringing forms of popular cultural expression directly into the center of its narrative art. Bypassing the narrative forms of official culture, the film fuses vernacular idioms such as docudrama, grainy, tabloid-style still photographs, television images, and home movies, to create a carnivalesque style of narrative texture replete with examples of "bad taste." The cultural and social landscape of late-twentieth-century America is embedded in the film's montage technique, through which, as one writer says, "different cultural worlds converge: a convergence of differences without uniformity."[19]

The nostalgic desire that permeates the film for a unified national culture, a culture of unisonance, a single national voice, is thus set against its modernist, montagist form, that draws on the multiple popular idioms of contemporary life. Cutting across the different social divisions and narratives of nation in the film, however, is the memory of violence, the memory of discontinuity emblematically figured in the death of Kennedy. In foregrounding the memory of violence, the film resists the reductiveness of a single, official history and defends the role and power of differentiated memories.

Perhaps *JFK*'s greatest strength is its use of the disjunctive style of the contemporary media as an act of cultural resistance and as a means for folding that message of cultural resistance into an appeal to national identity in a way that recognizes the media as a terrain; analogous to the role of the novel and the newspaper in the past. But this strength might also be seen as the film's greatest weakness, for in the end this message returns us to the dominant narrative of nation and assimilates to national identity all other possibilities of community and solidarity.[20]

notes

1. *JFK: The Book of the Film* (Applause Books, New York, 1992) contains an extraordinary collection of reviews, commentaries, editorials, and responses comprising several hundred pages, as well as Oliver Stone and Zachary Sklar's research notes for the film. In addition, *Cinéaste* (vol. XIX, no. 1) 1992 has published a special issue on *JFK*, and *American Historical Review* (April, 1992) includes a substantial special section on the film. *Media Spectacles*, ed. Marjorie Garber, Jann Matlock, and Rebecca Walkowitz (New York: Routledge, 1993) contains several articles that deal with the controversy and debate surrounding *JFK*.
2. Hayden White provides a particularly sophisticated treatment of these issues in relation to *JFK* in "The Modernist Event," in this volume.
3. Benedict Anderson introduces the term "unisonance" in connection with the singing of the national anthem and the impression of social parallelism and simultaneity the singing of it fosters. See *Imagined Communities* (London: Verso, 1991), 145.
4. The relation between nationalism and narrative form has been addressed by a number of writers. See, for example, Homi K. Bhabha, "DissemiNation: Time, Narrative, and the Margins of the Modern Nation"; and Timothy Brennan, "The National Longing for Form" in *Nation and Narration* ed. Bhabha (London: Routledge 1990); William Rowe and Vivian Schelling, *Memory and Modernity* (London: Verso, 1991); Partha Chatterjee, *Nationalist Thought and the Colonial World* (Minneapolis: University of Minnesota Press, 1993); and Benedict Anderson, *Imagined Communities* (London: Verso, 1991).
5. Anderson, 26. The phrase "homogeneous, empty time" comes from Walter Benjamin, *Illuminations* (New York: Schocken Books, 1969), 261.
6. Anderson, 25
7. Anderson, 25.
8. White, "The Modernist Event."
9. The phrase, "anticipation within retroversion" comes from Mieke Bal, *Narratology: Introduction to the Theory of Narrative* (Toronto: University of Toronto 1985), 67.

10. Timothy Brennan, "The national longing for form," in *Nation and Narration*, 49.
11. Renata Wasserman, "Mario Vargas Llosa, Euclides da Cunha, and the Strategy of Intertextuality," *PMLA* (May, 1993): 464.
12. See Ann Laura Stoller, "In Cold Blood": Hierarchies of Credibility and the Politics of Colonial Narratives." *Representations* 37, (Winter 1992). The phrase, "epistemic murk," comes from Michael Taussig, "Culture of Terror, Space of Death: Roger Casement's Putumayo Report and the Explanation of Torture." *Comparative Studies in Society and History* 26 (July 1984), 467–497.
13. Homi K. Bhabha, "A Question of Survival: Nations and Psychic States," in *Psychoanalysis and Cultural Theory: Thresholds*, ed. James Donald (London: Macmillan,

1991), 98. Bhabha here explores the limits of Anderson's concept of the "unisonance" of the imagined community, drawing on competing models of national consciousness as defined by Edward Said and Frantz Fanon.

14. Anderson, 11. See also Brennan, 50.
15. The iconography of D.C. monuments has been utilized in other film texts in relation to conspiracy in ways that contrast with *JFK*. In *Mr. Smith Goes To Washington* (Frank Capra, 1939), for example, the montage elicits a sense of democracy as transparent; in *All The President's Men* (Alan Pakula, 1976), by contrast, the official spaces of Washington are represented as signs that must be deciphered for their underlying, conspiratorial connections. But where *All The President's Men* presents conspiracy as a temporary aberration that can be purged through the apparatus of "the system" itself, *JFK* narrates a secret history that "derealizes" the dominant historical narrative. The monuments and official spaces of Washington become, in *JFK*, almost as indecipherable and "riddling" as the glyphs on an ancient tombstone.
16. In the script of the film, this scene is handled differently. Rather than a black man and his young son at Kennedy's tomb, the script has Garrison flashing back to documentary images of Dachau, with piles of bodies being bulldozed into a ditch. In the logic of the film, this change underlines the message of the importance of national community associated with the images of Lincoln and Kennedy. It asserts, under the banner of the national, a sense of black and white people having a common story and sharing the same fate.
17. Homi K. Bhabha, "DissemiNation," in *Nation and Narration*, 297.
18. William Rowe and Vivian Schelling, *Memory and Modernity* (London: Verso, 1991), 204.
19. Rowe and Schelling, 213.
20. See Dipesh Chakrabarty, "Postcoloniality and the Artifice of History: Who Speaks for "Indian" Pasts?", *Representations* 37, (Winter 1992). The concluding paragraphs of this article express well the dominance of national narratives over other possible narratives of social connection and stress the role of historical writing in furthering this condition.

seven

andrei rublev

the medieval epic as post-utopian history

denise j. youngblood

> Russians experience their history as a Holy Mystery in which every action, every step, every victory, and every tragedy are signs of a historical Revelation, since this, after all, is the history of a great, god-fearing people.
>
> —Aleksandr Dugin, "Organic Democracy," 1992

A Soviet movie about a fifteenth-century Russian icon painter no doubt seems an odd subject for an essay on the postmodernist ethos in cinema. But Andrei Tarkovskii's medieval epic *Andrei Rublev* (1966, released 1969–71) was the first Soviet film to challenge the sterile strictures of Socialist Realism and official history.[1] Its minutely detailed surface realism mocks the unreality and myth-making of Socialist Realism and, as we shall see, debunks the idea, cherished by Russians, that their history is a "Holy Mystery."

Andrei Rublev is a profoundly postmodern, or better yet, "post-utopian" work.[2] It is a damning and subversive challenge to totalities, authority, and the idea of Truth. Because of the extreme politicization of culture and history in the former USSR, the post-utopian aesthetic has held particular appeal to Soviet directors over the last twenty-five years (until *glasnost*) as a framework for political and artistic rebellion.

Andrei Rublev is an important film in a number of respects, both cinematic and historical. First, it marks the beginning of Tarkovskii's creative evolution from a "realist" to an avant-garde artist.[3] Second, *Andrei Rublev* became the *cause célèbre* of the 1960s in Soviet cultural circles as Tarkovskii unsuccessfully struggled with the Mosfilm studio and state censorship codes to get the film passed uncut. Despite his efforts, the film was heavily censored, and even so, could not be shown in the USSR until 1971, two years after it screened in Europe, winning a prize at the 1970 Cannes Film Festival.[3] Finally, and of particular importance to this essay, *Andrei Rublev* must be recognized as a serious interpretation of the past—a history of medieval Russia that is at least as relevant and revelatory as anything written about the tumultuous beginning of the fifteenth century.

Although *Andrei Rublev* has been much analyzed, specialists on Soviet cinema and culture tend to view it either as merely a fascinating stepping stone in the career of the director of *Solaris* (1972), *The Mirror* (1975), *Stalker* (1980), *Nostalgia* (1983), or as a purely political work, an allegory critiquing the USSR of the 1960s.[4] Although I will discuss the political aspects of the film in passing, I propose to explore this complex film in some of its more contradictory aspects in order to demonstrate that it is open to a third reading. More than a film *with* a "history" that serves as a paradigm for Soviet cultural politics in the 1960s, *Andrei Rublev* is also a movie that *is* a history, an experimental history of medieval times that confronts the truisms of positivist historical rendering.

The historical figure Andrei Rublev was an ideal choice for the subject of a post-utopian historical film. The greatest painter in a culture not especially renowned for producing paintings (with the exception of icons), Rublev is a complete enigma. Tarkovskii was thus never in danger of succumbing to facticity. (For that very reason, historians of what Robert Rosenstone has dubbed the "Dragnet School" of history—"Just the facts, ma'am"—avoid him altogether.)

Rublev was born around 1370 and died around 1430 and was most closely connected with the Andronnikov Monastery, now within Moscow's city limits. As late as the eighteenth century, there was apparently a marked gravestone in the monastery yard; it has since disappeared.[5] That is all that is known about Rublev's life, except for what can be inferred from his profoundly original and supremely beautiful art.

Rublev lived during a time of turmoil, violence, and trouble in Russia: the

Prince of Moscow, Vasilii I (1389–1425, son of the legendary hero Dmitrii Donskoi) was exceptionally weak, and declining Tatar (Mongol) influence led to increased Tatar raids on Russian cities in an effort to reassert control. Feuding between and among the various remaining minor princes contributed to the chaos. The Russian princes sometimes attempted to collaborate with the Tatars in order to enhance their own positions. Yet despite Vasilii I's inability to control his subjects and their enemies, as Great Prince he continued the centralizing traditions of the Princes of Moscow and devoted much energy to monument building (in his case, churches) to shore up his unsteady political position.[7]

Stylistically, *Andrei Rublev* fits the tenor of these times. Like Russian medieval chronicles, Tarkovskii's film consists not of a story but of fragmented episodes. In addition to the prologue and epilogue that frame the film, *Andrei Rublev* contains eight discrete episodes that are organized chronologically. These episodes, cryptic and disjointed, together exist as a filmic version of the literary chronicle's structure. Russian chroniclers, like their European counterparts, operated under principles of selection that are no longer obvious or rational to the modern reader. In a similar fashion, Tarkovskii depicts some years in great detail (one third of the film is devoted to the year 1408) while ignoring others completely (the disjuncture from the seventh episode to the eighth elides eleven years, which are never explicated). In chronicles people are treated as symbols; it is also difficult to consider Rublev as an individual, although he is present in each episode and gives the picture its title. More often, Rublev functions as a witness *to* history rather than a participant *in* it.

The cinematic elements used in constructing the film also contribute to the construction of an alternate discourse for history telling. There are few closeups, corresponding to the lack of emphasis on individuals. Frequent cross-cutting from exteriors to interiors and again to exteriors emphasizes the contrasts between the chaos and brutality of nature and of people with the stillness and artifice of art and intellectuals (like priests). Haphazard movement creates the impression of lack of purpose, futility, aimlessness rather than ordered progression. Finally, the often intrusive camerawork reminds viewers of the presence of yet another group of outsiders, the filmmakers.

The episodic nature of *Andrei Rublev* is apparent from the beginning. The film opens with a mysterious prologue about a hot-air balloonist preparing to take off in front of a church. Here the film's tone of disorder, decrepitude, and hostility toward change is set: As the camera follows the balloonist, we see the typical Russian landscape with its flat plains, low hills, and long rivers. We also observe the individual (the balloonist) in opposition to the group, a crowd watching in disbelief. The balloon loses air, and in a disorienting fall, the balloonist crashes into a river and apparently drowns. No transition, no explanation.

The first episode which follows the prologue, entitled "The Jester,"[6] establishes Tarkovskii's deceptively historicist approach. An intertitle informs us that it is the year 1400. We see three priests, accurately dressed for the period. But this historicism is immediately undercut when two of the priests—the well-established icon painter Daniil Chernyi and the up-and-coming artist Andrei Rublev—are anachronistically presented as "stars" in an artworld where paintings were never signed. The third priest, the ambitious and bitterly envious Kirill, is portrayed as a lesser talent.

These men seek shelter from blinding rain in a crowded peasant hut where a jester holds forth, vituperatively castigating the *boyars* (the native, as opposed to Tatar, nobility). The peasants are clearly uncomfortable in the presence of the priests (and vice versa); the jester leaves after finishing his angry tirade. Suddenly, through the fog, we see horsemen approaching the cabin, galloping in the deep mud. They have come for the jester and throw him violently against a tree, knocking him out before flinging him over a horse and taking off. Silence. Kirill, who has disappeared from view for a brief time, returns. From where we do not know, but it would seem that he, disturbed that the insolent jester "has been sent by the devil," may have turned the hapless man in. (In the final episode of the film, we learn that this supposition is correct.) The three priests leave their shelter as silently as they entered it. Across the lake, we see the horsemen in the distance.

Taking this fragment as a historical "document," what do we learn? The sequence establishes the major motifs of Tarkovskii's vision of Russian medieval history: the closeness to a nature that is palpable and not romanticized; the distance between the people and the intelligentsia (the priests) on the one hand and the people and the ruling classes (the *boyars*) on the other; the betrayal of Russians by Russians; the brutality between and among men. The episode also establishes Tarkovskii's views on the limits of history: in postmodernist fashion, the viewer, not the historian, does a great deal of the work of interpretation. As viewers, we are compelled to resort to ambiguous terms in constructing the meaning of the episode—"seem," "might have been," "perhaps"—the kind of "filling in" which discomfits the traditional academic historian but delights his or her postmodern counterpart.

Five years disappear into the void of History. There is no understandable transition to the second episode, "Feofan the Greek,"[7] which takes place in 1405 in Novgorod. In this episode, the craftsman-priest Kirill wanders around the foreground as a man is being dragged in the background to the gallows, crying that he is "innocent." Execution, torture, aimless motion ... these are the fabric of Russian culture. The film then cuts abruptly to an interior shot;

we see the legendary Greek icon painter Theophanes, known in Russian as Feofan the Greek, lying on the floor of a church. Kirill appears, and Feofan asks him if he might be the famous artist Andrei Rublev. This stings Kirill, who launches a critique of Rublev's work, castigating it for its "lack of faith and simplicity"—in our terminology, its nonconformity. Feofan, the dean of "Russian" icon painters, has a commission from the Great Prince to decorate the interior of the Cathedral of the Annunciation in Moscow and offers Kirill work. Ever undone by vanity, Kirill insists instead that Feofan come to the Andronnikov Monastery to fetch him. But when a *boyar* appears at the Andronnikov Monastery on Feofan's behalf, it is not to summon the expectant Kirill, but rather, Andrei Rublev. The price of fame is that Andrei loses the friendship, as it were, of both Daniil Chernyi and the hapless Kirill (the latter is expelled from the monastery after creating an ugly scene).

The Chorus of Skeptics in the audience must ask: What are the *historical* issues? The dazed meanderings of the main characters parallel the apparent aimlessness of the film. Episode three, 1406, which bears the film's original title, "The Passion according to Andrei,"[8] is little help in rendering narrative coherence to the film. Here, as in the previous two episodes, the viewer has to work hard to establish context and relationships between characters. Rublev and Foma, who is one of Rublev's boy apprentices, are walking through the wet, muddy, ant-filled woods. Rublev tells his young protegé that he will never be an artist because he is a "liar" who "eats too much." (Chorus, irritated: What does this have to do with *art*?) Rublev and Foma return to the church, whereupon Andrei has a chat with Feofan, another of those "random" conversations that later turns out to have established a key theme of the film. The ideas Feofan conveys are completely ahistorical in the modernist, positivist sense although they are very Greek. "Everything," he says, "is an eternal circle." His ideas are also profoundly cynical; in the Last Judgment, he says, "each will accuse the other of sins in order to defend himself," a pointed reference to the Stalin Terror.

Andrei, an unwavering idealist, responds that Feofan is right if "you only remember evil. Perhaps we must forget some things, but not all," a statement that appears to critique (or praise?) the selectivity of the historical record. Rublev goes on to identify the "Pharisees" (referring to the *boyars* who in turn may be understood to represent the Soviet elite) as "masters of deceit" but tells Feofan that "we must remind people that they are people. Russians are of the same blood." As the two great artists talk, the camera shifts to the outside, to the scene of what first appears to be a passion play but then is revealed as a real crucifixion that a group of *boyars* are observing.[9] (Or is this a fantasy? And if so, whose: Andrei's or Tarkovskii's? The film can be frustratingly ambiguous.)

By this point, the movie-goer accustomed to the happy narratives and clear-cut heroes and villains of Socialist Realism and Soviet history (or of Hollywood cinema and traditional American mythology) is likely to be distinctly uncomfortable, bored, and annoyed. It is reasonable to expect that half-way through a film, the viewer should have an understanding of its direction. Yet the usual aids to understanding are absent or deliberately misplaced. There is no voice-over narration, no descriptive intertitles. There is little dialogue, and when the characters do talk, their conversations are disjointed and intellectually pretentious. True, the film is visually realistic—but too realistic for pleasure. The people look dirty, hungry, and unhappy even when they are not being tortured. Vaunted Russian nature, prized by Russians and celebrated in the work of beloved "realists" like Turgenev or Tolstoi, here appears squalid, muddy, and uncomfortable, epitomized by the swarm of ants crawling up Foma's filthy leg.

The film begins to coalesce in the middle third, and Tarkovskii's objectives become clear. Episode four, "The Saint's Day,"[10] is the first of three sequences set in the year 1408. "The Saint's Day" is visually the most beautiful in the film, sharply contrasting with the stark and talky third episode that precedes it. On St. John's Night,[11] in early summer 1408, Andrei and his assistants (now including Rublev's old friend Daniil Chernyi, though we never learn how and when they were reconciled) are on their way to the city of Vladimir when they are startled by sudden noises and lights. They see people running naked through the woods to the river, casting spells with candles. The others are horrified, but Andrei is entranced, and, pulled by an invisible force, he heads for the scene of the pagan rites. Nude couples sink down into the tall grass, apparently copulating. Andrei stares in fascination. Suddenly he is set upon and seized by some angry participants, who tell him that they intend to drown him like a "black snake" when the festivities have ended. Andrei is taken to a hut and tied to a cabin pole. There, a young woman sheds her robe, kisses him, and with very little persuasion on his part, releases him.

The next morning, Andrei wanders back to his boat where his crew still awaits him. The viewer has no concrete idea what has transpired in the interim—whether Rublev had, for the first time in his life, a sexual encounter or remained a *voyeur*—but his face is scratched. He babbles some nonsense: the "locals are used to it." Obviously believing the worst, Daniil turns away from Andrei in disgust, asking, "Aren't you ashamed in front of your pupils?" Andrei is saved from answering by the sudden appearance of Authority: a gang of *boyars*, the Prince's men, have come to hunt the "pagans" down in yet another scene of extreme violence. Already in their own boat, the priests watch in deafening silence as a naked woman swims by them, attempting to escape the horsemen. This imagined scene *could* have happened, but it is, nonetheless, eerie and surreal. (Little is more surreal than realism, after all.)

Episode five, "The Last Judgment," continues the chronicle of the year 1408. Andrei and his artists have finally arrived in Vladimir, but although they have been there for some time, they have made virtually no progress on their task. The church's interior is blank: vast expanses of whitewashed walls. No one knows where Andrei is; the archbishop (like the viewer) losing patience with the artist's apparent lack of motivation, has sent a courier to the Prince to complain about the progress on the iconostasis, the screen of icons that separates the nave from the sanctuary. Andrei is, in fact, taking a stroll about a field with Daniil Chernyi—agonizing over how to depict the Last Judgment. The conversation between Chernyi and Rublev is worth quoting in some detail, since it provides a key to understanding Tarkovskii's interpretation of Russian history:

Daniil:	Why have we been talking for two months? You either paint the Last Judgment or you don't ... Sinners boiling in pitch; the devil with smoke coming from his nose.
Andrei:	I reject such a devil. It disgusts me.
Daniil:	It's the Last Judgment. I didn't invent it.
Andrei:	So it's dishonest. I never learned to cultivate integrity.

"*It's the Last Judgment. I didn't invent it.*" For Daniil, history is something real, not "invented." But for Andrei?

In the meantime, Andrei's crew prepares to abandon the seemingly hopeless project. Young Foma gathers his brushes to set off on his own; the masons head out for Zvenigorod to build a palace for the Prince of Moscow's younger brother. Andrei dejectedly wanders around the empty church, staring at the blank walls, biting his nails. The Great Prince has in the meantime arrived with his small daughter and immediately complains that what has been painted should be "brighter," rebuffing Andrei's autonomy as artist. The lovely little princess plays merrily, oblivious to adult angst and irritation.

Outside (and we have come to expect this contrast between interiors and exteriors that underscores the chasm between the elite and the masses), the scene is quite different. The Great Prince's *boyars* are tracking down the artisan "defectors" in the forest in order to blind them so that his hated younger brother will not have benefit of their services. This scene, shot with a constantly moving camera and without benefit of closeups is one of startling ferocity, even given the frequent, casual violence of the film up to now.

Shrieks of pain and spurting blood are juxtaposed with birdsongs and spattered paint.

Andrei has flung paint against the walls out of anguish at the tragedy that has befallen his comrades. He weeps. A young woman (Irma Raush), mute, clearly mentally impaired and therefore representing a "Holy Fool,"[12] enters the church. Distressed at the riot of disordered, and for her meaningless, color on the walls, she too begins to sob hysterically. She then walks toward the camera and out the door, abandoning "art" (Rublev and all he represents) to return to "nature" (the driving rain).

"*So it's dishonest. I never learned to cultivate integrity.*" But what does "dishonesty" mean in a society such as this? What is "integrity"? No one believes in anything, let alone in the Church. The people use saints' days to practice pre-Christian rites; they mock the priests; the Prince is so remote from real life that he can play with his daughter while Russians are being maimed at his command.

The final episode in this crucial year 1408, "The Raid," reinforces Tarkovskii's dark view of Russian history and his critique of Russian national character. It begins with a long shot of a prince's camp outside Vladimir. At first it is not clear exactly which prince's camp it is because the Great Prince and his envious younger brother are played by the same actor (both are played by Nazarov, in a curious piece of casting, suggesting that neither prince is preferable to the other). The Tatars are approaching and begin entering the frame. The spectator's confusion continues since these Tatars initially appear friendly, rather than hostile. We then see Russians and Tatars together seeking a place to ford the broad river.

Once again, we have to fend for ourselves for meaning, with little guidance from Tarkovskii. It becomes apparent that the prince is not the Prince of Moscow but his younger brother when he says to his Tatar counterpart, "Vladimir is deserted. My brother is in Lithuania." The Tatar warlord cheerfully retorts, "How you love your brother!" and laughingly explains that he and his army are late because they "could not resist" attacking a village en route. Which is worse? The foreign oppressor or the native collaborator?

What follows is a scene of unparallelled violence and mayhem. With the two warlords—Tatar and Russian—directing the affair, the citizens of Vladimir are massacred—men, women, and children. In the smoke and riotous panic, we see women being carried off to be raped, men and children run through with swords, split by arrows, hacked with axes. One man cries despairingly, "We are all fellow Russians!", to which he receives the reply, just before his death at the hands of another Russian, "You Vladimir bastard!"—accurately evoking the local, rather than national, identification that characterized the times.

The troops take a battering ram to the church. The Tatar warlord (a detached, but oddly sympathetic character) is sitting outside watching in bemusement while the camera cuts to the terrified people cowering inside the church. People are praying, and Andrei, finally stirred to action by this horror, attempts to lead the Holy Fool to a place of safety. At last, the church is penetrated, its sanctity forever violated. Andrei can now understand the meaning of the Last Judgment, as Russians and Tatars charge in on horseback to slaughter what remains of the population of Vladimir. A Russian soldier seizes the Fool and carries her upstairs to rape her. Andrei follows, takes the man's ax, and in an action quite extraordinary considering his character's passivity thus far, kills the soldier (he does this off screen; the viewer only sees the body tumble down the stairs). Rublev has at last crossed the line, becoming part of "real" Russian life. Outside madness prevails, the town is in flames, people are stealing horses and everything else they can. We cannot determine who these people are, which side they are on. For Tarkovskii, history is no soothing balm.

Back inside the church, it is quiet. Almost everyone has been killed, and the Tatar warlord is strolling among the corpses, admiring the icons, as though he were at an art gallery. The prince attempts to explain the Virgin Mary to the Tatar, but the Tartar cuts the prince off, laughing: "How can she be a virgin if she has a son? Interesting things happen in Russia!" As they casually converse, a man is being tortured in order to force him to tell where the church's gold is hidden. He shrieks at the prince: "You've sold Rus' [as Russia was called in the fifteenth century]; betrayed her."[15]

The soldiers begin torching the icons; the Tatar warlord continues to look amused as he too is denounced and damned by the torture victim. Those angry words soon stop as boiling pitch is poured into the wretched man's mouth, and he is tied to a horse and dragged out of the church to his death. As the Great Prince's treacherous younger brother slowly wanders up the stairs of the ruined cathedral, screams fill the air.

Cutting to the outside, we see large white birds filmed from on high—a beautiful moment—and then Rublev's apprentice, Foma, running. Foma, who escaped the massacre in the previous sequence, is apparently going to succeed again—but no, he does not; an archer shoots him in the back. As Foma falls into the stream, the camera lens is splashed with water—a deliberate reminder of the presence of the storyteller, maddeningly remote though this one is. Yet what does the death of one person matter to the historian?

The warriors, Russian and Tatar, have left behind a devastated city. The church is filled with mutilated bodies, and the only two people who remain alive are Andrei and the Fool. The Fool sits braiding a dead girl's hair. Andrei is stunned by the horror of it all. Suddenly the ghost of Feofan the Greek appears, matter-of-factly leafing through the charred pages of a book. They have the following conversation:

Andrei:	I've spent half my life in blindness ... Aren't we one people, one faith, one blood? One Tatar smiled and said, 'Even without us, you'll cut each other's throats.' ... I'll never paint again.
Feofan:	You're committing a grave sin.
Andrei:	I killed a man—a fellow Russian ... I will offer the Lord a vow of silence ... How long will we be able to go on?
Feofan:	I don't know. Forever, probably. How beautiful this all is.

Feofan vanishes. It is snowing softly. A horse enters the church. The Fool sleeps. "*How beautiful this all is.*" And it is. Who has demonstrated the more profound understanding of history? Rublev sees the understanding in the horror of local events; Feofan the Greek embraces the long view: "*Forever, probably*."

The year 1408 has been, with its three episodes, the turning point; not only for the film, but also for Andrei. He is no longer the naif who can "reject such a devil," and he can no longer ignore the world. He has "known" a woman (presumably on St. John's Night); he has killed a man; he has witnessed human cruelty and treachery on an unimaginable scale; he has seen his false vision of Russia and Russians united shattered.

Yet Rublev stubbornly resists history's lure. He ignores his past. Episode seven, "The Silence," skips ahead four years to 1412, and it is as if the epiphany of 1408 has never happened. Andrei has returned, with a vengeance, to his self-absorbed passivity. Famine stalks Russia. In the snowy yard of the Andronnikov Monastery, the Fool wanders about with a mangy dog, searching for food. She tries to eat the bark of a tree and spits it out in disgust. The only food left at the monastery is rotten apples, and a visitor from Vladimir describes the deserted villages he encountered on his way to the Moscow region (as well as his own escape from a starving wolf). We recognize that the man is Kirill, much aged. Kirill learns that Rublev has taken a vow of silence and abandoned art and that Daniil Chernyi has disappeared. Nothing remains of the "Rublev School," and Rublev himself is bent on the destruction of his legacy.

Begging the bishop for forgiveness for his vanity, Kirill asks to be readmitted to the monastery; whether his motive is to obtain food and shelter in this time of famine or to be able to see his alter ego, Andrei, we do not know. Outside Tatars charge into the yard, throwing meat to the yapping dogs while Andrei, in a demented reverie, stokes the fire. The Tatars are led by the same warlord who sacked Vladimir. The Fool watches the Tatars feeding the dogs so longingly that they take pity on her and give her some as well. The Fool is attracted to the Tatar prince—or at least to his breastplate, which she polishes so that she can see her face in it. Ever in high spirits, he gives the Fool his helmet and announces that he will take her as his wife.

The Fool, paradoxically, once again stirs Andrei from the lethargy of the last four years, providing yet another example of Tarkovskii's dogged efforts to resist interpretation through keeping the viewer constantly off balance. Andrei tries to drag her away, to keep her in his fantasy world. She screams and spits in his face and the Tatars carry her off.

No segue. Will this movie end, or just stop? The final episode, "The Bell," is set more than a decade later in 1423. Tarkovskii once again declines to humor us with an explanation; we can only imagine what Andrei has been doing all these years. The Prince wants a bell cast, but the master bellmaker Nikolka and all his family except for one son, Boris, have died of the plague. The boy, desperate, without family or livelihood, suddenly claims that he knows the secret of casting bells; the *boyars*, though suspicious of the truth of this claim, so fear the Prince's wrath that they take him on. As they search for a place to dig the casting pit, the viewer becomes more aware than ever before of nature through Tarkovskii's use of many crane shots and overheads. We see the gentle hills, sweeping vistas, and broad, slow rivers that represent eternal Russia to Russians and to all who love Russia. Perhaps Feofan the Greek was right. Russia has survived, will survive.

From the beginning, Boris's casters are suspicious of his credentials. They refuse to help him dig where he wants to; he struggles alone down a slippery ravine in driving rain looking for "good" clay. But intuition wins out over knowledge. Boris finds good clay, and as he shouts with relief and joy, above him on a bluff is none other than Andrei Rublev, going by with a cart. Once again, Rublev is a *voyeur* rather than a participant.

Young Boris is as unlike Andrei as anyone could be. Determined, forceful, impulsive, he aggressively supervises the casting of the bell in a bustle of activity, intercut with many vistas of the surrounding countryside. Andrei is constantly on the site, watching. At one point, Boris rudely shoves him (Russia's greatest painter, then and now) out of the way. The man-boy Boris orders the flogging of one of his helpers "to show who's in charge"; we hear the screaming and the sound of the whip in the background as Andrei watches. Kirill is with him, haunting him like a ghost. The three of them form a Trinity of sorts. No matter how many years pass, Russia will continue her romance with art and with brutality.

A great deal of play (perhaps too much to succeed aesthetically) is given the mechanics of bell-making through a markedly increased use of closeups.

After Boris vociferously demands more silver from the Prince's emissaries, he laughs to himself bitterly, "Imagine if after all this, it doesn't ring." More and more people gather around the casting site, now a raging inferno since the firing of the bell has begun. Andrei continues his silent vigil through it all. When the clay is removed, we see that the bell has a beautiful bas-relief of St. George slaying the dragon. The anxious Boris falls asleep against it. Andrei, still the *flâneur*, strolls aimlessly through a field and runs into Kirill who apologizes for being an "ungifted creature" and verbally attacks Andrei for wasting his enormous talents for so many years.

The film cuts back to the preparations for the bell. Dignitaries are swarming up the hill; through a sequence of high traveling shots, we get a bird's-eye view that creates a sense of openness and freedom in contrast to the dark and closed inner spaces that have characterized much of the picture. The majesty of art and nature is, however, rudely subverted by the sight of Boris standing by the bell picking his nose. (Tarkovskii will *not* give the viewer any comfort.) The excited babble of voices gives way to total silence as Boris gives the order to bring the bell out.

The Prince, playing up to foreigners, has invited the Italian ambassador and his entourage to watch the event. As the ropes creak mightily, the ambassador expresses his doubts (in Italian, not translated in the Russian language version) to his secretary that a mere boy could cast a bell, remarking on the primitive means used and that Russians are "all peculiar." The secretary replies: "I think you underestimate these people," but the ambassador persists, noting that the Prince will stop at nothing, even having beheaded his own brother (this is the first we learn of an event that would occupy center stage in a more traditional account).

As a beautiful girl (the Fool transformed)[16] walks by leading a white horse, Boris gives the order to ring the bell. In a high back tracking shot, we see a panorama of the scene: the girl, people laughing and cheering, the muddy, forlorn landscape, the dignitaries riding away. But above it all, the pure, deep sound of the bell and the glorious sound of other bells that have joined it.

Boris lies sobbing in the mud as Rublev approaches, breaking his long silence to comfort the young bellmaker. Boris admits he had no idea what he was doing, that his father had never shared the secret of casting. Andrei, admiring the triumph of primal instinct over artifice, suggests that they go to the Trinity Monastery together to work, and the camera focuses in extreme closeup on Boris's torn trousers, baste shoes (woven sandals that symbolize primitive Russia), the smoldering coals. His sobs end in silence, followed by a freeze frame, and then a fade-in to color.

The fade-in to color is the most famous epilogue in Russian cinema, with Tarkovskii for the first time in the film showing us why we should care to watch a three-hour movie about the life of Andrei Rublev. It is long-delayed gratification, to be sure, but worth the wait. Rublev's icons, shot in extreme closeup so that only details appear, are breathtaking. These images, more than five hundred years old, transcend historical time.

So do art, courage, individuality, and creativity triumph over ignorance, cruelty, treachery? Action and responsibility over passivity? It is a comforting message, but hardly the one Tarkovskii intended, as both the prologue and the epilogue indicate. The prologue was enigmatic enough, but so is the ending. There is little in medieval painting more beautiful than Rublev's icons. But as the camera moves away, we see not beauty, but decay, mold, fissures. A thunder clap sounds as we are shown the blistering face of Christ. As the camera continues to distance us from the icons, we hear louder thunder, followed by a sudden closeup of blackened, peeling paint, dripping with rain. The film ends with a final fade-in to a herd of horses on an island in blinding rain. Nothing is eternal; not even art, not even beauty. When the icons are gone, what will remain of Andrei Rublev and what he represented? When there is no evidence, what remains of history? "*Perhaps we must forget some things, but not all.*"

The political ramifications of *Andrei Rublev* in the context of the Soviet Union in the Brezhnev era are obvious to those who understand these issues, so obvious that Tarkovskii could not possibly have believed he could make this film unimpeded by censorship.[17] Within the confines of the Socialist Realist aesthetic, the film is all wrong. Andrei Rublev, Russia's greatest painter, is no "positive hero," but a kind of Hamlet, a hyper-intellectual doubter who squanders his talent. (He does change throughout the course of the film, but never for long; we cannot be certain that his new-found enthusiasm at the end will last.) No challenges are successfully overcome (unless we consider Boris and the bell), no enemies vanquished. There is no story, no forward momentum. The film is ambiguous through and through, right up to the end, and it is fraught with overwrought symbolism (at least according to the puerile strictures of Socialist Realism).

In political terms, authority figures are cruel and treacherous, enemies rather than friends of the people. They collaborate with foreigners to the detriment of the people's welfare. The "people" themselves are little better—a dark, undifferentiated mass, lacking any sense of commonality or spirituality. Certain individuals are celebrated above this group and are clearly separated from it. The artist is working for himself, not for others. All such notions were taboo in Soviet society because they too closely replicated the truth of the present.

Tarkovskii's historical interpretations, like his political attitudes, also deviate from the norm. Since the 1890s, when Russian Marxism became a movement with political parties, it has been clear that the disorderly Russian past would not fit Marx's historical scheme without considerable distortion. The medieval period has been more problematic to interpret in a Marxist sense than any other, since Russia did not pass though a feudal phase. Nonetheless, theoretically it should have been acceptable for Tarkovskii to show the princes as villains, but theory has never counted for as much as it was supposed to in Soviet interpretations (and reinterpretations) of Russian history. In fact, since the 1930s, when Stalin began reinstituting a romantic-nationalist version of Russian history, the late apanage period has been construed as one of glorious heroism, with the Princes of Moscow uniting the Russian people to drive the Tatars out. (Dmitrii Donskoi, father of Vasilii I, had, after all, defeated the Tatars at the battle of Kulikovo Field in 1380.) Tarkovskii punctures the putative "heroism" of the period quite matter-of-factly in every episode of *Andrei Rublev*.

Revisionism, of course, does not necessarily make "good" history (not even when the revision opposes Soviet accounts). How can anyone argue that a film that is invented from beginning to end, that mocks long-standing historical conventions, is history at all? It strikes me that whether or not we can do so depends on our conceptualization of what history is and can be. It also depends on the sensibilities of the "inventor," in this case Tarkovskii. For one thing, the film is without a doubt accurate in terms of its physical, material, and folkloric detail. Tarkovskii was well-served by his historical advisors, and he has succeeded in bringing a heavily mythologized period of Russian history to concrete, brutal life. But this film is not, as Marc Ferro believes, merely an "object" film, overwhelmed by minutiae, whose sole rationale is to create cinematic *tableaux vivants*.[18]

The episodic structure of *Andrei Rublev* is not merely an effort to create verisimilitude by parroting the style of medieval chronicles, but rather is a largely successful attempt to challenge the Anglo-Germanic "scientific" narrative tradition of historical writing. Tarkovskii was surely familiar with the work of the greatest of all Russian historians, Vasilii Kliuchevskii, who believed in the value of the fragment, the telling moment, as the way to constructing historical truth *à la russe*.[19] Indeed, Kliuchevskii's ideas were not new in the Russian context. Another famous Russian intellectual, the decidedly Romantic and very Russian Alexander Herzen, had already put similar ideas into practice in his memoir *Past and Thoughts*, a brilliant example of nineteenth-century Russian historical writing. Herzen wrote: "I myself never seek to avoid digressions and episodes—every conversation proceeds that way, life itself proceeds that way."[20] And *Past and Thoughts* proceeds that way.

"*Life itself proceeds that way.*" Although Tarkovskii wrote about *Andrei Rublev* only sporadically in his book *Sculpting in Time*, his worldview was clear and representative of the postmodern approach to history:

> Had we gone for reconstruction of the picturesque tradition of the picturesque world of those times, the result would have been a stylised, conventional Russian world.... But for cinema that is not the right way....
>
> [You may be] rewarded with superficial acclaim: "Ah, what a feeling for the period!" "Ah, what cultivated people!" But you will be killing cinema.[21]

Such an approach is the death of history as well if one believes, as I do, that the detail is merely window-dressing that can obscure the meaning.

In *Andrei Rublev*, Tarkovskii succeeded in challenging convention. His "strange enough spectacle"[22] is a superb piece of post-utopian, postmodern filmmaking. By emphasizing the fragmentary quality of historical knowledge, he helps us to understand that the past is not orderly, but confusing, contradictory, cruel, and paradoxical. As Tarkovskii suggests in *Andrei Rublev*, no history, not even Russian history, is a "Holy Mystery," nor is it an epic tale of heroes and triumphs. There is no one meta-narrative.

But Tarkovskii by no means devalues the past by junking the conventions of those who see themselves its guardians. On the contrary, he sees the quest for the elusive and ultimately unknowable as nonetheless crucial for humanity's survival. How can it be that after all these years Rublev's Trinity icon is still "alive and understandable?"[23] Is it because "history is the real present,"[24] so deeply a part of all humans that it can never truly be "past"? If there is a message in *Andrei Rublev*, perhaps it is this.

notes

The research for this article was supported in part by the International Studies Program of the University of Vermont; my thanks to my research assistant Emil Lazarov. I am also grateful to Vida T. Johnson, Peter Kenez, Lisa Kernan, Frank Manchel, and Vivian Sobchack for their careful readings of a prior version of this essay.

1. *Andrei Rublev*. Produced by Mosfilm, 1964–66 [released 1969-71]; directed by Andrei Tarkovskii; screenplay by Andrei Mikhalkov-Konchalovskii and Andrei Tarkovskii; cinematography by Vadim Iusov; music by Viacheslav Ovchinnikov; art direction by E. Cherniaev; sets by E. Korablev; historical advisors: V. Pashuto, S. Iamshchikov, M. Mertsalova.

   Cast: Anatolii Solonitsyn (Andrei Rublev); Ivan Lapikov (Kirill); Nikolai Ginko (Daniil); Nikolai Sergeev (Feofan the Greek); Nikolai Burlaev (Boris); Irma Raush (the Holy Fool); Rolan Bykov (the jester); Mikhail Konov (Foma) Iurii Nazarov (the Great Prince and his brother). Russian with English subtitles; black and white/color; running time, 185 minutes. Distributed by Corinth; video by Fox Lorber Home Video.
2. For this term, and indeed for inspiration, I am indebted to Boris Groys's fascinating book *The Total Art of Stalinism: Avant-Garde, Aesthetic Dictatorship, and Beyond*, trans. Charles Rougle (Princeton, NJ: Princeton University Press, 1992).
3. The director had won international acclaim with his diploma film, *Ivan's*

Childhood, in 1962, though as Vida Johnson has pointed out in a letter to the author, Soviet critics never considered *Ivan's Childhood* to be "realistic" in the traditions of Socialist Realism.

4. Tarkovskii suffered the further indignity of seeing this already truncated version cut by forty more minutes in U.S. release for commercial, rather than political, reasons. For a good discussion of the problems Tarkovskii had making the film see Maya Turovskaya, *Tarkovskii*, trans. Natasha Ward, ed. Ian Christie (London: Faber and Faber, 1989), 46–49. The newly available Corinth/Fox Lorber version has been restored to the "original" 185 minutes.
5. It is mentioned in passing in virtually every history of post-Stalin film; see, e.g., the references in Anna Lawton, *Kinoglasnost: Soviet Cinema in Our Time* (Cambridge: Cambridge University Press, 1992); Andrew Horton and Michael Brashinsky, *The Zero Hour: Glasnost and Soviet Cinema in Transition* (Princeton, NJ: Princeton University Press, 1992); Graham Petrie and Ruth Dwyer, eds., *Before the Wall Came Down: Soviet and East European Filmmakers Working in the West* (Lanham, MD: University Press of America, 1990). For examples of more extended, explicitly political treatments, see Albert Leong, "Socialist Realism in Tarkovsky's *Andrei Rublev*," *Studies in Comparative Communism* 17, nos. 3/4 (Fall/Winter 1984): 227–33; Maria Ratschewa, "The Messianic Power of Pictures: The Films of Andrei Tarkovsky," *Cinéaste* 13, no. 1 (1983): 27–29. Interestingly enough, as Frank Manchel has noted in correspondence with the author, the film has been most highly regarded by film scholars who do not specialize in Soviet cinema; see, e.g., Nigel Andrews's October 1973 review in *Monthly Film Bulletin* 204 (October 1973), where he refers to the film's "awesome reputation" and calls it "the one indisputable masterpiece of the last decade." A very recent and laudatory Russian viewpoint which focuses on the film as a paradigm for the 1960s can be found in Lev Anninskii, *Shestidesiatniki i my: Kinematograf, stavshii i ne stabshii istoriei* (Moscow: Soiuz kinematografistov SSSR, 1991), 190–201; my thanks to Vida Johnson for bringing this to my attention. Johnson and Graham Petrie are at work on a book on Tarkovskii.
6. Mikhail Alpatov, who does not admire Tarkovskii's inventions in the film, has himself made a great deal out of very little hard data in his monograph *Andrei Rublev: Okolo 1370–1430* (Moscow: Iskusstvo, 1972), and earlier in the anthology under his editorship *Andrei Rublev i ego epokha* (Moscow: Iskusstvo, 1971). In English, see Tamara Talbot Rice, *A Concise History of Russian Art* (New York: Praeger, 1963), 113–24.
7. In Russian "Great Prince" is *velikii kniaz*. "Grand Duke," as most translations have it, is misleading in that it obscures the differences between Russia and the West: there were no duchies or dukes in Russia, only principalities and princes.
8. Or "The Buffoon."
9. "Theophanes" in the Corinth/Fox Lorber version.
10. A title which undoubtedly referred to the most uncontrollable of feelings, passion, rather than the Passion that Tarkovskii shows here.
11. For a discussion of crucifixion symbolism, see Linda J. Ivanits, *Russian Folk Belief* (Armonk, NY: M.E. Sharpe, 1989), 21, 137. Ivanits's excellent book provides explanation for many of the folk practices and symbols seen in *Andrei Rublev*; a cultural anthropologist would have a field day.
12. Translated in the Corinth/Fox Lorber version as "The Holiday," which is somewhat misleading.
13. Ivanits, *Russian Folk Belief*, 6, 10–11.
14. This character is called the "idiot" in the Corinth/Fox Lorber translation, which obscures her significance in Russian medieval culture. See James H. Billington, *The Icon and the Axe: An Interpretive History of Russian Culture* (New York: Vintage, 1966), 59.
15. Russia was called "Rus" in the fifteenth century.
16. As Vida Johnson has noted, letter to author.

17. For a brief summary of the critical reception, see Turovskaya, *Tarkovsky*, 48.
18. See Ferro, *Cinema and History*, trans. Naomi Greene (Detroit, MI: Wayne State University Press, 1988), 47.
19. It is not coincidental that Ferro also disparages Kliuchevskii in the same sentence in which he dismisses *Andrei Rublev*.
20. Herzen, quoted in Lydia Chukovskaya, *To the Memory of Childhood*, trans. Eliza Kellogg Klose (Evanston, IL: Northwestern University Press, 1988), v.
21. Andrey Tarkovsky, *Sculpting in Time: Reflections on the Cinema*, trans. Kitty Hunter-Blair (New York: Alfred A. Knopf, 1987), 78.
22. Tarkovsky, 79.
23. Tarkovsky.
24. Mira and Antonin Liehm, in their discussion of *Andrei Rublev*, make the interesting observation that Tarkovskii regarded "history as the real present." See their *The Most Important Art: East European Film after 1945* (Berkeley: University of California Press, 1977), 308.

eight

subject positions, speaking positions

from *holocaust, our hitler,* and *heimat* to *shoah* and *schindler's list*

thomas elsaesser

history, representation, cinema

History, when it is not just what's past, but what is being passed on, seems to have entered a conceptual twilight zone, not least because it has become a past that cinema and television can "master" for us by digitally remastering archival material.[1] While memory, especially when contrasted with history, has gained in value as a subject of public interest and interpretation, history has become the very signifier of the inauthentic, merely designating what is left when the site of memory has been vacated by the living. With the audio-visual media effortlessly re-present-ing that site, however, the line where memory passes into history has becomes uncertain, and the label "postmodern" is used to designate the fact that the divide is being crossed and recrossed in either direction. For how authentic is memory, even when events are still attached to a subject? "When I say 'I remember my fifth birthday', what I mean is: 'I remember the last time I told about remembering my fifth birthday'."[2] Or what of the memory of events which live in the culture because of the images they have left, etched on our retinas, too painful to recall, too disturbing not to remember? "Do you remember the day Kennedy was shot?" really means "Do you remember the day you watched Kennedy being shot all day on television?" No longer is storytelling the culture's meaning-making response; an activity closer to therapeutic practice has taken over, with acts of re-telling, re-membering, and repeating all pointing in the direction of obsession, fantasy, trauma. If civil wars, communal strife, and tribal violence suggest a compulsion to repeat at the level of action—because buried memories, rekindled by fresh hatred and local grievance, seek to re-dress wrongs suffered centuries ago—what obscure urge is soothed by the compulsion to repeat so typical of television? Perhaps it is not unconnected with the prevalence of events at once so apparently senseless and so predictably routine that neither narratives nor images seem able to encompass them.[3]

What part has the cinema had to play in this? In the case of the Vietnam War, movies have not given us the history, or even histories, but *The Deer Hunter* (Michael Cimino, 1978), *Apocalypse Now* (Francis Ford Coppola, 1979), *Full Metal Jacket* (Stanley Kubrick, 1987), *Platoon* (Oliver Stone, 1986) and *Dear America—Letters from Vietnam* (William Couturie, 1987). Those movies are re-enactments without credible closure, attempts at exorcism without promise of redemption. Yet because of these films and others like them, the "Vietnam experience" has taken on a shape, an identity, and a texture (for the United States, at least) that makes its history both possible and "academic," in the sense that the legend has established its own reality alongside the "truth" as in John Ford's *The Man Who Shot Liberty Valance* (1962).[4]

In this respect, the United States has been fortunate to have a public art (the cinema) that may be said to have done "mourning work" on behalf of the nation, thus allowing the Vietnam war to enter "history" and not just the history books. Not all peoples are either as lucky or as bold. One only has to think of Japan, a country that appears until recently not even to have begun reflecting on the fact that the memory others have of it requires opening up its "history" to outside scrutiny. Germany, on the other hand, has often either invited such scrutiny or has not been allowed by others to forget events that cannot be contained in consensus accounts or exempted from contested representation. The crimes of Nazism have demanded voicing and recollecting, be it by giving testimony or by acts of commemoration.[5]

In this light, one can examine the larger questions Steven Spielberg's *Schindler's List* (1993) raises, a movie that was made into a cultural event partly by opening so shortly after the opening of the Holocaust Museum in

Washington. These questions exceed the semantic field insinuated by the director's mega-hit *Jurassic Park* (1992): that the Holocaust might have become history's last theme park, because they touch the status of representation in contemporary culture in general, while in particular, they also involve the gesture of deference extended by Spielberg's film towards Claude Lanzmann's *Shoah* (1985), and link that to Lanzmann's violent rejection of both Spielberg's film and gesture. The collision between the two films implies aesthetic, moral, as well as religious differences, but it also includes that almost constitutive division in film history between Hollywood and Europe, itself a scene where the same drama seems destined to be played out over and over again. I want to take this case, and look once more at the relationship between historical events and their representations, but also at what it means to bear witness—especially when public history has inevitably superseded personal memory—and to speak for someone, or find oneself spoken by someone, in the medium of cinema.

If a need for speaking, for rendering accounts beyond any hope of settling them, imposes itself this century, above all for "Auschwitz," it is because the name has come to stand for so many questions relative to both history and the "end of history." But one of the most persistent questions has been, paradoxically, whether Auschwitz can stand for anything at all other than itself in its stark, ungraspable singularity. As such, it has become the touchstone of a number of debates around representation, or rather, it stands at the center of representation because it marks the very limit of representation.[6] The *Schindler's List/Shoah* controversy is thus not merely about to show or not to show (no pun intended).

Literary theorists have long discussed the paradoxical nature of an event such as the Holocaust that defies representation and yet demands it with equal finality.[7] Even when agreed that conventional narrative "emplotments" are inappropriate to an experience so unique and extreme as Auschwitz, the question remains of whether its singularity is betrayed by any account *other* than one of uncompromising literalness, where only the survivors' testimony, only names, dates can be allowed to speak, along with the documentary records of numbers and chronology.[8] Does not the very meaning-defying dimension of these horrors and their place in history create a duty to find ways of speaking about them, new discourses?[9] On one side are those who believe that in order to preserve the silence of respect, of honor to the dead, and in order to record the "permanent scar on the face of humanity," all forms of fictional narrative, dramatization, and figurative speech must be qualified as *mis*representations, not least because such forms imply a presence where there can only be absence.[10] On the other side, there is the fear that such literalness might itself be merely a mode of representation, a rhetoric which will confine the events to a fast receding point in time, thus preventing the possibility for invoking their actuality when similar barbarities of ethnic cleansing once more defy understanding and defeat the will to action.

This dilemma between representation and its limits is part of a philosophical discourse. In a now-famous simile, Jean-François Lyotard compared Auschwitz to "an earthquake [that] destroys not only lives, buildings, and objects but also the instruments used to measure earthquakes directly or indirectly."[11] Lyotard seems to suggest that between the hope of safeguarding the reality of Auschwitz through a form like realism, however epistemologically compromised, and the despair of remaining silent in the face of the incomprehensible, there may have to be a "sublation," or double negation: the effort to "preserve the fact that the unrepresentable exists."[12]

Given the gravity of this directive, it would seem sheer presumption even to ask whether the cinema has a part to play in mapping out the moral or conceptual space of the unrepresentable.[13] Much of the force of the injunction against misrepresentation, for instance, relies implicitly on a religiously grounded *Bilderverbot* (iconomachy), itself at least in part an acknowledgment of the power of images to elicit "effects of melodrama, sentimentality, prurience," debased and secularized responses to the divine power to exalt or move to fear and trembling.[14] It is this injunction that *Schindler's List* has transgressed, by the very fact of its existence.[15] One critic concluded his review of the film by urging, "we should never forget that in its short history [the cinema] has regularly appealed to fascists, the ideology that treasured showmanship."[16] Similarly, the most incisive and critical study of the "new discourse" on fascism, Saul Friedlander's *Reflections of Fascism,* relies for its examples heavily (though not exclusively) on the cinema.[17] Yet several European films have tried to grapple with fascism and the Holocaust in a spirit of critical commitment and even moral anguish, from Alain Resnais's *Night and Fog* (1955) to Hans Jürgen Syberberg's *Our Hitler* (1977). Many of them have done so *precisely by* focusing on the issue of representation. Jean-Marie Straub's *Not Reconciled* (1965), for instance, and Edgardo Cozarinsky's *One Man's War* (1981) painstakingly juxtapose sound and image in order to mark the gaps between the represented, the spoken, and the referential.

The overtly commercial or popular films of the past twenty years that have dared to represent the horrors of Nazism have not all been sensationalist. *Schindler's List* may be a rare example of a dramatization of ghetto life or of the "reality" of the camps, but it is not unique. Films made by Czech (Zbynek Brynych's *Transport from Paradise*, 1962), Polish (Andrzej Munk's *The Passenger*, 1963), and East (Konrad Wolf's *Sterne*, 1966) and West German directors (Peter

Lilienthal's *David*, 1978) come to mind.[18] As many commentators have noted, had *Schindler's List* been made in any of the Eastern European countries, or by anyone other than Spielberg, it probably would have passed unnoticed.[19]

More to the point, perhaps, is the question of whether the "effects of melodrama, sentimentality [and] prurience" do indeed constitute "limits" which any discussion of representation may have to confront, including one that takes Auschwitz as its starting point. However colored by negative judgments of taste and decorum these effects are, they connote an affectivity, and therefore an aspect of subjectivity, crucial not just to the cinema. Emotions, one could argue, ought to belong to any engagement with matters of life and death on the part of both those whom history has given the role of spectators and those who are charged with passing on compassion and preserving memory. *Schindler's List* has had some of its most fervent advocates among non-film specialists who argue that there is a need to invest history with such feelings and that the cinematic resources of drama, melodrama, suspense, and violence are legitimate means when deployed towards these ends:

> As a contribution to popular culture, it can only do good. Holocaust denial may or may not be a major problem in the future, but Holocaust ignorance, Holocaust forgetfulness and Holocaust indifference are bound to be, and *Schindler's List* is likely to do as much as any single work can to dispel them.[20]

This has a slightly patronizing air, suggesting that emotion is something the ignorant and the lazy need in order not to forget. But discussions of melodrama have also offered a more sophisticated analysis of the relation between representation and affect, and affect as representation, in the forcefield of the said and the unsaid, the excessive and the repressed. It is important, then, to understand the rhetorical tropes by which presence and absence, inclusion and exclusion signify each other.[21] Another non-film specialist, Bryan Cheyette, has argued that *Shoah* and *Schindler's List* are

> diametrically opposed representations [which are nonetheless] intimately related. What Lanzmann rightly insists is impossible to represent on screen, Spielberg does his best to put on screen. Much to Lanzmann's irritation, testimony contained in *Shoah* is turned into images in *Schindler's List*. For this reason, the popular realism and sentimentalism of *Schindler's List* cocks a snook at Lanzmann's intellectually unanswerable, but unrelenting, modernist scepticism.[22]

While the balancing act of this passage shows how difficult a terrain the juxtaposition of realism, melodrama, and modernism confronts, it is made more difficult still by polarizing the representation of fascism in the cinema across the divide between modernism and postmodernism. In this respect, I think Friedlander is right, for instance, to reject arguments that might seem to defend works by German filmmakers, say Syberberg's *Our Hitler*, or Fassbinder's *Lili Marleen* (1980) (two films Friedlander finds particularly problematic) on the grounds that they are deconstructive, pastiche or postmodern works; he is right to insist that the dominant modes of emotional engagement in these two films are indeed those of fascination, kitsch, nostalgia, and melodrama. However, Friedlander's argument is based on a modernist position which is as distrustful of any kind of "mimetic" affective engagement as it is aware of the inadequacies of conventional realist narrative. But insofar as the aesthetics of impersonality and understatement constitute his implicit representational norm, it is not unproblematic that so many of Friedlander's examples are drawn from the cinema. The film experience is, par excellence, a site of mimetic emotions. Its ambiguous, libidinally charged play of identifications is therefore responding to a "melodramatic" interpretation more obviously than a "modernist" hermeneutics. Cinema, in this respect, is on the side of the excessive, perverse, or compulsive, rather than ruled by an aesthetics of detachment and distance.[23] Even *Shoah*, a limit case both by its length and its methods of gathering evidence, is committed to a rhetoric of pathos, irony, and affect.[24] In this respect, the films perhaps are postmodern, but this question needs first to be confronted with a history, in particular with the history of the representations of fascism.

show time for hitler

All cinema, but German cinema in particular, has had an especially ambivalent relation with Nazism. This is true not only because, as I shall argue, the German "speaking position" is at stake, even without a debate about modes of representation getting in the way. Since "never before and in no other country have images and language been abused so unscrupulously,"[25] the fact that German fascism has left a more complete account than any previous regime of itself and its version of history in images and sound means that its specular self-presentation becomes part of what one could call the representational reality of Nazism. Moreover, German fascism was the first political ideology which borrowed the materials, the techniques, and the mise-en-scène of its self-image from the cinema and show-business. Fabric and drapery, floodlights and recorded sound, scaffolding and plaster became the preferred props and elements. What has been called *Stimmungsarchitektur* (mood-architecture) found its way from stage and screen into public life. As a result, cinematic representations of Nazism *after* Nazism are of necessity involved in a dimension of self-reference or *mise-en-abyme*. They are confronted with a choice of evils: either adhere to a stringent form of understatement and visual asceticism in order to counter the visual pleasure and seduction emanating from the regime's spectacular stagings of itself, or expose the viewer once more to the fascination, making the emotional charge residing in these images part of the subject matter itself.[26] While the rhetoric of sobriety and understatement became itself a clichéd way of dealing with fascism in post-war documentaries, the presentation of the fascination "from within" was precisely the mark of the "new discourse" detected by Friedlander in Italian, French, and German films of the 1970s. Yet regardless of the filmmakers' intentions, the regime's self-representation, its eroticization of power and charisma, is not only a "reality" with which filmmakers have had to engage; it is also a "signifier" of Nazism from which they could not escape. In this sense, visual fascination is as present in the German films made about Nazism in the late 1940s and 1950s, where a *film noir* atmosphere signified the "demonic" quality of Hitler and his henchmen, as it is when a more contemporary filmmaker practices an "aesthetics of resistance" against specular seduction, as did Jean-Marie Straub in *Not Reconciled*.

The watershed which signaled renewed interest in fascism as a film subject came around 1970 when Luchino Visconti's *The Damned* (1969) and Bernardo Bertolucci's *The Conformist* (1970) chose to do battle on the enemy's terrain, so to speak—the territory of fascination, sex, death, violence—not least because the enemy was also the enemy within: the cinematic self in another guise. The representational reality of this self rather than its historical meaning was what made fascism material for a certain (idea of) cinema in the first place. This in turn signaled the crisis of another and previous (idea of) cinema: that of neo-realism. This choice of topic, we have to assume, was neither naïve nor speculative, but one that recognized the legacy of Nazi aesthetics (even where its politics had lost its appeal) in present-day commodity culture, also given to conspicuous waste and spectacular destruction. In the age of the blockbuster, who does not recognize the seductive appeal of creating a substitute world, of treating power as a work of art, in short, of the *eros* and *thanatos* of objectification? Visconti and Bertolucci spoke to these thoughts, unequivocally.

But what about popular or commercial films, like Bob Fosse's *Cabaret* (1972) or Mel Brooks's *The Producers* (1968), which also made much of the affinity between fascism and show business, underlining this "aesthetization" of politics, already critical to Walter Benjamin, and later also analyzed by Susan Sontag?[27] Do they not confirm Friedlander's worry that the lure of kitsch and death carries over into films using fascism as a pretext for a love intrigue? Doesn't *Cabaret*'s spectacle of putting-on-a-show, or *The Producers*' song-and-dance routines, and especially its parodies of goose-stepping Nazis in a production number called "Springtime for Hitler," make light of the obscenity of a regime that put on the mask of entertainment and glamour, so as to hide the energy it put into destruction, terror, and contempt for human life?

Perhaps Liza Minnelli's Sally Bowles in *Cabaret* can serve both as an example and a counter-example. In the story of the night-club performer's friendship and entanglement with a homosexual Englishman and his lovers, several themes emerge which do and do not have to do with the nascent fascism that forms the backdrop, one of which is that of the fascination with the "other," the oscillation between alien and familiar. That the film portrayed Germans of all classes and convictions in a sympathetic, or at any rate non-judgmental, light was motivated by the central character's foreign perspective, and it marked a significant enough shift in Hollywood representations of Germans. But it was the fact that the film dared to use its Nazi setting for a musical that considerably raised the stakes. The association of such a sinister chapter of history with jazzy music seemed designed to court the charge of trivialization. Yet the radical shift in genre from somber Wagnerian music drama (for instance, in *The Damned*) to light entertainment was defiant in several respects: it made a claim for popular music and the musical as genre to be taken "seriously" (a complex cultural process that had taken place during the 1960s on a very wide front), and it also argued that sexuality be granted a "political" dimension. *Cabaret*'s discourse on perverse sexuality and dandyism as a form of political resistance cut across the stereotypical identification of fascism with sexual perversion. It opened the way for representing homosexuals as themselves a persecuted group and for understanding sexuality (in this case, the bisexuality and androgyny of the Sally Bowles figure) as a subject position that responds to this specific historical reality and embodies a form of heroism.

Cabaret's generic identity as a backstage musical about show people in Berlin on the eve of Nazism makes it a polysemic text. This polysemy, though, is not quite the same as postmodern openness. Rather, being a big budget, star-cast international commercial film, *Cabaret* tries, like all Hollywood vehicles, to address a wide audience, with very diverse entry-points into its diegetic world (including an entry-point for Germans—one of Hollywood's largest European markets—no longer willing to pay money to see their countrymen cast as cardboard villains). Instead of seeing the film suspended between critical intentions and misinterpreted reception, *Cabaret* (and its huge international success) must in the first instance be regarded a historical fact about 1972. As such, it records a number of (transgressive) cultural shifts (about popular music, gender, and sexuality) which have now become commonplaces, but which at the time perhaps needed to articulate themselves in the context of a referential world—Germany in the 1930s—which itself connoted transgression, danger, ambiguity. It could do so successfully because it rewrote a popular intertext, *The Blue Angel* (Josef von Sternberg, 1930), famous for (heterosexual) decadence in 1920s Germany. *Cabaret* represented its diegetic universe as a blend of youth, the politics of the street, impending apocalypse, and sexual adventure, suggesting a number of *Zeitgeist* parallels between the 1930s and the 1970s, that however shallow they may seem to a social historian, allowed the film to have a multi-vocal speaking position made coherent by its star, Liza Minnelli, who successfully "addressed" an audience.

It is easy to see how such an argument can also be made for *Schindler's List*. Spielberg's hero Schindler, as becomes clear well before the end-credits which dedicate the film to Steve Ross, the late Chief Executive Officer of Time-Warner, is a gambler, a risk-taker, a showman, whose hour of fame and moral courage is intimately connected to a situation of war, but is seen as any period in which the "real economy" is overlaid or suspended by a kind of "symbolic economy" of brinkmanship, bluff, and bravado—familiar to 1990s viewers from a more recent decade of mega-deals, merger-mania, and junk bonds. It is Schindler's self-definition (in his first major scene with Itzakh Stern) as the man who brings the knack of "presentation" to an otherwise banal transaction that allows the audience to "recognize" him, and, from then on, make his motivation as psychologically coherent as any Hollywood narrative requires.

taking back neo-realism

This move could be identified as typical of the new "discourse of fascism": an amalgam of kitsch and sentimentality, violence and nostalgia, adventure and show. One might counter that such is the emotional stuff the cinema has been accused of from its beginning, which no doubt is what led to the notion—half argued, as we saw, in reviews of *Schindler's List*, but already voiced two decades ago by Hans Jürgen Syberberg—that the cinema is inherently fascist. But such a perspective, while worth considering, is somewhat foreshortened.

A missing link in the debate, to my mind, is the fact that through the topic of fascism, the European art cinema of the 1970s and 1980s (particularly the Italian cinema) decisively broke with realism, the dominant post-war representational mode, whether one thinks of the neo-realism of Rossellini and De Sica or the realist ideology of virtually all the "new" cinemas of the 1950s and 1960s in France, Britain, Poland, or West Germany. Visconti's *The Damned*, Bertolucci's *1900* (1976), or Fellini's *Roma* (1972) had, in a sense, "taken back" neo-realism (which of course, in such textbook examples as Rossellini's *Open City* (1945) or Visconti's *Ossessione* (1943) was itself essentially melodramatic).[28] Moreover, these directors had made a subjectively slanted, melodramatically or operatically spectacular representation of history the dominant model of filmic representation.[29] With it, the Bazinian notion of the morality of cinema ("truth 24 times a second" as Godard put it) entered into a profound mutation, one that increasingly (in film theory) focused on the constructed or semiotic nature of realism and (in filmmaking) explored the media reality which the ubiquity of television, video, and their enormously enhanced power of imaging had created. This probing of the new image worlds of electronic reproduction and the breakdown of the divide between "inner" and "outer" reality which they entail is still the major preoccupation of the cinema, and it has brought an as yet unabated turn to melodramatic, erotico-pornographic, horror, and fantasy subjects, as typical of the post-1970s Hollywood as it is of contemporary European cinema.

Thus, one can, with some justification, identify within these major shifts and reorientations of both popular cinema and art/auteur cinema (shifts which postmodernism has tried, not altogether successfully, to theorize) a tendency in the 1970s that, especially for European filmmakers, made fascism a preferred reference point: Visconti and Bertolucci were followed, in quick succession, by Louis Malle's *Lacombe Lucien* (1973), Liliana Cavani's *The Night Porter* (1974), Lina Wertmuller's *Seven Beauties* (1976), Joseph Losey's *M. Klein* (1976), Ingmar Bergman's *The Serpent's Egg* (1978), and François Truffaut's *The Last Metro* (1980). Although these films hardly form a genre or even a coherent group, there are enough areas of contact to invite a more systematic analysis of their preoccupation with Nazi emblems, Nazi iconography, and the building up of a kind of stock repertoire of architectural props, clothes, haircuts, and accessories that began to function as instant signifiers of fascism.[30]

Such an analysis can proceed from different perspectives and, consequently, construct different "objects of study." Looking at the afterlife which Nazism appeared to lead in the popular media generally, Friedlander saw the films, with their ambiguous celebration of style detached from a clear moral and historical stance, confirm a dangerous confusion between critical distance in historical understanding and a form of exorcism that seemed to end up playing the devil's advocate.[31] Other analyses sprang from nationally specific points; for instance, the realization that quite a radical change in attitude had occurred in France with respect to the Occupation period and the Resistance. Michel Foucault attributed it to the demise of Gaullism in 1968–69 which dissolved the strategic post-war alliance de Gaulle had forged between the nationalist right (government-in-exile) and the collaborationist right (Pétain and Vichy). What Foucault feared from the sympathetic portrayal of collaboration (in *Lacombe Lucien*) and the revelations of just how widespread and highly placed collaboration had been in occupied France (in Marcel Ophuls's *The Sorrow and the Pity* [1970]) was not the glamorization of Nazism, but a negation of the Resistance, together with the denial of popular (socialist) struggles, and thus an erosion of what he called "popular memory."[32]

Jean Baudrillard, taking a characteristically wide sweep, analyzed the phenomenon in the context of a general nostalgia and detected in the cinema's "retro-fashion" a distinct "retro-scenario": Western Europe, locked into the political stasis of the Cold War, with the intelligentsia demoralized by the post-1968 defeat of its revolutionary dreams, nostalgically imagines through the cinema a time where a country's history still meant individual victims, still signified causes that mattered and decisions of life and death. The attraction of a return to history as story and image was the illusion it could give of a personal or national destiny: a need fascism had tried to gratify on a collective scale. For Baudrillard, too, retro-cinema was therefore less a move towards coming to terms with the past than the fetishization if not of fascinating fascism, then of another trauma located in the present: the absence of history altogether.[33]

historicizing vs. relativizing: different theories of fascism

What the debate about retro-fashion, nostalgia, and historicism highlights with respect to Nazism is a certain deficit in the traditional or even scholarly accounts of Fascism, a historical experience which, precisely, has lost none of its topicality at the end of the twentieth century. To the extent, however, that it is an historical experience, which in Europe alone has profoundly affected millions of people, it matters whether it is analyzed by historians, by ethnographers and psychoanalysts, or indeed by filmmakers and film scholars.

Historians in the 1970s became embroiled in what later was called the "fascism-debate," opposing "intentionalists" (German fascism as the systematic implementation of Hitler's racist and imperialist goals) and "functionalists" (Nazism as the ad-hoc alliance of divergent socio-economic interests, held together only after Hitler had declared war and bonded to the Führer by criminal complicity in the "Final Solution"). This gave way to the historians' debate of the 1980s, when Jürgen Habermas detected in the writings of certain German scholars (notably Ernst Nolte and Andreas Hillgruber) a revisionist project that was designed to relativize the Nazi period in order to "normalize" it, by comparing the extermination of the Jews to other genocides before (Stalin's gulags, the Ottoman massacre of the Armenian nation) and after (Idi Amin, Pol Pot).[34]

The latter argument became crucial to the issue of historical representation around the limit case of Nazism, because it was the reverse side of the attempt, so prevalent among German historians, to keep distinct the representation of the "Third Reich" from the representation of the Holocaust.

Precisely because these two realities are mutually interdependent and inextricably bound together *in history*, it is important to understand how and why they have been played off and against each other or are regarded separately in historical, narrative, or fictional representations. One of the tell-tale signs, for instance, of an apologetic discourse has always been to separate the "internal" history of the "Third Reich" from its "external" policies (the war, the extermination of the Jews) by pointing out that Hitler achieved the unification and modernization of Germany (where Bismarck and the Weimar Republic had failed) before the war undid it all. Another sign of an apologetic discourse is the argument that since out of a population of 700,000 German Jews "only" about 250,000 perished in the camps (and most of them in the years 1942–45), the majority of Holocaust victims died as a direct or indirect consequence of the war and therefore must be seen in the context of the exceptional situation created by war.[35]

On the other hand, an argument that sees the "Final Solution" not only as the implicit "telos" of Nazism, but as the single reality that informed every aspect of Nazi Germany from 1933 onwards risks separating Hitler's racial policy from the regime's other principal aims: the "overcoming" of democracy, the subversion and destruction of communism and organized labor, the domination of Europe by the German Reich, and the attainment of world-power status. That it nearly "succeeded" in one of its aims, the destruction of European Jewry, does not make the "failed" objectives any less part of the representational reality of the "Third Reich." But then so are other representational realities that may have to be looked at separately from any of the overt political and ideological aims of Nazism in order to grasp their meaning and connection with Nazism. Hans Dieter Schäfer, for instance, has analyzed some of the contradictory "life worlds" existing side by side in Germany during the 1930s and 1940s, which include such popular cultural phenomena as a lively trade in jazz and swing records, even though they were officially banned, or the thriving tourism by sea and road to countries (including the USA) on which Germany was to declare war. What Schäfer calls "everyday schizophrenia" becomes a little less inexplicable when seen against Nazism's (successful) promotion of a consumer culture which reconciled many Germans to the regime's curtailment of civil liberties.[36]

Such historical "revisionism" has itself to be seen in the broader context of "historicizing fascism." Initially, this had been the goal of Marxist analysis. One remembers Max Horkheimer's dictum from the 1930s: "He who does not wish to speak of capitalism should also be silent about fascism," taken up after the war in order to counter the "demonization" and personalization of fascism in the figure of Hitler.[37] The notion of Hitler as a uniquely aberrant individual and the Nazi elite as a gang of common criminals sanctioned the screening out of the political and economic factors that had made fascism part of the modernizing forces of industrialization and the crisis cycles of finance capitalism. Furthermore, it exculpated those sections of German society that had helped Nazism to power and had maintained it there, notably the banking establishment and heavy industry, the judiciary, the army, and the civil service. Declaring *tabula rasa* in 1945 allowed the Adenauer government to make its peace with most of these sections, a fact to which several of Jean-Marie Straub's protagonists are, precisely, *Not Reconciled.*

However, by the early 1970s the "historicizing" argument had moved on to focus on the inadequacies of the structural or conjunctural models that Marxists had been putting forward. Instead of calling fascism the "crisis management" of capitalism, the "new" debates either stressed the European or international dimension of the phenomenon (for instance, by taking up the earlier theses of Ernst Nolte[38]) or they gave the psychic-libidinal dimension a greater weight (Alexander Mitscherlich's attempt to explain, for instance, the allegiance of the masses to the Führer[39]). While the first argument has surfaced again in the historians' debate, the second, psychoanalytic approach did not find favor with historians, but was hugely influential among writers and filmmakers, especially in West Germany. Hence the paradox that a "theory of fascism," regarded as almost irrelevant by professional historians, came to assume a major cultural and explanatory power for filmmakers and film historians and led to the posited affinity of modern cinema and fascism.

In the European art cinema, the analogy was elaborated, but also limited, along at least three quite distinct lines: as the theme of specular seduction, show-business, and the technology of sight and sound (*The Last Metro, Lili Marleen*); as sexuality, in its vitalist, gendered and perverse dimensions (*The Conformist, Seven Beauties, The Night Porter*); and finally, as the loss of self, melancholy, and "mourning work" (*The Serpent's Egg, Despair* [Fassbinder, 1978], *M. Klein*).[40] At the same time, one needs to be cautious about the label "European." France, Italy, Germany: each country's cinema recorded these affinities and mirror-images in distinctive ways. While in Italian films, class decadence and deviant sexuality became major issues (*The Damned, Salo* [Pier Paolo Pasolini, 1975]), in German films, it was often the family and patriarchy that found themselves scrutinized via the Nazi setting (*Germany Pale Mother* [Helma Sanders-Brahms, 1979], *Lili Marleen*). As the divergent explanations offered by Baudrillard or Foucault show, even within one country, the specificity of historical reference must be addressed, or conversely, the films' polysemy needs to be seen within generic or institutional frameworks. If there is indeed a new discourse (as opposed to several discourses), and one symptomatic for the whole of Europe, it has to test itself through determined historical, generic, or geographical representations, not against them.

Among German historians, the ambiguity was a different one. A problematic symmetry opened up between those whose moral conscience insisted on the uniqueness and singularity of the Holocaust and those who in an ideological move wanted to make the same claim of uniqueness for Hitler and his regime in order to absolve the generations before and after from responsibility. Yet since any argument that would isolate the period of Nazism from the rest of German history was unsustainable on both historical and moral grounds, the conservative right put forward its own demand for historicizing fascism. This time, however, not in order to point to the continuities of fascism with Germany's social structure throughout most of its modern history, but in an attempt to relativize Hitler's policies, to compare the regime's crimes to those of other totalitarianisms, and, as already indicated, thereby to "contextualize" the Final Solution.

This skewed symmetry was to haunt West German public attitudes to recent German history throughout the 1970s and 1980s.[41] It is the soil on which the new (apologetic) right has grown, but it is in some sense also the background to West German filmmakers' critical turn to fascism as a film subject. Compared to what may or may not have been the motives in France and Italy, theirs was a more complex story of reaction, regrouping, and response. The New German cinema came to making fictionalized films about history late, almost a decade after Visconti's *The Damned*. For most of the 1960s and 1970s documentary approaches predominated.[42] Only when a series of political events, replete with uncanny historical parallels, led Alexander Kluge early in 1978 to gather together a number of his colleagues to make the film *Germany in Autumn* (1978) can one detect a different kind of self-reflexiveness in the cinema's relation to the fascist legacy, and also to its possible and impossible historicizations. In this film there are two funerals—a state funeral for Hans Martin Schleyer, West Germany's boss of bosses, assassinated by the Red Army Fraction and a reluctantly granted family funeral for Gudrun Ensslin, convicted member of the RAF, who presumably committed suicide in a Stuttgart high-security prison—that provide the framework for an oblique meditation on some of the asymmetrical repetitions in recent German history.[43]

As an "omnibus film," *Germany in Autumn* attempted to combine discursive and argumentative sections with dramatizations, which may explain why it had relatively little response among the general public. Barely a year later, another fictional treatment of fascism was to have a public impact of unexpected proportions: the screening on German television of the US-produced four-part series *Holocaust*.[44] Thus, the trigger for German directors to rethink the representation of history on film came, like the defeat of fascism itself, from outside. They stood under the shock of the enormous public response, and in particular, the overwhelmingly emotional response the story of the Weiss and Dorf families elicited from German television viewers.

> An American television series [...] accomplished what hundreds of books, plays, films, and television programs, thousands of documents, and all the concentration camp trials have failed to do in the more than three decades since the end of the war: to inform Germans about crimes against Jews committed in their name, so that millions were emotionally touched and moved.[45]

The emotions touched were themselves of a complex kind; while the metaphor of "floodgates opening up" recurred almost stereotypically, and expressions of guilt, shame, and remorse were made public with sometimes hysterical and sometimes exhibitionist fervor, there was also much outrage and condemnation about the screening.[46] Filmmakers were among those who charged the series with trivialization and embarrassing sentimentality, because it represented the unrepresentable and imaged the unimaginable—the concentration camps and gas chambers. While some felt perturbed that a Hollywood soap opera on *the* German subject should have moved millions to tears when their own films had been ignored, others felt roused to respond to the challenge. Not only was it the case that, in the words of Günter Rohrbach, head of drama at Westdeutsche Rundfunk, Germany's most prestigious television network, "after *Holocaust* television can no longer be what it used to be," the New German cinema also could no longer be what it used to be.[47] In quick succession appeared Hans Jürgen Syberberg's *Our Hitler* (1977), Rainer Werner Fassbinder's *The Marriage of Maria Braun* (1978) and *Despair* (1978), Helma Sanders Brahms's *Germany Pale Mother* (1979), Alexander Kluge's *Die Patriotin* (*The Patriot*, 1979), Volker Schlöndorff's *The Tin Drum* (1979), Fassbinder's *Lili Marleen* (1980), and finally, in 1984, Edgar Reitz's 11-part *Heimat*, begun in 1979. These are still among the titles most immediately associated with the New German cinema, its identity from then on fixated—and its fate sealed, it seems—by brooding ruminations about national history and identity.

ordinary fascism

Few directors of the 1980s represented Auschwitz or the Holocaust (although a screening of Alain Resnais's *Night and Fog* plays an important role in Margarethe von Trotta' s *The German Sisters* [1981]).[48] Instead of "historicizing" fascism along the left/right divide, many of the films, especially those made for television, found a primary orientation in what among historians came to be known as *Alltagsgeschichte* (the history of everyday life). As a form of micro-analysis of history, it gave the perspective of "ordinary people," offering itself as a perspective on ways of recording life in Germany through the years between 1933 and 1945: Nazism as a daily reality, as a "normality" putting to the test individual attitudes and human behavior. Its historiographic pedigree is the French school of the *Annalistes*, in celebrated studies of the Middle Ages such as Ferdinand Braudel's *The Mediterranean and the Mediterranean World in the Age of Philip II*, or LeRoy Ladurie's *Montaillou.*[49]

Getting people to study Nazism in terms of everyday history had been a point of contention among historians since the late 1970s. Martin Broszat, for instance, had argued that, in order to be able to talk about the "Third Reich" as "the German people's own history" and thus for individuals to take responsibility for what had occurred, Germans had to cease viewing it as external and separate, and to mobilize private or family memories.[50] Rather than having people regard Hitler as the nation's pied-piper and they themselves as having acted in a trance ("the Nazi-spell" was a common term of post-war disavowal), personal stories and reminiscences had to be evoked and told in order to get out of what one historian called "the quasi-hypnotic paralysis of most of the German people with regard to the Nazi past."[51] Opponents of this viewpoint heralded it at the very least as a dangerous simplification, the return of the "barefooted historians."[52]

Several successful television series (for instance, Eberhardt Fechner's *Tadellöser & Wolf* [1974/75]) and countless documentaries were to be based on this concept, yet the international apotheosis of filmed everyday life was Edgar Reitz's *Heimat*, a film that followed the destiny of the Simon family from 1918 to 1982. If *Heimat* suggested that the German cinema, too, had recourse to melodrama for its view of history, then this was both its strength and weakness: its strength in that it reached a large audience in Germany and elsewhere, giving unusually detailed and engrossing insights into rural life before 1945; its weakness in that *Alltagsgeschichte* can indeed be apologetic in tendency if not intent. Reitz soon found himself accused of having used the revisionists' ploy for "normalization" and "routinization," especially when his decision to leave out the death camps was justified on the debatable grounds that few "ordinary" Germans would have experienced the deportations and exterminations first-hand. Jim Hoberman, for instance, spoke of "blatant tokenism" and "born-again Germany."[53] *Heimat* also confirmed Baudrillard's thesis when one considers that the insistence on the family had something of a fetish-function because it clung to a notion of the authentic in "everyday experience" as if it was a quality that could somehow be recovered and represented on film.[54]

Yet *Heimat* could also be seen as "deconstructing" some of the conservative values it appeared to extol, notably the "blood-and-soil" rootedness of its main characters and the authenticity that their close-knit family life represents. For what appears to be the motor and motive of historical change is ultimately technology and consumer culture. Reitz shows no rural, pre-industrial idyll, and instead his characters' lives and histories are transformed by modern communication technologies: the women go to the movies (to see a film called *Heimat*) and the men either spend their time with ham-radio sets, are busy with precision optics, or have a passion for still photography—when not on active duty as newsreel cinematographers on the Eastern front.

the postmodernist argument: rewriting history as film history

An equally deconstructive turn is present in another, even more controversial, response to *Holocaust*: Hans Jürgen Syberberg's *Our Hitler*. One of the central arguments of this film is that the Nazi deployment of radio broadcasts, live transmissions, mass rallies, and civilian mobilization campaigns turned the State into a twelve year state-of-emergency, experienced by many Germans as communality, participation, and direct address. Syberberg's polemical point is that Hollywood cinema and more recently television, in the name of democracy and the right to consume, have made the Riefenstahl aesthetic of *Triumph of the Will* (1935) the international television norm: politics has become a series of photo opportunities, public life a perpetual festival of presence, action, live-ness, where spectacles of destruction, or feats of prowess and the body beautiful are feeding national or individual fantasies of omnipotence. Together with Fassbinder's *Lili Marleen*—the most obvious example of a postwar German film to take Nazi history and turn it into a representational mode of excess, melodrama and contradiction—the mega-films/mini-TV series of Syberberg and Reitz might therefore qualify for the epithet "postmodern," in the sense of their three specific areas of intervention: pastiche and rewriting, show business and power, and the media reality of radio and cinema.[55] If Reitz's contribution to breaking down the divide between high culture and popular culture is a tour de force of *Alltagsgeschichte,* Fassbinder's attitude to popular culture implicitly responds to Syberberg's *Our Hitler* where an uncompromisingly high-culture proposition (that modern show business is in some sense more fascist than Nazism) underpins the rather shrill and cranky bracketing together of Hollywood cinema and Hitler.

By representing fascism and the cinema at the level of the referent by way of citation and cliché (sidestepping issues of how "accurately" a film can "deal with" fascism or "convey" its horror or seduction), these filmmakers concentrate on the (technological, emotional, rhetorical, and psychic) machinery which fascism has in common with cinema. They draw attention to one particular history of the cinema's (and television's) power-potential: that of creating a public sphere ("mobilization") and affective/emotional engagement. But where Syberberg, and indeed Reitz, differ from Fassbinder is in their barely disguised anti-Americanism, which gives them critical leverage against fascism while not obliging them to engage with the Holocaust. *Our Hitler* in particular is recognizable as the high-water mark of a certain post-1968 anti-Americanism, whose critique of Hollywood can also be found in Godard's demand for "two or three Vietnams, in the heart of the Hollywood-Mosfilm-Cinecittà-Pinewood Empire," or in the British avant-garde's calls for a "cinema of unpleasure."[56]

Once again, the parallels with the *Schindler's List/Shoah* debate are inescapable. First of all, most of the critical reactions to *Schindler's List* went over the same ground the *Holocaust* debate in Germany had raked up more than a decade earlier. First *Holocaust* and its reception posed a double problem for German filmmakers. The series had "successfully" combined the representation of the "Third Reich" with the representation of the Holocaust: it had made of it one story. Secondly, it had been able to arouse strong feelings by personalizing history, concentrating on two individual cases, juxtaposed and counterpointed, and—utilizing the strategies of Hollywood dramaturgy most discredited by film theory—it had manipulated spectator empathy and identification. Then again, it had neither "historicized" fascism in the left-wing sense, nor "relativized" it in the right-wing sense. It had not treated the Holocaust as unique either because by choosing the genre of the family melodrama it was offering identification to each and every viewer. Put differently, *Holocaust* had provided a coherent subject position, but it did so at the price of de-historicizing fascism altogether, universalizing it as a soap opera against the background of natural catastrophe.

Although *Schindler's List* is, in every respect, a more serious and sophisticated film than *Holocaust*, there are parallels, if only to the extent that both deploy melodrama, spectacle and viewer identification. Spielberg, too, presents life in the camps, and in one controversial scene he shows women undressing and entering the shower rooms. But he is careful in this scene also to direct the eye towards the background, to a long column of figures disappearing into an underground bunker that the viewer need not be told stands for the gas chambers. Here suspense and melodrama are in the service of a moment of tragic irony in which the viewer is obliged to infer what cannot be shown, while the manipulation of expectation, suspense, and relief that the women the spectators identify with were "only" sent to the shower rooms and in fact rescued by Schindler from Auschwitz creates an appropriately extreme counterpoint.

Spielberg, too, personalizes. But unlike *Holocaust* he confronts the problem of how to identify individuals and yet represent the collective. The very notion of "the list" is a powerful device to retain in view a collectivity, a group, while the repeated act of naming gives each the dignity of an individual fate. At the same time, as some critics have pointed out, Spielberg has the rare gift of imparting dramatic sweep and emotional resonance to the depiction of a crowd, notably in the scene "in which the children are trucked away to something worse, and the mothers surge forward as involuntarily as a groan."[57]

Nonetheless, the most persistent criticism of *Schindler's List* is Spielberg's focus on one individual, tilting the narrative away from the destiny and destruction of a people towards the story of Schindler, a man whom Lanzmann has called "merely a small-time German gangster."[58] Yet it is also arguable that a mode that encompasses the oblique and the unstated, along with the explicitly horrific, requires a story told "against the grain" of all the narratives we have in our heads about the Holocaust. Spielberg, while remaining within the terms of Hollywood dramaturgy, relies on some of the "classical" devices of the historical novel, filtering events through a middle-of-the-road hero, the nature of whose involvement positions him at the margins of the stage of history, neither prime mover nor victim.[59] Similarly arguable is whether the optimistic ending is a necessary device for getting the story to a mass public in the first place and thus a "concession to Hollywood," or an unforgivable insult to the six million who died during the transports and in the camps. Those who might want to reply that it makes little sense to accuse Spielberg of concession to popular taste (what is Spielberg if not the incarnation of popular mass-entertainment?) end up appearing cynical, shallow, or worse. Cheyette, for instance, concludes his piece with an exasperated *cri de coeur*: "Surely it is possible to try and comprehend both Lanzmann and Spielberg without being accused [...] of being a Holocaust 'denier.'"[60]

Given the intensity of feeling, such apparently reasonable liberalism may miss the mark: even a reviewer has to choose, it seems. But I would argue that the filmmaker *has* chosen. Above all, he has chosen for the cinema and its history: whether this makes him a postmodernist, and whether a postmodern stance makes him necessarily either morally or historically irresponsible towards the Holocaust, is a point worth pondering. In contrast to *Holocaust*, *Schindler's List* is both highly "intertextual" and "deconstructive." Spielberg is aware not only of his film's Hollywood and U.S. television predecessors, but of the European cinema from the 1970s that had fascism as its subject. Circumstantial evidence even suggests that he has also looked at some of the German films under discussion: the brief turns to color he uses were first used to similar effect by Reitz in *Heimat*. Other parallels, in particular with Fassbinder's films, also impose themselves. By bringing together an entrepreneur (Schindler), whose only gift is showmanship, and a sadistically torturing and self-tormented psychopath (Goeth), Spielberg outlines what one could indeed call a "postmodern" analysis of fascism: around the topos of absolute power and the cancelling out of values in a situation of crisis. The quasi-Dostoevskian discussion the two men have, where, according to Schindler, true power lies in pardoning a presumed transgression rather than punishing it, poses a metaphysical crux which in Goeth merely confirms the random arbitrariness of all life and human actions, while underscoring that Schindler's own power at this point arises from the fact that an economic and a moral system have been put "under erasure." The barter between supply and demand, human life and human labor, cupidity and vanity which makes the Schindler "scam" successful follows the logic of a black market, in which both currency and value have been brusquely suspended.

Like Spielberg's vision of the links between Schindler's factories and the camps, Fassbinder's emplotment of the "Third Reich" in *Lili Marleen* stresses the frighteningly surreal logic of symbolic and material exchange.[61] It designates the point where a postmodern reading of the film misses a historical dimension, precisely because Fassbinder refers himself to a specifically German film history. He makes melodrama and excess his subject not only because he wanted to address a mass audience; but because Nazism was that period in German history when, paradoxically, the division between high culture and mass culture began to seem less definite. Already in the 1930s, Ernst Bloch had warned the German left about abandoning to the right the energies inherent in popular culture.[62] In light of the "schizophrenic consciousness" alluded to above, one can see popular culture as the site of an ambiguous struggle, manifesting itself in big-budget Ufa studio films, in popular music, and in radio-broadcasts to the masses of classical music concerts. Mass culture in 1930s and 1940s assumed a new historical significance, precisely because of the enormous investments that were made in the technology of sound and vision. This general process, however, took on an added *political* and national significance because of the regional and folk cultures that were selectively taken in charge by the centralized state. The modern technologies of representation at the fascists' disposal became the material basis for calling the Nazi entertainment cinema "propaganda," not so much because of what it showed, but because of what the perpetual show *hid* from view: the fanatic ruthlessness with which the regime repressed, destroyed, and eradicated other cultures and crafts on an incalculable scale.[63] Fassbinder's black-market melodramas, from *Despair* and *Lili Marleen* to *Maria Braun* and *Berlin Alexanderplatz* (1980), record some the fallout of this wider process, even where they focus on the nuclear family and the couple: the very excess of the emotional turmoil wracking the characters points to the dislocations caused, in Fassbinder's case, by capitalism's modernization processes as well as by the first society of the spectacle it gave rise to.

Conveying a specifically Jewish point of view, *Schindler's List* has the stamping out of skills, the destruction of cult objects and cultural artifacts as one of its many themes. The tracking shots which follow the ghetto inhabitants' luggage into the recesses of the railway station (where the contents are, with assembly-line efficiency, sorted, sifted, weighed, and dismantled) are a heart-rendingly eloquent image of a culture's wholesale desecration and obliteration. Spielberg here sees the fate of the Krakow ghetto also in the context of a general devaluation of material culture which goes hand in hand with the industrialized production and warfare, the relocation, exploitation, and dehumanization of labor for which black-market conditions are both necessary prerequisites and symptomatic manifestations.

These themes, however, are also very close to *Shoah*, substantiating the gesture of acknowledgement Spielberg seems to have extended towards Lanzmann. Spielberg cites a number of specific scenes from *Shoah*, but these are in a mode so different from *Shoah* that the "modernism" of Lanzmann is put in brackets by the homage Spielberg pays him, an homage which as we saw, one critic went so far as to call "cocking a snook."[64] But this is to interpret rather narrowly a relation of some complexity, where acknowledgement of a debt goes hand in hand with what, in a somewhat different context, Harold Bloom has called "an act of creative correction that is actually and necessarily a misinterpretation."[65]

For Spielberg's film, in ways that this essay can only hint at, is quite intimately bound up with a European film history as well as with European filmmaking. The fact that he decided to shoot in post–Cold War Poland, that the style he chose reminds not only Wim Wenders of Andrzej Wajda, that at one stage he asked Roman Polanski to direct it, suggest a dimension to *Schindler's List* which makes it part of the ongoing dialogue between so-called post-classical American cinema and the art and auteur cinema of Europe,[66] extending a special tribute to Poland and Polish cinema. At the same time, Spielberg, no less than other directors of his generation, such as Coppola and Scorsese (but also Spike Lee), is a self-consciously American director, and, furthermore, an ethnic director. In this respect, *Schindler's List* is a sort of *Godfather* on *Mean Streets*. The dedication to Steven Ross makes the connection to the movie moguls (and to the Jews that "invented Hollywood"), and there can be little doubt that Spielberg himself identifies with the Jews as well as with Schindler (whose alter ego is, of course, Goeth). Thus, at one level his protagonists Schindler, Stern, and Goeth figure in a drama that allegorizes, not all that obliquely, the physics and metaphysics of power. As a filmmaker, too, one is master over life and death in a world both volatile and virtual. More concretely, Spielberg also situates himself within the tradition of classical American cinema. According to Armond White, the reference is explicitly to D. W. Griffith:

> As with the *Orphans of the Storm* separation of the sisters in *The Color Purple*, [the scene in *Schindler's List* of the women separated from their children] recalls Griffith's command of primal emotion and narrative vigor. The Spielberg twist (and plus) comes with the very Hollywood principle of "proportion." A single mother separated from a child is usual.... But 200 women running after their abducted children belongs to a most powerful artistic vision. It's a moment in which Spielberg has successfully reimagined the terror of the Holocaust in an original way.[67]

White goes on to remark that, compared to Spielberg's other films, *Schindler's List* is both less bold and less imaginative in the very territory it purports to make its own: that of genocide and of representing history in a popular medium. As a film about race and oppression, *The Color Purple* (1985) seems to White to "attempt a first—applying Hollywood's entire fictional apparatus to create a romance about African Americans, [...] the most successful example of the Eighties' interest in cultural signs and signifiers of African-American and Hollywood history." And *1941* (1979) and *Indiana Jones and the Last Crusade* (1989) "give serious attention to the WWII era and the fascist thrall of Nazism," with Spielberg accomplishing "a postwar, postmodern miracle in those films—criticising the political gestalt of the virtuous, victorious, prosperous West with the pop ethos of Hollywood fantasy, the tradition of which he is the truest heir." Yet, *Schindler's List*, by contrast, is "circumscribed ... by the culture industry that has accumulated around the subject of this century's European Holocaust."[68]

Such vigorous claims for a postmodern Spielberg seem at first glance contradicted by the director's equally vigorous affirmation of one of Western culture's *grands récits*, that of human progress. But once one concedes that one cannot get very close to *Schindler's List* by arguing whether Spielberg was right in showing 1,000 Jews rescued where six million perished, it is possible to recognize in his films a typically postmodern hubris, namely the faith that the cinema can redeem the past, rescue the real, and even rescue that which was never real. As Leon Wieseltier put it:

> *Schindler's List* proves again that, for Spielberg, there is a power in the world that is greater than good and greater than evil, and it is the movies. He is hardly alone in this cinéaste's theodicy.[69]

whose history?: public parapraxes and personal speaking positions

If the cinema should have attained the status of a reality in its own right, it is a reality still bounded by history—more precisely, it is bounded by the fact that cinema exists in the public sphere. Films such as *Schindler's List*, just like *Holocaust*, *Our Hitler*, *Heimat*, and *Lili Marleen*, were, beyond their existence as films, also media events, discursive realities cascading through the representational reality of television, phone-ins, newspapers, leader columns, learned journals. The question of the subject positions they created and the speaking positions they assumed were vital aspects of their reality in culture. While in *Holocaust* the subject positions offered led to a facile identification with the victims of the Holocaust, *Our Hitler* and *Heimat* were anti-*Holocaust* in that they tried to open a more tortuous and underground path to subject positions of the divided German self (the monologue of the schizophrenic child-murderer from Fritz Lang's *M* (1931), or passages from Himmler's Posen speech at crucial points in *Our Hitler*) and of a retreat to the domestic self (Reitz in *Heimat* creating a Mother Courage who doesn't lose her children to the war). If *Holocaust*'s naiveté in assuming that showing people go to the gas chambers in a film could give an idea of "what it was like" was a deeply offensive presumption, how is one to take the analogy between the child-murderer in *M* and Adolf Hitler (in *Our Hitler*), and how does one "become naive" in Reitz's *Heimat* about the persecution and deportations of Jews, barely mentioned throughout 16 hours of film?[70] For Reitz, it was Hollywood's speaking position that made *Holocaust* offensive, while for some viewers of *Heimat*, it was the speaking position of a barely disguised anti-Americanism that offended.[71] By dividing Germans into those who stayed and those who went away (to the United States, as emigrants or exiles), and by speaking from a German New Left position (for which the United States was the enemy) while trying to identify with the old German left (wiped out by Hitler and Stalin), Reitz's film appeared to be speaking from the "green-red" position of the German ecology movement.

Both Syberberg and Reitz may argue that their films are in a "double frame," so to speak. *Heimat*, for instance, is for Reitz a story within a story ("thousands of stories based on irritatingly detailed experiences which do not contribute to judging or explaining history, but whose sum total would actually fill this gap"[72]), and thus a (single) story of the Simons family that is "framed" by the many stories (too well known, according to Reitz, to need retelling) of the Holocaust. Similarly, the multiple ironies and incongruities constructed in *Our Hitler* could be seen as the *mise-en-abyme* of all possible speaking positions and thus proof of the impossibility of speaking "as a German" about the Holocaust and the "Third Reich," while needing to testify that the unspeakable happened. However, in light of the directors' public interventions (Syberberg's having become increasingly political[73]), it is important both to protect the films' *mise-en-abyme* or framing ironies from their makers' personal statements and to acknowledge the difficulties the cinema has as a mass medium to institutionalize preferred readings other than by creating ambiguous subject positions.[74] There had been, after all, those "hundreds of documentaries" about fascism and the Holocaust, none of whose unambiguous subject positions provoked either the emotional outbursts following the screening of *Holocaust* or the debates occasioned by *Heimat, Our Hitler,* and *Schindler's List.* The question is thus one of the "political unconscious" of a popular text that by definition exceeds the control of the maker and which becomes a cultural or historical fact precisely because of this excess.

It is this configuration which allows one to speak of the "identity politics" involved in the representation of fascism and the Holocaust. In some instances, it can involve a whole nation's speaking position. The identity politics of Germany, for instance, surface not only when the speaking positions of, say, the films of the New German Cinema are at issue, but when official (West) Germany manifests itself with a speaking position on public occasions—especially when dates are commemorated or historical events are celebrated. There is, for instance, May 8th, the date in 1945 of the German Reich's unconditional surrender. The many mishaps and misunderstandings which this day has given rise to in the last forty years could fill an entire book, documenting how the Federal Republic has never been able to decide whether the nation is celebrating its liberation or mourning its greatest defeat, or both, or neither.[75] Perhaps the best-known blunder around this date was when Ronald Reagan, then President of the United States, joined Chancellor Helmut Kohl to commemorate the fortieth anniversary of the end of World War II in 1985, by a visit to the town of Bitburg, long famous for its beer and now for a previously unremarked military cemetery which contained graves of Waffen-SS officers. After worldwide protests from the Jewish community, another visit was hastily arranged of the memorial at the former concentration camp of Bergen-Belsen.[76]

May 8th, however, is not the only instance in (West) German public life where history as the return of the repressed suddenly intervened to draw unwanted attention to the speaking positions of prominent Germans. On November 9th, 1988 a ceremony took place in Bonn to commemorate the fiftieth anniversary of the *Kristallnacht,* the beginning of the open persecution and deportation of German Jews. Philipp Jenninger, the President of the Upper House of the German Federal Parliament, gave a keynote speech that caused so much consternation that he was obliged to resign. Reading the speech in print, one is struck by the writer's intense and emotional identification with the victims, especially in the passages where he quotes at length and in horrifying detail an eye-witness report of mass-executions.[77] But speaking as a German rather than a Jew, he also tried to think himself into the minds of the ordinary German of 1938. Jenninger's speech might be called a post-*Holocaust* and post-*Heimat* attempt to address two constituencies simultaneously: Germans and Jews, the memory of those who lived in places like Schabbach (Reitz' fictional village in *Heimat*), and the memory of those who were transported to camps like Auschwitz. Jenninger's attempt singularly failed, not only because there is no historical discourse in which these two realities can coexist as compatible subject positions, but also because he had entirely misunderstood his own speaking position. What might conceivably have passed if spoken as an individual deeply troubled by a sense of responsibility and the need for atonement apparently could not be said by the representative of the highest elected body of the nation. Representation here taking on its full meaning of representing an event while also speaking on behalf of someone, those on whose behalf Jenninger spoke clearly did not feel the event was represented as they wished to hear it. By trying to remove the frame that separated these two incompatible discursive registers, Jenninger was left without a place from which to say anything at all. Since then, the *Kristallnacht* anniversary has become, in another historical turn, once more an overdetermined date, allowing two quite dissimilar events and their reverberations to superimpose themselves on each other, one "silencing" the other.[78]

On such occasions, history has a way of overtaking the most carefully scripted speaking positions so that mastering the past also implies an "unmastering" of history, accepting the "parapraxes" which can insert themselves into one's speaking positions. The historical semiotics at work here can be studied all over Eastern Europe, and they extend beyond individuals and texts: they comprise, for instance, the way a nation speaks to itself about its history in the form of public holidays and public memorials, or when naming streets and designating sites as part of national history. It was surely no accident that Jürgen Habermas, for instance, when starting the polemic which subsequently became the historians' debate, made a connection between the writings of scholars like Nolte and the German Federal Government's plans to fund two new historical museums, one in Bonn for the history of the Federal Republic, one in Berlin for the history of the German nation—even though Nolte had taken no part in these decisions. The government's attempt to distribute history strategically, so to speak, and create an asymmetrical duality was itself proven premature thanks to the irruption of another historical event: the fall of the Wall and German unification.

By what is therefore also no coincidence, the publication which Habermas singled out for comment shows the same dual structure of dissimilar events that are obliged to share one and the same representational or discursive space that so often typifies divided and now united Germany's dealing with representations of its recent history. Similarly, Andreas Hillgruber's *Zweierlei Untergang* ("Two Kinds of Ruin") combines in one volume an essay on the "Shattering of the German Reich" and one on the "End of European Jewry."[79] This brought into a deceptive and, as it would turn out, provocative symmetry the story of the collapse of Hitler's Eastern front in the last year of the war and an assessment of the "Final Solution," its planning and ruthlessly methodical implementation. The provocation resided not in the texts themselves nor the case they put forward.[80] More problematic was the parallel that the juxtaposition seemed to draw between the evacuation and expulsion of the German population from the provinces east of the Oder, and the extermination of Jews, herded from all over Europe into the death camps of the East. Yet what caused major offense was Hillgruber's candid admission that, as a German historian, he could not but empathize with the injustice, suffering, and death inflicted on the German population during the cold winter months of 1944/45. Had Hillgruber, who was himself part of the exodus, made these statements in the context of a biographical account, "few would have quarrelled," as Perry Anderson put it. But by claiming empathy and identification while speaking as a German historian, Hillgruber had "slipped with one step from the understandable to the indefensible."[81]

identification, identity politics: what price empathy?

In one sense, the reason for the indefensible is obvious: the position of empathy assumed by Hillgruber creates in the same space of narration two kinds of victim, each competing with the other: the Holocaust's singular and exemplary fate is in a sense invalidated by dramatizing it back to back with the possible or actual Soviet retribution meted out to the civilian population of Germany's former Eastern provinces.

But surely, one could object, even the Germans must be allowed to mourn their dead? Might Hillgruber not be understood as following the advice of Alexander Mitscherlich who had suggested that West Germans suffered from a particular kind of self-alienation, an "inability to mourn," that meant that they were also unable to love, either themselves or others.[82] Significantly, it was German filmmakers who took up the call for mourning work, and this forms the central idea in *Germany in Autumn* as well as in *Our Hitler*. For Syberberg, for instance, an aesthetics of mourning as he conceived it is radically opposed to dramatic enactments and restagings and thus counters the mechanisms by which the classical fiction film creates coherent viewing subjects. Instead, his is a counter-cinema, based on a bricolage of kitsch objects and sentimental mementos, clichéd images and romantic music. Such a poetics of "mourning work" is also a politics, and as the example of Syberberg or Hillgruber shows, it carries a high risk. Too often, it has seemed to commentators, "mourning work" stops short at the stage of self-pity and sentimentality ("What is terrible about Germans is not their brutality, but their sentimentality," the Jewish writer Amos Oz once remarked), thus acknowledging compassion only at the price of playing victims off each other in the vain hope of squaring accounts. It has even been argued that much of the New German Cinema presented a view of history in which Germany appears as a nation of victims, either through its choice of women as protagonists, or by its allegorizing the country as a female body, vulnerable and maltreated—in both cases without leaving room for other victims.[83]

Here too, the discursive reality of the New German Cinema implied a collective speaking position which history itself called into question. Internationally recognized, albeit briefly, the speaking position became fruitfully caught up in the ambiguities that had attached themselves to the signifier "German" after 1945. The film directors, showing the same love-hate relationship which other prominent post-war Germans—above all artists and writers—displayed towards the Federal Republic, protested alienation from their country while being nevertheless eager to represent it, especially abroad. In the movement's heyday during the 1970s and 1980s, Werner Herzog, Syberberg and Wim Wenders ritually saw themselves as international spokesmen, even as ambassadors, of a "good" Germany, often taking the moral high ground. Wenders, for instance, wrote:

> I speak for everyone who in recent years, after a long drought, has started once again to produce images and sounds in a country which has an unceasing distrust of images and sounds that tell its story, which for this reason has for forty years greedily soaked up all foreign images, just as long as they have taken its mind off itself.[84]

Other directors, in the spirit of Willy Brandt's genuflection at the memorial to the Warsaw ghetto, did public penance, such as Herzog's pilgrimage to Lotte Eisner or his assertion that his films represented "legitimate German culture." Others still, rather more sceptical or cynical, played the court jester and on occasion were not afraid to openly bite the hand that fed them (the Bonn Government, its film funding system, or the Goethe Institute that sent them abroad). For example, Herbert Achternbusch's "politics of identification" in a film like *Das Letzte Loch* (1981) represented one of the more radical ways of confronting Nazism and the "Final Solution" by trying to literalize the destruction of six million human beings.[85]

Similarly, Fassbinder refused to act the honorary diplomat, and instead threatened to become a street-sweeper in Mexico while misbehaving at home: his play *The City, Garbage and Death* caused a scandal even after his death, for it touched a taboo area of West Germany by representing official philosemitism as an attempt to blot out an anti-semitism whose persistence after 1945 had never been publicly acknowledged or debated. Using the crudely Manichean dramaturgy of a Jacobean revenge tragedy, Fassbinder featured his villain as a character simply called The Jew, an Auschwitz survivor and property speculator who derived power from the guilt feelings he could call upon thanks to his official victim status, while being himself used by the political establishment to do their dirty work. If, understandably, it caused grievous offence to the Jewish community, especially in Frankfurt, where the play is set, it also became the scapegoat of a debate which never took place; though by virtue of becoming a scandal, it forced into the open those external limits which the representational arts may have to test.[86]

One of the casualties of unification has been the right and the obligation felt by the German literary establishment and film authors to speak on behalf of Germany, to "represent" it. In the complex process of yet another impossible squaring of accounts between East and West Germany, a period of reassessment is under way, perhaps not yet of German history, but of some of those who until now have been its artistic custodians. With this reassessment, the idea of "mourning work" to respond to one's own experience of loss as a prelude to acknowledging the loss of others has begun to sound hollow: not least because it overvalues the political importance of the aesthetics of moral rectitude, but also because official Germany seems once again to be lording it over others while still standing in line for sympathy. *"Die Schuld lassen wir uns nicht nehmen"* ("We won't let them take away our guilt") once read the caption to a West German cartoon of Chancellor Kohl laying a wreath at a concentration-camp memorial.

But if "mourning work" cannot open up that space of otherness, what can? What kinds of affect might possibly "unlock" numbness, apathy, indifference and reconcile memory and hope, commemoration and forgetting, or mediate between pity, sentiment, and shame? This question unites those who applaud a popular filmmaker like Spielberg with those who condemn him. It is at such a juncture that the mimetic emotions of cinema, including nostalgia, sentimentality, and melodrama, have a direct bearing and purchase on the idea of representation, perhaps because these are emotions of the (narcissistic) self over which the cinema and the audio-visual media in general have a not inconsiderable power, even if that power does not amount to that of a "theodicy."

Here, a term comes to mind which in its use and over-use is symptomatic of a certain dialectic of power and powerlessness: the word is the German *Betroffenheit*, which roughly translates as "the affect of concern" but in its root-meaning includes "recognizing oneself to be emotionally called upon to respond, act, react." It thus covers empathy and identification, but in an active, radical sense of being "stung into action." This concept, so widely used when matters of "politics after politics" (such as the question of human rights, of ecological action, or racist violence) are debated that it has become a cliché, nonetheless tries to convey subject positions that lie beyond sentimentality and yet touch a point where the self itself knows and can experience otherness. In the face of narcissistic forms of identification in conventional narrative and fictional dramatization, such an "affect of concern" is meant to break through any coherent and thus comforting subject position and shock spectators into recognition. Yet such strategies of shock, increasingly used to convey the suffering caused by human or natural disasters, also imply the deeply ambiguous modes of address typical of news broadcasts and current affairs programmes: soliciting (emotional) response, while disempowering (civic, political) action.

The dilemma refocuses the divide between fiction film and documentary discussed at the beginning of this essay. It is now possible to compare these two genres not in terms of what they show or do not show, whether one is more "authentic" than the other, but in terms of the ambiguous or extreme subject positions they are able to sustain. In films like *The Sorrow and the Pity*, *Memory of Justice* (1976), *Hotel Terminus* (1988), and *November Days* (1990), Marcel Ophuls, a documentary filmmaker whose work focuses on European history, has turned his camera and microphone on people whose self-deception is only rivalled by their sense of self-importance, thus creating a credibility gap crucial to Ophuls's method. Yet what seems equally typical is Ophuls's ability to transform himself as interviewer into a character, often playing the clown, not afraid of having a door slammed in his face like a traveling salesman, thus eliciting a whole range of apparently inappropriate feelings, from comedy to sadistic pleasure, from farce to prurience. Dissimulating his own emotions and convictions, in order to make (some minor protagonist of) history "speak," Ophuls not only remains a spiky presence on screen or through his off-screen voice, but also once compared himself to Columbo, Peter Falk's awkward, stooping, serio-comic detective, always asking one more question. Crucial is the fact that Ophuls understands the need to create for the viewer a complex subject position, even if this connects him to a speaking position which is that of a quasi-fictional character.

In *Shoah*, Lanzmann also creates a persona for himself. With his relentless questions he turns into something like his subjects' super-ego, at once insistent and firm. The dialectic of who speaks and who is silenced in an image becomes the very core of the enterprise. Lanzmann's care over bureaucratic detail, the exact description of place and circumstance, the way he goads the memory of surviving prisoners, guards of concentration camps, and farmers who merely looked on, suspend all preconceived narratives and explanations. *Shoah* does not invalidate them, nor does it complement them. Instead, Lanzmann works with each individual's memory as a unique "archaeological" site, requiring different tools and different techniques. Whether he flatters someone's complacency or patiently stalks another's evasiveness, whether he takes the man who shaved the women at Treblinka back to his barber shop or listens to the prisoner from Chelmno tell how his singing voice saved his life, Lanzmann creates a multitude of speaking positions by separating them as sharply from each other as possible, while embedding them in sympathy, even when they must have appalled him or when pity threatened to overwhelm him.

The "affect of concern" emanating from the films of Ophuls and Lanzmann is to make one see things which are not on screen and listen to voices speaking from within oneself. In contrast to *Holocaust*, where omniscient narration generates a unified subject position, the restricted narration of *Shoah* and *The Sorrow and the Pity* holds viewers in place through the presence of the filmmaker as interviewer/detective/father confessor without disambiguating these roles or making them transparent. The films can begin to do "mourning work," not because they give us fictional victims or actual villains, but because like Dante's encounters in hell, they fill the mind's eye and ear with voices and presences: they will forever speak of a history for which there is neither redemption nor exorcism.[87] Yet, paradoxically, however painful and arduous the films are to watch, neither Ophuls's nor Lanzmann's speaking position threatens the coherence of the viewer's identity: to this extent they are classical, or classically modernist, works. Thus if fracturing the viewers' identity is the very condition that makes the radical otherness of an extreme historical experience representable, then there may be a limit to the documentary methods employed by Lanzmann and Ophuls. The limits of the fiction film, by contrast, would have to be defined differently.

For instance, Joseph Losey's *M. Klein* is a film built around the construction of one such moment of fractured identity, aiming to recover the point at which the spectating subject loses his/her bearings, all the while carried along by the processes of fictional identification typical of the popular feature film. The story of a Parisian art dealer during the Occupation who, not a Jew, can make his fortune buying up collections from Jews anxious to escape France, *M. Klein* hinges on the fact that despite his morally suspect behavior, we totally identify with the hero when one day he is arrested by the Gestapo and taken to the Vel d'Hiver. For the fact that Klein does not protest and instead gets on the train with all the Jews that have been rounded up, makes the spectator want to say, on behalf of the hero: "But you've got the wrong man: he isn't a Jew"—until with a sudden shock one realizes that all the people on the train are "the wrong men." Identification, historical foreknowledge and the logic of classical narrative have here conspired to lull the senses into "accepting" the transported Jews as normal until the moment we want to rescue our hero, and, realizing that we need to rescue them all, we are shattered by the knowledge of our total impotence; but which is also the knowledge of our own collusion and complicity.

It might almost be an axiom of the difference between documentary and fiction films about fascism that the latter, in order to have any kind of credibility, must not create sympathy for the victims of the Holocaust, since that very sympathy trivializes and betrays them. Thus, in a sense the particular strength of the fiction film is, precisely, its ability to "shatter" subject positions, including those of empathy. Such moments of recognition as I have tried to describe in *M. Klein* and *Schindler's List* are unique to the cinema, and they demand aesthetic strategies—resources of narration and identification for instance, but also of contrast, excess, and violence (as in the children's transport, or the shower scenes)— that are not only more complex than the literary representational self-restraint of naming and documenting, but perhaps also more perverse, even more threatening than the realist/modernist ones often held up as the critical norm.

Readings that frame the subject positions of the films' mode of address, I argued above, are culturally agreed or discursively negotiated and, as in the examples I gave, can amount to manifestations of an historical unconscious, itself part of "representing history." However, it is part of the "postmodern" condition of contemporary cinema that the "text" no longer speaks for the author. No modernist defense like "exile, silence and cunning"[88] can protect the filmmaker as author, but the public arena of magazine and television interviews, published diaries and essays, the promotional machinery that makes the director "speak." These speaking positions, I think, need not refer to biographical individuals, nor even to "auteurs," but are instances of historical and personal accountability. It is in this context that one can view the one-sided exchange between Lanzmann and Spielberg. In order to put this dimension into a political context and a moral perspective, it may be helpful to recall two responses to *Holocaust* from the 1970s. When the series first aired in the U.S., Elie Wiesel, in an article in the *New York Times*, wrote

> The film is an insult to those who perished and to those who survived. In spite of its name, this "docu-drama" is not about what some of us remember as the Holocaust.... I am appalled by the thought that one day the Holocaust will be measured and judged

> in part by the NBC television production bearing its name.... The Holocaust must be remembered. But not as a show.[89]

Wiesel clearly could invoke both personal testimony and a notion of the authentic against a product of the entertainment industry. A year later, in May 1979, after *Holocaust* had been screened in Germany, Edgar Reitz published a kind of manifesto, entitled "Let's work on our memories":

> Authors all over the world are trying to take possession of their history ... but they often find that it is torn out of their hands. The most serious act of expropriation occurs when people are deprived of their history. With *Holocaust*, the Americans have taken away our history.[90]

Reitz also appealed to memory, and thus to a category of the authentic. Indeed, at first glance, these two statements are identical in judgment and sentiment. They condemn the series' fictionalization and trivialization and fear for the survival of history as validated experience. But their speaking positions could not be further apart. In the case of Reitz, one is bound to ask: who is speaking? How can a German who grew up under Hitler lay claim to this history, appropriate it, and not speak in sorrow or shame, but rather complain that the Americans have "expropriated" it? If "our history" means causing the death of twenty million people, one wishes the Americans could take it away! What the Americans did take away was the scourge of fascism from the face of Europe, a detail that seems to have escaped Reitz's moral and aesthetic sensitivity. To the postmodernist argument that in the battle over representations, Reitz has the right to "rewrite historical texts" since there can be no history outside texts, one can answer that it is Reitz's speaking position that is outside the text, where it has to confront its formal similarity and historical incompatibility with Wiesel's speaking position.

However, what gives Reitz's position its air of rectitude is that the "postcolonial" discourse of Hollywood/European cinema (shades of Godard's "two or three Vietnams") has superimposed itself on another historical discourse, that of Auschwitz and 1945. In the process, aggressors and vanquished have changed places. Reitz, by claiming "our history," is claiming victim status. Hollywood ("the victor") makes a film called *Holocaust* that "conquers" world markets, while the Germans (the vanquished) make films called *Our Hitler* and *Heimat*: the intended irony of these titles pales to an un-postmodernist white irony, as one blushes to realize the larger irony that cancels it—that "Hitler" and "Heimat" connote once more the very causes of the Holocaust.

Nothing quite so crass frames and unframes the speaking positions of Lanzmann and Spielberg, but their disagreement prompts similar thoughts about the historical, geographical, and indeed spiritual horizon that their films touch and their identity politics cannot transcend. Whatever one may finally think of either *Schindler's List* or *Shoah*, the subject positions they offer the spectator are on the one hand determined by their respective genres and on the other hand are united by the fact that both films work, with admittedly different means, on the borders of what I have called the "unified" and the "shattered" self. These subject positions, however, stand in stark contrast to their respective economic status and thus to their place in the public sphere. Where *Shoah*, although screened in many countries, had to contend with minority television channels or at art-cinema venues, *Schindler's List* was one of the major international Hollywood releases of the 1993–94 season. This difference of access to a public means that, in the absence of a "level playing field," they cannot be simply compared "as texts," and instead compete with each other in one of the discursive realities that Spielberg's film has opened up. Both Lanzmann and Spielberg make use of the media interest fanned by *Schindler's List* to construct for themselves speaking positions. While Lanzmann volunteered comment on Spielberg's film in articles and talk shows, Spielberg gave interviews and issued statements, before, during, and after the shooting of *Schindler's List*. With such a media intervention to establish his (biographical, ethnic) right to speak on the issue of the Holocaust, the normally rather media-shy Spielberg seemed anxious to define the terms of a "preferred" reading of his film.[91] By and large, he was successful: the film, even before it was awarded the endorsement of seven Oscars, received wide coverage and a mostly favorable press. Although it is thus possible to impute to Lanzmann professional pique (but to what purpose?) or let the matter rest on the difference beween a modernist and a realist aesthetics, the ensuing one-sided exchange may well point to other, equally relevant differences.

Interviewed by the BBC, for instance, Lanzmann argued that Spielberg had made a film "typical of American Jews, wanting to appropriate the Holocaust."[92] Startling as this assertion may be, its shock comes from the way it echoes Reitz's remarks some fifteen years earlier, that "with *Holocaust*, the Americans have taken away our history." Both statements are united by an anti-Americanism in which the Hollywood/Europe divide allows other agendas of identity to intrude upon the moral issues at stake. For Lanzmann might, in giving vent to a resentment, have hinted at deeper incompatibilities, throwing into relief the fact that Spielberg had indeed "interpreted" the Holocaust. Had he not told the story of Schindler and his Jews as a double, if not triple allegory, that in each case promises salvation? Ending as it does at his graveside, with the survivors paying tribute, Schindler can be seen as a Moses figure, leading his people out of an Egyptian captivity, while he, like all true prophets, is barred from reaching the promised land. But where the Israelites danced around the Golden Calf, the Schindler Jews smelt gold to make of it the ring they present to Schindler as token of their gratitude. This gives, in turn, an almost mythic authority to their reappearance on the horizon, carrying with them the sacrifices of a past into a nation-building future. Spielberg has, and this Lanzmann perceived perhaps rightly, appropriated a particular version not so much of the Holocaust as of Jewish redemption, overlaying it with a recognizably American, immigrant, settler, and founding-fathers rhetoric.

As such, it is a play with "master-narratives," transgressing the taboo against any kind of narrative emplotment, that is part of the "European" identity of the Holocaust. Like *Cabaret*, discussed above, *Schindler's List* provides several entry-points for its audiences; it is a polysemic text, which is to say a popular text. Yet it is a popular text also because it contains a meditation on two kinds of survival from the two kinds of ruin Auschwitz connotes to survivors like Wiesel and Lanzmann: that of a people and that of the idea of humanity. Spielberg first of all gives a surprisingly literal reading to "whoever saves one life saves mankind" for he has dared to "count" and "reckon" the Schindler Jews not against those that perished, but by the number of their descendants. He has enveloped in a generational pragmatism (or "family history") *the* historical event which, by general consent, nullifies all reckoning, all rendering, or squaring of accounts.

Two kinds of eschatology, then, seem to confront each other: the tragic vision of life of the European Jew Lanzmann, and life-affirming vision of the American Jew Spielberg. But beneath the eschatology, there is the "theodicy," to take up once more the phrase of Wieseltier, or perhaps, more precisely, the rule of synecdoche. By affirming that whoever saves one life, saves mankind, Spielberg accepts the principle that the one can represent the many, that the part can stand for the whole.[93] *Shoah* is based, explicitly and emphatically, on the exactly opposite premise: that no one can stand in for anyone else, no one can speak for anyone else. After six hours of testimony in *Shoah*—a testimony that, in different ways, records only absence, one is left with the overwhelming thought that no history can contain, let alone signify or represent, the palpable reality of so many individual, physical deaths.

By contrast, now that Spielberg has made the film, a palpable reality exists, a space filled with faces, voices, bodies, objects. It has even called into being realities that did not exist. The streets and places in Krakow, for instance, where he shot on location, exist as a new kind of historical reality. Tours can be booked that take you to the site of the ghetto, made meaningful because a famous movie was shot there.[94] By association with a trivial event, this or that street has become historical, and even though, of course, it is a "false" (postmodern) history, it can now remind visitors of, and thus credibly stand for a "real" history. A cinéaste's theodicy, after all. More generally, and more paradoxically, Spielberg, by putting into circulation a discourse which suggests that this was a "personal" film, has given himself the license to do exactly the opposite, namely to speak on behalf of others, to make the step from direct testimony and personal memory, to narrative and history.

Thus, neither the normative argument of generic emplotment nor the institutional constraints imposed on professional historians to validate their evidence can altogether satisfactorily be invoked when the representation of history in the cinema is at issue. Yet while there may be no internal limits, as it were, which constrain a filmmaker to "stick to the facts" or observe the dictates of good taste, there are a number of external constraints, as we saw, which operate even more stringently in the case of popular cinema. For to the extent that a film creates a public sphere, a space for discourse, confrontation, and debate, it is this space that produces the speaking positions which in turn are the external limits of representation.

One reason for dwelling on these examples at such length is that they underscore the difficulties, when taking fascism as a "limit case" of historical representation, of determining any text's or author's speaking position, yet also assert the necessity of doing so in each case. Detailing the inversions, reversals and at times perversions of such speaking positions, hopefully, extends beyond a mere academic exercise. At a time when history has returned to Central and Eastern Europe, to Africa and elsewhere, while the legacy of Fascism as well as Stalinism has to be confronted by the whole of Europe, the crimes named by Nazism and the Holocaust cannot possibly be "our" history, just as it need not only be "our" testimony or mourning work. Therein lies a hope, but also an obligation.

notes

1. "Mastering the past" is the phrase used in English to translate the German *Vergangenheitsbewältigung*, literally: "coming to terms with the (fascist) past."
2. John Rowse, speaking about "Human Memory and the Computer" on John Tidmarsh's *Outlook*, BBC World Service, 15 August 1994.
3. The notion of narratives without closure, demanding a degree of attentiveness and participation one associates with information that might vitally affect one's life, recalls what Hayden White has defined as "modernist events." See "The Modernist Event," in this volume.
4. At the end of *The Man Who Shot Liberty Valence*, the newspaper editor says to James Stewart, "If you have to choose between the truth and legend, print the legend."
5. See Ian Buruma, *The Wages of Guilt: Memories of War in Germany and Japan* (London: Jonathan Cape, 1994), about these two countries' very different ways of "mastering the past."
6. See Saul Friedlander, ed., *Probing the Limits of Representation* (Cambridge, Mass: Harvard University Press, 1992).
7. One would like to think that Adorno's often-quoted remark about the impossibility of poetry after Auschwitz refers to this paradox rather than positing a proscription.

8. See Hayden White, "Historical Emplotment and the Problem of Truth," in *Probing the Limits*, 37–53.
9. This has been the position, notably, of George Steiner, in *The Portage to San Cristobal of A.H.* (New York, Simon & Schuster, 1982)
10. Jürgen Habermas, *The New Conservatism: Cultural Criticism and the Historians's Debate*, ed. and trans. Shierry Weber Nicholson, intro. Richard Wolin (Cambridge, Mass.: MIT Press, 1989), 230.
11. Jean-François Lyotard, *The Differend: Phrases in Dispute* (Minneapolis: University of Minnesota Press, 1988), 57.
12. Jean-François Lyotard, *The Postmodern Condition* (Minneapolis: University of Minnesota Press, 1984), 78.
13. See, however, Ilan Avisar, *Screening the Holocaust: Cinema's Images of the Unimaginable* (Bloomington: Indiana University Press, 1988).
14. Berel Lang, "The Representation of Limits," in *Probing the Limits*, 317.
15. "What's wrong with the film is essentially what's wrong with nearly all popular culture, namely that its means of expression are debased and debasing." Letter to the Editor, *Times Literary Supplement*, April 1, 1994, 15.
16. David Thomson, "Presenting Enamelware," *Film Comment* (March/April 1994): 50.
17. Saul Friedlander, *Reflections of Fascism* (New York: Harper & Row, 1983).
18. For a comprehensive list of titles, see Robert C. Reimer and Carol J. Reimer, *Nazi-Retro Film: How German Narrative Film Remembers the Past* (Boston: Twayne, 1992).
19. Most recently, this was noted by Wim Wenders, in a public discussion with the author, at the Desmet Cinema, Amsterdam, July 8th, 1994.
20. John Gross, "Hollywood and the Holocaust," *The New York Review of Books*, 3 (February 1994), 16.
21. Cf. Peter Brooks, *The Melodramatic Imagination* (New York: Columbia University Press, 1985).
22. Bryan Cheyette,"Schindler's List," *The Times Literary Supplement*, 1 April 1994, 15.
23. For an argument about the "melodramatic" as an autonomous representational mode, see Christine Gledhill, "The Melodramatic Field: An Investigation," in Gledhill, ed., *Home is Where the Heart is* (London: BFI Publishing, 1987), 5–41.
24. See my discussion of *Shoah* in *New German Cinema: A History* (London: Macmillan, 1989), 258.
25. Wim Wenders, "That's Entertainment: Hitler." Originally in *Die Zeit*, 5 August 1977, translated in Eric Rentschler, ed., *West German Filmmakers on Film: Visions and Voices* (New York: Holmes & Meier, 1988), 128.
26. The reference point for the Nazi regime's staging of itself is, inevitably, Leni Riefenstahl's *Triumph of the Will* (1935).
27. Walter Benjamin, "The Work of Art in the Age of Mechanical Reproduction," in *Illuminations* (New York: Schocken Books, 1971); and Susan Sontag, "Fascinating Fascism," reprinted in Bill Nichols, *Movies and Methods* I (Berkeley and Los Angeles: University of California Press, 1980).
28. See Robert Burgoyne, "The Imaginary and the Neo-Real," *Enclitic* (Spring 1979): 16–34.
29. There were, of course, in Italian cinema, illustrious precedents, both in the popular cinema (the long tradition of the "peplum") and in auteur cinema, notably Visconti's *Senso* (1954) and *The Leopard* (1963).
30. Anton Kaes notes, "The Third Reich itself was often reduced ... to a semiotic phenomenon: SS uniforms, swastikas, shaved napes, black leather belts and boots, intimidating corridors and marble stairs have become mere signs unmistakeably signalling fascism." *From Hitler to Heimat* (Cambridge, Mass.: Harvard University Press, 1989), 22.
31. *Inside the Third Reich: Memoirs*, trans. Richard and Clara Winston (New York: Macmillan, 1970). The so-called "Hitler-wave" broke with Albert Speer's memoirs in 1968, Joachim Fest's *Hitler* biography (Frankfurt, 1973) and subsequent film,

Hitler—A Career, in 1977. It reached its high-culture watermark with novels by Michel Tournier and George Steiner and ebbed away with the farcical fraud around Hitler's diaries in 1986. Its symptomatic importance lies also in the fact that it encompassed the whole spectrum of culture, from garish comics and pornographic magazines, accessories in sex shops and s/m boutiques, glossy reproductions of period photographs in coffee-table books, to the growing shelves of novels, biographies, autobiographies, and scholarly publications devoted to the "Third Reich," to Hitler, and to every conceivable aspect of Nazism.

32. Michel Foucault, "Film and Popular Memory," originally in *Cahiers du cinéma,* 251/2 (July/August 1974); in English in Sylvère Lotringer ed., *Foucault Live* (New York: Semiotexte, 1989), 89–106.
33. Jean Baudrillard, "Holocaust," *Cahiers du cinéma* no 302, (July–August 1979).
34. Among an extensive literature, one can usefully consult Charles S. Maier, *The Unmasterable Past* (Cambridge, Mass: Harvard University Press, 1988), and Jürgen Habermas, *The New Conservatism* (Cambridge, Mass.: MIT Press, 1989).
35. This is the line taken, for instance, in parts of Joachim C. Fest, *Hitler.*
36. Hans Dieter Schäfer, *Das gespaltene Bewußtsein: Deutsche Kultur und Lebenswirklichkeit 1933–1945* (Munich: Carl Hanser, 1981).
37. Max Horkheimer, "*Die Juden und Europa,*" *Zeitschrift für Sozialforschung* VIII 1/2 (1939): 115.
38. Ernst Nolte, *Three Faces of Fascism* trans. Leila Vennewitz (New York: Holt, Rinehart and Winston, 1969).
39. Alexander and Margarethe Mitscherlich, *The Inability to Mourn: Principles of Collective Behavior,* trans. Beverley A. Plaszek (New York: Grove Press, 1975).
40. For a discussion of "mourning work" and cinema, see my *New German Cinema: A History* (London: Macmillan, 1989), 239–248; and Eric L. Santner, *Stranded Objects* (Cornell University Press, 1990).
41. Cf. Dan Diner, ed., *Ist der Nationalsozialismus Geschichte? Zu Historisierung und Historikerstreit* (Frankfurt/Main: Fischer, 1987); and Reinhard Kühnl, ed., *Streit ums Geschichtsbild* (Cologne: Pahl-Rugenstein, 1987).
42. Cf. Eric Rentschler, "Remembering not to Forget: Alexander Kluge's *Brutality in Stone,*" in *New German Critique* 49 (1990): 23–41.
43. The autumn in question was the highpoint of the RAF, the politically motivated assassinations, the cutbacks in civil liberties, the crisis of the social democratic government under Chancellor Helmut Schmidt. On the question of historicizing fascism, the film took an unambiguous leftist position. It suggested the continuities between Hitler and the Federal Republic, between deep-seated authoritarian attitudes and hysterical over-reaction among the population, between lack of courage in public life and official censorship. For a more detailed discussion of *Germany in Autumn,* see Anton Kaes, *From Hitler to Heimat,* 26–27, and my *New German Cinema: A History,* 260–264.
44. NBC 1978, directed by Marvin J. Chomsky, screenplay by Gerald Green. The impact of *Holocaust* in West Germany has given rise to a sizeable literature. For a comprehensive assessment, see Michael E. Geisler, "The Disposal of Memory: Fascism and the Holocaust," in B. Murray, C. Wickham, eds., *Framing the Past* (Carbondale, Ill.: Southern Illinois University Press, 1992), 220–260.
45. Heinz Höhne, in *Der Spiegel,* quoted (and translated) by Anton Kaes, *From Hitler to Heimat* (Cambridge, Mass.: Harvard University Press, 1989), 30–31.
46. The exhibitionist side was in some sense highlighted by the fact that, as every German commentator pointed out, the world's eyes were on Germany to see how it would react to the series. Anton Kaes, *From Hitler to Heimat,* 31–35 has an account of the international dimension of the *Holocaust* reception.
47. Quoted in Anton Kaes, *From Hitler to Heimat,* 31.
48. There were, however, a vast number of documentaries dealing with both the

"Third Reich" and the "Final Solution." See, for example, Volker Lilienthal, "Das gepriesene Schreckbild," in Joachim Schmitt-Sasse (ed.), *Widergänger: Faschismus und Anti-Faschismus im Film* (Münster: MAks, 1992), 173–201.

49. Ferdinand Braudel, *The Mediterranean and the Mediterranean World in the Age of Philip II*, 2 vols., trans. Sian Reynolds (New York: Harper & Row, 1972–3); and Emanuel LeRoy Ladurie, *Montaillou: The Promised Land of Error*, trans. Barbara Bray (New York: G. Braziller, 1978).
50. Martin Boszat, et al., *Alltagsgeschichte der NS-Zeit. Neue Perspektive oder Trivialisierung?* (Munich/Vienna: Oldenbourg, 1984). For a concise statement of Broszat's position in English, see Martin Broszat, "A Controversy about the Historicization of National Socialism," in *New German Critique*, 44 (1988): 85–126.
51. Christian Meier, quoted in Kühnl, *Streit ums Geschichtsbild*, 258.
52. For a review of the debate, see Martin Jay, "Songs of Experience: Reflections on *Alltagsgeschichte*," *Salmagundi*, Winter 1989): 29–41.
53. Jim Hoberman, "Once Upon a Reich Time," *The Village Voice*, April 16, 1985, 52.
54. For a critique of the the notion of "authenticity" as used by German filmmakers, see my "The New German Cinema's Historical Imaginary," in Murray Wickham, eds, *Framing the Past*, 282–285.
55. For a fuller version of this argument, see my review of *Heimat* in the *Monthly Film Bulletin*, February 1985, 48–52; and *Myth as the Phantasmagoria of History* in the *New German Critique* 24–25 (Winter/Spring 1982): 108–154.
56. As in Laura Mulvey's "Visual Pleasure and Narrative Cinema," *Screen* 16/3 (Autumn 1975): 17.
57. David Thomson, *Film Comment*, 44.
58. Claude Lanzmann, in a discussion program aired by TV 5, 12 January 1994.
59. See Georg Lukács, *The Historical Novel* (London: Merlin Press, 1962) for an analysis of characterization and plot structure in Walter Scott, Stendhal, and Leo Tolstoi among others.
60. *Times Literary Supplement*, 1 April 1994, 15.
61. See my *Fassbinder, Fascism and the Film Industry*, *October* 21 (1982): 115–140.
62. Ernst Bloch, "Non-Contemporaneity and Obligation to its Dialectic," in *Heritage of Our Times*, trans. Neville and Stephen Plaice (Berkeley and Los Angeles: University of California Press, 1991), 97–144.
63. Fassbinder's reworkings of the Ufa melodramas of the 1940s give an intimation of what feelings of fear, loss and guilt Germans living during the Nazi period might have been repressing, in order for films like Veit Harlan's *Die goldene Stadt* (1942) or *Opfergang* (1944) to "harvest" them so efficiently and perversely in the form of female masochism, self-sacrifice, and the yearning for death.
64. Such as the picture of the empty chairs or the throat-slitting gesture Polish peasants are reported to have made to passing cattle-trucks headed for Auschwitz.
65. Harold Bloom, *The Anxiety of Influence* (Oxford: Oxford University Press, 1973), 30.
66. Many of the "epic" scenes, as indeed in earlier Spielberg films, show the (acknowledged) influence of David Lean.
67. Armond White, "Toward a Theory of Spielberg History," *Film Comment* (March/April 1994): 55.
68. White, "Toward a Theory of Spielberg History," 54, 55.
69. *The New Republic*, 24 January 1994, quoted by David Thompson, *Film Comment* (March/April 1994): 44.
70. Cf. Gertrud Koch, "How Much Naivety Can We Afford?" *New German Critique* 36 (Fall 1985): 4–6.
71. See Eric L. Santner, "On the Difficulty of Saying 'We': The Historians' Debate and Edgar Reitz' *Heimat*," in B. Murray and C. Wickham, eds. *Framing the Past*, 273–4.
72. Edgar Reitz, "Statt *Holocaust* Erinnerungen aufarbeiten," *medium* 5/79: 21.
73. Cf. for instance, Hans Jürgen Syberberg "*Wie man den neuen Haß züchtet*," in *Frankfurter Allgemeine Zeitung*, September, 12, 1990.

74. Enno Patalas, director of the Munich Filmmuseum, once contrasted the public's reaction on showing Veit Harlan's *Kolberg* (1945), where no one protested, with that of showing Harlan's *Opfergang* (1944), after which he received threats. (Quoted in Bernadette Klasen, "*Eine Frau wird erst schön durch die Liebe*," in Joachim Schmidt-Sasse, ed., *Widergänger*, 38). It seems that audiences have a secure subject position in a film they "know" to be propaganda (*Kolberg*), but feel threatened when a strong emotional reaction to a melodrama (*Opfergang*) conflicts with their awareness that this is a "fascist" film.
75. See Norbert Seitz, ed., *Die Unfähigkeit zu feiern* (Frankfurt: Verlag Neue Kritik, 1985), quoted in my "Bitburg and Bergen-Belsen: The Inability to Celebrate," in *On Film* 14 (1985): 36–40.
76. See Eric Rentschler, "The Use and Abuse of Memory: New German Film and the Discourse of Bitburg" *New German Critique* 36 (Fall 1985): pp. 67–90.
77. Philipp Jenninger, "Von der Verantwortung für das Vergangene" [On the Responsibility for the Past], *Die Zeit*, 25 November 1988.
78. On November 9, 1989, a year after Jenninger's speech, East Germans first crossed the Berlin wall. Eric Santner has spoken of a "mnemonic readjustment" taking place, making November 9th "newly available for libidinal investment." Eric L. Santner, "History Beyond the Pleasure Principle," in *Probing the Limits*, 144.
79. Andreas Hillgruber, *Zweierlei Untergang: Die Zerschlagung des Deutschen Reiches und das Ende des europäischen Judentums* (Berlin: Siedler, 1986).
80. Perry Anderson has a high regard for the historical merits of Hillgruber's analysis. See "On Emplotment: Two Kind of Ruin," *Probing the Limits*, 62–63.
81. Perry Anderson, "On Emplotment; Two Kinds of Ruin," *Probing the Limits*, 58.
82. I have discussed Mitscherlich's theses, in "Primary Identification and the Historical Subject: Fassbinder's Germany," reprinted in Phil Rosen, ed., *Narrative, Ideology, Apparatus* (New York: Columbia University Press, 1986), 544–548.
83. Eric Rentschler makes this point in "Remembering not to Forget: Alexander Kluge's *Brutality in Stone*," in *New German Critique* 49 (1990): 38.
84. Wim Wenders, "That's Entertainment," in Rentschler, *New German Filmmakers, Visions and Voices*, 127.
85. Cf. with my "Achternbusch and the German Avantgarde," *Discourse* 6 (Fall 1983): 92–112.
86. For a detailed documentation, see Heiner Lichtenstein, ed., *Die Fassbinder-Kontroverse* (Königstein: Athenäum, 1986).
87. The Dante analogy I owe to an excellent review of *Shoah* by Michael Hollington, "Naming, Not Representing," *The Age Monthly Review*, March 1988, 9–11.
88. James Joyce, *Portrait of the Artist as a Young Man* (Harmondsworth: Penguin Books, 1966), 128.
89. Elie Wiesel, "Trivializing the Holocaust: Semi-Fact and Semi-fiction," *The New York Times*, April 16, 1978.
90. Edgar Reitz, "Statt *Holocaust* Erinnerungen aufarbeiten," 21–22.
91. See among others, Jeremy Isaacs, *Face to Face: Steven Spielberg*, BBC2 Television, March 24, 1994, which featured details about his Jewish upbringing and family, and touched on the story of himself as a boy, taunted and bullied at school.
92. Claude Lanzmann, interviewed on "Moving Pictures," BBC2 Television, 4 December 1993.
93. "Except to the people whose lives he saved, Schindler made no difference to the outcome of the Holocaust. But the film's aim is to show that he made a huge difference, for he is meant to prove that remarkable individuals can outsmart evil." Jason Epstein, "A Dissent of *Schindler's List*," *New York Review of Books*, April 21, 1994, 65.
94. Julian Borger, "'Visit Places from Schindler's List': Site of Schindler story repackaged as city of the film," *The Guardian*, May 16, 1994, 20.

part three

the end(s) of history

nine

historical *ennui*, feminist boredom

patrice petro

> [I]t is particularly tempting to write a history of feminist theory—precisely because it is feminist—which stresses or even implies "progress." Yet, it is important to acknowledge that, even perhaps especially within feminism, there is the ever present potential of regression, uneven development, failure and disillusion, not to mention misunderstanding. For some, what had once been enabling is now perceived as a restrictive and tiresome paradigm, which generates analysis after analysis, but little new insight. There is a kind of *ennui* which haunts the project of feminist film criticism at the moment and which has become increasingly visible.
>
> —Janet Bergstrom and Mary Ann Doane

In their introduction to a special issue of *Camera Obscura* devoted to the female spectator, Janet Bergstrom and Mary Ann Doane offer the above intriguing remarks about history, *ennui*, and feminist film theory. There is a pervasive sense of exhaustion and disillusion within feminism today, they suggest, a kind of *ennui* which now "haunts the project of feminist film criticism."[1] Although described as something "increasingly visible," this *ennui* seems more precisely visceral, affective: a feeling of weariness and discontent traceable to at least two sources. On the one hand, it derives from a teleological, progressive, even generational view of history, one which sees feminist film theory (particularly in its Mulveyan or modernist mode of the seventies and eighties) as somehow exhausted or completed—merely a stage in the development of the next new thing. On the other hand, it results from the "ever present potential of regression, uneven development, failure and disillusion" to which, Bergstrom and Doane point out, "even perhaps especially" feminism is prone.[2]

Needless to say, Bergstrom and Doane at once acknowledge and reject the *ennui* they so aptly diagnose. (Not all repetitions are redundancies, they imply, given the potential within feminism for uneven developments, not to mention misunderstandings.) If, as they maintain, it is tempting to write the history of feminist theory in terms of progress—in other words, in terms of novelty or innovation that leaves the past behind—it is nonetheless important to also write its failures and regressions, since failures, like successes, both impede and generate change.

I would like to approach the question of the relationship between feminism and historical representation by introducing terms similar to Bergstrom's and Doane's; namely, modernism and feminism, boredom and history. I intend to show in this essay how modernism, like feminism itself, is best understood not as a *novel* way of representing history but as a *banal* way of representing novelty as well as gender difference. Thus understood, both feminism and modernism open up ways in which to historicize and destabilize gendered experiences of *ennui* as well as modern experiences of time. As I hope will become clear, the current state of feminist film theory—its sense of boredom, exhaustion, and fatigue—might be seen within this perspective as more enabling, less restrictive and less novel, than it does at first glance.

modernism, postmodernism

It is significant, I think, that most discussions of *ennui* and boredom today take place within discourses of postmodernism (where the status of modernism, rather than gender, is usually at stake). From Baudrillard's remarks about banality and fatality to Jameson's work on boredom and aesthetics to Lyotard's ruminations on boredom and the sublime, it would seem as though various postmodernisms evoke a language of exhaustion, repetition, and decline. To take but one example, in his book, *The End of Modernity: Nihilism and Hermeneutics in Postmodern Culture* (1988), Gianni Vattimo sees the contemporary or postmodernist experience of history as the experience of the "end of history." By this Vattimo means the end of a certain sense of history, what he calls a "banal vision" of an "already articulated order" which he links both to modernism and to the experience of modernity. For Vattimo, historical *ennui* is the most enduring legacy of modernity, with its logic "of novelty become obsolete and replaced by new novelty in a process that discourages creativity in the very act of demanding it."[3] Paradoxically, he claims, it is the modernist cultivation of the new which inhibits novelty and produces a pervasive feeling of historical *ennui* in the present—"the feeling that the weight of history would effectively suffocate the possibility of any new creation in the culture at large," as one critic has described it.[4] According to Vattimo, the only way out of this condition is to deny historical novelty all meaning and to reject its vulgar (i.e., progressive and cumulative) vision of time. Instead of novelty, and against banality, Vattimo proposes a recollection and a rethinking of the past—what he calls *Verwindung* (overcoming, getting over, recuperating) and also *pietas* (devoted affection, respect).

From a feminist perspective, Vattimo's diagnosis of both the condition of and the solution to postmodernity raises interesting issues and questions. (The historical *ennui* he describes, for example, seems remarkably similar to that described by Bergstrom and Doane.) To begin with, what has banality meant for women modernists as well as for women more generally in modernity? Is the sense of historical *ennui* he describes gender coded? More to the point, what does a stance of "devoted affection" or "respect" for the past have to offer feminist historians? And to what extent do they need to get over, overcome, or recuperate from what has been counted and recounted as history? Indeed, to what extent has the weight of the past actually "suffocated" women's creativity and the very possibility of social and political change? Is it, in fact, the weight of the past or the leaden quality of the present that inhibits feminist novelty and produces *ennui*?

In her book *The Gendering of Melancholia* (1992), Juliana Schiesari poses similar questions, and argues that the politics of lack and loss, as articulated in postmodernist discourses of "history at an end," themselves have a long and venerable history:

> After two decades of proclaiming new beginnings and new sciences of all sorts, contemporary theoretical discourse seems given over to a rhetoric of loss and to a general sense that things are at an "end".... Where the "ends" of man, modernity, or Western metaphysics were once greeted with morbid glee and anarchistic celebration, now the apocalyptic tone of such pronouncements seems somewhat hollow, and even tinged with a sense of defeat and anguish.... Of course, this is not the first time

> that melancholia has surfaced as a dramatic cultural phenomenon among a Western intellectual elite, even to the point of signifying what it means to be a thinker, scholar, or poet.[5]

Schiesari explains that the discourse of melancholy and historical *ennui*, a specific representational form of male creativity familiar to philosophy and literature, was "inaugurated by the Renaissance, refined by the Enlightenment, flaunted by Romanticism, fetishized by the Decadents, and theorized by Freud, before its current resurgence."[6] This discourse, moreover, functioned to convert feelings of disempowerment into privileged cultural artifacts: male losses were transformed into representational gains and, in the process, women's losses and disempowerment in culture were systematically devalued and excluded. "[T]he great melancholic of yesteryear," writes Schiesari, "would have been a tortured but creative male genius, but the stereotypically depressed person of today is an unhappy and unproductive woman." Schiesari continues:

> Nothing more eloquently expresses what I call the gendering of melancholia than this split between a higher-valued form understood as male and a lower-valued one coded as female ... And not only is the male form empowering and the female one disempowering, but melancholia is romantically garbed in the past while depression is given only the banality of the present.[7]

This analysis of melancholy underscores the ways in which banality and *ennui* are gendered in intellectual discourses of the "ends" of man, modernity, and Western metaphysics. There are, of course, important and historically continuous relationships among melancholy, *ennui*, and boredom, not to mention those among modernism, mass culture, and postmodernism. Nevertheless, in marked contrast to melancholia, which remains "romantically garbed in the past" in intellectual discourses of the present, boredom offers a peculiarly twentieth-century conception of self as well as a subjective, and less exclusively masculine, experience of history and the banality of time.

boredom, melancholy, *ennui*

> Throughout the nineteenth and into the early years of the twentieth century, a reasonably exhaustive study of boredom progressed in the West ... This philosophy put forth the idea that human suffering oscillated along a continuum between anxiety/privation and boredom/satiety. The former carried a connotation of commonality, a quality abhorrent to post-romantic thought, while the latter had more of a connotation of nobility

... [T]he modernist aesthetic takes the narrative in the other direction. Rather than having the connotation of nobility, boredom became an attack on the mundane aspects of fragmentation and redundancy, ... It became a democratic affliction that affected everyone, ... less a problem due to shortages of production (privation) than it was a problem of the monotony of production itself.[8]

Although various disciplines have recently contributed to the study of melancholy (including psychoanalysis, sociology, and literature), for the most part boredom remains somewhat undertheorized in contemporary scholarship, relegated to the status of an uninteresting subset of the more general phenomenon of *ennui*. For example, in an expansive study of Western fiction, entitled *The Demon of Noontide* (1976), Reinhard Kuhn excludes four types of boredom from his analysis of melancholy since he believes they are tangential to the metaphysical concerns of a properly literary history. These are: momentary boredom (what he calls "désoeuvrement"), psychosomatic boredom (which he describes in relation to the typical portrait of the female suburbanite), sociological boredom (or the boredom that results from industrialized labor and leisure), and anomie (or the "total loss of the will to life").[9] In what amounts to the virtual exclusion of every form of boredom known to twentieth-century life, Kuhn argues for the value of melancholy as a creative male condition that is grounded in the explicit exclusion of women. "It is a generally accepted interpretation," he writes of one of the founding texts of literary modernism, "that Flaubert's Emma Bovary presents symptoms similar to those felt by the bored suburbanite."

And yet to reduce her ennui to this level is to misunderstand the very complex condition to which she is victim. The former suffers from a metaphysical malady, and the latter only feels a superficial and vague disquiet. It is this difference in dimension that makes of the one a great literary figure and of the other an undistinguished and uninteresting representative of a group.[10]

Kuhn's remarks confirm what Schiesari sees as central to the tradition of male melancholy: the way in which melancholia is made to represent—is literally represented as—a sensitive or exquisite male illness, which is then said to characterize representation itself, whereas the "lower" form of boredom is characterized by its materiality, by its associations with femininity and by an incapacity to "translate symptoms into a language beyond its own self-referentiality as depression."[11] What Kuhn's example of *Madame Bovary* unwittingly reveals, however, is that the very "superficiality" of boredom links it to a more modern, more gender-specific and female experience of self. Indeed, as Andreas

Huyssen has argued, although "critics have gone to great lengths to show what Flaubert had in common with Emma Bovary—mostly in order to show how he transcended aesthetically the dilemma on which she foundered in 'real life'"—the novel itself became known in its own time as giving representation to a "woman who tried to live the illusions of aristocratic sensual romance and was shipwrecked on the banality of bourgeois everyday life."[12] (188)

This is not to deny the misogyny of Flaubert's text or the way in which Flaubert fetishized his own sense of loss (through an imaginary identification with femininity) while simultaneously sharing his own period's hostility towards women. Nevertheless, if melancholy and boredom are both defined by a certain self-consciousness, in melancholy, self-consciousness is painful precisely because the perception of otherness comes at the cost of exclusivity. In boredom, by contrast, self-consciousness is more "vague" and "superficial"—in Kuhn's example, more apt to bring into representation women's experiences of everyday life. Whereas melancholia is about loss, and about converting male losses into representational gains, boredom, at least in the twentieth century, is about excess, sensory stimulation, and shock (generated as much by the existence of others as by the media and overproduction). What is ever-present in melancholia and seems palpably missing from boredom is thus an overriding sense of nostalgia for an exclusive fantasy of privileged suffering which separates the self from others. In boredom, there is no sense of privilege or nobility. Indeed, in the twentieth century boredom becomes both "a democratic affliction" and a great leveller, bound up with changing definitions of work and leisure, art and mass culture, aesthetics and sexual difference.

Boredom, in other words, is at once an empty and an overflowing conceptual category—empty because it has no ultimate, transcendent meaning; overflowing and excessive because even when it appears fixed it still contains within it definitions that are denied or suppressed. In a sociological study entitled *Overload and Boredom: Essays on the Quality of Life in the Information Society* (1986), Orrin Klapp suggests that the transformation of everyday life in the twentieth-century accounts for the variety of meanings attached to boredom as well as the proliferation of words that refer to boredom as a modern condition. "The following list," he writes, "may suggest that there is more boredom than people recognize by that particular name":

> accidie (acedia), anhedonia, apathy, arid, banal, banality, blasé, burn-out, chatter, chatterbox, glazed eyes, hackneyed, harping, ho hum, humdrum, inane, insipid, insouciance, repetitious, routine, rut, sameness, satiety, soporific, stagnant, stagnation, sterile, chitchat, chore, cliché, cloying, dismal, doldrums, drag, dreary, dry, dull, dullness, effete, enervation, ennui, flat,

> irksome, jade, jaded, jejune, languor, lassitude, listless, long-winded, monotony, museum fatigue, pall, platitude, prolixity, prosaic, prosy, stuffy, stupefying, surfeited, tedium, tedious, tiresome, torpor, trite, trivia, uninteresting, verbosity, weariness, wearisome, world weary.[13]

Klapp concludes the list with the following speculation: "That we have so many words plausibly suggests that modern people have need for them just as the Eskimo has so many words for snow."[14] Otherwise expressed, if boredom is a signifier that fluctuates and resists interpretive closure, it is also a term that attests to cultural changes that are at once psychical and aesthetic, economic and political.

This very instability, moreover, confounds the oppositions—between work and leisure, nobility and commonality, inertia and action, excess and lack, fullness and emptiness, masculinity and femininity—that had once characterized the understanding of melancholia (and its difference from boredom) in the eighteenth and nineteenth centuries. With the rise of visual culture, mass society, mass production, and consumerism, boredom came to describe the modern experience of time as both empty and full, concentrated and distracted (the experience of temporal disruption in the sense of "dead time" as well as temporal duration in the sense of "killing time"). If the division of labor produced sensory deprivation in the overload of repetition, so, too, did mass culture produce boredom in the distracted fullness of a leisure time become empty. As contributors to the journal *Documents* have recently put it, the expansion of boredom in the twentieth century "breaks the boundary of the nineteenth-century narrative that separated boredom/satiety and anxiety/privation. There is high-velocity crash, and the two once separate qualities are twisted together in an inseparable entwinement."[15]

conformity and subversion

Given the "inseparable entwinement" of opposing terms within twentieth century boredom, it is not surprising that the politics of banality have been the subject of an intense and protracted debate. Is boredom about resistance and opposition, a refusal of the novel in the anticipation of something truly new? Or is boredom about conformity and repetition, the banalization of identity or of novelty in the very act of demanding it? In other words, does boredom involve an uncomfortable yet creative self-consciousness, or does it merely reinforce sameness, disinterest, and apathy—a resignation to the status quo? "Monotony nourishes the new,"[16] wrote Walter Benjamin in the notes to his unfinished Arcades project, where he also remarked, "boredom is the threshold of great deeds."[17] Some thirty years later, the Situationist International declared: "Boredom is always counterrevolutionary"[18]

Whether boredom and banality take on qualities of resistance or conformity obviously has much to do with historically specific and competing views of mass culture and mass society. But the political instability of the term also has something to do with assessments about the inevitability and, indeed, the very desirability of the fragmentation of identity and of history. The role of gender is not innocent here, but neither is it obvious or self-evident. To be sure, a split persists in the twentieth century between a higher-valued form of boredom understood as male and a lower-valued form of boredom understood as female. But in the modalities of boredom that proliferate in the twentieth century (modalities which include *ennui*, resistance, subversion, conformity, dullness, nonidentity), women's losses and disempowerment in culture begin to come into representation, and thus into historical view.

This is especially true of certain modernist representations of boredom, which, as I suggested earlier, are distinguished both from eighteenth- and nineteenth-century views of melancholia and from some current versions of postmodernism by their emphasis on the banality of the present, now understood in gendered terms. For instance, in her early journalistic writings as well as in her later novels and plays, Djuna Barnes performed a critique of *fin-de-siècle* attitudes towards women and heterosexual romance and in the process offered another way of understanding the banality of the present and its pervasive sense of historical *ennui*. For Barnes, historical *ennui* is produced by gender and sexual difference. She therefore focuses on the condition of modern women in the city, where new freedoms prove to be only relative and contingent and where gendered dichotomies limit and contain women's desires for sexual transformation and social change. The possibility of imagining a way out of this situation haunts all of Barnes's writings but is especially apparent in her early interviews with women whose activities exceeded traditionally defined feminine roles: Mother Jones, the suffragettes who endured force-feeding, women boxers, a policewoman who wrote poetry. Barnes's attempt to render the everydayness of these women's activities in mass culture is, in part, an effort to defamiliarize the familiar understanding of gender and sexual difference in modernity—not by seeing things anew, but by seeing them as no longer novel, thus perceiving difference in banality.

In her 1917 interview with stage actress Helen Westley, for example, Barnes explores *ennui* from a woman's perspective and shows how the estrangements and banalities of modern life are fundamentally bound up with experiences of sexual difference. Barnes begins by asking Helen Westley to offer advice to young women who aspire to work in the theater, to which the actress responds that there is no advice, only the experience of *ennui*:

> The history of the world has been one not of conquest, as supposed; it has been one of ennui. Why do we fall in love? Because we are filled with ennui. Why do we fall and break our limbs? Because of ennui. Why do we fall ill and remain unconscious for hours? Ennui, my dear. Ennui sends us to our death; ennui sends us to the battlefields; ennui sends us through the world, and ennui takes us out of it. If this were not so, do you suppose for a moment that we would permit ourselves to fall in love once we had heard of its effects?....
>
> Give me despair, and I am at my best. Give me sorrow, and only then are my shoulders worthy of me...Where have I learned this trick of the half-turned shoulder, the cold, drooping eyes? Through sorrows and difficulties. There's nothing like it for developing the figure and making one supple; it's better than dancing or swimming. Oh, yes, I can face all things.[19]

At once serious and frivolous, provocative and self-mocking, Barnes's interview with Helen Westley challenges the assumption that *ennui* is a male condition and exposes its status as theatrical gesture or pose. This is not to say that the pose is without reference to real suffering or disillusionment—or to real women. It is rather to suggest that women's suffering and disillusionment in the present have less to do with novelty than with banality, with feelings of weariness and discontent despite (apparent) sexual freedom and social progress. In the middle of the interview, Westley and Barnes break into laughter at the recognition of this fact, and admit the futility—and banality—of *ennui* for women:

> Westley: Well, let's stop.
>
> Barnes: We can't, not yet; I have at least three more pages to fill.[20]

Here, as in her later writings, Barnes at once mimes and subverts the conventions which both demand and inhibit novelty and prevent the possibility of anything new. In this early interview, for instance, she targets the interview form and the traditional discourse on *ennui*—the former of which was historically in the business of selling novelty and the latter of which was considered the preserve of a tortured but creative male genius. Paradoxically (or, perhaps, not so paradoxically) it is the acknowledgment of boredom which relieves anxiety through laughter. If melancholy had previously been the measure by which the novelty of historical *ennui* was assessed, Barnes destroys this measure by insisting on the significance of *ennui* for women and then by undercutting this significance and replacing it with boredom—the empty pages to be filled.

Barnes was not, of course, the only modernist writer to explore *ennui* in relation to modernity and sexual difference. T. S. Eliot—Barnes's editor, friend, and consistent critic—took up remarkably similar issues in a celebrated 1930 essay on Baudelaire, in which Eliot seems to speak of nineteenth-century France, but is in fact referring to twentieth-century mass culture. "The possibility of damnation," he writes of Baudelaire's poetry in this essay, "is so immense a relief in a world of electoral reform, plebiscites, sex reform, and dress reform, that damnation itself is an immediate form of salvation—of salvation from the ennui of modern life, because at least it gives some significance to living."[21] Glossing this quote, literary critic Gregory Jay explains,

> The list of modern life's boredoms is itself significant: it includes the spread of democracy to women and the lower classes, the replacement of governmental authority by popular votes, the liberation of sexual activity from state and church dictates, and the disappearance of rigid dress codes for men and women in public. Behind each of these threats is a breakdown in hierarchical differences, an unleashing of possibilities of relation and meaning.[22]

Whereas Eliot insists on *ennui* as the meaning of the modern age, Barnes opts for boredom in an effort to dislodge meanings that appear fixed in modernity. As the examples I have cited from their writings suggest, if *ennui*, melancholia, and boredom are all defined by a certain self-consciousness, this very consciousness involves an implicit notion of the gendered self. For Eliot, self-consciousness is painful because the perception of otherness comes at the cost of male exclusivity—the spread of democracy to women and the working class. For Barnes, self-consciousness remains more vague and superficial because it lacks this sense of privileged suffering that separates self from others. Whereas modernity and sexual difference are thus the explicitly named sources of Eliot's *ennui*, for Barnes they are the sources of boredom—a boredom which at once denies and asserts the novelty of historical suffering by acknowledging women's discontent, and thus a notion of a gendered self, previously denied representation.

modernism and historiography

As the examples of Barnes and Eliot suggest, the relationships among modernism, *ennui*, and boredom must be reassessed if we are to understand what Hayden White sees as the dissolution of the historical event in the unrepresentability of such twentieth-century phenomena as two World Wars, the Great Depression, and the Holocaust. In his recent writing on modernism and historiography, for instance, White has drawn extensively on the work of modernist writers (notably Virginia Woolf and Gertrude Stein) in an effort to detail and defend the modernist tendency to unleash possibilities of relation and meaning, to de-realize the distinction between fact and fiction, and to dissolve the event into a specter of non-meaning. It is nonetheless significant that White never addresses the role of gender in historiography and fails to consider the way in which sexual difference is either represented or unrepresentable in the modernist experience of boredom—of a time without event.

As I have attempted to demonstrate, gender and sexual difference are central to this experience of time in modernity—the time between the event and the uneventful, between that which happens and that which fails to occur. If, as Fredric Jameson has claimed, "history is what hurts," then, as Djuna Barnes, Virginia Woolf, Gertrude Stein, and other women modernists have shown, history is also about what *fails to happen* (something about which female artists and feminist women in the twentieth-century have long been painfully aware). This, it seems to me, is the significance of the modernist derealization of the historical event as something objective, discrete, teleological, and uncontested in twentieth century feminisms. All too often, when history "hurts," pain is expressed in the tradition of male melancholia. This tradition, I have argued, not only excludes women's experiences of the non-eventful—and thus their experiences of history—but it also elevates male suffering as a sensitive or privileged illness which apparently characterizes representation and, in recent debates about postmodernism, the very possibility of history itself.

This is why boredom offers such a useful conceptual language to begin thinking about the fading of the historical event and the status of history in twentieth-century representational forms. Indeed, similar to modernism and like gender, boredom is a term that appears fixed and yet whose meaning remains contested, open-ended, always in flux. It is perhaps not surprising, then, that so much feminist work over the past decades—from the literary writings of Djuna Barnes to the experimental work of feminist filmmakers to the critical writings of feminist film theorists—has involved an aesthetics as well as a phenomenology of boredom: a temporality of duration, relentless in its repetition, and a stance of active waiting, which, at least in their feminist formulations, allow for redefinition, resistance, and change. For women modernists, aesthetic and phenomenological boredom provided a homeopathic cure for the banality of the present—a restless self-consciousness (a "desire to desire") very different from the ideal of disinterestedness that characterizes traditional historiography. It seems to me that the same kind of self-consciousness is available to feminist film theorists today. Indeed, the *ennui* that currently haunts the feminist project (and that has haunted feminism in the past) may ultimately prove creative and enabling rather than a cause for *ennui* or despair. Boredom and repetition, of course, have long been central to feminist aesthetics as well as to mass culture and women's experiences of everyday life. And although some now find feminism (rather than the limitations placed on women) tiresome and repetitive, it is important to remember that dead moments and dead ends in the present have been the source of new ideas and new creations in the past. Feminist insights therefore bear repeating (not all repetitions are redundancies, given the ever-present potential for failure, not to mention misunderstanding) in the ongoing attempt by women to create spaces for reflection, renewal, and change.

In any event (and perhaps especially in this time without event for feminism), a feminist historiography that takes its inspiration from modernism must reject the tedium of conventional representation (including what has now become a conventional representation of feminism itself) in order to reclaim the banality—in the sense of the everydayness—of gender, sexuality, and sexual orientation. At the same time, however, it must refuse postmodern melancholy and its discourse of lack and loss, of "history at an end," if it is to represent women's (past) losses and imagine their (future) gains. To put it slightly differently, in this time of historical *ennui*, even (perhaps especially) within feminism there remains an ever present need to struggle against the everyday on behalf of the everyday. And this will involve, as it has always done, a struggle not simply against boredom, but also for it.

notes

1. Janet Bergstrom and Mary Ann Doane, "The Female Spectator: Contexts and Direction," *Camera Obscura* 20/21 (May–September 1989), Special Issue "The Spectatrix," 15.
2. Bergstrom and Doane.
3. Gianni Vattimo, "*Verwindung*: Nihilism and the Postmodern in Philosophy," *Substance* 53 (1987): 8.
4. Daniel Barbiero, "A Weakness for Heidegger: The German Root of *Il Pensiero Debole*," *New German Critique* 55 (Winter 1992): 163.
5. Juliana Schiesari, *The Gendering of Melancholia: Feminism, Psychoanalysis, and the Symbolics of Loss in Renaissance Literature* (Ithaca and London: Cornell University Press, 1992), 1–2.
6. Schiesari, 3.
7. Schiesari, 16.
8. *Documents* 1: 1-2 (Winter 1993), Special Issue "On Boredom," 91–92.
9. Reinhard Kuhn, *The Demon of Noontide: Ennui in Western Literature* (Princeton: Princeton University Press, 1976), 9.
10. Kuhn, 9.
11. Schiesari, 16.
12. Andreas Huyssen, "Mass Culture as Woman: Modernism's Other," in *Studies in Entertainment: Critical Approaches to Mass Culture*, Ed. Tania Modleski (Bloomington: Indiana University Press, 1986), 188.

13. Orrin Klapp, *Overload and Boredom: Essays on the Quality of Life in the Information Society* (New York: Greenwood Press, 1986), 23
14. Klapp, 23.
15. *Documents*, 92.
16. Walter Benjamin, *Das Passagen-Werk*, ed. Rolf Tiedemann, 2 vols. (Frankfurt: Suhrkamp, 1982), 962.
17. Benjamin, 162
18. Quoted in Geoff Waite, "On the Politics of Boredom: (a communist pastiche)." *Documents* 1:1–2 (Winter 1992): 102.
19. Djuna Barnes, *I Could Never Be Lonely Without a Husband: Interviews by Djuna Barnes*, ed. Alyce Barry (London: Virago Press, 1985), 253–55.
20. Barnes, 258.
21. T. S. Eliot, *Selected Essays* (New York: Harcourt Brace, 1950), 379.
22. Gregory S. Jay, "Postmodernism and *The Waste Land*: Women, Mass Culture, and Others," in *Rereading the New*, ed. Kevin Dettmar (University of Michigan Press, 1992), 238.

ten

the future of the past

film and the beginnings of postmodern history

robert a. rosenstone

THESIS: The argument of this (sketch for an) essay can be stated simply: among theorists of and apologists for postmodernism (the two categories overlap), there are a few who take time to discuss a new kind of historical writing—a postmodern history which, apparently, brings the way we know or think of the past into line with the post-structuralist critique of current historical practice. As examples of this tendency, these theorists point towards the work of certain historians, or to particular genres of historical writing, or to individual works of history. But something odd happens between the notions of postmodern history and its exemplars, for as any fool can plainly see (as my father would have said), the historians, genres, and works of history named by these theorists do not really fulfill the notions of postmodernism as outlined by these theorists themselves. Works that fulfill their notions of this new kind of history do exist, but not at all where the theorists are pointing. For while professional historians continue, with but a few exceptions, to write in a highly traditional manner, some little-known filmmakers and videographers have begun to create a kind of history that we can truly label postmodern, producing works that provide a distinctly new relationship to and a new way of making meaning of the traces of the past.[1]

CONFESSION: Pardon the digression, but I feel the need to explain that I come to this issue not as a theorist (you can tell that already), but as a historian. One trained some thirty years ago in the Dragnet School of History—*Just the facts, Ma'am.* Intellectual developments in the quarter century since then—the poststructuralist revolution—have clearly altered my beliefs, but have not wholly destroyed them. Even if I now know that we historians constitute our objects of study on the basis of ideological and political agendas and create narratives (or even analytic articles) shaped not by data but by linguistic rules and prefigured tropes, I still believe we have something important to learn from studying long-gone people, beliefs, moments, movements, and events (yes, we need these, too). So if my faith in the truth of what we can know about the past has diminished (and it has), my need for such knowledge remains firm. From Dragnet History I have moved on to Samuel Beckett History—*I can't go on; I'll go on.*

POSTMODERN HISTORY?: The notion of postmodern history seems like a contradiction in terms. The heart of Postmodernism, all theorists agree, is a struggle against History—with a capital "H." A denial of its narratives, findings, and truth claims. A view of it as the great enemy, the Oedipal father, the metanarrative of metanarratives, the last and greatest of the White Mythologies used to legitimate Western hegemony, a false and outworn discourse that fosters nationalism, racism, ethnocentrism, colonialism, sexism—and all the other evils of contemporary society.

One (unusually) clear statement of the case against History has postmodernism questioning the following: "(1) the idea that there is a real, knowable past, a record of evolutionary progress of human ideas, institutions, or actions, (2) the view that historians should be objective, (3) that reason enables historians to explain the past, and (4) that the role of history is to interpet and transmit human cultural and intellectual tradition from generation to generation."[2]

SURPRISE! A few theorists of Postmodernism nonetheless display a certain amount of interest in, even sympathy for, a study of the past—for doing history with a small *h.* Among them are the following: Linda Hutcheon, Elizabeth Deeds Ermarth, Pauline Rosenau, F.R. Ankersmit, and Hans

Kellner. It will violate their individual views to do so, but let me present a kind of pastiche, taken from their writings, that describes the history they admire:

History that "problematizes the entire notion of historical knowledge." That foregrounds the "usually concealed attitude of historians towards their material." That reeks with "provisionality and undecidability, partisanship and even overt politics...." That "engages pulse and intellect simultaneously...." That "breaks down the convention of historical time ... and subsitutes a new convention of temporality ... rhythmic time." That aims not at "integration, synthesis, and totality." That is content with "historical scraps." That is not "the reconstruction of what has happened to us in the various phases of our lives, but a continuous playing with the memory of this." That is expressed not in coherent stories but in fragments and "collage."[3]

ONE ODDITY: When these theorists attempt to cite examples of postmodern history, they tend to wave in the direction of categories and genres instead of dealing with the specific works.

For Linda Hutcheon, *postmodern* or *New* history (she elides the terms, as do others) includes a wide range of approaches, from the *Annales* school to histories that highlight the past experiences of the formerly excluded: women, ethnic minorities, gays, losers (rather than winners), regional and colonial peoples, and the many (rather than the few, or the ruling elites).[4]

Pauline Marie Rosenau sees postmodern—or New—history as employing "deconstruction, subjective interpretation, and a symbolic construction of reality, rather than quantitative, structural, or functional methods ... it seeks to unravel texts, raise questions about meaning in the text, and invent micronarratives as alternatives to history." Rosenau's list of genres points to works written by feminists, African-Americans, neo-Marxists, psychoanalytic, and "discourse oriented" historians.[5]

ANOTHER ODDITY: When these theorists attempt to name individual historians responsible for works of postmodern history, they point towards two kinds of scholars:

(1) Other theorists. People like themselves who do not (apparently) deal with the *pulse* of the past at all. That is, historians who ignore textualized events, movements, individuals, in order to analyze textualized texts, works of high culture, the writings of philosophers, critics, and historians. The common names given: Hayden White, Dominick LaCapra, Jacques Derrida, Michel Foucault.

(2) Fairly traditional historians who have broadened the discipline by approaching topics with tools drawn from other disciplines, especially

anthropology, literature, philosophy, critical theory, gender studies. Or who have helped to open up new subject areas—working-class, ethnic, feminist, subaltern, gay. The common names, mentioned repeatedly: Emmanuel LeRoy Ladurie, Georges Duby, Carlo Ginzburg, Natalie Davis.

A THIRD ODDITY: When these same theorists attempt to name actual works of postmodern history, they provide a (very) few titles, over and over: Emmanuel LeRoy Ladurie, *Montaillou*; Natalie Davis, *The Return of Martin Guerre*; Carlo Ginzburg, *The Cheese and the Worms.*

A FOURTH: Opponents of postmodernism take the same slash-and-burn approach. In a piece entitled "Telling it as you like it: Post-modern history and the flight from fact," the most outspoken of these opponents, Gertrude Himmelfarb, has great difficulty in actually locating examples of the new kind of history she trashes with such ferocious glee. Denouncing both Joan Scott and Theodore Zeldin without ever mentioning their actual historical works, she points to a single example of postmodern history—Simon Schama's *Dead Certainties*,[6] yet this is a book comprising what the author himself calls two "novellas ... works of the imagination, not scholarship."[6] Clearly, specificity is much less fun than soundly thrashing the *usual suspects*: White, LaCapra, Foucault, Derrida.[7]

BORGESIAN HISTORY?: Hutcheon and Rosenau, Himmelfarb, and the other theorists have, apparently, forgotten only the kitchen sink. Maybe it won't fit in their conceptually overstuffed grabbags. The problem is that the lists of genres, historians, and works of history are oddly unparallel, largely mistaken, curiously unrevealing, and highly self-contradictory. The *Annales* (named by Hutcheon) began (and continues) as an attempt to make history more scientific, not more problematic; to this day, *Annales* historians are likely to call themselves *scientists* rather than *humanists*. As for the formerly excluded (named by all theorists)—whether one points to subject matter (ethnics, gays, colonials) or approach (psychoanalytic, neo-Marxist)—at least two things must be said: First many of the categories (African-Americans, the working class) and approaches (say neo-Marxism) are not new, but have been part of traditional history for decades now and are an accepted part of historical discourse. Second other categories (losers, or regionals, or colonials) may be considered outsiders only from certain standpoints—it is increasingly recognized by historians now that one person's margins are always someone else's center. For a historian of India, Senegal, or Viet Nam, Western Europe can now be considered the periphery.

THE POINT: The historians, the genres, and the individual works mentioned by theorists who discuss works of history do not at all fulfill the theorist's own critique of traditional History or the notions of Postmodern history that they elaborate.

This is not to deny that in the past quarter century historians have opened up vast new areas of study (pointed to by the theorists) and created many new approaches for excavating and rethinking the remains of the past. Indeed, the achievements of the New Social History and of feminists and postcolonial historians in giving voice to those previously voiceless (women, ethnic minorities, industrial workers, peasants, the colonized) are so extensive and well known that one can hardly remember a time when they were not part of our historical picture. But in their presentations of the past, in the way they write, these historians have not strayed from very traditional notions of realistic narrative, logical explanation, linear argument, traditional cause and effect. Indeed, so tame is their prose that one has to wonder whether the theorists have actually read the historical works they label postmodern. (What one suspects, of course, is that they ignore works of history in favor of reading other theorists.)

Emmanuel Le Roy Ladurie's *Montaillou*, where multiple voices speak and interpenetrate with that of the historian, may be the single work of history to move any real distance towards formal literary innovation. None of the other scholars cited goes so far. None (including Le Roy Ladurie) uses pastiche or collage. None creates a world that includes new notions of temporality, such as *rhythmic* time. None problematizes major assertions. None presents a world comprised of *scraps*, or gives up traditional modes of analysis. And when these histories foreground the politics and ideology of the author, they do so in the preface—exactly where historians have always felt free to bare their souls and ideologies.[8]

The examples of the so-called postmodern history touted by the theorists are, to anyone who has a taste for the new, a real disappointment. Certainly they have nothing in common with the postmodernism exhibited in other fields and art forms. These histories contain none of the dash, the humor, the mixing of genres, the pastiche, the collage, the odd juxtapositions, the temporal jumps, the wacky illogic of the architecture, theater, or literature we label postmodern. Ultimately they seem to fill nobody's notions of the postmodern—not the theorists, not mine, and not—(may I assume?)—yours.

FILMMAKERS TO THE RESCUE: If you long for new kinds of history, if you think we need new ways of relating to the past, don't despair. Postmodern history has been born and is currently alive and well. It exists less on the page than on the screen and is the creation of filmmakers and videographers. By both traditional and modern standards, this should not be surprising. The visual media have become our chief means of telling each other about the world. And filmmakers clearly have much less invested in traditional ways of rendering the past than do historians—though they have no less investment in its meaning.

What do these (real) postmodern history films do to the past? Lots of things, including some or all of the following: (1) Tell the past self-reflexively, in terms of how it has meaning for the filmmaker historian. (2) Recount it from a multiplicity of viewpoints. (3) Eschew traditional narrative, with a beginning, middle, and end—or, following Jean-Luc Godard, insist these three elements need not necessarily be in that order. (4) Forsake normal story development, or tell stories but refuse to take the telling seriously. (5) Approach the past with humor, parody, absurdist, surrealist, dadaesque, and other irreverent attitudes. (6) Intermix contradictory elements: past and present, drama and documentary, and indulge in creative anachronism. (7) Accept, even glory in, their own selectivity, partialism, partisanship, and rhetorical character. (8) Refuse to focus or sum up the meaning of past events, but rather make sense of them in a partial and open-ended, rather than totalized, manner. (9) Alter and invent incident and character. (10) Utilize fragmentary and/or poetic knowledge. (11) Never forget that the present is the site of all past representation and knowing.

To exemplify how such elements are used, I shall move to some descriptions of postmodern history films, doing so in the full knowledge that these descriptions should not be on a page but on a screen—as film or video; or, better yet, as an interactive CD-ROM that mixes text, moving image, and sound; or over the Internet, which can already carry moving visual images along with text. These media are, I think, uniquely capable of dealing with the multiple, complex, and overlapping elements that comprise historical film. Already one work of history and one of cinema studies have appeared on or utilized CD-ROM.[9] A few years down the road, articles on the visual media will routinely appear in such formats. But at this moment, even as I write in a style designed to shake up normal academic forms and expectations and to approximate, however distantly, the cuts and juxtapositions of the visual media, I must confess to being hyper-aware of the difficulties and limitation of telling films in words—especially obscure films that you, the reader, may not have seen. All this means you will have to trust the author of this article even more than you usually trust the author of a scholarly essay. A similar problem of trust is posed by the historical film, pre- or postmodern. Because films lack footnotes, bibliography, and other scholarly apparatus, they have difficulty justifying the accuracy of their vision of the past to the audience. The usual strategy is to overwhelm with drama, color, sound. My strategy is to disarm you by giving this apparent confession as a warning. But take heed: before you accept my arguments, go get these films and see them for yourself.

WELCOME TO THE SHOW: With something as new as postmodern history, division into smaller categories seems premature. Yet to show the range and diversity of such films, I shall describe works that, were they written pieces of history, might well fall into such widely-recognized categories as contemporary, ethnic, national, cultural, gender, and comparative history.

CONTEMPORARY: Jill Godmilow's *Far From Poland* (1983), shot at the beginning of the Solidarity Movement, deals with a contemporary topic in a self-reflexive way. It foregrounds the life of the filmmaker in order to show how personal matters impact both upon the film and the history of Solidarity that it renders—a history, like almost all works of history, created a great distance away in time and/or space from the events it depicts and analyzes.[11]

Far From Poland begins with the filmmaker talking from note cards directly into the camera. Explaining that she happened to be in Poland when the shipyard strikes began in Gdansk in 1980, Godmilow tells us she flew back to New York, raised some money, hired a camera crew, and bought tickets for Warsaw. Her aim: "to tell the real story." Godmilow's image is replaced by that of a worker with a helmet and blowtorch who says: "Let me tell you a story." His tale is not, as we might expect, about the shipyards, but about a documentary filmmaker, steeped in the traditions of the left, who "searched the world for the face of humanity" and found it in Poland at the time of the strikes. The camera pulls back and we see that the worker's image is on a video monitor in an editing room, with Godmilow watching it and groaning. In voiceover, she tells us that this is her current friend, Mark Magill, a performance artist whose notion of Marxism is of the "Harpo, Zeppo variety." The real Mark enters through a door and they argue over the film she is making: she talks about the struggles for truth and justice; he claims that, like everyone else, she only wants to use Solidarity to prove her ideas are right.

The competing voices in this opening sequence continue; the debate over what this work of history can mean grows ever more urgent as other voices join in. Once the filmmaker learns she cannot get a visa for Poland and decides to make a film anyway, in New York, her quandary over how to deal with Solidarity becomes part of the history she tells. The variety of methods she uses to present this history are inventive: along with the filmmaker's domestic drama and direct address, *Far From Poland* utilizes American TV footage, video shot for Godmilow by Solidarity cameramen, re-enactments of interviews with workers that were published in the Polish press, interviews with Polish emigres, letters from a friend in Poland, flashcards, midnight conversations (the screen is black) between Godmilow and Fidel Castro over the meaning of Socialism; a laugh track; and out-takes from a fictional movie, ostensibly shot by famed director Andrzej Wajda in 1988 (five years after *Poland* was released), showing Polish dictator General Jaruzelski living under house arrest imposed by a new people's government which has succeeded his regime.

What sort of history does all this make? Godmilow not only learns, while making the film, that she cannot tell *the real story*, she learns why nobody else can tell it either—for there is no real story to tell, but only a series of ways of representing, thinking about, and looking at the Polish movement. Yet for all the open admission of the personal stake of the filmmaker-historian in the outcome of the work and the problematics of representation and knowledge that the film underlines, *Far From Poland* ends up by making strong claims for the importance of the history of Solidarity (about which we do learn a good deal). The film suggests Solidarity is a highly significant human and social movement, a harbinger of change for Poland and, perhaps, for other parts of Europe and the world. Not a bad prediction for a work which refused to take itself absolutely seriously.

ETHNIC: Rea Tajiri's *History and Memory* (1991) is also self-reflexive, but this video about the American relocation camps for Japanese during World War Two foregrounds the personal stakes of the historian in uncovering the past.[12] Early in the film, Tajiri, in voiceover, tells us, "I began searching for a history, my own history, because I knew the stories I had heard were not true—and parts of them had been left out." During this voiceover we see a woman, her back to the camera, standing in a dusty place and filling a canteen with water. This vision of Tajiri's mother is her sole legacy from the camps, a place she has never been but which she somehow can remember; a place of "great sadness" that has haunted her life.

Tajiri's desire to understand that single image fuels the film. Her problem of how to create a usable past that will ease the personal pain that history has caused is a double one: she must find a way around both social and personal amnesia—she must combat the lies, evasions, and partialisms of official history and the popular media, and get past the silence of the older generation of Japanese-Americans about the camp experience (made literal in Tajiri's case by her mother's inability to remember anything at all).

In its resurrection of the past, *History and Memory* uses a good deal of the kind of archival film to be found in a great number of current documentaries. The film includes Japanese and American military footage of the attack on

Pearl Harbor; clips from Hollywood films, like *From Here to Eternity* (Fred Zinneman, 1953), *Bad Day at Black Rock* (John Sturges, 1955), and *Come See the Paradise* (Alan Parker, 1990); newsreels that show Japanese-Americans going off to relocation centers; an Office of War Information propaganda film about the necessity for the camps and the happiness of the internees; interviews with relatives who were incarcerated; footage of the filmmaker's personal journey to Poston, Arizona, where her family was held; and sequences from some illegally-shot (cameras were banned) 8-mm footage of daily life in the camps.

The film also includes some elements less common in documentary: dramatic re-enactments of family scenes and, perhaps most unusual, a black screen with text scrolling over it to "show" us those important events that take place while no camera is watching, such as the condemnation and removal of her family house by a government agency.

The structure that holds together the images and voices of *History and Memory* is not a traditional linear narration of the past; nor is the message a simple one of condemnation of the official racism sanctioned by war. Certainly the work contains enough information to give us a sense of the dimensions of the great injustice done to one group of Americans, and after a half-century, the hyper-patriotic and feverish distortions of the media starkly reveal themselves. But the filmmaker's purpose goes beyond recapturing the past and redressing grievances. *History and Memory* is a work that creates a different notion of the past in its insistence that fact, fiction, and memory—including their distortions—are equally important elements of historical discourse.

NATIONAL: Ross Gibson's *Camera Natura* (1986) looks at the history of Australia from the earliest convict settlements to the present day—but not in the way national histories are traditionally told.[13] In this work there is nothing about economic development, social change, and political reform, for Gibson sees his country's history in terms of the relationship between the European population and the continent's landscape. The vast, inhospitable, and often intractable terrain has been central to the construction of the nation's mythologies and ideologies, to notions of the Australian *character* and *destiny*.

Early in the film, we see a re-enactment of an incident from the life of Tom Watling, an eighteenth-century transported convict and artist who was given the job of creating paintings that would transform the harsh landscape around him into something tame and homey for people back in Britain. Before doing his first work, Watling says directly to the camera, "I know what I'm supposed to do," then we see the strokes he uses to soften and prettify the scene before him. For the filmmaker, Watling clearly is the traditional historian, molding the past to our comfortable expectations of neat and tidy Progress. Overtly disdaining just this kind of approach to the past, *Camera Natura* goes on to create a far more elusive and disturbing kind of history.

What we see is a history comprised of fragments assembled into a work that is neither linear, cyclical, dialectical, nor any other discernible shape. The film moves backwards and forwards in time, ranging over the landscape (literally and figuratively) of past and present with a vast array of materials: maps, paintings, clips from fiction films and military documentaries, TV advertisements, dramatic recreations. Points are made not through linear or even necessarily clear argument; instead one senses the themes here: the land as threat and the land as spiritual inspiration; the wilderness as the foundation of both community and individualism; the evolution of the media—from eighteenth-century painting to nineteenth-century photography to twentieth-century moving images—as both reflection and cause of historical change. Eros and gender are themes in this film too, often in sublimated form. "Women and the earth," proclaims a hero in a film: "I've always felt they were much the same, only the earth more exciting." There is also an ongoing affair with changing modes of transportation—recurrent images of the horses, cars, and airplanes necessary to conquer the vast spaces of the continent.

The fragmentation that shatters the surface of *Camera Natura* is not the only aspect that marks it as postmodern. Most unusual for a work of history, particularly a national history, is its refusal of closure, an unwillingness to conclude that two hundred years of Australia add up to some particular notion or cluster of notions that are particularly good or bad for residents of the land. The final image of the work, a TV advertisement for fast food that shows sacred mountains suddenly transformed into a hamburger and french fries, may suggest things about the processes of secularization and commodification in the contemporary world—but the message, like all the other messages in this work, consciously creates an interpretive challenge for anyone wishing to come to grips with the Australian past.

CULTURAL: Juan Downey's *Hard Times and Culture* (1990) views its much-studied subject, "*fin-de-siècle* Vienna," from the point of view of the contemporary moment.[14] The first image is of New York skyscrapers, while on the soundtrack rappers sing over and over a quotation from George Kubler: "An epoch of staggering difficulties above which painting, poetry and the theater flowered imperishably." An African-American woman speaks to us on screen: "Out of the cesspool beautiful flowers come out of there, you know?" A cab driver looks in a rear-view mirror—and sees Vienna at the time of Franz Josef.

The history that follows is as offbeat as the film's opening. Or perhaps one should say *histories*, for several approaches to the past jostle each other in this work. Political developments are expressed in three ways: as waltz, as soap opera, as bad TV drama. A narrator tells us: "Like a waltz, the history of the empire can be played in triple meter, in three beats." Each beat represents a death in the royal family—the murder of Kaiserin Elizabeth, the suicide of Prince Rudolf at Mayerling, and the assassination of Archduke Franz Ferdinand and his wife at Sarajevo. Framed by a stylized TV screen, each death is presented in a factual but highly theatrical and melodramatic manner, with stage blood oozing and actors intoning fatuous (but sometimes historically documentable) lines: "Sophie, Sophie," cries Franz Ferdinand. "Don't die. Stay alive for the children."

The undermining of traditional fact by juxtaposition, framing, and mode of presentation is a strategy pursued in the all-important (for Vienna) realm of culture. Indeed the relationship of data to interpretation is often vague. We hear lectures on the instability of the empire from a professorial type who is shakily riding a bike around the Ringstrasse; we learn that the Emperor maintained a box at every theater in the realm but never attended a single performance; we hear that Bruckner had a "counting disease" that drove him to the edge of insanity while we see a billboard in America counting the mounting national debt; we see decadent Klimt portraits and learn they were painted for the newly rich; we look at Freud's consultation room; we see a reenactment of Von Hoffmannsthal's work about Lord Chandos, a writer for whom language had lost its meaning. Such scenes are intercut with images from America—homeless people in New York, the African-American woman lecturing on the exploitation of Black musicians, newspaper headlines from the Gulf War, tracking shots in a cemetery while dogs bark out the Death March.

The ordering of all this material may seem random, but the collective impact of image and sound is difficult to escape: assassination, suicide, political stagnation; the closeness of war; the divorce of the practical from the cultural; the obsession with numbers and objectivity; the increasing inability to communicate through shared language; the retreat into commercialism, the unconscious, silence—sound familiar? *Hard Times and Culture* is not the first work of history meant to function as a critique of the present and is certainly not the first to insist that the past has a great deal to teach us about where we stand in our political and cultural life. Indeed, for all its visual and verbal pyrotechnics, the aim of the work may be seen as almost conventional. When its narrator at the close tells us that in Vienna *modernism* was not aimed towards the future but was, rather, an attempt to understand the past by "establishing the conditions that render the present possible," the remark is self-referential. But to grasp those conditions in terms of today's consciousness, one must use, as Downey's film suggests, vastly new and different modes of representation.

GENDER/COMPARATIVE: Trinh T. Minh-ha's *Surname Viet Given Name Nam* (1989), no doubt the best-known of the films described here, is a work that both delivers a *history* of Vietnamese women at home and in the United States since the mid-seventies and continually works to problematize its own assertions.[15] The basic strategy becomes clear only halfway through the film when the viewer learns that the women apparently interviewed in Viet Nam during the first half of the film were actually Vietnamese women living in America who have been acting out interviews from published texts. To make matters more complex, the women, when in Vietnam, speak heavily accented, sometimes unintelligible English, but playing themselves in America they speak subtitled Vietnamese.

Surrounding the interviews of women telling their lives are stories and ruminations, told in the filmmaker's voice, about women in Vietnamese history, along with footage of traditional dances, religious ceremonies, street scenes, markets, women at work, and poetic images of countryside, boats, and rivers. The sum of this material is a historical argument at once anti-patriarchal and anti-Confucian, an argument carried out in terms of both form and content. The film is not structured like the documentary as it has developed in patriarchal society—it is not linear, self-assured, omniscient. The form of its history is that of the women's dance which is the first image we see, a dance of patterns that recur but are never exactly the same. There is a paradox here, one that the filmmaker refuses to resolve: in its structure the work both insists on timelessness as a female characteristic and yet repeatedly shows how specific events (the war, migration) drastically change the contours and possibilities of women's lives.

To say *Surname Viet Given Name Nam* delivers a *history* is to redefine the term, but that surely is one of the points of a film in which the director, speaking over images of masses of marching women while a train whistle blows (the engine of history?), says: "There is always a tendency to find historical breaks, to say this begins here and ends there, while the scene keeps recurring: as unchangeable as change itself." And yet I would argue that, for all its attacks on common notions of historical practice such as fairness, clarity, chronology, and completeness, this film still provides a world of significant data and arguments about common women in the market, heroes, traditional roles, social practices, suffering, marriage, and ongoing gaps between rhetoric and reality that we can recognize as *historical*. One could even say that, in its own way, it undertakes four of the traditional tasks of history—recounting, explaining, and interpreting the past, and attempting to justify the way it has undertaken those tasks.

The film *recounts* the lives of (some) Vietnamese women over the last twenty years, showing the impact upon them of both revolution at home and emigration to America. It *explains* that underneath surface changes—for example, the fact that women can now become engineers and doctors—continuities from the past such as Confucianism and patriarchy still have a major role in defining women's activities and lives. It *interprets* the female-male struggle as ageless and ongoing, something that continues to occur no matter what the new social order or national context. And it *justifies* itself by dejustifying the traditional form of the historical documentary and suggesting that the forms of our knowledge about the past need to be changed. How else to explain the inclusion of large amounts of data that do no more than add texture to the portrait—memories of the special taste of ice cream in Viet Nam, dreamy images of moonlight on rivers, the lament of love songs and lullabies.

Ultimately, *Surname Viet Given Name Nam* refuses notions of causation or development and creates history through poetic overlays of sounds, images, words, and ideas. Certainly its historical world overflows with recurrent images and themes: women and dance, women and marriage, women as mothers, women and sacrifice, women and war, women and boats, women as heroes, women and sex, women and song, women and revolution, women and exile. If in exploring these themes, the film raises many more questions than it can possibly answer, this too may be seen as part of a new approach to the past, a method that provides yet another critique of patriarchal historical practice in which ambiguity and doubt are replaced by certitude.

OUT-TAKE: The postmodern historical film is not (yet) a genre, a movement, nor even (heaven help us) a trend. Perhaps it is best seen as a tendency—a growing tendency. If exemplars are still limited, it is important to emphasize that the five works described above represent neither the sum total of nor the full range of possibilities for this new kind of history. Among other examples/additions to the tendency, let me add the following:

Women's History: Mitzi Goldman's and Trish FitzSimons's *Snakes and Ladders* (1987).[16] A history of higher education for women in Australia which, taking the child's game of the title as both its central metaphor and narrative strategy, does not insert women into a conventional historical framework but forsakes linearity in favor of a multi-voiced work that is both open-ended and self-questioning.

Labor history: Kevin Duggan's *Paterson* (1988).[17] An often lyrical work that mixes many elements—events in the present and the past, documentary footage and dramatized fictional scenes, poetic evocation and traditional hard-nosed realism—as it probes the questions of what, whether, and how past union battles and major strikes (in this case the Paterson silk strike of 1913) can mean something to working people today.

Political Biography: Raoul Peck's *Lumumba: Death of a Prophet* (1992) manipulates time and chronology in what seems to be the manner of an African griot or oral historian.[18] Its images and narration shift effortlessly from past to present, from the public sphere to the private, from historical data to the filmmakers' personal ruminations in a work that is at once a visual and oral meditation on the brief life of Patrice Lumumba and the promise of African indepedence, thirty years ago and today.

Social Biography: Terese Svoboda's and Steve Bull's *Margaret Sanger: A Public Nuisance* (1992).[19] Underscored by a jaunty ragtime piano, this sound film is shot in the style of the silent era, with contemporary re-enactments that are as grainy and scratchy as its archival footage. In its presentation of historical analysis, the work can be unabashedly funny as it uses a team of pie-in-the-face vaudevillians to comment upon serious events in Sanger's life and upon the birth of birth control in America.[10]

Intellectual Biography: John Hughes's *One-Way Street* (1992).[20] Composed in accordance with Walter Benjamin's ideas—of history, knowledge, fragmentation, modernism, the priority of images, and the difficulties of narrative—this film about Benjamin's life, beliefs, ideas, loves, and death shuffles and reshuffles images, text fragments, dramatic re-enactments, talking heads, and archival footage into a cinematic version of one of the philosopher's own essays.

These examples suggest a larger point: postmodern historical films are made everywhere these days—in the United States, Europe, Australia, Latin America, and Africa. Most of them are low-budget works shot for the small screen. Most grow out of the documentary tradition, though the inclusion of dramatized episodes has become a common enough practice. Occasionally a feature-length dramatic work of history will fulfill notions of postmodernism—say Alex Cox's *Walker* (1987), an absurdist and overtly anachronist account of the invasion of Nicaragua in 1856 by a troop of Americans led by William Walker, or Carlos Diegues's *Quilombo* (1984), which gives us history as musical spectacle as it presents the grim story of Palmares, a country created by runaway slaves in the jungles of Brazil in the sixteenth century.[21] Occasionally a cinematic work of postmodern history may achieve a big reputation (but still have a small audience)—say Hans-Jürgen Syberberg's six and a half hour work, *Our Hitler* (1978). And occasionally touches we can call postmodern will inflect an otherwise conventional narrative film—for example Michael Verhoeven's *The Nasty Girl* (1990). But for the most part, the postmodern historical film is little known to the general (or even the scholarly) public because the economics of production and distribution work to keep any offbeat movements, trends, or tendencies in film buried. My hope is that by naming and describing them, I can help to begin to create a larger audience for these suggestive works which open up new possibilities for historical representation.

WHY CALL IT HISTORY?: Because such films are serious about describing and understanding, in however unusual a form, the beliefs, ideas, experiences, events, movements, and moments of the past. Because they accept the notion that the weight of the past has somehow helped to shape (us in) the present, even if they are not certain about how to assess that weight. Because even though they refuse to think in terms of linear cause and effect or to accept the idea that chronology is necessarily useful, and even though they insist that past material is always personal, partial, political, problematic, it is still possible to see them fulfilling traditional tasks of history and telling histories—of Solidarity as seen from America; of the Japanese internment camps as seen through the experiences of one family; of Australia in terms of its landscape, real and imagined; of Vienna just before the empire collapsed; of Vietnamese women since the revolution.

A RANDOM CONCLUSION TO A RANDOM SORT OF HISTORY: Postmodern history is history that does not necessarily call itself History with a capital *H*. It is history practiced by people who do not necessarily call themselves Historians with a capital *H* or even a little *h*.

Postmodern history is serious about making current meaning from the traces of the past. But it (obviously) suspects logic, linearity, progression, and completeness as ways of rendering that past.

Postmodern history weds theory and practice, the pulse of the past and ways of thinking about what that pulse means. It is always conscious of itself as a search of the past for present meaning.

Postmodern historians seem to have as their aim the desire to free themselves from the constricting bonds of metanarratives and the Historical discipline (the way history is taught in schools). They are often visually oriented people who attempt to make the past count in their and our lives once again. (The mainstream documentary or the dramatic film, with their sense of a linear and completed moral story would be suitable as visual forms for anyone who finds the Historical discipline and its metanarratives satisfactory.)

Postmodern historians have not given up on the past or (lower case) history—only on History as professionalized, institutionalized, History as a support for a social and intellectual order whose foundations perpetually need to be questioned.

Postmodern history makes us rethink the possibilities for history—indeed, the films described in this essay are a beginning of such rethinking—and for creating a new kind of relationship to the past. That we may not fully understand their *contribution* (an important word for historians) can be explained by what Jean-François Lyotard says in another context about creative artists: one may see the work of postmodern historians as in part a search for the rules by which their sense and practice of history will eventually be judged.[22]

ADDENDUM: The recent debate surrounding the possibility of representing the history of the Holocaust impinges upon the notion of the postmodern historical film. Whether it is historian Saul Friedlander lamenting the possiblity of finding a rational explanation for events so monumentally irrational, Jean-François Lyotard demanding that historians of Auschwitz lend an ear "to what is not presentable under the rules of knowledge," or Hayden White claiming that only *modernism* in historical writing can handle the *modernism* of Auschwitz, the result is a sense that traditional history has in this century run up against the limits of representation.[23]

One way around these limits has been suggested by White, who calls for a telling of the past in a voice at once new and old, a voice that lies somewhere between the objective voice of scholarship and the subjective voice of fiction and poetry.[24] This *intransitive middle voice* would be that of the historian not describing and analyzing but encountering and experiencing events of the past. To me it seems clear that such a voice, if one includes a visual component, is precisely that of the filmmakers whose works are described in this essay. As expressed in postmodern historical films, this voice becomes part of an attempt to forge a more meaningful relationship with the past. Clearly, it is a voice that refuses to take as the lesson of Auschwitz the notion that historical understanding is no longer possible, a voice that refuses to think about the question of whether or not history is a rational discourse describing rational phenomena, a voice that knows that as part of our humanity we humans can never stop the effort to talk about and make meaning of the past.

notes

1. Similar "amateur" experiments in seeing the past anew and creating a sort of postmodern history also seem to be taking place in other fields, such as theater, performance art, and dance. But on an international level it is easier to track and experience such changes in the visual media, which circulate so easily around the world.
2. Pauline Marie Rosenau, *Post-Modernism and the Social Sciences* (Princeton: Princeton University, 1992), 63.

3. Quotations taken, in order, from the following: Linda Hutcheon, *A Poetic of Postmodernism: History, Theory, Fiction* (New York: Routledge, 1988), 89, 74; Elizabeth Deeds Ermarth, *Sequel to History: Postmodernism and the Crisis of Representational Time* (Princeton: Princeton University, 1992), 8, 12, 41, 14; F. R. Ankersmit, "Historiography and Postmodernism," *History and Theory* 28, no. 2 (1989): 149–151. See also Hans Kellner, "Beautifying the Nightmare: The Aesthetics of Postmodern History," *Strategies* 4/5 (1991): 289–313.
4. Hutcheon, *Poetics of Postmodernism*, 91–95.
5. Rosenau, *Post-Modernism and the Social Sciences*, 66.
6. Presumably, Himmelfarb is attacking Scott for her work, *Gender and the Politics of History* (New York: Columbia University, 1988) and Zeldin for his two-volume study, *France 1848–1945* (London: Oxford, 1972, 1977). The former, a strongly feminist reading of history, is straightforward and traditional in its rhetorical style; the latter is, formally, more unusual—a topically-arranged portrait of France which to some extent makes moot the notion of chronology in favor of a kind of ahistorical "impressionism." Zeldin's effort may be seen as a move towards a new kind of written history that one might wish to label "premature postmodernism."
7. Simon Schama, *Dead Certainties (Unwarranted Speculations)* (New York: Knopf, 1991), 322, 320.
8. Gertrude Himmelfarb, "Telling it as you like it: Post-modernist history and the flight from fact," *Times Literary Supplement*, (16 October 1992).
9. There have been a number of attempts towards formal innovation in the writing of history in recent years, but these seem largely to have escaped the theorists who have written about postmodern history. For a brief introduction to this tendency, see Robert A. Rosenstone, "Experiments in Writing the Past," *Perspectives* 30 (December 1992), 10, 12, ff. That essay has led to the formation of an as yet unnamed group of historians who held a first Workshop-Conference at the California Institute of Technology, 1–2 April 1994.
10. Authored by Roy Rosenszweig, Steve Brier, et al., *Who Built America?* (Santa Monica: Voyager, 1993), is a CD-ROM version of a textbook by the same authors with the same title. Marsha Kinder, *Blood Cinema* (Berkeley and Los Angeles: University of California, 1993) is a study of recent Spanish cinema that has an accompanying CD-ROM.
11. *Far From Poland* (1984). Directed by Jill Godmilow. Color. 109 Minutes. Distibutor: Women Make Movies, 462 Broadway, Suite 501, New York, N.Y. 10013.
12. *History and Memory* (1991). Directed by Rea Tajiri. Color/BW. 32 Minutes. Distributor: Women Make Movies.
13. *Camera Natura* (1986). Directed by Ross Gibson. Color. 32 Minutes. Distributor: Australian Film Commission, Sydney, Australia. A copy of this film, for study but not for circulation, may be found in the UCLA Film and Television Archive.
14. *Hard Times and Culture—Part 1, "Vienna, Fin-de-siècle"* (1990). Directed by Juan Downey. Color. 34 Minutes. Distributor: Electronic Arts Intermix, Inc., 536 Broadway, New York, N.Y. 10012.
15. *Surname Viet Given Name Nam* (1989). Directed by Trinh T. Minh-ha. Color. 108 minutes. Distributor: Women Make Movies.
16. *Snakes and Ladders* (1987). Directed by Mitzi Goldman and Trish FitzSimons. Color. 59 minutes. Distributor: Women Make Movies.
17. *Paterson* (1988). Directed by Kevin Duggan. Color/BW. 37 Minutes. Distributor: Kevin Duggan, Paterson Film Project, 121 Fulton St., 5th Floor, New York, N.Y. 10038.
18. *Lumumba: Death of a Prophet* (1992). Directed by Raoul Peck. Color. 69 Minutes. Distributor: California Newsreel, 149 Ninth Street, San Francisco, CA 94103.
19. *Margaret Sanger: A Public Nuisance* (1992). Directed by Terese Svoboda and Steve Bull. Color/BW. 27 Minutes. Distributor: Women Make Movies.

20. *One-Way Street* (1992). Directed by John Hughes. Color. 58 Minutes. Distributor: John Hughes, fax 011–613–565–4209..
21. See my essay, "*Walker*: The Dramatic Film as (Postmodern) History," in *Revisioning History* ed. Robert A. Rosenstone (Princeton, N.J.: Princeton University, 1994).
22. Jean-François Lyotard, *The Postmodern Condition* (Minneapolis: University of Minnesota, 1984), 81.
23. Saul Friedlander and Jean-François Lyotard are both quoted in Anton Kaes's excellent and suggestive essay, "Holocaust and the End of History: Postmodern Historiography in the Cinema," in *Probing the Limits of Representation: Nazism and the "Final Solution"* ed. Saul Friedlander (Cambridge, Mass.: Harvard, 1992), 206–222. Hayden White's views may be found in "Historical Emplotment and the Problem of Truth," in the same volume, 37–53.
24. White, "Historical Emplotment and the Problem of Truth."

eleven interrotroning history

errol morris and the documentary of the future

shawn rosenheim

Truth isn't guaranteed by style or expression.
Truth isn't guaranteed by anything.
—Errol Morris

Is there hope for television's representation of history? The answer to this question may at first seem obvious, for television has probably never been more intensely bound up with the representation of historical events than in the last few years. In 1991, for example, Ken Burns's twelve-part *The Civil War* became the most widely watched show in the annals of PBS, and the video of the series sold millions of copies. With its mawkish score and star-driven narration, I take *The Civil War* as an example of the intellectual poverty of historical documentaries on television. Television has also played a complex role in the production of recent history. In the live broadcasting of the 1992 Los Angeles riots that followed the acquittal of police in the Rodney King–beating trial, television images of looting and burning became a feedback loop intensifying the events themselves. Local viewers were not only informed by live broadcasts, but, in ways unintended by the producers, were also spurred to action, told by implication where to go and what to do. Similarly, when O. J. Simpson was visually apprehended by helicoptered TV crews following his white Ford Bronco, all three national networks forsook their scheduled programming to capture events as they unfolded. Despite broadcasters' attempts to maintain objectivity, here too the presence of television itself irrevocably altered events (would the L.A.P.D. have so respectfully followed Simpson's Bronco without the escort of the media?).

As historical representations, it seems clear that *The Civil War* and television coverage of such popular historical events as the Reginald Denny or O. J. Simpson trials are antithetically defective. In its manipulative way, *The Civil War* presents a romantic history that demands a continual empathy from its viewers. Caught in the trap of Burns's nostalgia, viewers feel, rather than think, the meaning of the war, experiencing pity, fear, but above all, a self-congratulatory affirmation of loss and redemptive nationhood that ennobles Northerner and Southerner alike. The media frenzy over Simpson represents an inverse situation. Despite the massive television coverage (and such ancillary creations as the CNN interactive CD-ROM, *The People Versus O. J. Simpson*), the crime and its consequences have remained shapeless and badly told, as journalists have attempted to master the situation through repetition, meaningless updates, and mutual self-reference. Though such coverage was in its way often riveting, the reporting of Simpson's case only rarely interpreted the real issues of race, gender, and celebrity the case has raised. Due in no small part to the televisual ideology of presentness, the live coverage has often threatened to dissolve into a meaningless collection of factoids, stereotypes, and possible scenarios.[1]

But television need not only have to choose between arid chronicle and sentimental myth. In what follows, I would like to consider such an alternative, a proposed documentary series which might fairly be described as *mentalité* TV. The weekly series analyzes not only what happened in particular criminal cases, but also the texture of historical experience that so frequently allows justice to be perverted or confused. Simultaneously modernist and postmodernist, the series—entitled *Errol Morris: Interrotron Stories*—insists on the importance of "what happened" even as it exposes normative histories as tissues of myth. The agent for such revelations is in large part an interviewing device called the Interrotron. Why this bit of technology should have such resonant historical implications will be the burden of this essay.

Here's how the pilot begins. (Since *Interrotron Stories* has not yet been aired, I will describe the opening of the first episode in some detail.) Lights up on a television studio. A chair is perpendicular to the viewers, facing a camera set-up. To thrumming drums and horns, a man strides onto the set and sits. The camera pans right, past the cameraman, past another technician, to an identical camera and chair set-up. Cut to a medium shot of the man—now visible as Errol Morris—peering at the snow on a video monitor and then to an asymmetrical shot of a television monitor, on which Morris's face appears. As Morris speaks, the camera cuts between tilting close-ups of his face, the monitor image, and its distorted, blue-black reflection on a perpendicular glass surface. "What do you do when someone kills somebody and there's nothing you can do about it? Where if you say anything, they may come to kill you, too. Where nobody cares. And nobody wants to know. Meet John Shows, the man who spent almost forty years hunting the killer. And meet Diane Alexander, the woman who finally heard the truth." As Morris says "the truth," the camera cuts to an extreme close-up of his right eye, the eyebrow raised in emphasis. The music builds to its climax. A logo: *Errol Morris: Interrotron Stories*. Cut to black.

Mixing high-tech studio interviews, news footage, and dramatic recreations, the *Interrotron Stories* are designed to upset the prevailing conventions of reality TV. Although ABC, for whom Morris originally developed the series, has not yet purchased it, the network has paid for an additional pilot episode, as has Fox Television. (As this essay goes to print, Fox has just announced plans to air five hours of *Interrotron Stories* in the Fall of 1995.)[2] Morris's plan was to create a format based on his quirky sensibility, treating news stories ranging from national scandals to far more obscure incidents that engaged his imagination. Each episode was to be narrated wholly by participants in the case. Central to the series's conceit is the Interrotron, an interview device that allows subjects to look directly into the lens of the camera, instead of off to one side at an interviewer. Essentially a series of modified teleprompters, the Interrotron bounces a live image of Morris onto a glass plate in front of the interviewee, just as the director—"off in a booth somewhere, like the Wizard of Oz"—addresses a video image of his subject. In the same way, interviewees respond to an image of Morris that floats directly in line with the camera. The result is "the birth of true first-person cinema," as subject and interviewer stare at each other down the central axis of the lens.[3] Such direct contact intensifies each interview: larger-than-life, chiaroscuroed faces stare from the television with an unnerving intimacy, warily focused on the roving camera's lens. For Morris, "every look takes on a completely different significance. The inclination of the head suddenly takes on enormous dramatic power."[4]

On one level, the Interrotron is merely a gimmick, a device to give the series a memorable profile. The 1950s science fiction-sounding name recalls earlier instances of TV auteurism, such as *Alfred Hitchcock Presents* and *Rod Serling's Night Gallery*.[5] Morris himself admits that he "still can't tell whether the Interrotron is a joke or something truly wonderful." But in either case, the Interrotron offers "one more technique in a whole arsenal of techniques that you can bring to bear on nonfiction," and one that provides a remarkable means for visually dynamizing on-camera interviews. The formal originality of Morris's filmmaking has always centered on his treatment of the interview. From his first film, *Gates of Heaven* (1978), Morris practiced a reticent style of interviewing designed to eclipse his relation to the camera. During interviews, most shot with a fixed-focus 25-mm Zeiss high-speed camera, Morris would sit listening with his head pressed to the side of the camera lens, interrupting his subjects as little as possible. The resulting sense of his subjects' effortless self-revelation was heightened by editing that removed Morris's questions, even as the filmmaker's invisible hand produced a foreboding sense of overdetermined worlds. The Interrotron refines this process, allowing Morris to dissolve completely into the cinematic apparatus, thereby closing the dynamic circuit between camera and viewer and intensifying the viewer's cathexis to the screen. The device intensifies the psychoanalytic valence of the film camera, operating as the equivalent of the impassive analyst in classical Freudianism.

We may take the Interrotron as an exaggerated figure for the documentarization of the world. Docu-dramas, The Discovery Channel, amateur pornography, *TV Nation*—as cable channels proliferate, one increasingly encounters forms of nonfiction programming.[6] Yet if the documentary camera is ubiquitous today, it is also less tethered to direct visual perception. Any number of miniaturized, digitized, or magnetic image technologies are shattering the Newtonian scale that has always dominated the cinema. *Interrotron Stories* demonstrates a social corollary of this fact, as we see that human relations, too, are deeply inflected by our reliance on machines. The truth it reveals is not an empirical claim about the world, but a social fact, produced by the interaction between the camera, the studio setting, and the interview subject. Faced with the lens's interrogative eye, most subjects feel pressed to fill the dead time with words until something surprising is unintentionally revealed. In *Interrotron Stories*, speeches are not relational acts between people, but between a subject and the film apparatus. The Interrotron's mediatory system of cameras and monitors qualifies the truth of direct vision, particularly when—as in the recreations—such vision originates in odd, anxiety-producing angles, or epistemologically dubious points of view. Such effects are enhanced by the Interrotron's disturbing mobility. With their nervous, tilting cameras, misleading dramatic re-enactments, and monomaniacal narrators, the completed *Interrotron* episodes produce an effect Morris likens to "a real-life *Twilight Zone*."

Like the dioramic worlds built for *A Brief History of Time* (1992), the

Interrotron is part of a shift in Morris's work toward extreme artifice. Just as Stephen Hawking and his friends and colleagues were filmed not in their real homes or offices but in imaginary domestic environments built on a London soundstage, so the idea for *Interrotron Stories* was "to bring people to Boston, construct sets in Boston, and do all of the interviews in studio."[7] Morris originally created the Interrotron out of a longstanding interest in "the possibility of being very, *very* close to someone, and see them speaking absolutely naturally, and yet directing their primary attention to the camera." Given his earlier filmmaking practice, such drastic close-ups were not possible, since they would have magnified the angle between the camera's lens and Morris's face, wrecking the cinematic illusion of first person address. The Interrotron was developed during a series of commercial shoots, working out the mechanics of the piece by trial and error (as a mark of his success, Morris is now hotly sought after by companies interested in the device's distinctive visual signature).[8] At first, the Interrotron work was "very much like all the interviews I've done in the past," with a static, locked-down camera. But then it gradually became apparent that "if I'm no longer seated next to the camera, the camera can really do anything," including panning, tilting, and dutching. The resulting material

> enabled interviews to be edited in a way I've never seen anything edited before. I could essentially put together a seamless piece of interview, that might have a hundred cuts in it. Obviously the cuts are there, but because everything is dutched with respect to everything else, you don't notice them. You have the benefit of montage without having to interrupt what someone's saying, or resorting to jump cuts.

The Interrotron represents Morris's version of Dziga Vertov's *kinoglaz*, a cinema eye that insists on the necessity of mediation and manipulation. Morris enacts this through the constant iteration of eyes and unusual viewpoints and above all in the "dutching" of the series as a whole, which takes a canted approach to its own narration. Here, no authority asserts itself; no clear narrator emerges to resolve the truth of each episode. In this sense, the artifice of *Interrotron Stories* represents, if not *cinema vérité*, then the psychological *vérité* of cinema.

While the aesthetic implications of the Interrotron are interesting in themselves, they become even more so in light of the difficulties Morris has had getting *Interrotron Stories* on the air, suggesting the extent to which television circumscribes the possible relations of documentary to historiography. Having perfected his Interrotron technique, Morris shopped his series to various networks. At ABC, the director screened a rough cut of "Stalker," the story of a postal supervisor who was blamed when a former employee went on a murder spree in a Michigan post office. "People were just speechless," the filmmaker remembers. "I don't think anybody knew what to make of it." ABC ordered a pilot. But just as he was about to begin filming the final dramatic recreations, the network's office of Standards and Practices issued a hold on the production, claiming it violated a policy not to film any subject in which litigation was pending.

With "Stalker" blocked, Morris was asked to submit new episode ideas. ABC picked "Digging Up the Past," a tale of the deathbed murder confession of an Alabama Klansman. Set in the past, it was plainly less risky material. Yet while Deborah Leoni, ABC vice president for Dramatic Series Development, described the show as "riveting," the series was not picked up, partly because of a conflict with *Turning Point*, a new ABC news show, and partly for fear that future episodes would raise similar legal tangles.[10] Leoni explained that while the news division is allowed to present particular points of view on current stories, "We weren't and aren't the News. We at Drama are not allowed that same liberty." "Interrotron Series"—true stories filmed to feel neither exactly like fact, nor exactly like fiction—was deemed too dramatic for news and too real for drama.

Morris next took *Interrotron Stories* to Fox, which ordered its own pilot, "The Parrot." Yet Fox also had difficulties in placing the series. Though Fox executives said that the problem was one of timing, according to Morris the real problem was the show's excessive novelty.[11] Television viewers, Morris remembers an unnamed Fox executive saying, "'don't want twenty percent, twenty-five percent new. They want at most ten to fifteen percent new. Now what we have here, Errol, this looks to me like forty percent new. This might be even fifty percent new. There's just too much new here." The irony is striking: while certain of Morris's films, including *Gates of Heaven*, *Vernon, Florida* (1981), and *The Thin Blue Line* (1988), helped to invent reality programming, networks, threatened by the formal innovation of his series, left the filmmaker caught in a programming no-man's land.[12]

The debate over *Interrotron Stories* had less to do with Morris's choice of stories than with the stylistic ambiguity of their telling. By revealing the confusion, self-deception, and ambiguity clouding these murder cases, these episodes explicitly destabilize our perception of what counts as televisual history. To an audience used to the pieties of *The Civil War*, there is something troubling about the indeterminacy of these cases, particularly when the episodes invoke the finesse and closure of fictional TV programming. As Stu Smiley, a former Fox executive, puts it, the series represents "reality TV with a real dramatic narrative. It's reality *as* fiction. Which sounds crazy, but that's what Morris does best."

For all their interest in the bizarre and the grotesque, the *Interrotron* plots are the stuff of tabloids. "The Parrot" tells the story of Jane Gill, a penniless real-estate agent posing as a wealthy developer, who was apparently strangled by a business partner named as the beneficiary of her life-insurance policy. On its face an ordinary story of murder for profit, "The Parrot" turns unexpectedly when the defense produced as a key witness Max, an African grey parrot, who observed his owner's murder, and whose cries of "Richard! No! No! No!" were taken by the defense as evidence of the innocence of its client, Gary Rasp, and the possible guilt of Richard Mattoon, a close friend of Jane Gillis. Morris further twists the tale by leaving open the question of the bird's evidentiary capacity. The audience remains unsure of whether the parrot's throttled "Richard! No!" represents a traumatic repetition of the murder or just a memory of the bird's previous owner reprimanding his two-year-old son.

"Stalker" recounts the celebrated case of Tom McElvaine, the fired Michigan postal worker who killed six of his fellow employees. It gives the story a surprise point of view, narrating the event from the perspective of Bill Kingsley, the killer's former supervisor, whose career was shattered after he was first stalked by the disgruntled McElvaine and then blamed by the press for pressuring McElvaine to violence. Kingsley is a brilliant natural narrator, who, seen in the tight close-ups Morris favors, fixes viewers with his stern, brooding eyes and hyperarticulate speech, as he recounts his story in a stream of words too fast to process. We tour Kingsley's face, shot against a series of scrims, too close for a comfortable televisual relation. The camera staggers and halts, stutters in panning across faces, as voices out of synch with the action precede or follow the images. Kingsley is an electronic Ancient Mariner, a troubled face staring out of the screen directly at *our* eyes, buttonholing viewers.

And then there's "Digging Up the Past," which recounts the alleged confession of a Klansman named Henry Alexander to the 1963 murder of Willie Edwards, a black truck driver from Detroit who was forced by four members of the KKK to jump from a bridge to his death. (Edwards emerges as a metaphorical cousin to Randall Adams, the man wrongly accused in *The Thin Blue Line:* another victim of malign chance. Having stopped his truck to buy a soda, Edwards—who was making his very first trip through the South—was mistaken for another man.) The drama of the episode develops out of gradual revelation of Henry Alexander's participation in the 1963 murder. This process of discovery culminates after Alexander's death, when, following his instructions, his wife Diane digs up a buried chest of Klan memorabilia, including yellowed clippings about the murder of Willie Edwards, thus bringing the crime to a partial, if extrajudicial, resolution.

In its recreation of a racial crime from the height of the Civil Rights period, "Digging Up the Past" is the most historically situated of the existing episodes. It is also a mosaic of different kinds of documentary evidence, including reproduced photographs, newspaper articles, location footage, and so on.

Interrotron Stories distinctively engages historical narration on four levels. The first two are long-established conventions of documentary film. First the series includes such familiar documentary images as photographs, newspaper articles, location footage, and other factual representations of aspects of the case at hand. Second, *Interrotron Stories* uses new documentary footage concerning the past, generated by the filmmaker through his interviews with subjects who participated in some way in the original narrative.

Third, *Interrotron Stories*, like *The Thin Blue Line*, also includes dramatic recreations of events based on interview testimony. While such recreations are anathema to most documentarians, Morris's willingness to incorporate such scenes suggests that he recognizes how what might be called a *tabloid* interest in dramatic verisimilitude and sensational representations of scandal forms a crucial element in the popular understanding of history. Here, too, *The Thin Blue Line* serves as Morris's model, because from its opening dissolves between maps of Dallas and aerial shots of that city, the film exploits the uncertain distance between events in the world and their documentary representations. As the record of an investigation into the trial of Randall Dale Adams, an out-of-town worker sentenced to death for the 1976 killing of a Dallas policeman, *The Thin Blue Line* powerfully indicates how, through their reluctance to prosecute a local teenager named David Harris, the Dallas police and judiciary effectively conspired to put an innocent man on death row. Crosscutting between a judge's memories of his father's work with the FBI and an old feature about Dillinger, Morris provides an objective correlative for the judge's thoughts, even as he shows how our impressions of guilt are filtered and shaped by the American media machine. Nor, as Morris recognizes, is *The Thin Blue Line* exempt from this same process of manipulation. The film's concluding scenes are built around a montage, combining David Harris's confession, his reminiscences of his brother (drowned at age three), and childhood photographs of Harris swimming with his brother, in which Morris *seems* to suggest that Harris's sociopathy stems from his guilty failure to save his sibling. But the artifice of these scenes (in their color coordination and repeated use of water imagery), like Harris's sense of being *prompted,* reveal psychoanalysis as just another model for making sense of Harris's life. Far from explaining the mystery of Harris's violence, these formal and thematic elements work to expose the audience's hunger for narrative logic and dramatic order.

Unlike *The Thin Blue Line*, however, *Interrotron Stories's* fourth level of historical narration contextualizes all these different levels within the dialectical frame represented by Morris's opening and closing remarks, where he comments on the episode. While such commentary might initially sound like the naturalizing narrators of *911* or *Eye-Witness Video*, by mixing Morris's direct address to the audience with his skewed, Max-Headroomish presence on the teleprompters, *Interrotron Stories* carries its dialectical use of narrative levels even into its surrounding framework.

The evidence mustered in "Digging Up the Past" functions both as an important element in Morris's thickly textured visual form, and as a baseline account of the story's presence in the world. But the evidence such documents provide quickly proves tainted or inconclusive. *Interrotron Stories* is built on the dissonance between the story told in the documentary record and that adduced by Morris's interview subjects in the present. Morris dramatizes Diane Alexander's story both through recreations of the night on the bridge and by intercutting into his interviews re-enactments of Alexander walking through the woods, digging, and then unearthing the chest. The metaphor of the buried past is old, even stale, with its implied archaeology of guilt as past crimes are brought into the light. In "Digging," Diane Alexander responds to the crisis of her husband's guilt first with her own grief, and then (in an excerpt borrowed from a *Donahue* show) in a scene in which Alexander meets and embraces Willie Edwards's widow, as tears stream down their faces. The *dénouement* seems familiar: social ills resolved through sentimental expiation, true to the form of daytime television.

But more is at stake in these reenactments than is apparent through a casual viewing. Despite the way that Morris's dramatic recreations seem to conform to a cheesy televisual logic (the Klan members are cartoon backwoods racists, and the twangy, *Deliverance*-style banjoes of the score are used to signify "danger in the South"), all three episodes denaturalize their representations through excessive or anomalous camera work. As Willie Edwards jumps to his death, Morris cuts from a shot of the killers on the bridge to an underwater shot of Edwards's body knifing into the water; years later, when the body is discovered, the camera swoons blurrily toward the skull, its jaw yawed open in death. The very staginess of the KKK recreations should remind us that these scenes are faked.

In "The Parrot," the audience is treated to a literal bird's eye view of the murder, as we watch Jane Gill through the parrot's green-tinted vision. Such an outlandish perspective is complemented by very intimate close-ups of the parrot's eyes: looking through the transparent lens of the bird's eyeball into the dark pool of the iris, we see the instrument of our seeing. There is a striking inverse relation between the hyperreal clarity of the bird's appearance and the filtered, tinted shots representing the bird's point of view—an implicit admission that the technologies of storytelling inflect the unverifiable rhetoric of narration. Like Morris's use of the stylistic *cinema vérité* now ubiquitous in television, it is a way of keeping reality claims at bay—warding off presumptions to direct representation. Such shots belie the verisimilitude implicit in the bland, saturated color and high-key lighting that many of Morris's recreations share with network television.

Further, the very staginess of the KKK recreations should remind us that these scenes are faked. Like *The Thin Blue Line*, *Interrotron Stories* reveals its director's training as a former private investigator and as a graduate student of philosophy obsessed with issues of criminal evidence. In a procedure diametrically opposed to that of other reality shows, Morris uses his recreations not to show "what really happened," but to illustrate the slipperiness of memory. Insisting that "such scenes are not *evidence* for anything," Morris employs his mini-dramas as "ironic commentaries" on his narrators, which "call our attention to the fact that what we see may be a lie" or only one of many possible interpretations of an event. "If you use a re-enactment, the main thing that you need to do is articulate to the audience right away that you're showing them a lie." Otherwise, documentary film is simply a way of easing the audience out of the work of interpretation.

In "Digging Up the Past," the re-enactments are not literally false—Diane Alexander really *did* dig up the evidence of her husband's crime—but they are nonetheless misleading. That is because the episode isn't really about tracking down a smoking gun; it isn't really a tale about the locatability—and hence expiability—of guilt. Indeed, Diane Alexander's behavior in her interviews offers an object lesson in the structure of self-deception, as her common-law husband's power (Henry Alexander was a prominent local businessman) and her weakness conspire to corrupt the historical record. This logic of self-justification, in which only the victors are allowed to write history, comes to a breathtaking head when, as we listen to Diane Alexander's voice observe the similarities between Henry Alexander and Willie Edwards, Morris cuts from a shot of Edwards's decrepit wooden grave to Alexander's marble stone, prominently engraved with the single word "SAVED." The juxtaposition of the shots returns us to the realm of metahistory, as Morris's camera captures the way in which Henry Alexander used his wealth and racial privilege to rewrite his life into a fiction of Christian salvation.

Morris is drawn to murder cases because they precisely illustrate the limits of historical narration and the operations of law and justice. Murder investigations are, he claims, "a model of historical inquiry," and one which, postmodern narratology notwithstanding, has at its heart a concrete (if not necessarily knowable) set of events. In the words of Henry David Thoreau, "some circumstantial evidence is very strong, as when you find a trout in the milk."[13] Just so with murder: faced with a body shot in the back, one may generally presume a crime. Obviously, not all historical narratives can be definitely resolved: in the case of events dispersed in time and place, like the rise of Hitler or the sources of the Great Depression, no single explanation will be satisfactory or final. And even murder cases often turn less on a particular action than on the interpretation of motive and context: knowing who fired the gun, we still must ask about provocation, self-defense, and other extenuating circumstances.

Far from doing away with the difficulty of adjudication, murder cases reveal the stakes involved in the interpretation of seemingly unambiguous events. This approach is largely responsible for the curious mixture of stylistic elements within Morris's films. In their play of referential levels, frequent quotation and allusion, and lack of originating authority, Morris's films are thoroughly postmodern. Perhaps the most oddly memorable shot in *The Thin Blue Line* is an extreme close-up of a chocolate shake, thrown by a police officer caught off guard in her patrol car as her partner was shot down. Pirouetting slowly through the air, glopping heavily on the pavement, the shake partakes of a hyperreal postmodernity, mesmerizing us in excess of its status as an index of the policewoman's confusion. But the film's implicit hermeneutics mark Morris off as the last modernist, obsessively concerned with controlling his complex, ironic, but essentially coherent authorial intention. Morris's films are confident that there *is* a there out there: a world in which Randall Adams *or* David Harris killed the Texas state trooper, in which Gary Rasp *or* Richard Mattoon killed Jane Gill, but not one in which the problem can be given up with a shrug or by apportioning blame equally to everyone involved. The problem, the film and the series suggest, is that while an objective physical world does exist, we have no secure way of judging the way in which "the lenses that we are," to use Ralph Waldo Emerson's phrase, are warped, dirty, or otherwise flawed.

In *The Thin Blue Line* it seems necessary to grant Morris the validity of his old-fashioned claims to knowability and consequence. If that film holds up the police and legal systems for derision (on the grounds of their culpable self-deception) it is not a postmodern parable of the detective caught in his own web, in the manner of Paul Auster or Jorge Luis Borges. When the evidence (which culminates with a chilling taped confession by the actual killer) is properly researched and weighed—a task Morris undertook both in the film itself and in his own private researches—the conclusion that Adams is innocent becomes nearly unavoidable, and to attack it on rhetorical grounds ("what about the suppressed homoeroticism?" critics have asked, for example, as if the chance that Adams was cruising Harris made him complicit in the murder) is to collude with the Dallas authorities in sending an innocent man to jail.

The same logic holds true in *Interrotron Stories*. Sometimes, as in "The Parrot," Morris struggles to pack too much information and too many characters into the twenty-two minutes of each episode. But when the scale is right, as in "Stalker," whatever is lost in intricacy is made up by the vividness of these fables of miscarried justice. Although "Digging Up the Past" ends with the suggestion that Alexander died tormented by his crimes of long ago, this seems more a rhetorical convenience than a conclusion suggested by the evidence of the episode. The real story is not Diane Alexander's repudiation of her husband's past, but her own complicity. As Alexander recounts it, having heard suspicions of her husband's involvement in the crime, she "made a pact with God" that He would send a sign if Alexander was guilty. With no sign forthcoming, she went ahead with the marriage. It was, says Morris, "a pact with God to be self-deceiving," a kind "which I'm not sure you can find precedent for in the Bible."

Not only does Alexander's testimony reveal her convenient willingness to absolve her husband of his possible crimes but, as the episode makes clear, she is *still* protecting the last living member of the KKK posse involved in the murder, out of fear of retribution. Alexander's refusal to identify a certain Sonny Kyle Livingston as the fourth suspect explodes the sentimental conclusion which *The Donahue Show* and other journalists tacked on to Alexander's story. In Morris's version, by contrast, "the whole thing is really dreamlike. It's the ultimate faux-redemptive ending—the search for some overarching principle of justice or God." In his Interrotron coda, Morris directly involves the audience in the interpretation of the story just seen. Framed askew in the monitor, a video image of Morris's face asks: "What do *you* think? *Was* Henry Alexander ever punished for his crimes? Were there other people on the bridge that night? I'm Errol Morris, and this is *Interrotron Stories*. Good night; and [big smile] sleep well." Only the bad sleep well, Morris implies; despite Morris's own efforts and those of lawmen before him, Sonny Kyle Livingston still walks the streets a free man.

In its treatment of the Edwards murder, "Digging Up the Past" bears out Linda Williams's comments on Morris's filmic practice, that "while there is very little running after the action, there is considerable provocation of action." In *The Thin Blue Line*,

> The preferred technique is to set up a situation in which the action will come to [Morris]. In this privileged moment of *vérité* (for there finally are moments of relative *vérité*) the past repeats. We thus see the power of the past not simply by dramatizing it, or reenacting it, or talking about it obsessively (though these films do all this) but finally by finding its traces, in repetitions and resistances, in the present.[14]

In its direct address to the viewer, as in its refusal of external "expert" discourses (no judges or trial lawyers testify here), "Digging Up the Past" continues Morris's practice from *The Thin Blue Line*, where he requires his viewers to act for themselves as historical interpreters, detectives sifting the evidence not for a simple verification of guilt, but for the ramifying ways in which acts like Edwards's murder are written into the daily lives of those near the crime, rendering them, too, a part of its lies.

Though Walter Benjamin's "The Work of Art in the Age of Mechanical Reproduction" has long been a chestnut for film studies, just how much of the essay is concerned with the documentary value of film (what Benjamin calls "actuality") has gone relatively unnoticed. Benjamin brilliantly captures how the aesthetics of a documentary realism in film depends upon the effacement of technology: "The equipment-free aspect of reality here has become the height of artifice; the sight of immediate reality has become an orchid in the land of technology." For man today, Benjamin adds, "the representation of reality by the film is incomparably more significant than that of the painter, since it offers, precisely because of the thoroughgoing permeation of reality with mechanical equipment, an aspect of reality which is free of all equipment."[15]

Morris's series represents something like the fulfillment of Benjamin's prediction, where the permeation of mechanical equipment permits not the direct representation of reality, but the presentation of the *rhetoric* of direct reality. The series establishes a dialectical relationship between its opening sketch of the Interrotron, Morris's direct address to the audience, and the transparent realism of the recreated scenes that have effaced technology just as Benjamin has described. The interviews represent a median point between these modes, since although they provide the direct address to the audience by the "real figures," the illusionist lighting, the canting camera, and the swirling scrims behind the interviews remind us of televisual mediation. To his credit, this does not mean that Morris has sacrificed his films' claims on the world. The specificity of evidence he adduces and the way he puts his storytelling skills into the service of his version of each tale remind us that the peculiar charge of nonfiction filmmaking still lies in the privileged claims it can make about the world.

Interrotron Stories stands as both a symptom of and a response to the crisis now taking place within the domain of historical documentary. While postmodern historiography has long proclaimed the death of objectivist history, popular culture now reflects this same conclusion in various ways, including the general loss of what might be called a historical sense. Yet historical fictions still matter, and increasingly these partake of documentary or pseudo-documentary modes of representation. Besides such resonant traditional documentaries as the PBS series *Eyes on the Prize* or Barbara Kopple's *American*

Dream (1989), one can also name more formally innovative or personal films such as *Who Killed Vincent Chin?* (Renée Tajima and Chris Choy, 1988) or Michael Moore's *Roger and Me* (1989), to say nothing of the way that a filmmaker like Oliver Stone has adapted documentary rhetorics and styles in films as different as *Platoon* (1986), *JFK* (1991), and *Natural Born Killers* (1994). Stone has, of course, come in for a great deal of criticism for *JFK*, for the historical liberties he takes with his material, for his megalomania, and for his taste for conspiracies. Much of the hostility seems to have been generated by his freehand mixing of documentary, feature, and pseudo-documentary footage, as for example in his intercutting of Gary Oldman as Lee Harvey Oswald with real Oswald footage in such a way as to be almost undetectable without recourse to a videorecorder on slow. In a world in which large numbers of people will turn to films like *JFK* for much of their historical sensibility, Morris knows that it is pointless to ask for a stylistic purity or representational austerity in documentary filmmaking. Hence the Interrotron foregrounds the seductive and manipulative powers of the camera, even as the omnibus stylistic mixture of the *Interrotron* episodes becomes both a source of pleasure and a way of acknowledging the contingency of representation.

For many viewers today, I suspect that the epistemological and ethical distinctions between features and documentaries have almost completely dissolved. Raised on MTV's *The Real World*, this generation simply does not find the *propriety* of documentary rhetoric to be much of an issue. Which is another way of saying that the historical configuration of the documentary as, in Bill Nichols admirable words, a "discourse of sobriety," of high-minded, voiced-over, authority, may have largely come to an end.[16] While we cannot do without myths of history, *Interrotron Stories* suggests an alternative to the queasy sentimentalism and self-absorption that has characterized the television handling of such celebrated cases as Simpson's almost endless trial. Morris's series constitutes a remarkable double-critique of history, interrogating both the reductive accounts of human behavior offered by the popular press and the hegemonic accounts offered by *The Civil War* and kindred films, and leaving viewers instead with the uncertain testimonies of the filmmaker's subjects, struggling to understand their own and others' behavior—accounts that necessarily precede attempts to write grander social or national histories.

In the end, then, Morris is able to put the Interrotron to good social-historical use, because the psychoanalytical dimensions of the device are subordinated to the production of a *mentalité*-style history which refuses to treat traditional narrative histories as a natural category. The series represents a televisual analog to such works of cultural history as Carlo Ginzburg's *The Cheese and the Worms*, which recounts the life of Menocchio, the sixteenth-century miller who is ultimately executed for his blasphemous belief that the earth was born out of a mass of rotting cheese.[17] Like Morris, Ginzburg trains his considerable analytical powers on the behaviors of the marginal and the bizarre as a way of obliquely illuminating the zeitgeist of a given moment. It is worth stressing that for Ginzburg the case of Menocchio is especially compelling because of the way the challenge posed by this harmless eccentric mobilized the power structure of the Roman Catholic Church—a fact at least as telling about the Renaissance as anything Menocchio himself invented. Just so, *Interrotron Stories* are also profoundly tales of the dysfunction of the law, of the discrepancy between our prurient interest in scandal, outrage, and crime, and of the narrative models available to the law to adjudicate such behaviors.

If I claim *Interrotron Stories* as the documentary of the future, it is because the series forgoes the conventions of authority predicated on the neutrality and objectivity of the camera. *Interrotron Stories* represents historical filmmaking for the MTV generation, in which what is at stake is not the authority of the camera (its pretense towards autonomy and objectivity), but its implicative dexterity and seductive force. By incorporating the interview subject into the televisual apparatus, *Interrotron Stories's* self-reflexive text simultaneously sutures the viewer to television and reveals how that suturing occurs. Long after the particulars of the Willie Edwards case are reduced to a paragraph in the history of civil rights, "Digging Up the Past" and its companion pieces might conceivably represent a moment in which television faced up to its enormous role in our cultural imaginary. In so doing, the show negotiates a shift worth pondering—from a conception of television as a forum for delivering more or less inadequate historical representations, to one in which we can begin to reckon with the convoluted ways in which television itself forms so large a part of the history of our time.

notes

My epigraph is taken from "Truth Not Guaranteed: An Interview with Errol Morris." *Cineaste* 17 (1989), 17. Thanks to Vivian Sobchack and to Cassandra Cleghorn for expertly reading earlier versions of this essay.

1. The CNN CD-ROM is particularly bad in this respect, repeatedly describing Nicole Simpson as "the blond in the convertible," and illustrating its text with Quick-time video clips not of Simpson, but of a half-dozen *other* Los Angeles blonds in convertibles, who generically substitute for Nicole herself.
2. Britain's Channel Four is also negotiating to buy the existing pilots.
3. Philip Gourevitch, "Interviewing the Universe," *New York Times Sunday Magazine*, August 9, 1992, 53.
4. From an interview with the author, September 25, 1994. Unless otherwise noted, all quotations by Errol Morris come from this interview.
5. From a telephone conversation with Deborah Leoni, Vice President for Dramatic Development, ABC, October 7, 1994.

6. According to Leoni, "the appetite for reality material has diminished." Despite critical acclaim, *TV Nation*, the Michael Moore nonfiction series, was not renewed by NBC, and *Cops*, one of the venerable originators of reality programming, hovers near last place in the Nielsen ratings.
7. The Interrotron is further removed from ordinary documentary provenance by its origin in television commercials. For the last several years Morris has largely made his living as a director of commercials, primarily because of his difficulty in financing his feature-length projects. His ongoing projects include *Fast, Cheap, and Out of Control*, an omnibus film shot partly by Robert Richardson, Oliver Stone's cinematographer, and *Honeymoon in Auschwitz*, a portrait of the electrocutioner and Holocaust revisionist, Fred Leuchter.
8. Morris's Interrotron commercials include spots for 7–11, American Express, and Ford.
9. On *kinoglaz* and related subjects, see Dziga Vertov, *Kino-Eye: The Writings of Dziga Vertov*, ed. Annette Michelson (Berkeley: University of California Press, 1984), especially the introduction by Michelson, and 32–64.
10. In a fitting case of irony, *Turning Point* was cancelled in November, 1994.
11. According to Stu Smiley, a former Fox executive, by the time Fox received "The Parrot," "the pilot season was already winding down." Telephone conversation, October 4, 1994.
12. Ari Emmanuel, Morris's agent, describes the series in conflicted terms that are interesting in this context: "I don't think this is reality TV. Errol Morris is not reality. Somebody's gotta get the vision that this is not reality TV. This is the next generation. Essentially, you've got the filmmaker that created reality television, and now he's taking it to the next generation." Telephone conversation September 30, 1994.
13. Ralph Waldo Emerson, "Thoreau," quoted in *American Literature*, vol. 1, ed. Emory Elliot, et al. (Englewood Cliffs, N.J.: Prentice Hall, 1991), 1453.
14. Linda Williams, "Mirrors Without Memories: Truth, History, and the New Documentary." *Film Quarterly* 46: 3 (Spring, 1993): 15.
15. Walter Benjamin, "The Work of Art in the Age of Mechanical Reproduction," in *Illuminations*, trans. Hannah Arendt (New York: Shocken Books, 1969), 233.
16. Bill Nichols, *Representing Reality: Issues and Concepts in Documentary* (Bloomington: Indiana University Press, 1991), 3.
17. Carlo Ginzburg, *The Cheese and the Worms: The Cosmos of a Sixteenth-Century Miller*, trans. John and Anne Tedeschi (New York: Penguin Books, 1982). Writing of Menocchio's complex relation both to the elite written and the oral peasant culture, Ginzburg observes that "an investigation initially pivoting on an individual, moreover an apparently unusual one, ended by developing into a general hypothesis on the popular culture (more precisely, peasant culture) of preindustrial Europe, in the age marked by the spread of printing and the Protestant Reformation" (xii). In much the same way, through their combined involvement both with the American legal system and with television, the eccentric subjects of the *Interrotron Stories* become representatives of much larger and more diffuse cultural processes.

the professors of history

twelve

dana polan

"But I'm not an intellectual. Only a historian. And maybe not even that. Maybe just a compiler, a synthesizer, a ... "

—Historian in Helen Hudson's *Meyer, Meyer* at being called an intellectual (ellipsis in original)

A "Peanuts" cartoon from a few years back suggests the difficulty the public often has in imagining the teacher as a real person. Sally is writing Christmas cards and asks her brother Charlie for advice: "Is it proper," she wonders, "to send your teacher a Christmas card?" "Sure," Charlies replies, "Why not?" Looking at her card with puzzlement, Sally then inquires, "Where do I send it?", to which her brother gives the direct reply, "To her home." But this answer only leads to more bewilderment on Sally's part. In the final panel, she is as perplexed as she was at the beginning: she now wonders, "Teachers have homes?"

Sally's conceptual difficulties here derive from what I would term the problem of the pedagogue's embodiment. By "embodiment," I refer to the way in which teachers take up their activity of professing as living, breathing figures with specific looks, specific identities. That teachers have bodies may seem evident (although embodiment itself may undergo transformation as the information age discovers new ways to undertake teaching—for example, transmission of knowledge not through bodies but through computer screens). Nonetheless, I would argue that reigning philosophies of pedagogy all too often take embodiment to be a secondary, contingent, extricable, nondeterminant aspect of education: knowledge is knowledge, a radiant conveyance of thought that is so strong, so inspiring, so integral, that it generally reaches its goal no matter how seemingly ineffective the specific vehicle (i.e., the specific embodied teacher) might appear to be. And as we move ever more into the realms of higher education, we find less and less attention paid to practical issues of pedagogy—teacher-training, classroom evaluation, mentoring—the assumption seeming to be that in higher education one is dealing with a knowledge so pure, so important, that its mere declaration or declamation suffices (and in the very notion that this is "higher" education, there is perhaps the sentiment that such knowledge is a matter of spirit, rather than of the lower and lowly realm of bodies and matter).[1]

The flip side of this spiritualizing attitude *within* the philosophy of pedagogy as maintained by the professoriate is the insistence on the embodiment of professors that goes on almost everywhere else within the educational process. All a professor has to do, for example, is overhear students chatting in the hall or read an insider's guides to a university (including those teacher evaluation guides published by student organizations that are not the university's official means of teaching evaluation) to see the extent to which, for the students, teachers are easily, inevitably, irremediably, and often comically embodied—thought of as types, categorized according to clichés, attended to not only for what they say but for how they say it, for how their lessons are mediated by the particularities of their person.

In the following pages, I want to look at another popular means by which the inevitable embodiment of the professor is insisted upon: namely, the representation of the professor in popular fiction and film. Again, just as professors don't often attend to the issues of how they come off in class, of the image they convey—preferring to see their embodiment as epiphenomenal to the integrity of the knowledge they have to impart—they don't often attend to the popular culture images that circulate around them. Professors prefer to treat the stereotypes that circulate as laughable and, by consequence, dismissable. I would argue, though, that images that appear laughable to one segment of the pedagogic process (the teachers themselves) are not necessarily ineffective, unbelievable, or even laughable for other segments (for example, the students, their parents, the legislators). This gap in perception can have major consequences for the support given to, or taken away from, the academic enterprise. To take just one example, I have seen many of my liberal colleagues laugh at the image of academia (short hours, silly subjects, rejections of tradition, and so on) presented in the various neoconservative attacks on the supposed wastefulness of academia (I'm thinking, for instance, of books such as Charles Sykes's *Profscam*[2] or Roger Kimball's *Tenured Radicals*.[3] But it is often such books, rather than the liberal academics, that gain the attention and even the support of the popular press and of various legislatures (local, state, and federal).

In this essay, I want to look at the particular ways the embodiment of the professor is offered up in popular representations of the profession of history. The history profession's own traditional conception of itself as a lofty transmission of the truths of history is at variance with the image that novels and films present of the everyday activity of the professionals within the discipline.

Early in the introduction to his majestic 1988 study of the guiding ideologies of American historiography, *That Noble Dream: The "Objectivity Question" and the American Historical Profession*, Peter Novick notes one irony in engaging in meta-reflection on historians' practices: for all their interest in delving into the motives of past historical agents, historians themselves are hard put to understand their own activities as driven by any sort of motives, by anything less than a pure, transparent, and innocent desire to let Truth speak out:

> For many, what has been at issue [in debate on the "objectivity question"] is nothing less than the meaning of the venture to which they have devoted their lives, and thus, to a very considerable extent, the meaning of their own lives.... Except with very good friends, it is considered tactless and discourteous to suggest that someone's views are a reflection of his or her background, prejudices, or psychic needs.... When historians discuss the most deeply rooted beliefs of "ordinary people"—workers, generals, priests, businessmen—we hardly ever assume that those beliefs are arrived at as a result of logical considerations. Out of understandable but misplaced tact and courtesy we apply a different standard when writing historically about historians—particularly, of course, living historians.[4]

Historians traditionally institute then a split conception of human agents: there are the ordinary people, driven by earthy and earthly desires and passions, and above them, cognizing them from a position of pure and unfettered intellect, are the spiritual beings of academia.

Consequently, as Novick's account reveals, there are in fact two myths of objectivity at work in the historical profession. On the one hand, there is the notion that Truth exists, that it is a positive entity that can conclusively be discovered and adjudicated. On the other hand, there is the assumption that the historian out to seize this truth can (and must) make his or her own method objective—that the path to finding truth lies in rendering one's system as transparent, as unprejudiced, as professional as possible.

As Novick reminds us, historiography, ironically, has to a large extent not worked towards perfecting these myths of their profession so much as it has helped make them vulnerable to a series of challenges. Novick's story tells of challenges from within the discipline of history in the university where Truth comes to be seen by critical historians as something constructed and where the tools of construction come to be seen as deriving from deep-structural preconceptions on the part of the historian (see, for example, Hayden White's tropological researches in *Metahistory* that imply that no historical work is ever really transparent).[5]

But it is also from *outside* the discipline and academia that the historical profession's commitment to objectivity is challenged. In the following pages I focus on one form of this external challenge: cultural representations (filmic and literary especially) that argue the impurities within historical objectivity. For instance, if one mark of literary modernism was its challenge to the notion that Truth exists objectively, it seems appropriate that some of the key works of modernism have specifically worked this challenge out in the form of allegorization of the work of the historian. In this modernist writing, historians often fail, and they do so because their own lives are failures and, even more, because all attempts at meaning-making (in this case, making meaning of the past) are doomed to fail. In extreme forms of this representation, the historian's seemingly professional drive to know the meaning of the past for purely scholarly reasons, for the joy of knowledge for its own sake, finds itself so thwarted that professional crisis becomes existential crisis. After all, this crisis seems to imply that if one can't know the meanings of lives disconnected from one's self, what chance is there for any sort of knowledge of the self? If objective knowledge, which might seem easy to obtain, is in fact unattainable, how can one harbor any hope for the attainment of the more difficult subjective knowledge? In the classic of the tradition, Sartre's *Nausea*, the protagonist Roquentin's crisis of self is inextricable from his crisis of professional commitment; the two crises work together in *Nausea* to make a text of fissure and gaps, of dialogisms (even within the insistent single-voicedness of Roquentin's journal), of digression, and of vague hopes for aesthetic salvation.[6]

The notion that a crisis of historical research—one that is confounded by the question "What is the past?"—leads into a larger existential crisis—one that involves big questions such as "Who am I? Why do I matter?"—receives perhaps its most extreme rendition in Alain Resnais's film, *L'amour à mort*

(1984), where the main character, a historian of ancient Greece, literally dies and comes back to life miraculously. The second chance that this rebirth gives him pushes him to reevaluate and eventually reject his previous professional life that was dominated by what seems a worthless preoccupation with the past (he had been studying garbage-disposal patterns in classical Greece).

But the adoption of the modernist style doesn't guarantee that a specific artwork necessarily or automatically deconstructs historical objectivity (just as, as we'll see later, some works of popular culture do not use such style, yet are capable of challenging the historical enterprise at levels other than that of style). In his essay in this volume, Hayden White seeks justification for *JFK*'s palimpsestic textuality by inscribing the film within the modernist tradition with its devotion to montage, to relativism, to fractures of narrativity. To be sure, in Oliver Stone's film, Jim Garrison's quest for the Truth reveals itself to be a highly complicated matter. Yet, no matter how tendentious his version of history is, Stone still seems to nevertheless assume a univocality and a unicity of historical meaning: his is a liberalism that admires the strong hero who can cut through the crap of obfuscation and obstacle (including, in a sexist trope, the obstacle of Garrison's wife's inability to understand that a man's got to do what a man's got to do; not for nothing does Kevin Costner come to this film after a film of—however liberal—Western heroism, *Dances With Wolves* [1990]). It is significant that the slam-bam montage style of the film—history as a collision of little bits of fury and fever—slows down in the end-of-film trial sequence which instead uses langorous closeups of Garrison's face as he delivers the Truth of politics to the American people.

Despite the ways in which its sledgehammer editing style gives it an air of perspectivist modernism, *JFK* still adheres to an objectivist conception of Truth. We can appreciate this best if we compare the film's use of flashbacks to that in a much more radically modernist inquiry into the assassination, Richard Condon's wacky paranoia literary thriller, *Winter Kills*[7] and the equally complex and zany filmic adaptation of the same name from 1979. Condon's novel and William Richert's film don't merely talk of the confusions and explicit obfuscations of history, they perform them. The novel's and film's flashbacks—each introduced by characters who claim to tell the questing hero, Nick Kegan, how the assassination happened—all turn out to be lies, exploiting in the manner of Hitchcock's *Stage Fright* (1950) those readerly or spectatorial conventions that lead us to take the scenes before us as verities enounced from no point of view but emanating rather from Truth, from an authorless presence. There is little or none of this sort of radical play in *JFK*. In this more recent film, the flashbacks are put forward as unequivocal and unchallengeable bits of verity. Through Garrison's perception and ours, a totalized and radiant Truth is to be built up out of these bits.

And yet in another way, while claiming to tell a Truth, *JFK* does challenge historiographic objectivity according to Novick's model. In its very concentration on Garrison's obsessive drive to go after the truth, the film figures the second of the two challenges to objectivity: while it believes in a Truth out there, it shows that the historian is him- or herself hardly a transparent conduit for that truth. History is written out of motives, desires, obsessions, prejudices. Furthermore, for those generations of filmgoers who, like myself, remember the real Garrison trial, there is another, ironic element to Garrison's quest as it is represented in the film: despite the film's glowing admiration for Garrison, many of us still think of him (whether rightly or wrongly doesn't matter) as a nut, a conspiracy quack whose case unravelled itself wildly and destructively. We remember Garrison as a far-from-objective witness to Truth. One can watch *JFK*, then, as a dismantling of the historiographic venture, even if the film seems to still believe in the Truth of History.

Of course *JFK* is not a film about a professional historian, and yet in its inability to picture the quest after past truths as independent of present-day motives and passions on the investigator's part, it would seem congruent with the fictional representation of the historian as a figure for whom transparency is never really possible. In that representation, historians are embodied in that whatever investigation they conduct is tied to who they are, to their very being. Insofar as the fiction film, by its very photographic bases, can only represent the academic's work as embodied in on-the-screen figures, and insofar as the conventional realist-narrative novel narrates the moves and maneuvers of embodied personages as well, filmic and literary fiction seem destined to render and disclose the historian's research practice in motivated actions, in gestures overladen with personality. The meanings of action in the realist narrative novel and the classical fiction film are meanings to be tied to the specific personality, to the particular body, of the flesh-and-blood characters performing them.

Take, for instance, a 1958 academic novel, *Purely Academic*, by Stringfellow Barr.[8] Here the hero, a professor of diplomatic history named Schneider, uses his knowledge of the ways and means of diplomacy not only to interrogate the world of the past but also the present world around him. Like many academic novels, *Purely Academic* fully eschews Peter Novick's image of professions driven by a dream of objectivity to assume instead that professions by their very nature are irremediably driven by rivalry, by personal aggrandizement, by petty desires. And if here the contest of faculties is embodied by professors squabbling over resources (a foundation has promised to grant some of the social sciences some big bucks and now everyone is fighting for a piece of the pie), Barr's novel goes one step further and implies that such embodiment is directly evident, immediately visible: through a striking mimesis, each professor incarnates his academic subject in his very body, in his look, and all Schneider has to do is scrutinize his allies and opponents to intuit their situation and role in the diplomatic battle. Like the closeup of Garrison in *JFK* that implies that truth comes radiating out through his look, the description of scholars in *Purely Academic* implies that *their* truth derives from a perfect coincidence of the person's physicality and the intellectual work he is doing.

In an important way, however, Barr's novel, and many other narrative-realist novels and films of academia, go beyond *JFK* in their rendition of embodiment. As I said before, Garrison is not a professional historian and even if he is like a historian in his dogged pursuit of past truths, he differs in that he isn't, strictly speaking, a *teacher* of those truths. Garrison's problem, we might even suggest, comes from the fact that he is *not* a pedagogue: finding the facts is less important in itself than convincing others of them, and this is what he is unable to do even in the passions of his end-of-trial summation.

In much academic fiction and film, though, a scholar is incomplete if he / she is not a teacher. In Willa Cather's *The Professor's House* (1925), for example, the main character, St. Peter, an historian of the Spanish in the New World, wants to consider his research alone to be the defining characteristic of his life (so much so that his family activities are organized around his work, as mere adjuncts to it) but he realizes that teaching forms a sort of completion to the research project. He has two lives in fact—not research-life and home-life but research-life (with home-life a subset of research) and teaching-life. As the novel puts it,

> All the while that he was working so fiercely by night, he was earning his living during the day; carrying full university work and feeding himself out to hundreds of students in lectures and consultations. But that was another life. St. Peter had mangaged for years to live two lives, both of them very intense. He would willingly have cut down on his university work, would willingly have given his students chaff and sawdust—many instructors had nothing else to give them and got on very well—but his misfortune was that he loved youth—he was weak to it, it kindled him. If there was one eager eye, one doubting, critical mind, one lively curiosity in a whole lecture-room full of commonplace boys and girls, he was its servant.[9]

To the anti-objectivist notion that a scholar invests his or her research with all sorts of personal obsessions, the fictional representation of scholarly endeavor frequently adds a second and complementary conception: namely, that knowledge is not only to be acquired but to be radiated outward in an act of glorious and inspiring instruction. Thus in *Purely Academic*, one of the few instances where academia retains any vitality for the increasingly cynical

Schneider occurs when he lectures passionately on the modern age and, out of a class of intensely bored students, spots one student lighting up with inspired interest at what he is saying.

Such infectious inspiration is represented as so powerful that it can occur even without planning. In fact, according to the ideology of education that underlies the notion of inspiration, it is preferable that such inspiration be unplanned, spontaneous, direct. In Carl van Doren's novel, *The Ninth Wave* (1926), the historian-hero's vision of pedagogy as he takes up his first university post is presented as follows: "He would make no effort to attract any of [his students], but he would, he heroically planned, fill his nook with the air of lofty teaching, and the most kindred spirits would be drawn into it by the kindred impulses of their blood" (78).[10] At the extreme, then, this notion of the professor as radiant teacher tips into a new form of mimesis: the teacher so affects his or her student that the student comes to take on the same obsessions or desires as the teacher. *The Dead Poets Society* (Peter Weir, 1989), a film about a prep-school teacher, offers perhaps the most extreme version of this infectious mimesis as the students come to organize their very being around the doings of their instructor: they imitate his gestures, try to replay his student days, and generally tie their own maturation to an obsessive acting out of what they imagine their teacher's life to be like.

But the instructor in *The Dead Poets Society* is an English instructor, and here we might note a particularity of representations of the historian: of all the academics who might show up in film and fiction, history professors are the fewest and most far between. This relative absence, I would suggest, is itself significant. It may be that it is difficult to come up with effective public and popular cultural representations of the historian and his or her work, and this difficulty may have implications for the larger acceptability of history within everyday culture.

Science and the humanities are figurable within popular mythology (although each in its own way). Think, for example, of all those films of professors posing before beakers and test-tubes, pouring out strange clouds (an image in such films as *The Nutty Professor* [Jerry Lewis, 1963], *It Happens Every Spring* [Lloyd Bacon, 1949], *The Absent-Minded Professor* [Robert Stevenson, 1961]). Science here is the province of the real and the visibly spectacular, of the nitty-gritty, of the professor rendered as a researcher (rather than pedagogue) who, using tools, directly engages with a physical materiality (in *The Absent-Minded Professor*, we never see the titular character in a classroom; in *The Nutty Professor*, the "hero" is a very bad pedagogue—as if to say that scientists are workers for whom teaching is irrelevant, an imposition from without).

Humanities professors, by contrast, are rarely represented as effective doers of knowledge-gaining research. At best, the English professor's lessons are imparted by accident (unbeknownst to the professor, a spark of inspiration is ignited in a student) or enacted in an arena other than the classroom (for example, in encounters between the professor and students out in the "real" world). A most curious image of an active-doer humanities professor occurs in the film *Confidentially Connie* (Edward Buzzell, 1953), made at a historical moment when the G.I. Bill encouraged college education; when a college jock tells an English professor he is dropping out to go into professional football, the professor arm-wrestles him to the ground while quoting Shakespeare to show that the lessons of literature can give one practical force in the everyday world. This image of humanities professors suggests that they can become real only through gestures that intervene in the concrete world *outside* the classroom (hence, the common representation in film of the male English professor as a seducer of his young female students; he finds his reality in the potency of bodily engagement and not in classroom pedagogy). At worst, images of humanists often suggest that they are off in clouds of unreality or are an irrelevancy themselves. A *New Yorker* cartoon from a few years back catches this image of the ethereal humanist. In a bar, a professorial type (balding, glasses, short height, necktie) sits at the counter surrounded by working-class types (coveralls, caps, physical bulkiness). With a gleam in his eyes, the professor-type is declaring, "My work is to stare into space."

Science finds its identity in a mythology of the practicality and visibility of physical research; the humanities finds its identity in the mythology of its ethereality (a good identity when it is depicted as a radiant, inspirational transmitter of knowledge; a bad one when it is depicted as being in the clouds of irrelevance; a mixed one in the case of the professor as seducer). If there is currently a crisis in the university over literary disciplines—as evidenced by neoconservative attacks on new forms of criticism—this may in part come from the public visibility of literary study: it is easy for neoconservatives like Roger Kimball to make fun of certain highly visible titles from the Modern Language Association or other humanities conventions and to mock the ostensible extent to which English professors especially are sexualizing the field of literary study. But there may also be a public crisis of history—one that comes, in contrast, from its invisibility, its public nonfigurability (newspapers will make fun of the M.L.A. but don't even mention the American Historical Association).

A 1986 academic detective novel, *The Student Body*, by J. S. Borthwick, captures some of the essence of the polar opposite mythologies of the sciences and of the humanities in terms of their plenitude or lack of concreteness and practicality. In this novel, an overly ambitious undergraduate student has been murdered—most likely by an English department faculty member—and the incident and the reactions to it are depicted as symptomatic of the conflict among faculties:

> The next few days brought to the college the realization that something was indeed rotten in Denmark—that is to say, in the English Department—and with it came a certain satisfaction. English departments are always suspect, a nest for mad poets, confused socialists, misguided communists, and closet fascists, all straw brains viewed as arguing endlessly over the value of porno novels, fighting over new critical heresies, or nattering about the trivia of grammar, mode, and genre. The faculty and students of those schools and departments that supposedly dealt with the world of acts—engineering, mathematics, physics, the life and earth sciences—took particular relish in the murders and went about shrugging to each other. Well, what did you expect? Look at that Pruczak dame, some kind of witch; and Amos Larkin, drunk as a skunk at the hockey game; and Lacey, makes Don Giovanni look like a boy scout—you call them a faculty?[11]

Note that history is not included among "those schools and departments that supposedly dealt with the world of acts" (unless we are supposed to assume it is a "life science"). It is also, however, not included among the humanities disciplines and exists at best in an a-topia. As a discipline, history has long hovered between several identities: this indecisiveness is most evident in the very fact that in some colleges and universities it is included among the Social Sciences and in others, among the Humanities. This bureaucratic ambiguity replays debates raging within the discipline itself, as well as within other disciplines: is history about laws? is it empirical or hermeneutic?, is it descriptive (of concrete situations) or predictive (of possible trends)? and so on and so on. Within the discipline there is not assurance as to what history is, and I suggest this is also true outside academe—in public consciousness and mythology—where the work of history is some sort of vague, undefined non-entity.

We might note, for example, that one seldom sees images of the historian in the work of active research—on site, in the archives, conducting interviews, and so on. Scientists, it is assumed, do research. Although the popular mythology of science is empiricist in nature (it assumes there are positive facts out there), this is a depth empiricism that assumes facts are not evident, that they have to be dug out with tools and gizmos and intensive effort. Hence films of patient scientific discovery like *Madame Curie* (Mervyn LeRoy, 1943) or *Young Tom Edison* (Norman Taurog, 1940). And hence the standard iconography for the scientist-researcher: wearing a lab-coat and standing in front of various gadgets and looking out steadfast, ready to engage in complicated experiments on a resistant materiality. An episode of the TV series *Class of '96* makes the point in an almost uncannily explicit way that different disciplines have different relations to hard truth. A montage offers up a number of different professors announcing to their students the nature of the upcoming midterm exams. The economics professor reminds his students that there is only one right answer; the English professor reminds the students of the endless open-endedness of possible interpretations. Between them, we see a history professor who tells her students that there are many (but not an infinite number) of possible factors behind historical causality—confirming the perception that history is neither hard enough to be a real science or soft enough to be a real branch of the humanities.

In a sense, it may be that the image represented of historians is troubled by the very success of the myth of objectivity. Insofar as historical facts are assumed to exist positively, the historian is then assumed to be little more than a conveyer of knowledge that antedates him or her. I imagine that this is the way many of us remember our elementary- and high-school history teachers (assuming we were in schools where history was a separate field and not simply subsumed under that curious category, "Social Studies"): the history teacher told us things about the past that we were to take as givens, and we were never supposed to wonder how the teacher in fact knew them (for example, we certainly do not imagine our high school teachers rummaging around in archives).

At best, then, within popular imagery the history teacher is little but a skilled lecturer, repeating truths that were established before he or she retold them. This again gives history an awkward position among the disciplines. The scientist gains justification in the making of new truths in a dramatic encounter with the real (see, for example, the heroic narrativity of *The Double Helix*, the bestselling story of the discovery of DNA,[12] later made into a TV movie with Jeff Goldblum starring as the originally gawky James Watson). The humanist gains justification in the making of new poetic or metaphysical truths through unfettered reflection and through exorbitant philosophizing. One common image of the English professor is that of Socratic enabler, pushing his or her students to come up with new insights (see, for example, the English professor in the TV series *Class of '96*: he sits back while the students fight out the interpretation of *Moby Dick*, an argument he has skillfully encouraged). But the history professor's "making" of fact or truth is derivative, second-degree, a mere reportage both of historical events that are old and of the historical facts or truths that precedent figures have produced. At best, the historian is a skilled lecturer, at worst an irrelevant antiquarian.

In those novels and visual works that do feature history professors, there often are scenes in which the lecturer gets so caught up in rhetorical skills that he or she gets carried away in unreal flights of rhetorical discursive fancy. It may not be coincidental that some of the novels of history professors show them suddenly departing from their prepared lecture (a neutral narrative account of the past) to engage in flights of philosophical reflection, thus either losing the attention of their students in the process or touching only a very few and special souls. The history professor stands out only when he or she abandons the traditional role of the history professor. Such moments stand in contrast to the typical representation of the humanities professor lecture. Take, for instance, Howard Fast's *Silas Timberman*,[13] an anti-Red Scare novel, where the titular figure, an English professor, gets in trouble not because he adds to his lessons but, quite the contrary, because he sticks to his lesson plan and teaches a work that others consider subversive (namely, Twain's *The Man That Corrupted Hadleyburg*[14]). English professors have something to teach (even if it turns out to be subversive), but historians are commonly represented as having little that is worth saying unless they deviate from the proper paths of traditional pedagogy to engage in the sort of metaphysical reflection associated with humanists. Historians, in other words, become compelling or pedagogically gripping only when they cease to be historians.

The extreme example of the image of the history professor as someone who either blandly sticks to his nondescript (and undescribable) work or who goes off into irrelevant detours occurs perhaps in Robert Nathan's 1947 novel of a history professor having a mid-life crisis, *Mr. Whittle and the Morning Star*.[15] Robert Whittle's crisis is simultaneously professional (he has produced no work of merit), personal (his homelife has become boringly regularized and he no longer cares much for his wife), sexual (he has a crush on one of his undergraduates, Penelope Andrews) and historico-metaphysical (he is convinced in the postwar moment of the Atomic Age that humankind is about to destroy itself). Mr. Whittle is quite simply in a rut, and this manifests itself in a new flamboyancy in his lectures: he begins to add codas to his formerly bland and factual historical narratives, announcing portentously that the apocalypse is imminent. Mr. Whittle's public declarations that the world is coming to an end are taken (by other characters and ultimately by the novel itself) to be betrayals of the fundamental and modest responsibility of the historian simply to report what happened in the past: by trading an account of the past for prediction, positing a teleology to historical flow, by converting "objectivity" into scare-tactic fatalism, Whittle has gone against the grain of the historical profession.

Fundamentally a conservative novel, *Mr. Whittle and the Morning Star* narrates the return of the history professor to the modesty of his lot. After some furtive and futile necking with his undergraduate and after a night of doubt-filled and self-torturing errancy under a stormy heaven, Mr. Whittle returns home and decides to accept the ordinariness of his career and marriage. It may be significant that his reconciliation with the routine of his life occurs at home and with no mention of what this implies for any specific thing he will or will not now do in his teaching; the assumption is that his career is a mere epiphenomenon whose fate is fully determined by the stabilities of his private life. By profession Mr. Whittle may be a historian, but in no way does that profession have any deep or fundamental impact on the nature of who he is as a man. History doesn't matter, it is an indifferent component of an indifferent life.

Earlier I mentioned the affinity of modernist fiction and modernist film for tales of historians who simultaneously try to make sense of history and of their own lives and find that both the objective past and their subjective present resist comprehension. In these works of modernism, such as *Nausea*, the hero's identity as an historian is intimately connected to his or her overall inability to make meaning of life. Significantly though, those more narrative-realist works that also deal with historians' existential crises—such as *Mr. Whittle and the Morning Star*—often make the fact of the protagonist's being a historian less central to his or her attempt to make sense of his or her personal life. Being an historian in these works doesn't make one more vulnerable to doubt—being an historian has no bearing on one's fundamental existential identity. In much of the popular fiction about academia, the hero's academic appurtenance is treated as inessential, as a virtual sideline. In modernist works, the fact that a protagonist is a historian serves as one of the marks of crisis (see, for instance, Gide's *L'Immoraliste*[16] where the protagonist, Michael, is unable to find his usual pleasures in historical work after having experienced the malaise of existence); for the popular narrative-realist work, the fact of being a historian has no bearing on one's propensity for crisis or for the resolution of that crisis. *Mr. Whittle and the Morning Star* resolves its crisis within the space of domestic life and even suggests that Mr. Whittle's career is irrelevant to this resolution. Insofar as history is in fact not about life but about past and dead facts and, in addition, is not in any directly meaningful relation to the life of the person teaching that history, it follows that the profession of history is of little help in working through one's existential crisis. History is treated as a past-time, rather than an investment of self that could or would in any way call that self into doubt.

Take, for instance, Edmund Fuller's 1963 novel, *The Corridor*. The hero, Malcolm Adamson, is a history instructor who wanders the corridor of a hospital when his wife begins hemorrhaging after a miscarriage. Malcolm and Jean had already begun to lose their deepest love for each other, and now Malcolm wonders how this happened and what their life will be like if Jean survives. The bulk of the novel consists of Malcolm's reflections and his memories of key moments in the trajectory of their marriage. But even though Malcolm finds it important to delve into his past, his professional work as historian is not really key to this archaeological effort. Significantly, we learn virtually nothing about Malcolm's work in history, nothing about his area, nothing about his approach, nothing other than the facts that his overall field is American history and that he is helping his department chair write a textbook. *The Corridor* does allow that Malcolm indeed has a specialty within history: "[W]hen he began to write—that essential of an academic career—he battled through every draft with her [Jean], and she pressed him relentlessly, however specialized his subject matter, toward style, independent thought, and creativity—away from the suffocating bogs of learned writing" (100–101), but the novel never elaborates, as if academic specialization is a mere and obvious given not worth spending time on. Ironically, Malcolm's one publication—an essay on the "shift and decline in the American dream, developed out of the close-reading of certain of De Crèvecoeur's more euphoric rhapsodies"[17]—is said specifically to represent a new departure for him, but we do not learn from what base he is departing. Significantly, the job in a small New England college that Malcolm lands on the basis of this article centers around his helping an older professor revise his American history textbook: Malcolm has no real existence as a historian and even the one heart-felt essay he writes leads to him becoming more divorced from personal work as a historian (he has, for example, less time to devote to his own dissertation).

Early in *The Corridor*, asking himself whether the dangerous operation Jean had was necessary, Malcolm reflects: "Is it necessary? What does it mean to be necessary? Could not that question be regressed endlessly, back through one's own life to birth, back through the history of the race, the planet, the whole creation? History was the subject Malcolm Adamson taught, but history had taught him little about the necessary."[18] History as profession, then, is incidental to the real existential work of historical reflection a man must engage in to figure out his place in the cosmos. History has nothing to do with one's present (it is not about the self, but about others), and the past that it is concerned with is a history fully exterior to the historian, not connnected with the historian's own personal past. Indeed, Malcolm's college shows up in the novel only as a vague background, a place where he works but that has no major consequence for the deeper significance of the life he lives: as the novel puts it, on his way to the hospital, Martin "drove the short way farther to the hardtop, then on through the village and beyond, past the grounds of Camden College. His classes were covered for today. He bore onward along the winding, misty road toward town."[19]

It may be that the indefinability and insubstantiality of the historical vocation within popular representation explains why novels about history professors show these professors engaging in quite physical ways with the "Real." But the novels suggest that such engagement is enacted only in situations outside the classroom or fully outside the professor's research work. To be sure, many academic novels and films include moments where the professor leaves behind the ethereal abstractions and unrealities of academia for a more pragmatically direct realm (for instance, Robert Reeve's "Professor Thomas Theron" series, about an English professor turned gumshoe) but the history professor novel seems more consistently to pit the historian's academic life against some other life judged more immediate and valuable. (Few novels go so far, though, as Robert Scribner's 1957 *Eggheads in the End Zone*,[20] about a history professor who becomes a football player when his college [a thinly veiled transformation of St. John's in Maryland] decides to make the professors, rather than the students, play in competitive sports!) Even Cather's *The Professor's House*, in many ways quite admiring of Professor St. Clair's research on New World Spanish history, offers numerous moments of the professor taking off from his research to go swimming with his sons-in-law and, even more important, in its central section, the novel abandons its academic narrative for the Old West tale of Tom Outland, one of the professor's students who led the sort of real life that most of the academics in St. Clair's life have no ability to appreciate. Although many novels and films about English professors take it as a given that these professors will sleep with their students (*National Lampoon's Animal House* [John Landis, 1978], *D.O.A.* [Rocky Morton, 1988], and see also the episode of *Quantum Leap* in which the character Sam is a drunken English professor who's involved with a starry-eyed undergraduate), there is virtually no major embodiment of the history professor as effective seducer: Mr. Whittle has a few furtive kisses with undergraduate Penelope Andrews; Malcolm in *The Corridor* is almost seduced at a historical association convention by an old flame, Evie Johnson, but pulls away at the last minute, and later on he almost seduces the wife of a chemistry professor (who significantly, has consummated love affairs) but she passes out from too much drinking. Insofar as they seem to do nothing scholarly, (no real research of their own, just repetitions of the facts of the past), history professors are judged against a world of active doing and are found wanting. An extreme example perhaps is the Rodney Dangerfield film, *Back to School* (Alan Metter, 1986) which offers a range of images of professors, including a libidinal English professor (played this time by a woman). In this film the hero, a millionaire who has gone back to school, listens to a young history professor talk of a Second World War he has obviously never participated in and whose facts and interpretation he is getting all wrong. Through commonsensical but pointed comments, the millionaire shows up the hip, young historian as the really ignorant fool he actually is. In a world made up of millionaires who have never gone to college but have a street-wisdom that allows them to intervene actively in the present and English professors who can act in the present through their demonstration of carnal desire, the history professor is treated as an oddity: not merely does *Back to School*'s history professor have no life in the present (he is shown only in one scene, being shown up as a fool by the millionaire) but he even has only an inauthentic grasp of the past, since he teaches inadequately about things he never experienced himself.

Many of the notions I have been considered are condensed in a 1925 novel, *The Ninth Wave*, by Carl Van Doren. *The Ninth Wave* is a *bildungsroman* that recounts the growth of Kent Morrow from farmboy to middle-aged and highly respected historian at the local university. While Kent does end up married to one of his students (thus portraying him as somewhat different than the non-sexualized history professors in the other novels I've mentioned), the growth of their relationship is handled as a prim-and-proper courtship rather than a seduction (in fact, the student goes after the timid Kent) and leads to a respectable and traditional marriage. So much is the novel about the proper banalities of domesticity and their privilege over everything else (including the possible glories of an academic career) that the culmination of the novel turns out not to be the moment in which Kent wins a prestigious history award and caps off his career, but one in which his daughter gives birth to a child and leads Kent to muse on the continuities of families across the generations.

At one point in *The Ninth Wave*, Kent is entertaining his old childhood friend, Mel, who has become a big New York lawyer. Mel has just read Kent's biography of Jefferson and offers him a compliment but with one reservation: "I've read your book on Jefferson, Kent. It's the best life of him I know.... But there's one thing about him which you don't make clear." "What's that?" replies Kent. Mel explains:

> How he got his idea of abstract justice.... Oh, I don't mean where the idea came from before his instinct made him accept it. Of course such ideas were common in Virginia during his youth. I agree with you that he didn't need to go to France or to read French books to get them. But what was there in his nature which prepared him? Every man who reads or thinks is simply washed with ideas, like an island which the tide covers. But one idea takes root in you, and another takes root in me, because we are the different people we are. There's the mystery, as they call it, of character. I know what Jefferson's ideas were, especially since I've read your book, but I still want to know why he responded to those particular ones, when others looked as convincing to men who had been brought up very much as he had.[21]

At this, Kent is forced to admit what he sees as the limits and limitations of his profession: "You're probably asking the historian to go further than his business takes him. He has to begin with the axiom that men are different, just as he begins with the axiom that men exist at all. Why there should be men, or why they should be unlike each other, is a question that only theologians are cheeky enough to tackle."[22] He admits that the profession of history is concerned only with the past, in its dryest components, and it has no power to deal with the big questions of the meaning of the past or the present, of others and of one's self.

Ironically, though, *The Ninth Wave* implies that there is someone else "cheeky enough" or capable enough to offer insights about these more metaphysical questions: namely, the novelist him- or herself. For all the declarations by Kent that history can't account for the emotive and intellectual singularity of each potential historical agent, the novel *The Ninth Wave* is fully confident that its narration can offer precisely such accounting. Like other realist-narrative fictions discussed in this essay, *The Ninth Wave* makes a distinction, through its very confidence in the ability of its narration to interpret the facts of life, between the powers of fictional discourse and the ineffectuality of historical discourse (which at best narrates nothing but a bunch of dead facts). As a *bildungsroman, The Ninth Wave* easily tunnels into Kent's unconscious, into his point-of-view, and lays out the factors and motivations that made him who he is. The novel takes as one of its stated themes that the self cannot know others but assumes that its own projections of aesthetic imagination are capable of a confident knowing. The novel may tell us that "The best a man and a woman could do was to walk ... along parallel roads. They could keep calling out to each other as they walked. They might even have so thin a dividing line that they could whisper through it. But there was no denying the wall. Loneliness was the rule of life."[23] But fiction, then, will be the force that surmounts all barriers, that scales all walls, to enter into a multiplicity of minds and of points of view and make all seemingly isolated egos one in the identity of the artist.

Ironically (or not so ironically), such fiction refuses a similar power to historiography. History, in the popular conception, is not about imagination, is not about re-construction, but at best about positivist restoration, about a non-interpretive mastery of bits of facts. Hence, for example, the best-seller appeal of E. D. Hirsch's *Cultural Literacy*[24] and the variant editions for diverse age groups, in which Hirsch implies that the past comes down to us as univocally identifiable bits of cocktail-party trivia, conforming to a stereotype of the past as fixed pieces of knowledge and of history as positive retrieval. The function of history, in such a conception, is not to interpret the past, but simply to replay it, at best to make its facts come alive. Interpretation, when such a conception finds a place for it, becomes little more than a flourish, the icing on the cake that makes the dryness of the inert history lesson a little more flavorful. In the high school film, *Teachers* (Arthur Hiller, 1984), the history teacher is popular because he dresses up as each historical character he is teaching. While a poetics of history like that in Hayden White's in *Metahistory* revolutionized the professional field of history by treating the historical text as textuality—precisely as active discursive fashioning—one wonders if this has had any effect on the popular conception of the profession, where it is probably the case that popular consciousness assumes (and hopes) history is little more than a reliable mimesis of the past and not a poetic construction of it.

The wavering of the disciplinary images of professors in *Class of '96* (economists find objective laws, English professors demand endless interpretations, history professors hover somewhere in-between) may be a mark then of the fact that certain disciplines have no real identity or significant purpose within public imagery. History, it seems, is one of these professions. Take, for instance, the case of James Bartlow, history professor-turned-screenwriter in the Hollywood melodrama, *The Bad and the Beautiful* (Vincente Minnelli, 1952). The complications start in this film with a very confused notion of what a historian does professionally: although the bookjacket from Bartlow's Pulitzer-prize-winning novel describes him as a former professor of "Medieval History," he seems to write nothing but Southern local-color books (the adaptation of his first vaguely looks like *Gone With the Wind*; his third is about his own Southern-belle wife). Moreover, it is significant that although Bartlow describes his first book as a "scholarly work about early Virginia," the film clearly identifies this work and his subsequent efforts as works of fiction. In other words, even as the film makes some gestures toward recognizing "scholarly work," it still has to imagine this work within the generic terms of gripping fiction (the Hollywood producer who has bought Bartlow's first novel even compliments him on how cinematically he writes). A historian, in this representation, has no real work of his (or her) own and is nothing more than a novelist or screenwriter-waiting-to-burst-out.

The fact that this historian is played by Dick Powell further disembodies the historian as historian and embodies him as other things—in particular, as a man of action, a man of the world. By the 1950s, Powell had two screen personae of the active man: the comic actor in musicals (at one point in *The Bad and the Beautiful* when he is forced to get up at 6:30 in the morning to work on his script, he mugs at the camera as if in one of his old Busby Berkeley comedies) and the tough-guy *à la* the *films noirs* he acted in in the 1940s (for example, *Murder, My Sweet*). Not for nothing, indeed, does this professor become a real tough-guy and punch out *The Bad and the Beautiful*'s protagonist in their last confrontation: as embodied by Powell, the history professor is insubstantial until he becomes something other than a professor.

If the history professor and his or her efforts tend to be disembodied in the popular literature and cinema of academia (or embodied only in inconsequential ways—for example, as collector of dull and irrelevant dry facts from a past disconnected from the present), this may have something to do with a public sentiment that the work of historiography accomplishes nothing of relevance. What is the point of history to Americans? The hard sciences parade their worth for the public sector as source of useful tools. In *The Absent-Minded Professor*, for instance, the branches of the military fight desperately over control of Flubber, the chemical product that gives objects anti-gravitational ability. The humanities find their worth in an ideology of self-help or of romance (English, for example, teaches writing skills, but even in its most ethereal moments, those of wacky interpretation, it enables the individual to establish selfhood through hermeneutic investigation; and creative writing enriches the soul). But history seems to have little relevance for the public: insofar as it is assumed to deal with inert facts and dead historical figures whose import does not extend into the present, history is perceived as a field without contemporary pertinence. It is for this reason that history in high schools has been annexed to that nebulous region of Social Studies since there, at least, history is obliged to announce its usefulness, its social role. But as a separate, integral field, history suffers the consequences of antiquarianism.

When history is distinguished from law and criminal detection in a film like *JFK*, it seems that history suffers in comparison to these other investigative modes insofar as it cannot make the claims of relevance they can. As modes of epistemology, law and detection are tempting subjects for popular representation in that they assume a direct and necessary connection of past and present.

If the history film often makes the identity and embodiment of the historian irrelevant to the dead facts he or she lectures about, the law story in contrast often doubly overdetermines the notion of the past's present relevance. Trials, which take evidence collected from a past to adjudicate its relevance to a present, solve things not only for defendants and plaintiffs but also for the lawyers insofar as the trial enables them to settle big existential questions where the lawyer solves something about his own life by solving the case (see, for example, not only *JFK*, but other trial films of personal remasculinization such as *A Few Good Men* [Rob Reiner, 1992] or *The Verdict* [Sidney Lumet, 1982]). Similarly, films of detection and investigation suggest that if one delves into the past, it is for reasons in and of the present. For example, Jim Garrison in *JFK* doesn't simply want to uncover the truth but he wants to resolve ongoing problems in America by that uncovering. As numerous scholars of detective fiction tell us, the detective story recounts two tales—the story of the crime and the story of its detection—and the latter actually becomes the forum in which the former is framed and even constructed. In addition, insofar as most detective narratives have to do with the investigation of a crime, the implication is that the past event (the crime) and the present are necessarily connected: not to explain the past would be to allow a criminal dangerously to continue his or her criminal acts in the present. The detective story, then, is ultimately and fully presentist. In contrast, history's public problem may be that it is too rooted in transpired events that can find no reason for present re-narration. History's story of the past has little pertinence for the ongoing story of the present.

Hence the interest of a popular film like *Bill and Ted's Excellent Adventure* (Stephen Herek, 1989). The film assumes that history's pedagogical deficiency comes from its inability, in contrast to other school subjects, to become a source of "Show and Tell." History's telling is normally disconnected from showing since there is nothing to be shown. In other words, since the past has passed, it can only exist in the present through the words of the historian and thus has nothing but insubstantiality. But if the heroes of *Bill and Ted's Excellent Adventure* offer in and for the present vitally embodied versions of dead figures from the past, we film spectators too are recipients of this offer: unlike a literary version which might have simply recounted Bill and Ted's adventure, the film *shows* us their adventure and its results and thereby gives body on screen to the figures of history. In this way, it pinpoints the ways in which the specificities of cinema as representational medium may create problems for the effective representation of the historian's work.

Insofar as it embodies its characters, popular film needs to give characters something to do. Fiction film, argued Mortimer Adler in *Art and Prudence* in 1937,[25] is the perfect Aristotelian art in that it offers the life of "men" in action, and while we might want to criticize the limitations of such a definition of film's vocation, we need also to realize that it catches something of the ideology and appeal of the classic fiction narrative film. The entertainment film is action, is action given body (but not the historian's body). But only in some cases do professors gain active bodies suitable for dramatic representation: the professor suddenly thrown into an active world which he or she is forced to be as active within (for example, the Indiana Jones films with its hero literally escaping from academia into a world of action); the professor as someone who leads dual lives of passivity and activity (for example, the stereotype of the seductive English professor who is respectable in class and wild in private); the professor as someone who has an active hero inside his- or herself if it can just be opened up. Scientists lend themselves easily to cinematic rendition since the assumption is that they are doers by nature (and the bubbling beakers and crackling electric gadgets then become metaphors of the energetic action they are engaged in); humanists lend themselves easily to cinematic rendition since it is assumed that there is an easy slide between the subject of their pedagogy—life itself—and their own lives (hence, one very common image in films of English professors has them lecturing on a literary work that just happens to parallel something in their own lives: for example, in *A Change of Seasons* [Richard Lang, 1980] the English professor [Anthony Hopkins] lectures about the literature of love, and we cut to a closeup of the student with whom he is in love). Here, though, lies the difficulty for the representation of the historian: he or she does little that meets the criteria of dramatic representation. Given especially the public assumption that historians don't "do" anything but repeat facts about the accomplishments of others, there is something essentially uncinematic about the work of history.

Embodying historical figures and implying that that embodiment is all that history is about, *Bill and Ted's Excellent Adventure* both criticizes the inert irrelevance of historiography and supports its underlying empiricism: on the one hand, Bill and Ted score points by bringing historical figures back from the past but on the other hand the pedagogical effect of their actions is little different than what school historians normally do, since Bill and Ted (and their classmates) take no useable lessons from the historical figures but act as if their mere presence in the present is sufficient. In other words, like the teacherly adult world to which they are so ostensibly opposed, Bill and Ted can offer nothing but history as a series of disconnected facts linked to vibrant personalities separated off from any meaningful sense of *longue durée*. On the one hand, the film pictures a circumvention of the mediating world of adults with their worthless lessons (and here the film shares the anti-school bias of numerous teen films—see, for instance, *Ferris Bueller's Day Off* [John Hughes, 1986]); on the other hand, the results of this seeming subversion merely confirm the status quo and imply the integration of the rebels within an epistemology that really and ultimately circumscribes them (and, in this respect, it is not ironic to find that Bill and Ted become cultural heroes of a future society or that Ferris Bueller can admit that he engages in misdeeds since he already knows that his financial and personal security as future yuppie are ensured for him no matter what mischief he enacts).

To the professional historian, a film like *Bill and Ted's Excellent Adventure* may seem light years away from the kind of disciplinary work he or she does. But it is the very distance between the profession and the popular representation that is important. Conceptions of the historical past are rampant in popular culture, but conceptions of the historian are few and far between. History as a professional activity appears to have little place in public consciousness precisely at a moment (the moment we often term "postmodernity") in which the question of the potentially public nature of history is of burning pertinence. The discipline of history may well need to examine the visibility or, more likely, the invisibility of its image so that it does not blithely continue a descent into cultural irrelevance.

notes

1. Sally's bewilderment is the mirror-inverse of the uncanniness I am sure many professors have felt in those moments when one of our undergraduate students mentions that he or she came across one of our published writings and was surprised to discover that we wrote. Given the centrality of publishing to academic success and advancement, we think of our research lives as obvious and integral parts of our professorly being; yet given how much of that publishing goes on in *professional* journals that, by their very nature, talk only to other professionals, this integral part of our lives is unknown to many of our students—indeed something they do not even suspect. (No doubt this also has something to do with another popular myth—that of the creative writer. Insofar as the popular mythology assigns the place of writing to this figure alone among academic professionals, it is not imagined, nor is it necessary or easy to imagine, that professors in other areas also write.) The uncanniness of the encounter—a student discovering with surprise that the professor writes—is, like the cartoon, caught up in issues of embodiment. We professors would like to believe that we find an embodied unity between our research work and our teaching, and it is potentially disturbing to find that others only know us in part.)
2. Charles J. Sykes, *Profscam: Professors and the Demise of Higher Education* (Washington: Regnery Gateway, 1988).
3. Roger Kimball, *Tenured Radicals: How Politics Has Corrupted Higher Education* (New York: Harper & Row, 1990).
4. Peter Novick, *That Noble Dream: The "Objectivity Question" and the American Historical Profession* (New York: Cambridge University Press, 1988), 11–12.
5. Hayden White, *Metahistory* (Baltimore: Johns Hopkins Press, 1973).
6. Jean-Paul Sartre, *Nausea* (Norfolk: New Dimensions, 1964).
7. Richard Condon, *Winter Kills* (New York: Dial Press, 1974).
8. Stringfellow Barr, *Purely Academic* (New York: Simon & Schuster, 1958).
9. Willa Cather, *The Professor's House* (New York: A. A. Knopf, 1925), 28.
10. Carl Van Doren, *The Ninth Wave* (New York: Harcourt, Brace, 1926), 78.
11. J. S. Bothwick, *The Student Body* (New York: St. Martin's Press, 1986), 157.
12. James D. Watson, *The Double Helix: A Personal Account of the Discovery of the Structure of DNA* (New York: New American Library, 1968).
13. Howard Fast, *Silas Timberman* (New York: Blue Heron Press, 1954).
14. Mark Twain, *The Man That Corrupted Hadleyburg and other Essays and Stories* (New York: Harper and Bros., 1902).
15. Robert Nathan, *Mr. Whittle and the Morning Star* (New York: A. A. Knopf, 1947).
16. André Gide, *L'Immoraliste*, (Paris: Mercure de France, 1986 [c. 1902]).
17. Edmund Fuller, *The Corridor* (New York: Random House, 1963), 162.
18. Fuller, 7.
19. Fuller, 4.
20. Robert Scribner, *Eggheads in the Endzone* (New York: Exposition Press, 1957).
21. Van Doren, 159–160.
22. Ibid
23. Van Doren, 181.
24. E. D. Hirsch, *Cultural Literacy: What Every American Needs to Know* (New York: Vintage Books), 1987.
25. Mortimer Adler, *Art and Prudence* (New York: Arno Press, 1978).

contributors

ROBERT BURGOYNE is Associate Professor and Director of Film Studies in the English Department at Wayne State University. He is co-author of *New Vocabularies in Film Semiotics* and is currently completing a book, *The Cinematic Rewriting of History*.

THOMAS ELSAESSER is Professor of Film and Television and Chair of the Department of Film and Television at the University of Amsterdam. His publications include *New German Cinema: A History*; *Early Cinema: Space, Frame, Narrative*; *Writing for the Medium: Television in Transition;* and, most recently, *Fassbinder's Germany: History, Identity, Subject*.

SUMIKO HIGASHI is Associate Professor of History and teaches film studies at the State University of New York at Brockport. She has published extensively on film and history and is the author of *Cecil B. DeMille and American Culture: The Silent Era*.

BILL NICHOLS is Professor of Cinema Studies at San Francisco State University. He has edited *Movies and Methods I* and *II* and is the author of *Ideology and the Image*; *Representing Reality: Issues and Concepts in Documentary*; and, most recently, *Blurred Boundaries: Questions of Meaning in Contemporary Culture*.

PATRICE PETRO is Associate Professor of English, Film, and Comparative Literature at the University of Wisconsin at Milwaukee. She is the author of *Joyless Streets: Women and Melodramatic Representation in Weimar Germany* and, more recently, the editor of *Fugitive Images: From Photography to Video*.

Dana Polan is Professor of English and Film at the University of Pittsburgh and Resident Director of the Paris Center for Critical Studies. He is the author of *Power and Paranoia: History, Narrative and the American Cinema, 1940-1950* and, most recently, of *In a Lonely Place*, published in the British Film Institute's Film Classics series.

Shawn Rosenheim is Associate Professor of English and teaches film and American studies at Williams College. He is the author of *Secret Writing: The Cryptographic Imagination from Edgar Poe to the Internet* and is working on a book about Errol Morris.

Robert A. Rosenstone is Professor of History at the California Institute of Technology. He is the author of the historiographically innovative *Mirror in the Shrine: American Encounters in Meiji Japan* and, more recently, *Visions of the Past*, a collection of his own essays. He also recently edited *Revisioning History: Film and the Construction of a New Past.*

Vivian Sobchack is Professor of Film and Television and Associate Dean of the School of Theater, Film, and Television at UCLA. She is co-author of *An Introduction to Film* and the author of *Screening Space: The American Science Fiction Film* and, most recently, *The Address of the Eye: A Phenomenology of Film Experience.*

Janet Staiger is Professor of Film, Television, and Cultural Studies at the University of Texas at Austin. Her recent books are *Interpreting Films: Studies in the Historical Reception of American Cinema* and *Bad Women: The Regulation of Female Sexuality in Early Cinema.*

Frank P. Tomasulo is Associate Professor of Film/Video in the Department of Communication at Georgia State University in Atlanta. He has published extensively on the popular media and is editor of the *Journal of Film and Video.*

Hayden White holds the distinguished system-wide title of University Professor at the University of California. He is author of *Metahistory: The Historical Imagination in Nineteenth-Century Europe*; *Tropics of Discourse: Essays in Cultural Criticism*, and *The Content of the Form: Narrative Discourse and Historical Representation.*

Denise J. Youngblood is Associate Professor of History at the University of Vermont. She is a specialist in Russian popular culture, has published extensively on Soviet cinema, and studied at the State Institute of Cinematography, Moscow. She is currently writing a book on the Russian movie industry at the turn of the twentieth century.

index

The Absent-Minded Professor (Robert Stevenson, 1961), 242
Adorno, Theodor, 17, 179–80n.7
Alfred Hitchcock Presents, 221
All the President's Men (Alan Pakula, 1976), 47, 125n.15
America's Most Wanted, 44
American Dream (Barbara Kopple, 1989), 231
Anderson, Benedict, 114, 121, 125n.14
Andrei Rublev (Andrei Tarkovskii, 1966/1969–71), 10–11, 127–143
Ankersmit, F.R., 202–203
Annales school, 2, 160, 203–204
Anti-Semitism, 63, 172
Antimodernism, 91–92, 97, 106, 107–108
Apocalypse Now (Francis Ford Coppola, 1979), 146
Art and Prudence, 254

Back to School (Alan Metter, 1986), 249–50
The Bad and the Beautiful (Vincente Minnelli, 1952), 252
Bad Day at Black Rock (John Sturges, 1955), 209
Barnes, Djuna, 194–96
Barthes, Roland, 71
Baudrillard, Jean, 155, 157, 188
Bazin, André, 53n.11, 82; and classical realist film theory, 71–72, 154; and the real, 75, 85
Beard, Charles, 94, 99
Becker, Carl, 94, 99
Bell, Daniel, 93, 106
Benjamin, Walter, 17, 24, 114, 151, 214
Bergstrom, Janet, 187–88, 189
Berlin Alexanderplatz (Rainer Werner Fassbinder, 1980), 164
Between the Acts, 27–29
Bhabha, Homi, 120, 122–23, 124–25n.13
Bill and Ted's Excellent Adventure (Stephen Herek, 1989), 13, 254–55
Bloch, Ernst, 164
Bloom, Harold, 165
The Blue Angel (Josef von Sternberg, 1930), 153
Boredom, 12, 188–98
Brennan, Timothy, 118
A Brief History of Time (Errol Morris, 1992), 222–23
Broszat, Martin, 160
Browne, Nick, 107
Browning, Christopher R., 30–31
Bruner, Jerome, 41
Buffalo Bill and the Indians, or Sitting Bull's History Lesson (Robert Altman, 1976), 73
Burgoyne, Robert, 10, 58, 61

C–SPAN, 7
Cabaret (Bob Fosse, 1972), 151–52, 178
Camera Natura (Ross Gibson, 1986), 209–10
Censorship, 128, 139. See also Production Code.

Challenger space shuttle, 23–24, 29, 32, 36, 84
A Change of Seasons (Richard Lang, 1980), 255
The Cheat (Cecil B. DeMille, 1915), 95
The Cheese and the Worms, 13. See also Carlo Ginzburg.
Cheyette, Bryan, 149, 163
The City, Garbage and Death, 172
The Civil War (Ken Burns, 1990), 3, 13, 219–20, 224, 232
Class of '96, 244–45, 252
Cold War, the, 10, 51, 111n.46, 155; and *The Ten Commandments*, 98–105
The Color Purple (Steven Spielberg, 1985), 166
Come See the Paradise (Alan Parker, 1990), 209
Conditional mood, 9, 57, 59–60
Confessions of a Nazi Spy (Anatole Litvak, 1939), 45–47
Confidentially Connie (Edward Buzzell, 1953), 243
The Conformist (Bernardo Bertolucci, 1970), 61, 151, 157
Conspiracy, 8, 10, 19, 64, 120–21, 240; and Oliver Stone, 45–46, 47–51, 232
The Content of the Form, 67n.3
Coppola, Francis Ford, 165
Cops, 42–43, 233–4n.6
The Corridor, 247–48, 249
Cultural Literacy, 251

The Damned (Luchino Visconti, 1969), 18, 40, 151, 152, 153, 157, 158
Dances With Wolves (Kevin Costner, 1990), 239
Das Letzte Loch (Herbert Achternbusch, 1981), 171
Dateline, 44
David (Peter Lilienthal, 1978), 148–49
Davis, Natalie, 204
De Man, Paul, 72
De-realization, 8, 24–26, 59; and *JFK*, 119
Dead Poets Society (Peter Weir, 1989), 242
Dear America—Letters from Vietnam (William Couturie, 1987), 146
Death by Hanging (Nagisa Oshima, 1976), 68n.15
Debord, Guy, 7, 70, 71, 84
The Deer Hunter (Michael Cimino, 1978), 146
DeMille, Cecil B., 10, 91–112
Derrida, Jacques, 70, 72, 80, 203–204
DeSica, Vittorio, 153
Despair (Rainer Werner Fassbinder, 1978), 157, 159, 164
Devereaux, Leslie, 65
Die Patriotin (Alexander Kluge, 1979), 159
Disney, 3–4; and *Pocahontas*, 6
Doane, Mary Ann, 187–88, 189
Docu-drama, 18–19, 40–41, 43, 44, 47, 222; and *JFK*, 49, 123
The Donahue Show, 227, 230
Doré Bible, 95, 98
The Double Helix, 245
Duby, Georges, 204

Eco, Umberto, 72
Eggheads in the End Zone, 249
El Chacal de Nahueltoro (Miguel Littin, 1969), 68n.15
Eliot, T. S., 196
Elsaesser, Thomas, 7, 9, 11
Ennui, 188–98
Epics, Biblical, 92, 101, 105, 107
Epics, historical, 10, 95, 100, 111n.33, n.41, 182n.66; and *Andrei Rublev*, 127
Epstein, Jean, 85
Ermarth, Elizabeth Deeds, 106, 202–203
Errol Morris: Interrotron Stories, 13, 220–233
Ethics, 30, 44, 232
Events, see Historical events.
Eye-Witness Video, 227
Eyes on the Prize, 231

Fackenheim, Emile, 30
Fanon, Frantz, 125n.13
Far From Poland (Jill Godmilow, 1983), 59, 207–208
Fassbinder, Rainer Werner, 163, 172, 182n.63
Feminism, 12, 188–89, 197, 213; and aesthetics, 198
Feminist film theory, 12, 187, 197
A Few Good Men (Rob Reiner, 1992), 253
Fielding, Raymond, 53n.7

Fisher, Amy, 43, 44–45
Flitterman, Sandy, 107
Forrest Gump (Robert Zemeckis, 1994), 1–4
Foucault, Michel, 70, 154, 157; as postmodern historian, 203–204
Freud, Sigmund, 77–78, 190, 222; and *nachträglichkeit*, 57
Friedlander, Saul, 31, 148, 150–51, 154, 216
From Here to Eternity (Fred Zinneman, 1953), 209
Full Metal Jacket (Stanley Kubrick, 1987), 146

Gates of Heaven (Errol Morris, 1978), 222, 224
George, Henry, 102–103
The German Sisters (Margarethe von Trotta, 1981), 159
Germany in Autumn (Alexander Kluge, 1978), 158, 170
Germany Pale Mother (Helma Sanders-Brahms, 1979), 157, 159
Ginzburg, Carlo, 13, 204, 232–33, 234n.17
Gitlin, Todd, 84
Glassberg, David, 92, 94
The Glenn Miller Story (Anthony Mann, 1954), 43
Godard, Jean-Luc, 162, 176, 206
Griffith, D.W., 166

Habermas, Jürgen, 155, 169–70
Hard Times and Culture (Juan Downey, 1990), 210–12
Heidegger, Martin, 70, 72
Heimat (Edgar Reitz, 1979), 11, 159, 160–62, 163, 167–69, 176
Herzen, Alexander, 140
Herzog, Werner, 171
Higashi, Sumiko, 10
Hill, Anita, 71
Hillgruber, Andreas, 155, 170, 171
Himmelfarb, Gertrude, 19, 204
Historians, 13, 94, 202–205. See also Professors of history.
Historical consciousness, 3–6, 13, 70, 82–83; and *JFK*, 119, 123; and modern events, 20–25; and nationalism, 94–95; and the film spectator, 8; and *Who Killed Vincent Chin,* 56–66
Historical events, 9, 39–45, 53, 66, 69–70, 179n.3; and *Forrest Gump*, 2; and ideology, 85; and *JFK*, 22–23, 37n.8, 116, 119–20; and memory, 145–46; and postmodernist literature, 51–52; and representation, 4–5, 8, 18–38, 58–59, 147; and *The Conformist*, 61
Historical relativism, 21, 94, 155, 158, 162
Historical revisionism, 30, 38n.22, 81, 234n.7; and fascism, 155–6; and *Heimat*, 160; and Hiroshima, 3; and *JFK*, 49; and Russian history, 140
History and Memory (Rea Tajiri, 1991), 208–209
The History Channel, 4, 7
Hitler: A Film From Germany (*Our Hitler*) (Hans Jürgen Syberberg, 1977), 11, 18, 40, 148, 150, 158, 161–62, 167–69, 176, 214
Hofstadter, Richard, 92, 93
Hollywood Goes to War, 45
Holocaust (1978 mini-series), 11, 18, 158–59, 167–69, 174, 175–76; compared with *Schindler's List*, 163; response to, 161–62, 177
Holocaust, the, 20, 30–32, 37n.9, 38n.22, 54n.35, 147, 148, 155–56, 158, 169, 178; and Hayden White, 196–97; and historical revisionism, 81; and *Hitler: A Film From Germany*, 168; and the Kennedy assassination, 51–52; and mourning, 179; and New German cinema, 159; and representation, 11–12, 39, 163, 216; and *Schindler's List*, 166, 168, 177
Horkheimer, Max, 156
Hotel Terminus: The Life and Times of Klaus Barbie (Marcel Ophuls, 1988), 59, 173
How'd They Do That?, 42–43
Husserl, Edmund, 82
Hutcheon, Linda, 36n.2, 51–52, 202–203, 204
Huyssen, Andreas, 191–92

Indiana Jones and the Last Crusade (Steven Spielberg, 1989), 166
Infotainment, 18, 40
Interrotron, 220, 221–22, 223, 231, 232, 234n.7
It Happens Every Spring (Lloyd Bacon, 1949), 242

Ivan's Childhood (Andrei Tarkovskii, 1962), 141n.3

Jameson, Fredric, 24–26, 32, 38n.15, 57, 65–66; and the body, 77; and boredom, 188; and the historical real, 83; "History is what hurts," 9, 73, 78, 197; and the waning of history, 107
Jay, Gregory, 196
JFK (Oliver Stone, 1991), 4, 7, 8, 14, 18–20, 22, 36n.2, 37n.5, 39–42, 45–54, 232, 240, 241, 253; and nationalism, 10, 113–18, 121–24; and *Who Killed Vincent Chin,* 61–62, 66
Joan the Woman (Cecil B. DeMille, 1916), 95
Jurassic Park (Steven Spielberg, 1992), 147

Kellner, Hans, 202–203
Kimball, Roger, 243
The King of Kings (Cecil B. DeMille, 1927), 97, 106, 111n.46
King, Rodney, 4, 9, 23, 44, 68, 69, 74–88; and television, 219–20
Klapp, Orrin, 192–93
Kliuchevskii, Vasilii, 140
Kristeva, Julia, 85
Kuhn, Reinhard, 191, 192

L'Amour à Mort (Alain Resnais, 1984), 238–39
L'Immoraliste, 247
LaCapra, Dominick, 70, 73, 80, 203–204
Lacombe Lucien (Louis Malle, 1973), 154
Ladurie, Emmanuel LeRoy, 160, 204, 205
Land of Liberty (Cecil B. DeMille, 1939), 99–101
Lanzmann, Claude, 176–77. See also *Shoah.*
The Last Metro (Francois Truffaut, 1980), 154, 157
The Last of the Mohicans (Michael Mann, 1992), 7
Lee, Spike, 165
Lévi-Strauss, Claude, 70
Lili Marleen (Rainer Werner Fassbinder, 1980), 150, 157, 159, 161–62, 164
Lumumba: Death of a Prophet (Raoul Peck, 1992), 214
Lyotard, Jean François, 70, 148, 188, 216

M (Fritz Lang, 1931), 167
M. Klein (Joseph Losey, 1976), 154, 157, 174–75
Madame Bovary, 191
Madame Curie (Mervyn LeRoy, 1943), 244
Malcolm X (Spike Lee, 1992), 54n.14
The Man Who Shot Liberty Valance (John Ford, 1962), 146
Mandelbaum, Maurice, 85
Marathon Man (John Schlesinger, 1976), 47
Margaret Sanger: A Public Nuisance (Terese Svoboda and Steve Bull, 1992), 214
The Marriage of Maria Braun (Rainer Werner Fassbinder, 1978), 159, 164
Marx, Karl, 65, 81
Marxism, 88n.58, 156–57, 139–40
Materialism, 9
Medium Cool (Haskell Wexler, 1969), 54n.34
Melancholy, 12, 189–98
Melodrama, 9–10, 26, 182n.63, 183n.74; and cinematic representation, 150; and *Confessions of a Nazi Spy*, 46; and historical representation, 110n.19, 148–49, 153–54, 160, 161, 164; and *Holocaust*, 162; and *JFK*, 119; and mourning, 11, 172
Memory of Justice (Marcel Ophuls, 1976), 173
Memory, 20, 34–35, 44, 55, 70, 145–48, 149, 155, 169, 203, 228; and *Errol Morris: Interrotron Stories*, 13; and *History and Memory*, 209; and *Holocaust*, 176; and *JFK*, 10, 49, 123; and melodrama, 11; and mourning, 172; and narrative, 32; and *Schindler's List*, 179; and *Shoah*, 173–74; and the Third Reich, 30, 160
Merleau-Ponty, Maurice, 71
Metahistory, 238, 252. See also Hayden White.
Metz, Christian, 84
Meyer, Meyer, 235
Middle voice, 12, 216, 59, 61
The Mirror (Andrei Tarkovskii, 1975), 128
Mitscherlich, Alexander, 157, 170
Modernism, 12, 38n.15, 97, 109, 111n.48, 189, 190, 196, 197, 239; and *Between the Acts*, 27; and Errol Morris, 229; and feminism, 198; and historical events, 30–32, 38n.22, 39–41; and *JFK*, 10, 123;

and *nachträglichkeit*, 57; and representation, 7, 8, 18, 21, 22–23, 114–15, 118, 150, 247, 194, 216; and *Shoah*, 165, 174, 177; and *Hard Times and Culture*, 211; literary, 24, 238
Morris, Errol, 12–13, 219–233
Mourning, 8, 52, 146, 171–72; and the Holocaust, 179; and narrative, 11, 31–32, 40; and *The Sorrow and the Pity* and *Shoah*, 174
Mr. Smith Goes to Washington (Frank Capra, 1939), 125n.15
Mr. Whittle and the Morning Star, 246

The Nasty Girl (Verhoeven, Michael, 1990), 214
National Lampoon's Animal House (John Landis, 1978), 249
Nationalism, 9, 10–11, 108, 114–16, 168, 202, 220; and New German cinema, 159; and Russian history, 134, 140; and *The Ten Commandments*, 102
Natural Born Killers (Oliver Stone, 1994), 232
Nausea, 25–26, 238
Neo-realism, 151, 153
Nichols, Bill, 8, 71, 73, 78, 82, 86n.10, 232
Nietzsche, Friedrich, 72
Night and Fog (Alain Resnais, 1955), 148, 159
The Night Porter (Liliana Cavani, 1974), 18, 154, 157
911, 227
1941 (Steven Spielberg, 1979), 166
1900 (Bernardo Bertolucci, 1976), 153
The Ninth Wave, 242, 250–51
Nolte, Ernst, 155, 157, 169
Nostalgia (Andrei Tarkovskii, 1983), 128
Not Reconciled (Jean Marie Straub, 1965), 151, 157
November Days (Marcel Ophuls, 1990), 173
Novick, Peter, 94, 99, 237, 240
The Nutty Professor (Jerry Lewis, 1963), 242

One Man's War (Edgardo Cozarinsky, 1981), 148
One-Way Street (John Hughes, 1992), 214
Open City (Roberto Rossellini, 1945), 153
Ophuls, Marcel, 173
Orphans of the Storm (D.W. Griffith, 1922), 166
Ossessione (Luchino Visconti, 1943), 153
Our Hitler, see *Hitler: A Film From Germany*

Pageantry, 27, 92–96, 99, 100, 105–106, 107, 108
The Parallax View (Alan Pakula, 1974), 47
The Passenger (Andrzej Munk, 1963), 148
Paterson (Kevin Duggan, 1988), 213–14
Peirce, Charles Sanders, 72, 86n.10
Performative discourse, 9, 58
Performative mood, 59–61
Petro, Patrice, 12
Platoon (Oliver Stone, 1986), 146, 232
Polan, Dana, 13
Polanski, Roman, 165
Porter, Edwin S., 41–42
Postmodernism, 36n.2, 38n.18, 24, 44, 84, 111n.48, 176, 194; and film theory, 154; and historical consciousness, 175; and historical representation, 7, 12, 18–19, 40–41, 73–74, 106, 118, 145, 150, 189, 201–16; and *JFK*, 8, 50–52, 123; and melancholy, 198; and *nachträglichkeit*, 57; and nationalism, 108; and *Schindler's List*, 163–64, 166, 178; and Tarkovskii, 127–28, 140–41; and *The Ten Commandments* (1956), 92, 107; and *The Thin Blue Line*, 229
The Producers (Mel Brooks, 1968), 151
Production Code, 46. See also Censorship.
The Professor's House, 241, 249
Professors of history, 13. See also Historians.
Profscam, 237
Progressive Era, 92–94, 100, 105
Purely Academic, 240–42

Quantum Leap, 249
Quilombo (Carlos Diegues, 1984), 214

Racism, 99, 155–56, 173, 202; and *The Color Purple*, 166; and *History and Memory*, 209; and *Interrotron Stories*, 225, 227; and Rodney King, 75–77, 81, 83–84; and *Who Killed Vincent Chin*, 56, 60–61, 62–64, 66, 68n.18

Rancière, Jacques, 85
Rashomon (Akira Kurosawa, 1950), 44–45, 81
The Real World (MTV), 232
Real, the, 9, 34–35, 52, 58, 72, 166, 231, 248; and historical events, 70; and *JFK*, 119; and re-enactments, 44
Realism, 11, 18, 21, 29, 60–61, 66, 114, 154, 133; and Cecil B. DeMille epics, 91–92; and "discourses of sobriety," 67n.8; and *Interrotron Stories*, 231; literary, 240, 251; pictorial, 106; and representation of fascism, 148, 153; and *Schindler's List*, 149–50; and the *Schindler's List/Shoah* debate, 177; and Andrei Tarkovskii, 128; and *The Ten Commandments*(1923), 96–97; and *Who Killed Vincent Chin*, 57–58, 62
Re-enactments, 8, 41, 42–45, 46, 53n.10, 146, 214; in *Errol Morris: Interrotron Stories*, 13, 221, 222, 224, 226, 227, 228, 230, 231; in *JFK*, 48, 49–50, 121; in *Camera Natura*, 209–10; in *Far From Poland*, 207–208; in *Hard Times and Culture*, 211; in *History and Memory*, 209; in *Hitler: A Film From Germany*, 169; in *Surname Viet Given Name Nam*, 212
Reitz, Edgar, 176
Rescue: 911, 42–43
The Return of Martin Guerre (Daniel Vigne, 1982), 18
Rod Serling's Night Gallery, 221
Roger and Me (Michael Moore, 1989), 36n.2, 59, 232
Roma (Federico Fellini, 1972), 153
Roots (TV mini-series, 1977), 18
Rosenau, Pauline, 202–203, 204
Rosenheim, Shawn, 12
Rosenstone, Robert, 11, 12, 128
Rossellini, Roberto, 153

Said, Edward W., 105, 125n.13
Salo (Pier Paolo Pasolini, 1975), 157
Sampson-Schley Controversy, 41–42
Santner, Eric, 31, 183n.78
Sari Red (Pratibha Parmar, 1988), 59
Sartre, Jean-Paul, 25–27, 38n.15, 63, 70, 238
Schafer, Hans Dieter, 156
Schama, Simon, 204
Schiesari, Juliana, 189–90
Schindler's List (Steven Spielberg, 1993), 4, 11, 18, 146–49, 153, 163–66, 178; and *Shoah*, 162, 165, 178. See also Steven Spielberg.
Scorsese, Martin, 165
Sculpting in Time, 140–41
The Serpent's Egg (Ingmar Bergman, 1978), 154, 157
Seven Beauties (Lina Wertmuller, 1976), 154, 157
Shoah (Claude Lanzmann, 1985), 11, 36n.2, 147, 149, 150, 173–74; and *Schindler's List*, 162, 165, 178
Show Boat (James Whale, 1936), 100
Silas Timberman, 246–47
Silverman, Kaja, 85
Simmel, Georg, 68n.19
Simpson, O. J., 3–5, 13, 35–36, 71, 220, 232, 233n.1
Snakes and Ladders (Mitzi Goldman and Trish FitzSimons, 1987), 213
Sobchack, Vivian, 80, 83
Socialist Realism, 10–11,127, 132, 139, 141–42n.3
Society for Cinema Studies petition, 79–80
Solaris (Andrei Tarkovskii, 1972), 128
Sontag, Susan, 151
The Sorrow and the Pity (Marcel Ophuls, 1970), 154, 173, 174
Spielberg, Steven, 172, 176–77. See also *Schindler's List*.
Stage Fright (Alfred Hitchcock, 1950), 239
Staiger, Janet, 8
Stalker (Andrei Tarkovskii, 1980), 128
Stein, Gertrude, 6, 32–35, 38n.15, 197
Steiner, George, 30, 38n.24, 181n.32
Sterne (Konrad Wolf, 1966), 148
Stone, Oliver, 37n.8. See also *JFK*.
The Student Body, 243–44
Subjunctive mood, 9, 59–60
Surname Viet Given Name Nam (Trinh T. Minh-ha, 1989), 212–13
Syberberg, Hans Jürgen, 153, 171

Tableaux vivants, 92, 93, 140
Tadellöser & Wolf (German television series, 1974–75), 160

Teachers (Arthur Hiller, 1984), 251–52
The Ten Commandments (Cecil B. DeMille, 1923, 1956), 10, 91–112; 1923 version, 91, 94–98; 1956 version, 91–92, 98–108
Tenured Radicals, 237
The Thin Blue Line (Errol Morris, 1988), 43, 53n.10, 224, 225, 226, 228, 229, 230–31
Thomas, Clarence, 71
Three Days of the Condor (Sydney Pollack, 1976), 47
The Tin Drum (Volker Schlondorff, 1979), 159
Tomasulo, Frank, 9
A Triumph of the Will (Leni Riefenstahl, 1935), 161
Turner, Frederick Jackson, 104, 111n.43
Turner, Victor, 51
Turning Point, 224, 234n.10
TV Nation, 222, 233n.6
Twilight Zone, 222

Unsolved Mysteries, 42–43

Vattimo, Gianni, 188–89
The Verdict (Sidney Lumet, 1982), 253
Vernet, Marc, 103–104
Vernon, Florida (Errol Morris, 1981), 224
Vertov, Dziga, 223
Violence, 8, 39, 42, 45, 146, 149, 151, 173, 175; and *Andrei Rublev*, 133–35; and *Confessions of a Nazi Spy*, 47; and *JFK*, 40, 52, 123; and Rodney King video, 78, 80–83; and *The Thin Blue Line*, 226; and *Who Killed Vincent Chin*, 62

Wajda, Andrzej, 165, 208
Walker (Alex Cox, 1987), 214
Warren Commission, 8, 48–49
Wenders, Wim, 165, 171
White, Hayden, 8, 50, 57, 67n.3, 83, 203–204; and historical events, 58–59, 84, 85, 196–97; and *The Content of the Form*, 69; and historical representation, 71, 73, 75, 77, 114, 118, 216; and *JFK*, 52–53, 239; and *Metahistory*, 4, 238, 252; and "The Modernist Event," 4–6, 39–41
Who Killed Vincent Chin (Renée Tajima and Chris Choy, 1988), 8–9, 55–68, 232
Why We Fight: The Battle of China (Frank Capra, 1944), 101
Wiesel, Elie, 38n.24, 175–76, 178
Wilden, Anthony, 55–56
Williams, Linda, 83, 230
Williams, Raymond, 107
Williams, William Appleman, 99
Winter Kills (William Richert, 1979), 239
Woolf, Virginia, 27–29, 38n.15, 197

Year of Decision (Paramount newsreel, 1941), 100
You Asked For It, 43
Young Tom Edison (Norman Taurog, 1940), 244
Youngblood, Denise, 10

Zapruder film, 4, 51, 70–71, 116

we have is language, rhetoric, and discourse. Indeed, it is almost axiomatic in contemporary media scholarship that "history is at once the living trajectory of social events as they occur and the written discourse that speaks about these events."[18] Dominick LaCapra says essentially the same thing: "All forms of historiography might benefit from modes of critical reading premised on the conviction that documents are texts that supplement or rework 'reality'."[19] Even Hayden White seems to concede this point: "The crucial question for any historical investigation is the evidentiary status of any given artifact, more precisely, its *referential* status.... The historically real, the past real, is that to which I can be referred only *by way of* an artifact that is textual in nature."[20]

It is one thing to say that the material world (reality) may exist subject to infinite perceptual mediation and conceptual interpretation; it is quite another, however, to deny that "reality" and "facts" exist at all. Referentiality is not just a philosophical and artistic matter, but a spatial and social one as well. Reality *is* reality, whether mediated or not. As Bill Nichols points out, "Material practices occur that are not entirely or totally discursive, even if their meanings and social value are."[21] Denying the existence of existence is tautologically absurd. As Nichols avers: "The world ... exceeds all representations. This is a brute reality .... The world, as the domain of the historically real, is neither text nor narrative."[22] Fredric Jameson seems to concur: "History is *not* a text, not a narrative, master or otherwise.... History is what hurts. It is what refuses desire and sets inexorable limits to individual as well as collective praxis."[23] Jameson's critique goes further: "In faithful conformity to poststructuralist linguistic theory, the past as 'referent' finds itself gradually bracketed out, and then effaced altogether, leaving us with nothing but texts."[24]

Annie Oakley: Why can't you show the truth, just for once?
Buffalo Bill: Because I've got a better sense of history than that!

—*Buffalo Bill and the Indians, or Sitting Bull's History Lesson* (1976)

Like Robert Altman's Buffalo Bill, the extreme versions of postmodernist historiography critiqued above provide the observer of real life and media phenomena with no meaningful mode of making meaning other than the "meaning effect." Jameson notes that "the signified ... is now rather to be seen as a 'meaning-effect,' as that objective mirage of signification generated and projected by the relationship of signifiers among themselves."[25] Under the thrall of postmodernism, latter-day neo-Marxists have all but forgotten that the philosophical underpinnings for their ontology is in dialectical materialism, a system rooted in matter, reality, and historical facts. Jameson observes,

"The concept of the postmodern [is] an attempt to think the present historically in an age that has forgotten how to think historically in the first place."[26] This situation leads to a loss of historicity that can hardly be replaced by media representations; in fact, film and videotape only exacerbate this new textual approach to history—this total replacement of event with its writing.

a (black) man is being beaten, or history is what hurts

[Rodney King's] name may well become an icon in the social and political history of the twentieth century. Scopes, Sacco and Vanzetti, Ethel and Julius Rosenberg, the Chicago Seven. Rodney King could join them one day—and it wasn't even he on trial.

—*Newsweek*, 26 April 1993

The controversial American trials mentioned in relation to Rodney King in the *Newsweek* article all had something in common beyond their notoriety: none of the evidence that supported the "guilty" verdicts in these cases was on videotape. In contrast, both the first Rodney King trial—in which four Los Angeles police officers were found "not guilty" of state charges of assault and excessive force in apprehending the suspect—and its "sequel"—a federal proceeding in which two of the defendants were found "guilty" of civil-rights violations—depended for evidence on a chance minicam recording of the pivotal incident, in which a supine Rodney King received two Taser blasts of 100,000 volts, seven kicks, and fifty-six separate metal baton blows from the "swarming" police officers.[27]

That videotape, in its raw black-and-white, grainy, shaky, and blurry form, was recorded by amateur videographer George Holliday on the night of March 3, 1991. Holliday shot from the balcony of his Lake View Terrace apartment (seventeen miles northwest of downtown Los Angeles) as twenty-seven Los Angeles police officers stopped, detained, beat, and arrested African-American motorist Rodney King after a high-speed (one hundred miles per hour) car chase. Later, Holliday sold his tape for $500 to a local television station, KTLA, which released it to Cable News Network (CNN) and thereafter to all the major American television networks for rebroadcast.[28]

Most Americans saw only an eighty-one-second fragment of Holliday's video recording of the event, which, *in toto*, ran almost nine-and-a-half minutes and was sandwiched between mundane scenes of Holliday family members playing Nintendo and the family cat licking its paw. Yet public judgments were made on the basis of this small video fragment that greatly affected the lives of the four police defendants, Rodney King, the L.A. police chief, the

L.A. district attorney, South Central Los Angeles, and (possibly) a mayoral and presidential election. Furthermore, those public judgments led to the worst riots in the United States in this century, with a toll of fifty-three people dead and $1 billion in damage. Holliday's attorney, James Jordan, was quoted as having said, "The George Holliday videotape is the most viewed and I daresay the most important videotape of the twentieth century."[29]

As presented on numerous TV newscasts and at the first trial in Simi Valley, California, the Rodney King videotape marks a controversial site for interrogating some basic historical, political, and pedagogical *partis pris*.

The vocabulary and mentality of poststructuralism have seeped into common parlance, relativizing everything and teaching that history is merely a text with no meaning beyond what can be read into it. The motto seems to be: when in doubt, doubt. Such systematic skepticism and polysemic indeterminacy about media imagery can be the intellectual harbingers of unexpected results, to wit: a jury that "emplotted" a racist beating as the lawful apprehension of a criminal perpetrator.[30] After all, Hayden White has said that people should be "free to conceptualize history, to perceive its contents, and to construct narrative accounts in whatever modality of consciousness is most consistent with their own moral and aesthetic aspirations."[31] Attorneys defending the L.A. police officers at this first trial did just that; they were able to provide sophisticated "spin control" of the beating by repeatedly showing the infamous home video recording (in slow motion) and by telling the jury that Rodney King was behaving irrationally and was resolutely disobeying the officers' commands to stop moving—a classic instance of the "reading against the grain," "structuring absence" methodology valorized by many film and video scholars.[32]

The "zero-degree" style of Holliday's small-format video recording aided and abetted in its use as an ambiguous object. Even if dictated by happenstance, the long-take aesthetic (occasionally punctuated by out-of-focus zooms) followed the preferred ethos of ethnographic and anthropological filmmaking in fieldwork situations—what Bazin called "self-effacement before reality."[33] The use of a single, uninterrupted shot effaced the overt presence of the videographer in favor of the transparent reality before the lens, creating a sort of "video vérité" observational mode. This noninterventionist, seemingly straightforward and objective mode of production allowed the videotape to be used as a national Rorschach test of sorts, whereby each citizen reacted to the scene according to his/her own subjectivity and experience (often based on gender, class, and race). It must be remembered, however, that with any form of photography "we behold someone's look at the world, and not the world itself."[34]

Mediation, not only *in* the tape, but also *of* the tape, however, was always occurring. Television anchorpersons, print journalists, attorneys and prosecutors, politicians and police chiefs all wanted to explain the raw footage by projecting a story onto it. For example, defense attorneys at both trials used slow motion and freeze-frame analysis to "isolate specific blows to King to justify each one and thus subvert the meaning of the rapid flow to provide the jury with an excuse for forgetting the 'excessive force' reading that comes from seeing the rapid series of blows."[35] The defense attorneys essentially turned Holliday's long take into a montage by "deconstructing" and decomposing it into isolated parts. In addition, attorneys added voice-over commentary and narration as they interpreted the defendants' actions and Rodney King's reactions at every second. If contemporary theorists are correct in suggesting that reality cannot be apprehended or is a useless construct, then there was no way to determine apodictically whether or not Rodney King was beaten (let alone beaten unjustly) outside of the discourse that accompanied the trial.

One must go beyond the text of the videotape to the larger text of society at a particular historical conjuncture to understand the meaning of the King videotape and the first jury verdict. It has been argued that "a carefully controlled defense strategy ... tapped into preexisting cultural assumptions about race, law enforcement, and justice. The video's possibilities for polysemic meaning were effectively squelched under the pressure of ideological practice."[36] In short, the lawyers for the accused police officers wanted to narrativize the incident from the perspective of beleaguered law enforcement authorities attempting to bring into custody an unruly and belligerent black scofflaw. Defense attorney Michael Stone was explicit about using such a strategy, admitting that he wanted the jury to view the beating "not through the eye of the camera but through the eyes of the police officers who were at the scene."[37] Similarly, the prosecution in the second trial attempted (in part by calling Rodney King to the stand) to have jurors identify with the beating victim, a sort of "Rodney King, *c'est moi*" strategy. In either case, a transfer of identification was sought: the spectator (juror) was moved from the position of an objective observer to being inscribed as a "spectator-in-the-text."[38] Beyond that, the historical fact of the beating was converted into an absolute, if undecidable, *text* in the Simi Valley and Los Angeles courtrooms, as well as in the courtroom of American public opinion.

Furthermore, the King video had to be converted specifically into a *narrative* text by both sides in the trial in efforts to seek support for their explicit interpretations of the event. Although some ambiguities did exist (were King's movements involuntary reactions to pain or volitional attempts to stand up, in violation of police orders?), the legal facts of the case were not particularly in dispute. What was at issue was the interpretation and morality of those facts. Hayden White has indicated that "every historical narrative has as its latent or manifest purpose the desire to *moralize* the events of which it treats."[39] In the Rodney King trials, juridical spectators needed to be conditioned and inscribed to see the tape and the beating from a particular moral viewpoint. To achieve that end, "jurors were encouraged to read the King video not as they would a piece of news footage, but rather as they would a classical Hollywood film."[40] In fact, during closing arguments, the defense lawyers referred to the police officers as the "thin blue line" that protected society from malefactors like Rodney King.

But read another way, the video text was not just a record of the specific beating incident that George Holliday taped. Rather, it was a social index of the institutional racism and police brutality in America's urban centers. Just as Adam Smith's "invisible hand" of the economy influenced the marketplace, so George Holliday's "invisible (video) hand" exposed the formerly invisible (and not very "learned") hand of racist police power.[41] As such, the return of the (racial) repressed of the United States' woes, like Rodney King's wounds, became instantly readable sociohistorical texts, the body of evidence, so to speak, of a social injustice. Fredric Jameson seems to have predicted the King incident when he said, "Finally the body itself proves to be a palimpsest whose stabs of pain and symptoms, along with its deeper impulses and its sensory apparatus, can be read fully as much as any text."[42]

Sigmund Freud's famous study "A Child Is Being Beaten" represents his most thorough examination of the motives for repression. The fantasy of a child being beaten—and the pleasurable sensations cathected to it—was a common one for the hysterical and obsessional neurotics who sought clinical treatment in Freud's day. In all cases, whether the fantasy involved the analysand as the beaten child (masochism) or his/her brother or sister (sadism toward the sibling rival), the father was the figure doing the beating. According to Freud, people who harbor such fantasies in their adult lives develop a special sensitivity and irritability toward anyone perceived to be a father or superego substitute (e.g., a male police officer, teacher, or president). For Freud, in the case of the male beating fantasy, being beaten stands for being loved (in a genital sense).[43]

What, however, if the Freudian scenario is not just an imaginary fantasy but part of the social reality in a racist culture? What if, instead of a child, a (black) *man* is being beaten by (white) male authority figures with phallic police batons—in full view of a video camera and eventually millions of television viewers? And what if the victim's name, King, is coincidentally linked to the famous civil-rights leader who once said, "We will no longer let them use their clubs on us in dark corners. We are going to make them do it in the glaring light of television."[44] What we have then is the return of the (social) repressed, a manifestation of the Althusserian Repressive State Apparatuses that society generally hides from view—the force, coercion, and violence perpetrated by the police, courts, and prisons.[45] Thus, just as Freud believed that the dream was the "royal road" to the personal unconscious, the Holliday videotape became the royal (indeed, the "Kingly") road to the American social unconscious—where our central contradictions of race, class, and violence secretly lurk and where the laws of socioeconomic fatalism supervene.

In the first trial, the prosecution referred to the videotape as its "star witness" and as "an automatic indictment." In the second trial, dubbed "Rodney King II" by Los Angeles locals, both the federal prosecutors and defense attorneys relied heavily on the tape, although King also testified on the witness stand. One juror in the second trial was quoted as saying, "We went through the video forwards, backwards, frame by frame, slow motion, regular motion. I think *the tape basically speaks* for itself. I would have to say that is what basically convicted [the two police officers]."[46] Another juror said, "We used the video like a frame to put all the pieces into. Without that video, there wouldn't have even been a trial." And a third juror added, "What we decided is to chuck all [the experts'] opinions. We said we're going to interpret [the video] ourselves. That's our job."[47]

the prison-house of video

The status of documentary film as evidence from the world legitimates its usage as a source of knowledge. The visible evidence it provides underpins its value for social advocacy and news reporting. Documentaries show us situations and events that are recognizably part of a realm of shared experience: the historical world as we know and encounter it.

—Bill Nichols, *Representing Reality*

Fredric Jameson's observation that "history is what hurts" is literally true for both Rodney King and South Central Los Angeles. History hurt in the sheer facticity of the physical beating of one individual and in the material, social, and economic scars wrought on a minority community. King's bruises, the L.A. deaths, and the property damage were concrete and real cultural traumas, not a free play of signifiers—no matter how they were interpreted. But televisually mediated history also hurt, by creating a media morality play that transfixed U.S. viewers and fractured the American social fabric.

The beating incident was not *perceived* by the machine but *mediated* by the